SCREENING GENDER, FRAMING GENRE:
CANADIAN LITERATURE INTO FILM

Screening Gender, Framing Genre

Canadian Literature into Film

Peter Dickinson

UNIVERSITY OF TORONTO PRESS
Toronto Buffalo London

© University of Toronto Press Incorporated 2007
Toronto Buffalo London
Printed in Canada

ISBN-13: 978-0-8020-4475-4
ISBN-10: 0-8020-4475-1

Printed on acid-free paper

Library and Archives Canada Cataloguing in Publication

Dickinson, Peter, 1968–
    Screening gender, framing genre : Canadian literature into film / Peter
Dickinson.

    Includes bibliographical references and index.
    ISBN-13: 978-0-8020-4475-4
    ISBN-10: 0-8020-4475-1

    1. Canadian fiction – Film and video adaptations.   2. Sex in motion
pictures.   3. Homosexuality in motion pictures.   4. Motion pictures –
Canada – history.   5. Canadian fiction – 20th century – History and
criticism.   I. Title.

PN1995.3.D53 2007   791.43′657   C2006-902647-5

University of Toronto Press acknowledges the financial assistance to its
publishing program of the Canada Council for the Arts and the Ontario
Arts Council.

This book has been published with the help of a grant from the Canadian
Federation for the Humanities and Social Sciences, through the Aid to Scholarly
Publications Programme, using funds provided by the Social Sciences and
Humanities Research Council of Canada.

University of Toronto Press acknowledges the financial support for its
publishing activities of the Government of Canada through the Book
Publishing Industry Development Program (BPIDP).

*for my parents
who took me to the movies,
for Richard
who taught me how to watch them,
and for my students
who taught me how to read them*

Contents

List of Figures   ix

Acknowledgments   xi

Introduction: Literature and Film, Gender and Genre   3

1 Sex Maidens and Yankee Skunks: A Field Guide to Reading 'Canadian' Movies   17

2 Feminism, Fidelity, and the Female Gothic: The Uncanny Art of Adaptation in *Kamouraska*, *Surfacing*, and *Le sourd dans la ville*   49

3 Images of the Indigene: History, Visibility, and Ethnographic Romance in Four Adaptations from the 1990s   77

4 Critically Queenie, or, *Trans*-Figuring the Prison-House of Gender: *Fortune and Men's Eyes* and After   104

5 Space, Time, Auteurity, and the Queer Male Body: Policing the Image in the Film Adaptations of Robert Lepage   129

6 Ghosts In and Out of the Machine: Sighting/Citing Lesbianism in Susan Swan's *The Wives of Bath* and Léa Pool's *Lost and Delirious*   162

7 Adapting Masculinity: Michael Turner, Bruce McDonald, and Others   186

Filmography   213

Notes   221

Bibliography   247

Illustration Credits   263

Index   265

List of Figures

I.1   *The English Patient* 6
1.1   *Rachel, Rachel* 19
1.2   *Déliverez-nous du mal* 26
1.3   *Les fous de bassan* 30
1.4   *The Handmaid's Tale* 32
2.1   *Kamouraska* 56
2.2   *Surfacing* 66
2.3   *Surfacing* 67
2.4   *Le sourd dans la ville* 72
2.5   *Swann* 75
3.1   *Black Robe* 84
3.2   *Shadow of the Wolf* 88
3.3   *Clearcut* 92
3.4   *Dance Me Outside* 97
3.5   *Atanarjuat* 100
4.1   *Fortune and Men's Eyes* 116
4.2   *Il était une fois dans l'est* 117
4.3   *Outrageous!* 118
4.4   The B-Girlz 121
4.5   *Better Than Chocolate* 125
4.6   *Le sexe des étoiles* 127
5.1   *Le confessionnal* 137
5.2   *Le confessionnal* 138
5.3   *Le confessionnal* 139
5.4   *Le confessionnal* 140
5.5   *Le polygraphe* 142
5.6   *Le polygraphe* 144
5.7   *Le polygraphe* 145
5.8   *Nô* 149
5.9   *Nô* 150
5.10 *Possible Worlds* 154
5.11 *La face cachée de la lune* 160
6.1   *Salmonberries* 167

6.2   *Fire*   170
6.3   *Lost and Delirious*   173
6.4   *Lost and Delirious*   178
6.5   *Mädchen in Uniform*   183
7.1   *Hard Core Logo*   195
7.2   *Hard Core Logo*   198
7.3   *American Whiskey Bar*   202
7.4   *Elimination Dance*   204
7.5   *Journey into Fear*   207

Acknowledgments

This book began as a proposal for a course that never got taught. I owe a great debt of thanks to Emily Andrew, who edited my previous book at University of Toronto Press, for encouraging me to expand that proposal in the form of a book prospectus; an equal measure of thanks must go to Siobhan McMenemy, my current editor, for waiting so patiently to receive the final manuscript, and for seeing it through the review process with such professionalism. As part of that review process, I received very generous feedback from the two anonymous assessors of my manuscript and from University of Toronto Press's Manuscript Review Committee. Their respective suggestions for clarifications and changes have strengthened my argument immeasurably. Frances Mundy helpfully and patiently answered my queries during the book's progress through its various stages of production, and Matthew Kudelka offered crucial improvements to my long sentences and even longer paragraphs.

I have also benefited from the advice, critical commentary, and scholarly example of the following individuals in film and literary studies: Jon Beasley-Murray, Michael Eberle-Sinatra, Judith Halberstam, Patsy Kotsopoulos, Helen Leung, André Loiselle, Lee Parpart, Jackie Stacey, Elspeth Tulloch, and especially Thomas Waugh, whose own work on the multiple narratives of gender and sexuality underpinning Canadian film remains an inspiration. In the Department of English at Simon Fraser University, I am lucky to work with colleagues who are not only supportive of my work, but also genuinely interested in hearing me expound on it in forums both more (departmental colloquia, reference books) and less (car rides home, dinner parties) academic. I wish to thank, in particular, Susan Brook, David Chariandy, Colette Colligan, Jeff Derksen, Carole Gerson, and Sophie McCall. It was also at SFU that I finally got to test in the classroom some of my theories on literature and film; for responding so enthusiastically, for challenging me to rethink some of my more entrenched views, and for opening my eyes to things on the page and on the screen that I had not adequately considered – or even seen – I thank my students, both undergraduate and graduate, all of whom are expert theorists of adaptation.

Research for this project was supported by funds from the Social Sciences and Humanities Research Council of Canada, for which I am most grateful. In particular, those funds allowed me to hire a succession of extremely smart, professionally astute, and critically savvy research assistants, whose material contributions to my thinking are registered on every page of this book. For this, I thank Wendy Foster, Sean Saunders, Jesse Battis, Alessandra Capperdoni, and Alison McDonald.

Portions of chapter 1, and earlier (much abbreviated) versions of chapters 4 and 5 appeared in the following journals: *Essays on Canadian Writing* 76 (2002); *Canadian Journal of Film Studies* 11.2 (2002); and *Screen* 46.2 (2005). My thanks to the editors of these journals for permission to reprint that material here. Copyright and permissions information relating to the various photographic stills and video frame-grabs reprinted throughout this book are listed at the end of this book. Every effort has been made to contact copyright holders, and I welcome the supplementing of any missing information. My profound thanks to all those artists, photographers, filmmakers, and producers who have generously waived fees in allowing me to reproduce their work here. For assistance in obtaining and sourcing images, I am indebted to Julienne Boudreau and Pierre Véronneau, both of the Cinémathèque québécoise, and to Lisa Fotheringham.

My parents have followed the progress of this project from its inception, and their abiding interest in my scholarly life is, I know, a heartfelt expression of their love. Richard Cavell remains my toughest and most trusted critic, and his contributions are everywhere in these pages. I have talked through virtually every section of this book with him over the past six years, he has listened to countless iterations of its contents in one form or another, and together we have watched, and watched again, hundreds of hours of film. That he has never waivered in his support of this project, or of me, is testament to his generosity and to his grace.

SCREENING GENDER, FRAMING GENRE

Introduction: Literature and Film, Gender and Genre

> Could you estimate the degree of frustration experienced by the one million Americans who tried to read *The English Patient* after seeing the film?
>
> Michael Turner, *American Whiskey Bar*[1]

Many readers of Canadian literature know that Michael Ondaatje's *The English Patient* won the Governor General's Award and shared the Booker Prize in 1992; many more know that Anthony Minghella's film adaptation, starring Ralph Fiennes, Kristin Scott Thomas, Juliette Binoche, Willem Dafoe, and Naveen Andrews, took home nine Academy Awards in 1997. In fact, it was the latter coup that was for a time heralded much more prominently on the cover of the Vintage/Miramax trade paperback that went into mass market circulation around the time the film was released. This is but one of the many ironies alluded to in my opening epigraph from Michael Turner's *American Whiskey Bar* (a novel that was itself adapted as a live television broadcast by Bruce McDonald in 1998, and about which I will have more to say in the final chapter of this book). As Turner suggests, those readers who came to Ondaatje's novel via the film were often confused by the text's poetical style, its non-linear plot, and its apparent narrative focus on Hana and Kip rather than Almásy and Katharine. Clearly, film and book were very different in form and in substance. How then to compare them?

For almost as long as films have been adapted from literature (which, as I point out in the next chapter, is a long time indeed), the critical frameworks used to compare them have been overwhelmingly indicative and evaluative. That is, we often measure the success of film adaptations by how 'faithfully' they adhere to their source material. However, as this book in part aims to demonstrate, transforming the written word into the visual language of film is necessarily an open-ended process, one that involves the quotation and intersection of a number of different 'texts,' not all of which may be recognizable as originary or even literary. There are, in other words, some things that a novel can do that a film cannot, and vice versa. At the same time, examining carefully the changes made between literary source texts and their film treatments often provides an additional critical framework for assessing the broader aesthetic and ideological debates that govern various considerations relating to genre and audience classifications in both media. In this regard, the example of *The English Patient* points as well to the basic economic imperatives that drive the film adaptation industry, influencing everything from which books get optioned in the first place to casting choices, and, yes, changes to the story (cue the egregious Hollywood happy ending).

Thus, while the chapters that follow take up, at various points, the narrative syntax common to close analyses of both fiction and film (such as point of view, voice, story/plot, character, and time and repetition), they are much more concerned with assessing what differences in the apprehension of this syntax within the locus of Canadian film adaptation might say about the – at times overlapping, at times opposed – reading and viewing audiences being hailed by the respective literary and cinematic texts under consideration, and about the social, cultural, and historical contexts governing their production and reception. More particularly, it is my contention that examining Canadian film adaptation through the specific context of gender – especially as it intersects with genre studies – offers a way of resituating and re-evaluating both the problematic fault lines of, and our continued investments in, fidelity criticism. In examining the links between ideology and narrative intrinsic to the adaptive process, my argument in this book essentially coalesces around the following question: To what extent might one's *reading* for the coherence of certain narrative codes relating to *genre* in literature be said to translate into *looking* for the destabilization of certain representational codes relating to *gender* in film? Let me return to the example of *The English Patient* as a way of articulating more clearly the development of my own thinking on Canadian film adaptation in relation to this question.

In an important essay on *Kissed*, Lynne Stopkewich's bewitching 1996 adaptation of Barbara Gowdy's short story 'We So Seldom Look on Love,' Lee Parpart, drawing on the work of Carl Plantinga and others, has written about the often visceral emotional response readers have when favourite works of literature are brought to the screen, especially if the resulting film is not altogether to their liking.[2] My reaction to *The English Patient* (and, it should be noted, to other films discussed in subsequent chapters), is typical in this regard. However much I had, and still have, problems with Ondaatje's novel on a stylistic level, I could not help thinking of Minghella's film as a 'whitewash' in terms of its politics. Of particular concern, in this regard, is the director's depiction of the events that precipitate Kip's departure from the Villa San Girolamo.

In the concluding 'August' section of Ondaatje's novel, it is the bombing of Hiroshima and Nagasaki that sets in motion 'the line of movement Kip's body followed out of [Hana's] life.'[3] The defuser of countless small bombs and mines over the course of the war, Kip is suddenly confronted with the image of 'a bomb the size, it seems, of a city, so vast it lets the living witness the death of the population around them' (*EP* 287). He is unable to fathom it; as Ondaatje writes in the novel, 'He knows nothing about the weapon' (*EP* 287). But he does know who dropped it, and who they dropped it on. Which is why Hana and Caravaggio find him staring down the barrel of a rifle at the English patient, however ersatz and burned beyond recognition he might be. Kip sees him as the representative of this 'tremor of Western wisdom' (*EP* 284): 'American, French, I don't care. When you start bombing the brown races of the world, you're an Englishman. You had King

Leopold of Belgium and now you have fucking Harry Truman of the USA. You all learned it from the English' (*EP* 286). Kip, of course, does not kill Almásy, even though Almásy begs him to; but his connection with the other inhabitants of the Villa does seem to be irrevocably severed. And so he hops on his motorbike and leaves for the south, 'travelling against the direction of the invasion, as if rewinding the spool of war' (*EP* 290). The penultimate image of Kip afforded the reader is of him skidding across a rain-soaked bridge, being thrown from his bike and into the river below (*EP* 295), which repeats at the same time that it elementally revises the opening image we have of Almásy's burning body falling from his plane 'into the desert' (*EP* 5).

   In chapter 1 of this book I deal at greater length with the growing body of literary scholarship around the cultural and racial politics of the film adaptation of *The English Patient*,[4] particularly as it intersects with and complicates poststructuralist film theory's response to fidelity criticism. Let me just add here that I, too, think that the ending of Minghella's film especially blunts Ondaatje's concluding critique of the so-called 'civilizing effects' of colonization and competing nationalisms. It does this by locating the impetus for Kip's departure from the Villa in the devastating personal loss he feels over the death of his friend Hardy, who is killed by a booby-trapped statue while partying in the town square following VE-Day celebrations (itself a key temporal shift from the novel). Indeed, while Kip's character had, earlier in the film, offered a scathing indictment of British Imperialism during a scene in which he reads Rudyard Kipling's *Kim* to the English patient, the film ends with him saying that Hardy, like Almásy, represented 'everything that's good about England,' and that Hardy was beyond reproach in his treatment of Kip as a friend and fellow soldier rather than as an exotic foreigner. Yet as ideologically suspect as these changes might be, they also help dynamize some of the paradoxes implicit in the study of film adaptation generally (and generically), and the hypotheses regarding the adaptation of gender which are at the heart of this particular study more specifically.

   That is, the generic tensions between historical epic and romantic melodrama that exist throughout Minghella's film come to a head in its concluding frames, during which various sound and image codes cue the viewer to a particularly normative reinscription of hetero-patriarchy. To explain. As Hana prepares to administer, at the English patient's request, a fatal dose of morphine (another major departure from the novel), she breaks down into uncontrollable sobs; it is this 'spectacle of a body caught in the grips of intense sensation or emotion' that Linda Williams has identified as a characteristic feature of the 'body genre' of melodrama, in which 'questions of gender construction as well as gender address in relation to basic sexual [and colonial] fantasies' necessarily intersect with the visual and narrative pleasures on offer in the film as a whole.[5] This becomes even clearer as Hana begins to read to the English patient from his Herodotus book, in particular from the final words composed by Katharine as she lay dying in the Cave of Swimmers. As Hana's character reads, her voice begins to overlap and merge with Katharine's; in the ensuing montage, the film cuts back and forth dialectically between shots of the Villa and the Cave of Swimmers, and mixes dialogically the words spoken by Juliette Binoche (Hana) and Kristin Scott Thomas

I.1   *The English Patient*: Hana (Juliette Binoche) reads to the English patient (Ralph Fiennes).

(Katharine) (see Figure I.1). In this way a thematic connection is established between the two women, who have both been abandoned by the men they love; at the same time, the image track suggests that colonial history (signalled through the epic, David Lean–like wide-angle pan of the desert) needs somehow to be 'domesticated' for more palatable mass consumption (cue the requisite interior melodramatic close-up of Hana in the home she tried – and failed – to make for herself and her motley family). Indeed, the editing of this concluding scene – cross-cutting as it does between the play of light and shadow over the sands of Africa and in the skies of Europe – combined with Gabriel Yared's mushy and bloated, string-heavy score – makes it clear that what transferred most success-fully between novel and film was Ondaatje's romantic aestheticism rather than his post-colonial politics.[6]

In focusing on Minghella's decision to play up the romance of a tragic and doomed heterosexual love rather than critiquing colonization, I don't mean to dis-miss the film out of hand. In fact, there are all sorts of reasons – formal, nationalis-tic, and, yes, emotional – why I must grudgingly admit my admiration for the film. In this representative example of the adaptation process, I am more inter-ested in highlighting how gender operationalizes both the film as historical epic and my critique of it as romantic melodrama. In other words, in both cases, Hana (and, latterly, Katharine) bears the burden of genre analysis: by virtue of her deci-sion to stay and care to the end for the English patient, and by her decision to let

Kip leave; by virtue of her ultimate possession of the Herodotus book, and by which story she chooses to read from among its interleaved pages.[7] She bears this burden in Ondaatje's novel as well, and in a way that, following from Laura Mulvey's insights in her foundational essay 'Visual Pleasure and Narrative Cinema,' one might say is fundamentally scopophilic.[8]

Readers of Ondaatje's novel will recall that it concludes with a coda or epilogue, which seems to affirm 'a mysterious connection across space and time between Kip and Hana.'[9] The omniscient narrator imagines Kip, now a married doctor with two children, sitting in his garden in India 'watch[ing] Hana, her hair longer, in her own country' (*EP* 300). And the image of voyeurism is important here, Kip's gift of second sight being expressly linked by Ondaatje to the apparatus of cinema: 'a camera's film reveals her, but only her, in silence' (*EP* 300). When one rereads this scene *after* having watched Minghella's film, it is hard not to interpret it as Ondaatje's own submission to standard novelistic conventions of romance and as a concomitant subsuming of his own (post)colonial critique; indeed, several critics have scolded Ondaatje for the way he seems to capitulate, after critiquing universalist assumptions about a shared humanist connection in previous pages, to those very principles here.[10] But those same critics are wont to ignore the expressly gendered aspect of this scene of surveillance – how Hana is positioned, to use Mulvey's discourse, as an erotic object of male phantasy, a fetishized image or spectacle to be looked at, and how Kip, as the one doing the looking, perforce becomes our surrogate subject, or focalizing agent.[11] This in turn highlights the fact that in generic classifications of Ondaatje's novel as post-colonial fiction, Kip is also routinely positioned as both the sole representative of the experience of colonization *and* of post-colonial resistance to that experience. Which is to ignore Hana's prior questioning of her own role, as a Canadian *and as a woman*, nursing the fighting men of an empire's former colonies (to say nothing of the complexities of Caravaggio, an Italian-Canadian immigrant coming 'home,' so to speak, as a spy). As Hana puts it in her concluding letter to Clara, an important document that students are likely to gloss over, 'I am sick of Europe ... I want to come home' (*EP* 296).

My reciprocal reading of Ondaatje's novel and Minghella's film foregrounds the three major axes of inquiry that I am seeking to bring together in this book. The first is the very basic and by no means original (although still contested) notion that the institution of cinema, like the institution of literature, reflective as it is of broader social ideologies (and reflecting them as well), plays a constitutive role in the production and dissemination of representations and definitions relating to gender and sexuality in our society. Related to this is the equally familiar idea that genres (both literary and cinematic) participate in this process of gender construction by virtue of various narrative codes, images, and signifiers, which are consciously and unconsciously conscripted (by authors and filmmakers, publishers and studios, reading and viewing publics) to at once hail an intended – and intentionally gendered – audience and to identify what that audience is consuming (discursively or spectatorially) as representatively masculine or feminine, heterosexual or homosexual, and so on. What may be less obviously axiomatic, and what this book is most concerned with illuminating, is how a specific focus on films adapted from literature can help expose the narrative/aesthetic *and* the ideological mechanisms that subtend the processes of genre recognition and gender identification in both of these artistic realms. Inasmuch as my understanding and use of gender (and, relatedly, sexuality; see below) in this book cannot be separated from other discursive and embodied markers of difference (such as race, ethnicity, and class), a corollary aim of this book is to examine how a specific focus on the Canadian adaptive contexts necessarily disrupts a reading of both our literatures and our cinemas as generically homogeneous, especially in terms of the hegemonic and counter-hegemonic national identifications they produce.[12]

My thinking on the interrelationships between genre and gender in cinema has been heavily influenced by the work of Steve Neale, especially in terms of the flexibility – one might say adaptability – with which he mobilizes both terms in his readings of classic Hollywood films. In the case of the former, Neale, following from Jacques Derrida, dismisses the idea that genre works through a process of exclusion, establishing discrete categories that are not to be mixed; instead, he claims not only that films can be 'multiply generic,' but also that genre itself is 'a multi-dimensional phenomenon' encompassing, for example, both a broad range of texts (not all of which are necessarily filmic) and the intratextual conventions and 'inter-textual relays' that govern the production and reception of those texts, including how those texts are marketed and distributed as they move across different media and, in the process, perhaps target different audiences.[13] As Robert Stam has recently put it: 'Filmic adaptations of novels invariably superimpose a double set of generic conventions, one drawn from the generic intertext of the source novel itself, and the other consisting of those genres engaged by the translating medium of the film. The art of filmic adaptation partially consists in choosing which generic conventions are transposable into the new medium, and which need to be discarded, supplemented, transcoded, or replaced.'[14]

In the chapters that follow, then, I am less interested in identifying and cataloguing the film adaptations I am analysing according to various narrative categories and subcategories, and applying the requisite generic labels (although I do, admittedly, do some of this); rather, I wish to examine how the supra-genre of adaptation is itself multidimensional, and multifunctional, at the same time that it contains within it certain expressly gendered expectations of what boundaries should and should not be crossed. Hence that old bugbear of adaptation studies – fidelity, about which I will have much more to say in chapters 1 and 2. All of this is another way of saying that if the term *genre* seems to disappear somewhat in the ensuing chapters, this is only because my deployment of the term *adaptation* in this book understands genre to be subsumed into – and therefore an integral part of – its rhetorical significations.

Neale is also among the first genre critics in film studies to link analyses of genre to issues of gender and sexuality. Significantly, he does so by building on Mulvey's important insights on the cinematic gaze in 'Visual Pleasure and Narrative Cinema.' Here is as good a place as any to acknowledge my own debt to Mulvey in this book, and in my understanding of the basic principles of spectatorship more generally. Mulvey's 1975 essay and its 1981 addendum[15] are not immune to critique (as I demonstrate, for example, in chapter 6); even so, I would argue that her work remains so current precisely *because* the observations that underscore her psychoanalytic theorization of the image and the look are so adaptable: in terms of the directions of, the identifications produced by, and the people positioned within the realm of the scopic.

As for Neale, in his 1980 monograph *Genre* he applied his synthesis of Mulvey to the *gendered* construction of genre as follows:

> As versions of mainstream cinema, offering systemised variants on its modes of meaning and pleasure, genres participate constantly in an ongoing process of construction of sexual difference and sexual identity. This is not simply a consequence of the fact that some genres (like the western and the war film) have traditionally been defined as aiming at a 'male' audience, while others (like the melodrama and the musical) have traditionally been defined as aiming at a 'female' one … [The cinematic institution] has contributed doubly to the construction and the maintenance of sexual identity and difference – by constructing, labelling and marketing films and genres according to (equally constructed) categories of gender and by simultaneously inscribing them with 'points of appeal' which it marks and defines as specific either to one sex [*sic*] or another. It is also a question of the fact that sexual identity and sexual difference are inscribed inevitably into a system of signification (especially one designed to narrate the actions and activities of human characters), and into the subject relations that that system, and its various processes, sustains.[16]

While the astute, post–Judith Butler student of gender will note some semantic slippage in this passage's mobilization of sex, gender, sexual identity, and sexual difference, I again appreciate the expansiveness with which Neale deploys his terms. Indeed, throughout this book I myself use the terms gender and sexuality not precisely interchangeably, but rather as co-implicated in the reciprocal production of and exchange between identity and desire, especially in terms of how *gender* identification and *sexual* desire are frequently conflated within what Butler calls the 'heterosexual matrix.'[17] To this end, in several of the chapters that follow (but most notably in chapters 4, 5, and 6), I am particularly concerned with how minority genders and sexualities are systematically excluded and marginalized by the generic rules of identification and desire set out by hetero-patriarchy. One such rule says that if you identify as one gender, you are supposed to desire sexually the opposite gender; another says that there should be some sort of coherence between your interior psychic gender identity and sexual desires and the external expression of that identity and those desires.

Moreover, Neale in some respects anticipates Butler's famous pronouncements in *Gender Trouble* by implying that genders, like genres, are constituted and labelled (as normative or non-normative, for example) through a process of repetition[18] – a process inscribed and circulated simultaneously at the level of individual signifiers on screen, at the level of product marketing, and at the level of spectatorial identification. And inasmuch as Neale, again like Butler, reminds us that this process of inscription is a bodily one, I find extremely useful – and most pertinent to my own study – his injunction that we examine how gender difference and 'sexual difference are focused in their construction on the representation of the human body, and the way in which such representations are specified generically.'[19] Throughout this book I attempt to keep Neale's comments at the forefront of both my readings of individual texts/films (and specific scopophilic scenes within them) and my analyses of the gendered metaphorics of adaptation itself.

When I began this project, I was a frustrated reader and an impoverished spectator: frustrated by what I saw as a general lack of scholarly attention to adaptation studies in the Canadian context (and especially to specific examples that I felt merited greater attention), and by my own inability to contribute as yet in any meaningful way to that discourse; impoverished by my own woeful ignorance of the historical canon of Canadian cinema, and by my inability to access, let alone see, much of that canon. As such, when I started to conceive the broad parameters of this book, the questions I initially – and rather naively – posed emerged directly from a fundamental, and fundamentally vast, deficit of knowledge. What gets lost when a novel by Margaret Atwood or a play by Robert Lepage or a book of poems by Michael Turner is transferred onto the screen? What, if anything, is gained? Are these losses or gains (if, indeed, we should be even thinking about them in such terms) compounded and/or mitigated by the nationality of the director or by the countries originating the productions or participating in the co-productions (if other than Canada)? How have production companies and government funding agencies – the National Film Board of Canada, the Canadian Broadcasting Corporation, Bravo!FACT, Alliance Atlantis, Telefilm Canada, Canadian Heritage – helped facilitate the adaptive process? And to what extent does the film and television canon that has resulted merely replicate the canon of Canada's literatures? What might we learn by comparing the critical and audience receptions of especially popular or especially controversial adaptations? How do questions of authorship, genre, spectatorship, identification, and narrative desire translate between print and visual media? And do they translate differently in English Canada and Quebec? How might a close examination of individual filmed treatments of Canadian literature evolve into a broader theory or model of adaptation in general? In what ways do films – and film 'adaptations' (however broadly interpreted), in particular – interpellate the viewer/reader, and how are they themselves interpolated within cinematic history and material culture? And, finally, to what extent, and effect, are such processes of interpellation and interpolation gendered?

   In the end, as I've already outlined, I have winnowed my focus down to a version of this last question. I seek, in part, to make sense of this question by focusing on the history, theory, and critical contexts of selected film treatments of Canadian literary texts. The chapters that follow are mostly structured around specific case studies, but at the same time they aim to address fundamental debates on the politics and semiotics of cinematic representation more generally. They cover a range of different topics, consider a diverse cross-section of 'texts,' and adopt a variety of disciplinary, methodological, and theoretical perspectives. In no way is this book meant to be a comprehensive overview of film adaptation in this country. There are obvious gaps in terms of topical, historical, generic, and regional coverage. Still, I hope this synchronic reading of individual adaptative moments within the overlapping diachronic narratives of Canadian literary and cinematic history will contribute to an emerging discourse on what – to paraphrase Gilberto Perez on Jean Renoir's *A Day in the Country* (itself an adaptation of a story by Guy de Maupassant) – we might call the landscape of fiction and film in this country, and that it will offer in the process 'a representation both of the world and an apprehension of the world.'[20]

A word about the selection criteria for the literary texts and film adaptations considered in these chapters. First, I have chosen for analysis only films produced since 1968. This was the year the Canadian Film Development Corporation (the forerunner of Telefilm) came into existence, with important consequences (discussed in chapter 1) for which film projects – including adaptations from literature – got greenlighted for funding. Closely allied to this chronological consideration is a related cultural (and economic) imperative that has governed my choices for individual case studies. That is, with minor exceptions, each of the films I have chosen to focus on in depth is either a Canadian production or a co-production; this will allow for some broad generalizations as well as for some specific comparisons between Canada's self- (and cross-) representations in its national literatures and those in its national cinemas. As well, this book makes virtually no attempt to analyse the rich tradition of televisual adaptations of literature in Canada; while this might seem a glaring oversight to some, I think that important differences in production, broadcast/distribution, narrativization/serialization, and spectatorship preclude an easy synthesis of the two media under the comparative rubric of adaptation (as my discussion of *American Whiskey Bar* in chapter 7 will in part reveal). Nor do I treat, in any comprehensive manner, the rich tradition of short films adapted from Canadian literature in this country, be it high-profile NFB-, Bravo!FACT-, or W Network–produced works based on canonical stories by Gabrielle Roy, Margaret Atwood, or Alice Munro, or less well-known (and more sexually adventurous and narratively experimental) independent fare such as Jason McBride's *Stargaze* (1998; based on the story by Derek McCormack), Jeremy Podeswa's *Touch* (2001; based on the story 'My Lover's Touch' by Patrick Roscoe), and Adrienne Campbell-Holt's *Autobiography of Red* (2002; based on selections from the long poem by Anne Carson).

Finally, in what follows I have decided to focus as much as possible on adaptations that have, generally speaking, been little (or under-) discussed by critics, literary and film alike. So, for example, in chapter 2 you will find sustained readings of the film versions of Anne Hébert's *Kamouraska* and Margaret Atwood's *Surfacing* rather than the more high-profile and critically contentious treatments of *Les fous de bassan* and *The Handmaid's Tale*. Similarly, when discussing images of the Indigene in early 1990s literature-to-film adaptations in chapter 3, I compare the largely forgotten (because, admittedly, largely forgettable) English-language adaptation of Yves Thériault's *Agaguk, l'homme du loup* (retitled *Shadow of the Wolf* for the screen) with the more high-profile treatment of Brian Moore's *Black Robe*. And in chapters 4 and 5, on the transposition of various gay images from stage to screen, though I do spend some time analysing such acclaimed adaptations as André Brassard's *Il était une fois dans l'est* (based on Michel Tremblay's 'Belles

Soeurs' cycle), Jean Beaudin's *Being at home with Claude* (based on the play by René-Daniel Dubois), and John Greyson's *Lilies* (an English-language treatment of Michel Marc Bouchard's *Les feluettes*) – all of which have been repeatedly dissected by other critics (although none more perceptively than André Loiselle[21]) – I devote most of my attention to sustained readings of Harvey Hart's unjustly ignored film adaptation of John Herbert's play *Fortune and Men's Eyes*, and Robert Lepage's entire adaptive oeuvre, which has generated much critical commentary, albeit very little of it framed in terms of issues of gender and sexuality.

The one place where I break all of these rules is in chapter 1. There I briefly survey the history of film *and* television adaptation in this country, from 1913 to the present. In so doing, I not only discuss the important roles played in that history by national bodies such as the CBC/Société Radio-Canada and the NFB/Office National du Film de Canada; I also perforce engage with what it seems only appropriate to call the Hollywoodization of Canadian literary texts (not to mention a concomitant Canadianization of Hollywood). This process has taken various forms, from the presence of American actors such as Richard Dreyfuss, James Woods, and Tom Berenger in homegrown adaptations of Mordecai Richler's *The Apprenticeship of Duddy Kravitz* and *Joshua Then and Now* and Stephen Vizinczey's *In Praise of Older Women*, to major American studio releases of films based on novels by Lucy Maud Montgomery (the 1921 version of *Anne of Green Gables*), Margaret Laurence (the Paul Newman-directed *Rachel, Rachel*, based on *A Jest of God*), Michael Ondaatje (*The English Patient*), and, yes, Margaret Atwood (I will be discussing at length Volker Schlöndorff's muddled take on *The Handmaid's Tale*). At the end of that chapter I undertake another survey, this one of theories of cinematic adaptation, and of the engagement of specific critics – from George Bluestone and André Bazin to Brian McFarlane and Robert Stam – with the ideologies of fidelity, translation, narration, and intertextuality.

Chapter 2 continues to probe the issue of fidelity – specifically, important feminist caveats to critiques of fidelity – via an analysis of the neo-gothic 'women's pictures' that resulted from the adaptation of three canonical novels by Canadian feminist writers. Hébert's *Kamouraska* and Atwood's *Surfacing* I have already mentioned; what makes these films especially ripe for comparison in this particular framework is that both were directed, in the space of eight years, by Claude Jutra. I examine the diegetic and extra-diegetic constraints faced by this eminent male director in bringing these seemingly 'unfilmmable' texts of female interiority to the screen, arguing that such constraints are paradoxically symptomatic of a fidelity to the exogamous sexual relations at the heart of the gothic marriage plot. To this end, I then go on to discuss Mireille Dansereau's 1987 film of Marie-Claire Blais's *Le sourd dans la ville*, demonstrating how the director subtly re-presents, or rescreens, the frightening as precisely that which is most familiar. Drawing on feminist literary criticism of eighteenth- and nineteenth-century gothic fiction and feminist film theory of the 1940s gothic woman's film, I focus in this chapter not only on the particular hauntings experienced by the female protagonists on screen, but also on the uncanny sense of doubleness and déjà vu that necessarily haunts the adaptation process as a whole.

Chapter 3 looks at 'images of the Indigene' as they have been produced and institutionalized within this country's literary and cinematic imaginaries. Among the adaptations I will be considering in this regard are four that appeared in quick succession – and to strongly mixed critical and popular responses – in the 1990s. Bruce Beresford's 1991 adaptation of Brian Moore's *Black Robe*, starring Lothaire Bluteau as Father Laforgue, and *Shadow of the Wolf*, Jacques Dorfmann's 1993 English-language treatment of Yves Thiériault's *Agaguk*, starring B-list Hollywood celebrities Lou Diamond Phillips and Jennifer Tilly, were both big-budget attempts to renovate the historical epic via post-colonial inflected screen representations of white–indigenous contact. Richard Bugjaski's *Clearcut* (1991), based on M.T. Kelly's novel *A Dream Like Mine*, and Bruce McDonald's *Dance Me Outside* (1995), adapted from a collection of short stories by W.P. Kinsella, are more social realist in bent and attempt to depict, from a predominantly indigenous perspective, the choices and constraints faced by contemporary First Nations peoples in resisting white cultural domination on and off the reserve. However, as I demonstrate by applying critical race theory and theories of Third Cinema, all four films draw mainly on the generic conventions of ethnographic romance; they play up the spectacle of a timeless screen Other – particularly where representations of gender and sexuality are concerned – in order, paradoxically, to render even more invisible the Indigene's absence from the scene/seen of history. I conclude this chapter with an analysis of Zacharias Kunuk's award-winning *Atanarjuat: The Fast Runner*, first examining the specific challenges posed by his treatment of an Inuit oral myth to adaptation studies' theories of (inter)textuality, and then looking more closely at how Kunuk's film works to foreground a resistance to and returning of the ethnographic gaze, making visible the very processes and mechanisms of representation and non-representation that the other films seek to elide.

In terms of the overlap between gender and genre, and between narrative and social space, that this book develops in the specific context of film adaptation, chapter 4 examines what I see as a significant subcategory of movies that emerged from Toronto and Montreal in the 1970s, in which the iconographic figure of the drag queen emerges as hero, one whose gender *and* narrative ambivalence challenges coherent, or normative, readings of the spectatorial production of desire. Into this subcategory we would need to place both André Brassard's *Il était une fois dans l'est*, his celebrated take on six of the plays from Michel Tremblay's 'Belles Soeurs' cycle, and Richard Benner's award-winning *Outrageous!*, adapted from Margaret Gibson's short story 'Making It.' Yet while I do indeed discuss both these films, chapter 4 focuses on *Fortune and Men's Eyes*, Harvey Hart's controversial 1971 adaptation of John Herbert's play about the dynamics of sex and power in a men's prison, which locates resistance to the institutionalization of dominant forms of masculine identity formation most forcefully – and most iconographically – within the character of Queenie, the flamboyant drag queen and self-declared 'cell mother' of both the play and the film. As I argue, her character has undergone substantial revision in the film; as a result, the play's narrative epistemology has been subtly revised and its dominant sexual epistemology has been radically shifted.

In chapter 5 I examine the intersection of auteurism and adaptation in Robert Lepage's cinema by focusing on the transposition of images of the queer male body from his theatrical source texts to their filmed adaptations. Drawing on the work of Gilles Deleuze, I look at how Lepage is able to police his cinematic narratives – that is, their form and content – more vigilantly than his theatrical ones. The temporal positioning of his self-translated films as in some senses superseding the theatrical collaborations on which they are for the most part based lends them a degree of spatial 'auteurity' in terms of the narrative and imagistic changes inscribed therein. I then focus more closely on how these changes relate to the reframing of the queer male body from stage to screen, arguing that the repeated image of the corpse in Lepage's cinematic oeuvre can be tied to the 'death' of certain important homosexual significations in his source texts.

In chapter 6 I attempt, via Patricia White, Judith Mayne, Teresa de Lauretis, and other lesbian-feminist film theorists, to negotiate between the historical 'ghosting' of the lesbian subject on screen and that of the lesbian spectator in mainstream feminist film criticism post-Laura Mulvey and Mary Ann Doane. I do so by developing, via Judith Butler and others, a theory of lesbian filmic citationality, a referential circuit of indirection and intertextuality that requires the viewer to look both at and beyond the image bounded by the screen, to pay attention to ghosts that lurk both inside and outside of the machine, to in effect see double. After a brief detour through Percy Adlon's *Salmonberries* and Deepa Mehta's *Fire*, I then apply this theory of cinematic ghosting and lesbian citationality to an extended discussion of *Lost and Delirious*, Quebec director Léa Pool's adaptation of English-Canadian author Susan Swan's *The Wives of Bath*, about the relationship among three teenage girls at a female boarding school. Here, the specific operations of lesbian citationality and spectatorial identification are doubly complex. That is, the novel is framed by its intertextual dialogues with Radclyffe Hall's *The Well of Loneliness*; furthermore, the film must be sited/cited both within the context of Pool's broader cinematic oeuvre (particularly her 1986 film *Anne Trister* and her 1999 masterpiece, *Emporte-moi) and* within the specifically *adaptive* history of lesbian cinematic representation, with which *Lost and Delirious* is itself in dialogue. From *Mädchen in Uniform* and *Olivia* to *The Children's Hour* and *The Prime of Miss Jean Brodie*: haunting Pool's film is less the ghost of Swan's original 'written' text than the combined spectre of these cinematic *inter*texts, each of which analyses the continuum of affective relationships among girls and women in the context of the boarding school, and each of which is also an adaptation of a work of literature (by Christa Winsloe, Dorothy Strachey Bussy, Lillian Hellman, and Muriel Spark, respectively).

In chapter 7 I turn from female to male homosociality. In so doing I attempt to contribute to the growing body of scholarship on representations of masculinity in gender studies, cinema studies, and Canadian cultural studies by focusing on the cross-genre and interdisciplinary work of Michael Turner as it has intersected with and been adapted by various male filmmakers and video artists in this country. In the first and most comprehensive part of the chapter I examine Bruce McDonald's 1996 film adaptation of *Hard Core Logo*, Turner's 'novel in verse' about a once-legendary Vancouver punk band that reunites for one last shot at fame and glory. I focus here on how McDonald's mock-documentary film trades as well on conventions of the road movie and the romantic melodrama to expose the invisible crisis of gender at the heart of both Turner's generically hybrid text and the masquerade of masculinity more generally. I continue my discussion of Turner and McDonald's adaptive collaborations, and the representations of masculinity at the centre of them, by focusing briefly on McDonald's 1998 live television broadcast of Turner's novel cum screenplay, *American Whiskey Bar*, and on the 1998 short film *Elimination Dance*, based on Michael Ondaatje's book of poetry, co-directed by McDonald and starring Turner in the pivotal role of the caller. Finally, in the concluding section of this chapter, I turn briefly to Turner's ongoing collaborations with celebrated Vancouver photographer and video artist Stan Douglas. My focus here is the 2001 video *Journey into Fear*, a complex adaptation, via Herman Melville's *The Confidence Man*, of the 1975 Daniel Mann film of the same name (itself based on a similarly titled 1942 film, which is in turn based on Eric Ambler's 1940 novel).

My main goal in this book is to analyse specific adaptations within the framework of gender and genre analysis. But in addition, I have two ancillary aims. First, I wish to situate Canadian film and literature not just intranationally but internationally. Thus the reader will find, scattered through the following pages, references to, and sometimes extended analyses of, books and films and performances by Percy Adlon, Sherman Alexie, Jacqueline Audry, Charlotte Brontë, Dorothy Bussy, Mart Crowley, Michael Cunningham, Stephen Daldry, Daphne Du Maurier, Stephen Elliott, Chris Eyre, Milos Forman, William Friedkin, Radclyffe Hall, Lillian Hellman, Alfred Hitchcock, Ken Kesey, Jennie Livingston, John Cameron Mitchell, Ronald Neame, Kimberley Pierce, Rob Reiner, Leontine Sagan, Muriel Spark, Robert Stevenson, Christa Winsloe, and William Wyler, among others. Second, I hope to use individual chapters – and the case studies around which they are structured – to engage more broadly with specific currents, theories, and debates in film theory. When a critic crosses disciplines, the 'kid in the candy store' syndrome tends to take over, with consequent attempts to absorb, digest, and regurgitate all the major critical paradigms. So before I get caught, let me be the first to admit that in the following chapters, my hands are in multiple jars. I have eagerly read – and in most cases found singularly instructive – a wealth of important film scholarship and theory; I hope that in the following chapters I have organized my application of this body of work with a degree of coherence.

For example, my focus in chapter 6 on feminist theories of cinematic representation and spectatorship is balanced in chapter 3 by a discussion of how critical race theory on film intersects with feminist theory around similar issues. My updating of the 'positive images debate' in early gay film criticism via Judith Butler's theories of gender performativity and heterosexual melancholia in chapter 4 finds a corollary in chapter 5, where I reread the queer images on offer in Lepage's films via an application of Deleuze's notion of the indeterminacy of the 'crystal image.' My opening discussion of film theory's intertextual and (inter)semiotic challenges to fidelity criticism in chapter 1 is contextualized by my examination of feminist narratology's concomitant challenges to critiques of the fidelity model in chapter 2. And permeating all of the chapters (to varying degrees) is my attempt to grapple with the basic tenets of apparatus theory, specifically as it has received, reconceived, and disseminated Lacanian psychoanalysis and Barthesian semiosis, and especially as it has been applied to the multiply gendered and generic adaptations of cinematic identification and narrative desire.

I hope my engagements with film theory (which reflect my own peculiar, some might say peculiarly literary, adaptations of some very basic tenets) do not obscure the close textual analyses of individual works of literature and film that form the core of this study. I hope, as well, that they do not obscure the pleasure I experienced in conducting that analysis. In the conclusion to his important and ground-breaking study *Stars*, on the ideologies governing the production and consumption of images of film celebrities, Richard Dyer offers some final ruminations on 'beauty, pleasure, delight,' noting that while he does not wish to privilege these aesthetic, emotional, and experiential responses over the 'cognitive' analysis he has just so exhaustively documented for us, neither does he want, 'in the rush to analysis, to forget what it is that I am analysing.'[22] Likewise, let me conclude this introduction by stating that although I approach the texts (both source and target) under analysis in this book as a critic, I also approach them as a fan, even when, as with *The English Patient*, I am asking of them deeply troubling questions about gender and genre.

1 Sex Maidens and Yankee Skunks: A Field Guide to Reading 'Canadian' Movies

A skunk and an American flag were introduced – both equally unknown in P.E. Island. I could have shrieked with rage over the latter. Such crass blatant Yankeeism!

> L.M. Montgomery, on the 1919 silent film adaptation
> of *Anne of Green Gables*[1]

This story could have been the most gross sexploitative film ever, sort of 'maidens on a sexual rampage.'

> Margaret Atwood, pronouncing herself satisfied
> with the film adaptation of *The Handmaid's Tale*[2]

The English Patient was, of course, not the first work of Canadian literature adapted for the screen to garner high-profile acclaim among *cinéastes* south of the border while at the same time being excoriated by offended readers back home. Phil Robinson's *Field of Dreams* (1989), based on W.P. Kinsella's novel, *Shoeless Joe* (1982), is another good example; changes in narrative content and setting were widely perceived as a sop to American audiences. Nor was *The English Patient* the first feature-length movie based on Canadian literary source material to score a slew of Academy Award nominations: *Rachel, Rachel*, Paul Newman's 1968 adaptation of Margaret Laurence's *A Jest of God* (1966), starring Newman's wife, Joanne Woodward, was nominated for four Oscars (Best Picture, Actress, Supporting Actress, and Adapted Screenplay), and took home a slew of other high-profile international awards (including Golden Globe and New York Film Critics Circle Awards for Best Actress and Best Director).

As with *Field of Dreams*, the most noticeable change in *Rachel, Rachel* is the shift in setting. Screenwriter Stewart Stern has transformed Laurence's fictional prairie town of Manawaka into a quaint New England hamlet, which Newman's opening shots (already in some senses adopting Rachel Cameron's point of view) capture in all its suffocating sameness; he cuts quickly from the horizon at dawn, to the cemetery, to the deserted main street (shown in wide angle), to the school where Rachel teaches, and finally to the house (which also doubles as the town funeral parlour) on Japonica Street where Rachel lives with her mother (Kate Harrington). The American locale requires another minor change, this one to the film's ending: Rachel and her mother depart for a new life in Oregon, rather than for Vancouver and a reunion with sister Stacey, as in the novel. Otherwise, the film is remarkably faithful to the book in terms of both narrative and narration. The novel's formal construction as an extended interior monologue is conveyed filmically through the frequent use of voice-over. This might seem a rather pedestrian and clumsy interpretation of Laurence's discursive style, but Newman complicates matters by presenting Rachel's voice-over not monologically, but polyphonically, as a discordant dialogue between the warring voices inside Rachel's head. Furthermore, Rachel's frequent fantasies, both paranoid and surreal, are rendered on screen in both present-tense daydream sequences and hallucinogenic flashbacks, with Newman using hand-held cameras, extreme close-ups, and different film speeds to convey the fragility of Rachel's mind.

In terms of the main focus of this book, the film is to be applauded for the way in which it exploits the genre of the melodrama and 'women's picture' to bring out more fully the anxieties surrounding gender that are at the heart of Laurence's depiction of the complicated relationship between Rachel and fellow teacher Calla Mackie (played in the film with exceptional brio by Estelle Parsons). That is, Rachel's horrified rejection of Calla's clumsy expression of same-sex affection (see Figure 1.1) is shown to be of a piece with Rachel's more general sexual repression. Thus, for example, the seduction scene with old boyfriend Nick (James Olson), which immediately follows the confrontation between Rachel and Calla, is equally awkward and unromantic, and culminates not with a languorous shot of Rachel in post-coital bliss, but rather with her engaging in the unpleasant business of douching.

Rachel, Rachel failed to win an Oscar in any of the categories for which it was nominated. Six years later, in 1974, Mordecai Richler and co-nominee Lionel Chetwynd would be bested in the category of Best Adapted Screenplay for their treatment of Richler's *The Apprenticeship of Duddy Kravitz* (Mario Puzo won that year for *The Godfather: Part II*). In 1984, however, the CBC-Atlantis production of Alice Munro's short story 'Boys and Girls,' starring Megan Follows as the put-upon Margaret, adjusting uneasily to some painful lessons in the gendering of social space, would take home a statuette as Best Live Action Short. And the following year, the NFB-Atlantis adaptation of Sinclair Ross's 'The Painted Door' would narrowly miss out in the same category. Still, it was *The English Patient*'s Academy triumph on that March night in 1997 – capping as it did a relatively strong box office run for a 160-minute historical epic (one decidedly more highbrow than James Cameron's *Titanic*) – combined with director Minghella's open and oft-cited admiration for the author, and Ondaatje's own close involvement in the film process (he was a familiar presence on the set and became a close friend not only of Minghella but also of editor Walter Murch[3]), that seemed to focus cinematic attention on Canadian writing and Canadian writers in new and unprecedented ways. At the same time, the collaboration highlighted important cultural and media elisions, many of which manifested themselves, tellingly, on Oscar night itself: There was that business about producer Saul Zaentz, in accepting the Oscar for Best Picture, momentarily forgetting and then subsequently mangling Ondaatje's name. And granted, the actress clutching the statuette for Best Sup-

1.1   *Rachel, Rachel*: Rachel (Joanne Woodward) collapses into Calla's (Estelle Parsons) arms at the tabernacle meeting.

porting Actress – Juliette Binoche – was French and not Québécoise. And while Minghella did take home the award for Best Director, he failed to win for Best Adapted Screenplay (losing out to Billy Bob Thornton for *Sling Blade*).

Such slights were perhaps to be expected. Hollywood, despite being in large part founded by Canadians (Mary Pickford was born in Toronto, Jack Warner in London, Ontario; and Louis B. Mayer had been raised in Saint John, New Brunswick), remains steadfast in its effacement of this country as anything other than an extended backlot of America, a source of cheap production crews. In the event, what we might call *The English Patient*'s Big Hollywood Adventure did have seismic reverberations back home in Canada. For publishing executives, literary agents, and cultural pundits there suddenly emerged, alongside international writing awards and prizes, and the standard domestic and foreign sales figures, another cultural yardstick by which to measure the global success of Canada's contemporary literatures: film rights. Selling them, and selling them quickly – preferably in a highly publicized bidding war to some marquee name with Hollywood clout – signals that an author has truly arrived. Never mind the actual quality of the finished picture.

Timothy Findley's *The Piano Man's Daughter* caused nary a blip on the radar screens of awards lists either inside or outside Canada, but it got an added jolt of adrenaline on the national bestseller lists when it was announced that none other than Whoopi Goldberg had purchased the film rights, and subsequently when it was announced that Stockard Channing had agreed to star. That the resulting made-for-TV film, directed by *Anne of Green Gables* impresario Kevin Sullivan, hardly registered with audiences when it was broadcast on the CBC in 2003 seemed almost ancillary. Margaret Atwood's official website proudly announces that three recent novels – *The Robber Bride, Alias Grace*, and *The Blind Assassin* – are all in various stages of film development, by Irish Screen Productions and Victor Solnicki, Working Title Films and Cate Blanchett, and the BBC, respectively (and this despite the decidedly qualified success of earlier adaptations of two of her novels: Claude Jutra's *Surfacing* [1981] and Volker Schlöndorff's *The Handmaid's Tale* [1990]). Carol Shields voiced her own reservations about Anna Benson Gyles's 1996 adaptation of her novel *Swann*[4] (with Miranda Richardson and Brenda Fricker), which turned a witty satire on academe into an overly earnest treatise on male violence against women; about that adaptation, I will have more to say in the next chapter. Yet neither that film nor Deepa Mehta's tepid film version of *The Republic of Love* has halted plans to adapt two other Shields novels: *The Stone Diaries* (to be directed by Cynthia Scott for Toronto's Rhombus Media) and *Larry's Party* (already adapted as a musical by Richard Ouzounian and Marek Norman for Toronto's Canadian Stage Company in January 2001). And director Anne Wheeler – whose previous credits include adaptations of Sinclair Ross's 'One's a Heifer,' Marilyn Halvorson's *Cowboys Don't Cry*, Brian Doyle's *Angel Square*, and Margaret Laurence's 'To Set Our House in Order' and *The Diviners* – failed to capitalize on the star power of either Cybill Shepherd or Brendan Fehr when she followed up her muddled take on Linda Svendsen's short story collection *Marine Life* with an equally confusing adaptation of Alice Munro's 'A Wilderness Station' in *Edge of Madness*. (Atwood, Shields, and Munro have fared much better with the series of short films based on a selection of their short stories that began premiering on the W Network in 2003.[5]). Despite these cautionary tales, the pages of publishing trade magazine *Quill & Quire* continue to be filled with regular announcements of other high-profile Canadian authors (including Ann-Marie MacDonald, Anne Michaels, Thomas King, Guy Vanderhaege, and Douglas Coupland, whose entire literary corpus seems to be under option by Hollywood) who have recently sold film rights to their works.

How many of these works actually make it to the screen is, of course, another question entirely. Still, it is worth noting that this kind of active optioning of literary texts is not unprecedented in Canadian film history, nor is it in literary and film history generally. Indeed, the concept of film adaptation is as old as the cinematic medium itself. As James Naremore noted recently in his introduction to *Film Adaptation*, several of the earliest feature films were derived from literary sources: *Oliver Twist* (USA, J. Stuart Blackton, 1909; UK, Thomas Bentley, 1912), *Quo Vadis?* (Italy, Enrico Guazzoni, 1912), *Birth of a Nation* (USA, D.W. Griffith, 1915), and so on.[6] In Canada, the earliest produced feature film – by the Halifax-based Canadian Bioscope Company – was *Evangeline*, a 1913 adaptation of the classic 1847 narrative poem by American Henry Wadsworth Longfellow, which tells the story of one of the darkest chapters in Canadian history.[7] Directed by Americans E.P. Sullivan and William Cavanaugh, the film was a huge commercial success, although it has all but slipped from this country's collective consciousness by now. In the spirit of cultural recuperation, then, in what follows I want to trace very briefly the history of film adaptations of literature in this country, paying particular attention to how the exigencies of Canada's emerging feature film and television policies helped shape this history, and pausing every now and then in my cataloguing of titles to offer more extended critical commentary on a selected few of these adaptations.[8]

As Peter Morris demonstrates in his important study of the beginnings of Canadian film production, literature and film have been intimately connected in this country since the silent era of the 1910s and 1920s. For example, in his chapter on rogue producer Ernest Shipman (husband of pioneering feminist actor, screenwriter, and director Nell Shipman), he notes that after enormous success adapting literary works *about* Canada written by the American James Oliver Curwood (including *Back to God's Country* in 1919, written by and starring Nell, and the most successful Canadian film of the silent era), Shipman next turned his attention to adapting several works by Ralph Connor, then English Canada's best-known and bestselling author.[9] Between 1920 and 1922 four films were produced based on Connor's novels – *God's Crucible*, *Cameron of the Royal Mounted*, *The Critical Age*, and *The Man from Glengarry* – all of them directed by Henry MacRae. Following this, Shipman produced *Blue Water* in 1924, based on the novel by Halifax writer Frederick William Wallace.[10] The film was directed by David Hartford and starred a then little-known Montreal ingenue by the name of Norma Shearer, soon to make a jump to the studio system south of the border and to forge a strategic alliance, both professional and personal, with MGM head Irving Thalberg. Unfortunately, many of the silent films adapted from Canadian literary texts during this period are now lost, including William Desmond Taylor's initial 1919 treatment of Lucy Maud Montgomery's *Anne of Green Gables* (which, as per this chapter's first epigraph, she reviled) and a fabled silent adaptation of Martha Ostenso's *Wild Geese* by Phil Goldstone, which was recently remade as a CBC miniseries by Toronto director Jeremy Podeswa (of *Five Senses* fame), with American acting icon Sam Shepard in the starring role of patriarch Caleb Gare.

However, during the silent and early talkies era, the Canadian writer whose work was featured most prominently, and most consistently, on screen was one who, strictly speaking, was not Canadian. Between 1915 and 1933, the former Scottish banker Robert Service saw the release of eleven films based on his poems and novels, all of which capitalized as much on the narrative drive of his work as they did on the 'Klondike craze' then sweeping through Hollywood movie making. These films included the following adaptations of poems from *The Spirit of the Yukon* (1907): *The Song of the Wage Slave* (USA, 1915, Herbert and Alice Blaché), *The Shooting of Dan McGrew* (USA, 1915, Herbert Blaché), *My Madonna* (USA, 1915, Alice Blaché), *The Lure of the Heart's Desire* (USA, 1916, Francis J. Gordon), *The Spell of the Yukon* (USA, 1916, Burton L. King), *The Law of the Yukon* (USA, 1920, Charles Miller), and another version of *The Shooting of Dan McGrew* (USA, 1924, Clarence G. Badger).[11] In addition, there were adaptations of three of Service's Klondike novels: *Poisoned Paradise* (USA, 1924, Louis J. Gasnier), *The Roughneck* (USA, 1924, Jack Conway), and *The Trail of 98* (USA, 1928, Clarence Brown). This frenzy of early cinematic adaptations of Service texts came to a head in 1933, when American director Ray Taylor brought out a twelve-part serial based on the poem 'Clancy of the Mounted Police,' included in the 1909 collection *Ballads of a Cheechako*.

A year later, the work of an ersatz Québécois underwent similar treatment when French director Julien Duvivier released his cinematic take on fellow countryman Louis Hémon's *Maria Chapdelaine* (1916), a novel that would eventually become canonized in this country as the quintessential example of the Quebec *roman de la fidelité*. Like *Anne of Green Gables*, Hémon's novel would spawn its own mini-industry of film adaptations. *Maria Chapdelaine* was brought to the screen twice more: in 1950, by another European director, Marc Allégret (the film was released in North America under the title *The Naked Heart*); and, finally, in 1983 in a splashy 'home-grown' production directed by Quebec auteur Gilles Carle that was released simultaneously as a theatrical feature and a television miniseries.[12]

Coincidentally, 1934 also saw the release of the second instalment in the *Anne of Green Gables* franchise – George Nichols, Jr's bowdlerization for RKO, starring the eponymous Anne Shirley in the title role. This adaptation runs a scant seventy-nine minutes. The plot of Montgomery's novel has necessarily been telescoped, with scenes being omitted or compressed, a single composite character standing in for a range of different types from the novel, and so on. Still, Matthew Cuthbert's miraculous deathbed recovery in the movie's final frames, and Gilbert Blythe's role in bringing this about, is – even in the context of Hollywood's long and notorious history of cultural borrowings and transformations – a rather egregious change.

The novel ends, following Matthew's death and Anne's decision to stay and teach in Avonlea, by highlighting the connection between Anne and Marilla as proud, independent, and capable women; by contrast, the film shifts the focus to the men, playing up the connection between Gilbert, who heroically saves the day by securing the aid of a specialist doctor, and Matthew, who remarks on his fondness for Gilbert and notes with regret that, had events gone differently, Gilbert might have been his own son. This is a reference to yet another major change in the film: the novel's background story about the aborted romance between Marilla and John Blythe, Gilbert's father, is altered to a rivalry between Matthew and John over Gilbert's mother. As Theodore F. Sheckels has recently put it, 'the movie's plot becomes *Romeo and Juliet* superimposed upon *Anne of Green Gables*, thereby marginalizing Anne as the passive victim of circumstances.'[13] Instead of functioning as her intellectual rival, as in the novel, in the movie Gilbert is positioned very clearly (and very early on) as Anne's romantic suitor. Gone, too, are the frequent paeans to 'ambition' and independent vision that Anne makes throughout the novel; the film suggests that a woman's greatest ambition in life should be marriage (as when Diana Barry's announcement of her engagement – another major departure from the book – provokes in Anne a crisis of faith about her studies).

As Benjamin Lefebvre has noted, Nichols's film is part of an ongoing series of cinematic 'deviations' from Montgomery's original texts – deviations that (as Lefevbre further points out) one must be careful not to condemn outright, if only because they raise broader issues around gender and genre.[14] Indeed, precisely *because* it focuses on male-female romance, the 1934 adaptation of *Anne of Green Gables* helps highlight the novel's contrasting focus on female-female friendship. The changes made in the film are so extreme, and so obviously designed to recoup the narrative as a patriarchal one, that they help transform what otherwise might be dismissed as a charming children's book into a radically proto-feminist text. As Sheckels puts it, a 'comparison between the movie and the novel alerts us to how Montgomery's novel offers a text that privileges community, especially that formed by women, and friendship among girls and among women, including intergenerational ones such as that between mother and daughter.'[15] Here, Marilla and Diana supplant the privileged position occupied by Matthew and Gilbert in the film and redirect our attention to the continuum of affective relationships established between girls and women throughout the novel, and to how those relationships gender the spaces (both interior and exterior) described in the novel as expressly female.

Finally, in 1935 yet another female Canadian writer famous for her serial fiction received the Hollywood treatment. That year saw the release of *Jalna,* directed by John Cromwell (who also directed *Of Human Bondage*), a cinematic amalgamation of the first four novels of Mazo de la Roche's Whiteoaks family saga: *Jalna* (1927), *The Whiteoaks of Jalna* (1929), *Finch's Fortune* (1931), and *The Master of Jalna* (1933). Given the influence that de la Roche's novels are said to have had on Margaret Mitchell,[16] it is interesting that the Jalna estate's incarnation on screen arrived four years before that of Scarlett O'Hara's beloved Tara in David O. Selznick's epic production of *Gone With the Wind*. Moreover, in the context of my preceding discussions of *Anne of Green Gables* and *Maria Chapdelaine*, it is worth noting that de la Roche's novels have also given rise to their own version of filmic serialization. In 1972 the CBC broadcast a miniseries, *The Whiteoaks of Jalna*, adapted for television by Timothy Findley and directed by John Trent. It was a critical and ratings disaster. Radio-Canada had better luck when in 1994 it broadcast a French-language version, also simply called *Jalna*, starring French diva Danielle Darrieux (lately of *8 Women* fame) as Gran.

The 1940s and 1950s witnessed two important developments in Canadian film and media history that directly affected the future of cinematic adaptations (and print culture more generally) in this country. The first was the creation of the National Film Board of Canada/Office National du Film de Canada (NFB/ONF), following the passing in Parliament of the *National Film Act* in 1939. English documentary filmmaker John Grierson, who wrote the report that highlighted the need for government-sponsored film production in this country, became the NFB/ONF's first commissioner, and Norman McLaren was quickly hired to head its animation unit. Documentaries and animated shorts governed the NFB/ONF's mandate during its early years, establishing its reputation internationally and helping rack up several prestigious awards (including the almighty Oscar); but the NFB/ONF quickly developed a parallel tradition of producing live-action, theatrical shorts and mid-length features, many of them based on works of Canadian literature. These included *Each Man's Son* (1954; dir. Roger Blais), based on the novel by Hugh MacLennan; *L'homme aux oiseaux* (1955; dir. Bernard Devlin and Jean Palardy), based on the story by Roger Lemelin; *La canne à pêche* (1959; dir. Fernand Dansereau), based on the story by Anne Hébert; *Morning on the Lièvre* (1961; dir. David Bairstow), based on the poem by Archibald Lampman; *Cornet at Night* (1963; dir. Stanley Jackson), based on the story by Sinclair Ross; *All the Years of Her Life* (1974; dir. Robert Fortier), based on the story by Morley Callaghan; *Le viellard et l'enfant* (1985; dir. Claude Grenier), based on the story by Gabrielle Roy; and of course the ubiquitous *Hockey Sweater/Le chandail*, an animated short shot in French and English by Sheldon Cohen in 1980, and based on the story by Roch Carrier.

Throughout the 1950s and early 1960s, Anne Hébert and fellow future novelists Jacques Godbout and Hubert Aquin worked as scriptwriters at the ONF. This was a time of exceptional creative efflorescence and collaboration in Québécois literary and cultural production, especially after 1956, when the NFB/ONF moved its headquarters to Montreal. There it quickly became the training ground for a generation of bold new filmmakers from Quebec, several of whom would later distinguish themselves as directors of films adapted from literature. These people included Claude Jutra (*Kamouraska, Ada, Dreamspeaker, Surfacing*), Claude Fournier (*Bonheur d'occasion/The Tin Flute*), Gilles Carle (*Les Plouffe, Maria Chapdelaine*), and Denys Arcand (*Le crime d'Ovide Plouffe, Love and Human Remains*).[17]

The second major development during this period, emerging directly from the Massey Report in 1951, was the creation of a national public television system, whose mandate in effect was to interpret Canada and Canadian culture to its viewers. Whatever we may think of the quality of programming that has resulted, it did give the Canadian Broadcasting Corporation (CBC) and the Société Radio-Canada (SRC) added incentive to tap the published literature as source materials for their productions. In 1953, Roger Lemelin's *La famille Plouffe* became the first *téléroman* broadcast on the SRC; it attracted weekly audiences in the millions (Gilles Carle's big-budget 1981 TV adaptation of the same novel was equally popular). The following year saw the soap opera's debut in English on the CBC, and the bilingual series ran on both networks until 1959. During the same period, Don Harron and Norman Campbell's musical adaptation of *Anne of Green Gables* (1956) and a serialization of Stephen Leacock's *Sunshine Sketches of a Small Town* (1952–3) also appeared on the CBC. While production of feature-length theatrical releases languished in English Canada during this period, Quebec was undergoing the first of several mini–film booms. Among the productions that resulted from this activity were Paul Gury's *Séraphin* (1950), based on Claude-Henri Grignon's classic novel, *Un homme et son pêché*; Gratien Gélinas's hugely successful *Tit-coq* (1953),[18] based on his equally popular play of the same name; and two ONF films by Bernard Devlin: *Les brûlés* (1959), based on the novel, *Nuages sur les brûlés*, by Hervé Biron; and *L'héritage* (1960), based on the story by Ringuet (Philippe Panneton).

As feature filmmaking in this country progressed throughout the 1960s and 1970s, aided in part by the founding of the Canadian Film Development Corporation (CFDC, the forerunner of Telefilm) in 1968, the source materials chosen grew progressively more risqué and the politics of marketing and assessing the resulting films increasingly controversial. One thinks, in this regard, of the firestorm that erupted over the release of Arthur Lamothe's high-profile treatment of André Langevin's *Poussière sur la ville* in 1967, which succeeded in polarizing critical opinion both on the state of Québécois filmmaking in general, and on the merits of fidelity to source materials more specifically.[19] Also during this period, what Thomas Waugh – in a slightly different context – has called the 'spatial iconographies' represented on screen[20] began increasingly to reflect (and reflect back upon) the two urban centres where film production was then largely concentrated: Montreal and Toronto. Examples include Don Owen's *Nobody Waved Goodbye* (1964); Claude Jutra's *À tout prendre* (1964); Irvin Kershner's *The Luck of Ginger Coffey* (1964; based on the novel by Brian Moore); Jean-Claude Lord's *Délivereznous du mal* (1965; released 1969; based on the novel by Claude Jasmin); David Secter's *Winter Kept Us Warm* (1965); Pierre Patry's *Caïn* (1967; with a script by Hubert Aquin and Jacques Proulx, based on Réal Giguère's unpublished novel, *Les marcheurs de la nuit*); Don Shebib's *Goin' Down the Road* (1970); Ted Kotcheff's *The Apprenticeship of Duddy Kravitz* (1974; adapted by Mordecai Richler and Lionel Chetwynd from Richler's novel); André Brassard's *Il était une fois dans l'est* (1974; a cinematic amalgam of the first six plays in Michel Tremblay's 'Belles Soeurs' cycle); Richard Benner's *Outrageous!* (1977; based on the short story 'Making It,' by Margaret Gibson); and George Kaczender's *In Praise of Older Women* (1978; based on the *roman-à-clef* by Stephen Vizinczey).[21] That so many of these films are adaptations should come as no surprise, given the context in which I am situating them; that so many of them also centre, in their content, around various 'crises' of masculinity and gender panic merits further attention, however, especially in terms of what Waugh elsewhere refers to as the 'discursive and material' intersections between the 'habitation/nation,' 'cinema/culture,' and 'sex/gender' systems at work in many of these films.[22]

To this end, in chapter 4 I situate the gender and narrative ambivalence at the heart of Brassard's *Il était une fois* and Benner's *Outrageous!* within a more extended analysis of *Fortune and Men's Eyes*, Harvey Hart's controversial 1971 adaptation of John Herbert's play about the dynamics of sex and power in a men's prison. Equally controversial in its representation of masculine self-identity and gender expression – not least in terms of its equation, as in Hart's *Fortune*, of homosexuality with emotional blackmail and inevitable suicide – is Jean-Claude Lord's adaptation of Claude Jasmin's novel, *Déliverez-nous du mal* (see Figure 1.2). Produced in 1965 by the independent Montreal studio Coopératio, which was fast

1.2   *Déliverez-nous du mal*: Director Jean-Claude Lord (l), novelist Claude Jasmin, and cameraman Claude Charron on the set.

gaining a reputation for releasing gritty, socially and psychologically realist features focusing on 'des personnages masculins angoissés' and 'en quête d'identité'[23] – many of them adapted from works of literature (including Pierre Patry's *La corde au cou*, also made in 1965, and also based on a novel by Jasmin) – the film's release was delayed four years, at which time it sank almost without a trace.

The story revolves around the fractious relationship between a wealthy gay man, André (Yvon Deschamps), and his erstwhile lover, Georges (Guy Godin), who seems mostly interested in André's money and who simultaneously bites the hand that feeds by relentlessly flirting with women, including André's married sister, Lucille (Cathérine Begin). Things come to a head at a hotel in the Laurentians when, despairing of Georges's newfound interest in a wealthy widow (Sophie Senécal), André attempts to hang himself – a scene that, as Waugh has shown, is greatly expanded from the novel and that Lord (who also wrote the script) uses to drive home his quasi-religious thesis about the ultimate evil of homosexuality, by linking sexual perversion with violent misogyny.[24] When said widow bursts in on André seeking his advice about Georges, who has just abandoned her, her reward for saving André's life is a savage beating by him. Also notable in this regard is the film's melodramatic ending. When Georges, who has since become engaged to an Anglophone heiress, asks André for one final loan of money, André snaps, and hires two hitmen to kill Georges atop Mont-Royal. This is consistent with Jasmin's text; however, whereas in the novel the hitmen successfully carry out the murder, in the film Georges sees his would-be assailants approaching with André and chooses instead to leap to his own death. This doesn't stop André from taking credit for the killing, and after a close-up of him announcing as much to Lucille, the camera cuts to a bucolic image of a country stream in springtime, over which is superimposed a closing title: 'ainsi soit-il' ('and so it shall be,' or more commonly, 'amen'). As Yves Lever has pointed out, read as the formal closing to the Lord's Prayer announced in the title to both the novel and the film, Lord's meaning is unambiguous: a new season will begin only when we have been 'delivered' from the evil of homosexuality.[25]

Thank goodness, then, for the bluff sexual swagger of the straight American actors Richard Dreyfuss and Tom Berenger, whose respective turns as Duddy Kravitz and Andras Vayda prove that when it comes to two of the more iconic Canadian film adaptations from the 1970s, the representational politics of masculine self-expression mostly amount to the working through of a sublimated Oedipus complex. That these films, by Ted Kotcheff and George Kaczender respectively, got made at all, and that on top of this they are on the whole quite good, is nothing short of a miracle, considering the creative closet into which Canadian filmmaking was thrust for most of the 1970s and early 1980s. This was the era of tax shelter films; investors were able to take advantage of government legislation that allowed them to deduct up to 100 per cent of their capital costs in 'certifiably Canadian films.' The result was high-water marks of cinematic excellence – in English Canada, at any rate – such as *Meatballs* (1979), *Prom Night* (1980), *Quest for Fire* (1981), *Porky's* (1982), and *Strange Brew* (1983). Geoff Pevere and Greig Dymond cynically summarize the outcome of this 'investment' in the

Canadian film industry in *Mondo Canuck:* 'A host of producers from around the world flocked to Canada to cash in on the bonanza by making movies that were Canadian only in the checklist sense. As they were usually the result of doctors, lawyers, dentists and other upper-income professionals less concerned with art than a tax dodge, a number of commercially, not to mention culturally, hopeless productions were rushed into production which otherwise would rightly never have seen the light of script development.'[26]

Pevere and Dymond rightly point out that the English-language dominance of such tax shelter productions (whose cast lists comprised a 'roll call of the once-weres, might-have-beens and whatever-happened-tos of American movies and TV') 'meant the virtual strangulation of the once-vibrant Quebec industry.'[27] But Québécois cinema bounced back much more quickly than its English-Canadian counterpart during the latter half of the 1980s, which witnessed another mini-boom in film production in *la belle province.* This had much to do with the emergence of a new generation of talented filmmakers. *Éminences grises* like Jutra (who would commit suicide as a result of the onset of Alzheimer's disease before the decade was out), Fournier, Carle, Michel Brault, and Arcand (who, slightly younger, produced some of his best work during this period, including *Le déclin de l'empire américain* and *Jésus de Montréal*) were still actively making films; but their ranks were being joined – and in many ways reinvigorated – by talented and brash directors like Jean Beaudin, Francis Mankiewicz, Mireille Dansereau, Léa Pool, Yves Simoneau, Jacques Benoît, Paule Baillargeon, and Jean-Claude Lauzon. All would eventually distinguish themselves in the specific area of film adaptation. They helped bring to the screen – not always without controversy – such texts as Yves Beauchemin's *Le matou,* René-Daniel Dubois's *Being at home with Claude,* Jacques Savoie's *Les portes tournantes,* Marie-Claire Blais's *Le sourd dans la ville,* Susan Swan's *The Wives of Bath,* Anne Hébert's *Les fous de bassan,* Dany Laferrière's *Comment faire l'amour avec un nègre sans se fatiguer,* Monique Proulx's *Le sexe des étoiles,* and even – albeit tangentially and very allusively – Réjean Ducharme's *L'avalée des avalés* (lines from which serve as a refrain throughout Lauzon's *Léolo*).

The Dubois/Beaudin, Swan/Pool, Blais/Dansereau, and Proulx/Baillargeon 'intertexts' will all be discussed at greater length in subsequent chapters. But it is worth pausing for a moment to situate Dansereau's film stylistically and narrationally alongside those of Simoneau, Mankiewicz, and Benoît. All four films were overshadowed at their time of release (in 1986, 1987, 1988, and 1989 respectively) by Arcand's *Le déclin de l'empire américain,* Lauzon's *Un zoo la nuit,* David Cronenberg's *Dead Ringers,* and Arcand's *Jésus de Montréal,* which garnered much more attention. Yet each merits critical reassessment, if only for the greater or lesser success with which each brought the formally experimental novels of Hébert, Blais, Savoie, and Laferrière to the screen, and – in the case of one of the resulting films – for the critical controversy this aroused.

The case I am referring to here is the film version of *Les fous de bassan,* which ran through three different directors and five different screenwriters (including Hébert herself) before the adaptation process was complete. The final product, as directed by Simoneau and scripted by Sheldon Chad, Simoneau, and Marcel Beaulieu, has largely been condemned by critics (and dismissed outright by the author herself) for the way in which it reduces Hébert's narratively complex and polyphonic novel to a single (male) point of view – that of Stevens Brown – and in the process effectively silences the resistant female voices of Nora and Olivia Atkins, who are raped and murdered on the beach of Griffin Creek, an English-speaking town on the Gaspé, by their cousin Stevens one August night in 1936.[28] In Hébert's novel, the narrative voices of Nora and Olivia – sometimes borne from beyond the grave and sometimes in conjunction with the natural elements (the wind, the sea, the birds) – interrupt and fracture the dominant patriarchal reconstruction of events by Reverend Jones, Perceval Brown, and Stevens, whose written record (he tells his side of the story through letters) only *appears* to lend his narrative an added degree of authority. By contrast, the film is, to use Elspeth Tulloch's phrase, singularly 'androcentric'[29] in its focalizing of the narrative aurally and visually through the male voice and the male gaze.

In this regard, the opening is paradigmatic. It begins out of sequence, with Stevens' (Steve Banner) murder of Olivia (Charlotte Valandrey) and the film's abrupt silencing of Nora's (Laure Marsac) intercut warning 'N'y vas pas.' It then flashes forward to a much older – and, it's implied, quite mad – Stevens (Jean-Louis Millette) shuffling about the town's run-down church, reconstructing aloud the events of that fateful night. That his voice-over will necessarily come to frame our interpretation of those events is reinforced visually through a succession of quick cuts between close-ups of the older Stevens and his younger self staring directly into Simoneau's camera. This is followed by a cut that returns us to the 1936 time frame and a POV shot of Perceval (Lothaire Bluteau), Stevens's mentally challenged brother, spying from atop the seaside cliffs on the Atkins girls as they swim. His voyeuristic vigil is interrupted only by his discovery of the hovering presence of his brother, newly returned to Griffin Creek. The significance of this scene of reunion between brothers – each in his own way pitted against and yet completely in step with the paternal order (Hébert's novel suggests that a motivation for Stevens's crimes is his unreconciled relationship with his domineering father) – will only become clear in the film's final frames, as Perceval comforts Stevens on an outcrop of rock following Olivia's murder (Nora is not killed in the film) (see Figure 1.3). As Tulloch notes: 'By freeze-framing the film's final image on the priapic, fraternal rock, Simoneau emphasizes the attainment, steadfastness, monolithism, and even permanency of Stevens' positive re-creation of his past self as a man.'[30] This is completely antithetical to the feminist politics of Hébert's novel, which suggest that Stevens's representative crisis of (Québécois) masculinity is a direct result of the twin forces of modernity and women's liberation. All of which necessarily returns us, as Tulloch suggests, to 'the question of feminism and fidelity,' specifically as it applies to male cinematic adaptations of women's texts.[31] I will explore this question below with respect to Volker Schlöndorff's high-profile 1990 treatment of Margaret Atwood's *The Handmaid's Tale*, and at much greater length in the next chapter in connection with Claude Jutra's adaptations of two other classic feminist texts by Atwood and Hébert, *Surfacing* and *Kamouraska*.

Marie-Claire Blais's *Le sourd dans la ville* is formally as complex as Hébert's novel. It is written as an extended interior monologue, but one that moves back

1.3   *Les fous de bassan*: Lothaire Bluteau (l) and Steve Banner as brothers Perceval and Stevens Brown.

and forth in time and even between characters. Dansereau wisely does not seek to replicate this stylistic device in the film; however, unlike Simoneau, she is able to suggest something of the text's interiorization and multifocalization by visually reinforcing the Hôtel des Voyageurs as an enclosed space, one that serves as a refuge against the harsh world outside for its denizens – particularly the fragile Florence (Béatrice Picard), recently separated from her husband, and Mike (Guillaume Lemay-Thivièrge), a young boy afflicted with a brain tumour – but that is also occupied by its own shadows. Indeed, as Gérard Grugeau has suggested in a review of the film, it is in part the cinematographic play of light and shadow that helps Dansereau achieve a 'poetically resonant' style on par with Blais's imagistic prose.[32] The connection between Florence and Mike is largely empathic in the novel, which eschews dialogue almost completely. Amazingly, that *tele*communication survives almost intact the transition to film. About this, I will have much more to say in the next chapter.

For his part, in the film of *Les portes tournantes*, Mankiewicz – who was at one time attached to the ill-fated adaptation of Anne Hébert's *Les fous de bassan* – attempts to capture cinemagraphically something of Savoie's similar narrative polyphony. This is accomplished as much aurally as visually, with the text's multiple focalizations and points of view being signalled on screen not only through the use of multiple flashbacks (shot through a gauzy, golden filter) but also through the extended use of voice-over narration and the foregrounding of Antoine's cassette recorder. Given its setting and subject matter, the novel's polyphonic structure is meant to suggest, formally, something of the syncopation of jazz, and to a certain extent it succeeds; the film is, I think, less successful. The extensive cutting between the dual time frames is an attempt to subvert traditional linearity; but despite all the emphasis on 'movement' in the book (the physical displacement of Céleste, first from her family in Val d'Amour, then in her escape to New York; Litwin's discourse on 'moving' pictures; the breakneck pace at which the music that Céleste enjoys is played; even the central image of the revolving door), the film is almost unbearably slow and leaden. To be sure, this counter-movement, or element of stasis, is also present in the book, represented as a force of inertia attempting to keep Céleste rooted in Campbelltown and the traditional ways of rural New Brunswick (manifested most explicitly in Pierre's parents). But the film's temporality, both in its nostalgic depiction of a fictive past and in the lugubrious pace with which that past unfolds on screen, seems to give in too easily to this impulse. Gabriel Arcand's brooding presence in the pivotal role of Madrigal Blaudelle doesn't much help, in this regard.

By far the least successful of these adaptations is Benoit's take on Lafferière. The film mistakenly and clumsily tries to capture the self-reflexive quality of the book's first-person narrative voice by having protagonist Fluke (Isaach De Bankolé) talk directly to the camera on more than one occasion; furthermore, it also tries to map a coherent story onto Lafferière's episodic narrative structure by framing Fluke's relationship with Miz Littérature (Roberta Bizeau) and his narcoleptic roommate Bouba (Maka Kotto) against a wholly new subplot involving three white drug pushers (led by a snarling Roy Dupuis), who are upset by the hovering presence of Fluke and his Remington typewriter in the Carré St-Louis.

1.4   *The Handmaid's Tale*: Margaret Atwood (l) talks to Natasha Richardson (as Offred) during a break in filming.

Even more problematic is the fact that in the film, the signifier 'nègre' – decontextualized from Lafferière's Fanonian musings on race and sexuality – takes on certain politically retrograde overtones, especially when read in the context of the film's ceaseless stereotyping of other racial and sexual minorities.

It's worth remembering that the 1990s – which in many ways culminated, adaptively speaking, in the much ballyhooed arrival of the Minghella/Ondaatje epic to screens across the country – began with a similar high-profile adaptation of a text by a canonical Canadian writer. The 1990 film of Margaret Atwood's *The Handmaid's Tale*, like that of Ondaatje's novel, had an impressive European-American pedigree, with Harold Pinter writing the screenplay, Volker Schlöndorff directing, and Natasha Richardson, Aidan Quinn, Robert Duvall, and Faye Dunaway starring (see Figure 1.4). However, what resulted from this assembled talent surprised many devoted fans of the novel, not least because it turned Atwood's darkly dystopian and ironic feminist text into a stock Hollywood romance, complete with a traditional happy ending where the boy presumably gets the girl. In the movie, not only does Offred – or Kate, as she is also known – heroically assassinate the Commander; she also manages to escape, with the aid of Nick and the Mayday underground, from the Republic of Gilead and her role as a Handmaid. The last shot we see is of Kate, heavily pregnant with Nick's baby, entering a trailer in a bucolic mountain stronghold controlled by the rebels. The voice-over indicates that she holds out hope for a reunion not only with Nick but also with her lost daughter by her former husband, Luke.

Leaving aside, for the moment, how the film's closing tableau reinscribes a patriarchal-heterosexual ideology based on the hegemony of reproductive sexuality – something that the novel would seem to challenge at every turn – it is important to note that the novel's ending is neither ideologically nor narratively so absolute. In the penultimate 'Salvaging' section of Offred's oral testimony, she confesses to her silent interlocutor – the 'you' who exists only through her telling – that the 'truth' of her story does not reveal her in a very good light – that towards the end especially, she 'did not behave well.'[33] Nowhere do we see any evidence of her resolve to kill the Commander, nor even to risk rifling through the papers in his office, which is, after all, all that the Mayday rebels are asking her to do. She tells Ofglen, when pressed by her, that she is 'afraid,' that she's sure she'll be caught, when 'the fact is that I no longer want to leave, escape, cross the border to freedom. I want to be here, with Nick, where I can get at him' (*HT* 255). Eventually, Ofglen begins to give up on Offred: 'She whispers less, talks more about the weather. I do not feel regret about this. I feel relief' (*HT* 255).

Offred's moral ambivalence is replicated in the novel's deliberately ambiguous and undecidable ending. The last we read of Offred she is being led away by two members of the Eye, Gilead's secret police unit, into an awaiting black van. Nick, who moments before had alerted her to the van's arrival, claiming that the arresting officers were members of the Mayday resistance in disguise, has now disappeared. Offred has no way of knowing if Nick is telling the truth, or if he has just betrayed her, or even if she will ever see him again. Her final words, with their emphasis on doubleness, on duality, on endings that might be beginnings, on strangers who might be friends, on darkness at the end of which might be light, underscore this ambiguity:

> The van waits in the driveway, its double doors stand open. The two of them, one on either side now, take me by the elbows to help me in. Whether this is my end or a new beginning I have no way of knowing. I have given myself over into the hands of strangers, because it can't be helped.
>
> And so I step up, into the darkness within; or else the light. (*HT* 276-77)

Of course, the mystery surrounding Offred's own personal end is compounded by the fact that Atwood's novel, much like Ondaatje's, ends not once but twice. Making sense of these various endings – both textual and cinematic – can lead to interesting classroom discussions, I have discovered. As part of my ongoing pedagogical mandate to teach more literature *through* film, I have made a *screening* of *The Handmaid's Tale* a corequisite to my students' *reading* of it. After seeing the film, it would be easy to forget about the 'Historical Notes' section that serves as a coda to *The Handmaid's Tale*, and that provides one final ironic twist on many of its themes. Thus, in debating the merits of the ending to Schlöndorff's film, and Kate's celluloid escape to freedom, I redirect my students' attention back to the novel's 'Historical Notes' and ask them whether what is transcribed there is any indication of Offred's textual freedom. My students are wont to interpret this question literally and to cite the presence of the appended notes themselves as evidence that, yes, she did eventually achieve freedom. In this they are following the logic of Professor Pieixoto himself, who remarks during the course of his presentation on the 'document' known as *The Handmaid's Tale* that 'the very existence of the tapes' proves that Nick 'must have helped "Offred" to escape' (*HT* 291).

Pushing the students a bit further, I encourage them to examine the text of Pieixoto's presentation a little more carefully. They start to pick up on the nature of his jokes and puns, their inherent misogyny (his reference to the 'archaic vulgar signification of the word *tail*' and 'bone' on page 283, for example, or his dubbing of 'The Underground Femaleroad' 'The Underground Frailroad'). After some further coaxing they also look more closely at how precisely Pieixoto sets about authenticating the tapes – how, in his own words, he attempts to 'establish an identity for the narrator' (*HT* 285). Pretty quickly, attentive readers discover that Offred herself is only incidental to this process, that in the end it is the identity of the Commander that Pieixoto feels provides the key. The ensuing debates surrounding the merits of Frederick R. Waterford or B. Frederick Judd as the likely candidate, and how they supersede the importance of Offred's own name, reinforce Atwood's ironic comment on how women's identities continue to be tied to those of men. Even here Pieixoto judges Offred's efforts to be a failure: 'She could have told us much about the workings of the Gileadean empire, had she had the instincts of a reporter or a spy. What would we not give, now, for even twenty pages or so of printout from Waterford's private computer! However, we must be grateful for any crumbs the Goddess of History has designed to vouchsafe us' (*HT* 292). As Mary Kirtz puts it in her comparison of the film and the novel, the latter's ending emphasizes the point that 'once again, a woman is rendered invisible and worthless within her own history.'[34] This point is obviated by the film, which seems to resolve the Handmaid's history most definitively.

Nevertheless, as I'm sure Kirtz would agree, another way a comparison of the different endings of the film and novel of *The Handmaid's Tale* can prove useful pedagogically is by redirecting students' attention to questions of narrative structure and time. By imposing a degree of closure lacking in the novel, the film linearizes the very complicated narrative of *The Handmaid's Tale*. To this end, the film opens with Kate's capture, the murder of her husband, Luke, and the abandonment to an unknown fate of her daughter. Thereafter, the film unspools in a fairly straightforward and chronological manner, ending with the heroic escape of Kate discussed earlier. This linear progression is disrupted occasionally by brief flashbacks in which Kate imagines her daughter wandering about aimlessly in the snow – the only clue in the film to the importance of the recurring 'Night' sections in Atwood's novel, which interrupt Offred's recounting of the strictly controlled and monitored events of her daily routine: 'Shopping,' 'Waiting Room,' 'Birth Day,' 'Salvaging,' and so on. Into this regimented, clock- and calendar-bound *collective* present (in which an entire society is organized around its Handmaids' reproductive cycles), Offred is able to interject a degree of temporal asymmetry by remembering, at night, her *personal* past, her pre-Gileadean life with her husband and daughter, her mother, and her friend Moira. As Offred puts it early on in the novel:

I lie, then, inside the room, under the plaster eye in the ceiling, behind the white curtains, between the sheets, neatly as they, and step sideways out of my own time. Out of time. Though this is time, nor am I out of it.

But the night is my time out. Where should I go? (*HT* 35)

As this passage makes clear, in the Night sections of the novel, time gets reordered into what Offred later calls 'a space-time, between here and now, and there and then, punctuated by dinner' (*HT* 211), a world in which past, present, and future all collide[35]: there is Offred's psychological recollection of past events ('she said we were going to feed the ducks' [*HT* 36]), her present narration of them ('It's also a story I'm telling, in my head, as I go along' [*HT* 37]), and her wish that what she has to say be listened to in some chronologically anterior future ('I'll pretend you can hear me' [*HT* 38]). That it does get listened to – albeit not perhaps by as sympathetic an audience as Offred might have hoped – is of course brilliantly foregrounded in the concluding Historical Notes section, which takes the novel 'out of time' yet again.

In a provocative and insightful article comparing the novel with the film, Glenn Willmott notes, with reference to Atwood's temporal dislocation of the reader in the Night sections, that 'only at night, when space and spatial order scatter in the dark, do the images of the centre's history arise, allowing the present to half-dissolve … Night plunges this place into *possibility*. Night is a time not only of history but of historicity, a time of relative freedom. At least a certain kind of freedom.'[36] Willmott directs our attention to Atwood's complex use of tenses in this regard, her mixing of the simple past, for example, with the past perfect, as in the novel's opening line: 'We slept in what had once been the gymnasium' (*HT* 3). Next to the waking nightmare that is Offred's present life in Gilead, her dreams of the past must necessarily seem more perfect, and perfectable, as must the future: 'I *would like* to believe this is a story I'm telling' (*HT* 37; emphasis mine). As Willmott and other critics have noted, Schlöndorff and Pinter are unable to convey – or, more properly, choose not to convey – this temporal complexity in the film; interestingly, apart from the occasional flashbacks (which, at any rate, have more to do with establishing emotional continuity of character rather than temporal discontinuity of plot), the only evidence we have of non-linearity comes in the form of a *textual* epigraph that appears on the screen in the film's opening frames, which reads as follows:

> Once upon a time
> in the recent future
> a country went wrong
> the country was called
> the Republic of Gilead

Easily missed upon initial viewing, the film's epigraph, like its ending, should send us back once again to Atwood's text. In particular, its recourse to a familiar narrative convention from centuries-old oral storytelling practice, and the disjunctive reversal of past and future within it, point to the fact that in Atwood's novel the power of Offred's story accrues precisely through the act of its telling: 'If it's a story I'm telling, then I have control over the ending. Then there will be an ending, to the story, and real life will come after it. I can pick up where I left off' (*HT* 37). Likewise, as Offred gradually comes to realize, an ending can be fore-stalled, through the reordering of events non-sequentially, or through their retelling multiple times, and in multiply different ways. What's more, the act of telling a story presumes an audience, an interlocutor, a listener, a 'you' – and '*You*,' as Offred reminds us, 'can mean more than one' (*HT* 37) – whose silent presence nevertheless bespeaks the possibility of response: 'But if it's a story, even in my head, I must be telling it to someone. You don't tell a story only to yourself. There's always someone else' (*HT* 37).

This emphasis on telling reflects what Willmott calls the novel's 'conversational' epistemology; whereas the film version, by virtue of the very medium itself, is necessarily governed by an 'ocular' epistemology. This means there are some things represented in the novel that the movie simply cannot do; for example, it cannot plunge the screen into darkness to signify the night sections (although it would have been interesting, had this been done, to judge the effect). By the same token, the cinematic medium allows Schlöndorff to exploit the themes of visual surveillance, of looking and being looked at, that permeate Atwood's text. As many commentators have noted, this even extends to a metafictional or metacinematic level, with the Eye of Gilead's secret police being associated with the mechanical eye of the camera, and with the Mulveyesque 'visual pleasure' of movie watching ironically – and inevitably – implicating the viewer in the thematics of masculinist surveillance and voyeurism critiqued by the novel.[37]

In the context of a discussion of the metarepresentational intricacies of Schlöndorff's film, I like to circle back with my students to the question of 'freedom' – not only Offred's, but also ours as readers/viewers. The film ends with Kate's escape, yet the effect of representing this on screen is, paradoxically, to imprison us viewers within a singularly dominant narrative epistemology.[38] In other words, what we see is what we get. We may not like what we see, but for the 149-odd minutes it is unfolding before us we have to accept its internal logic. Not so with Atwood's novel, which affords its reader, like its narrator, much more interpretive manoeuvrability. Contrary to the familiar adage, the author Atwood, like the author Offred – and unlike the auteur Schlöndorff – is suggesting that there are times when it is better to tell (or *not* tell, as the case may be) than to show. The film of *The Handmaid's Tale* seeks to provide answers, to leave us with a sense of visual certainty; by contrast, Atwood's text, ending on a note of aural/oral uncertainty leaves us with only questions (quite literally). ('As all historians know,' Pieixoto remarks by way of concluding his own assessment of 'The Handmaid's Tale,' 'the past is a great darkness, and filled with echoes; but what they say to us is imbued with the obscurity of the matrix out of which they come; and, try as we may, we cannot always decipher them precisely in the clearer light of our own day' [*HT* 293]). One such question must, I think, be this: What happens to texts by women when they are 'adapted' (in whatever way and for whatever particular context or medium) by men? This question applies as much to Pieixoto's reading of the Handmaid as it does to Schlöndorff's reading of Atwood, and it is one whose specific social and political teleologies I take up more fully in the next chapter.

That I have rather artificially bracketed my history of filmic adaptations of Canadian literature in this chapter with a discussion of glossy foreign productions of canonical texts by well-known authors is telling. A plethora of important adaptations have been produced or co-produced domestically since the mid-1990s that could have provided the basis for any number of additional case studies in this book. These include Richard Lewis's *Whale Music* (1994; based on the novel by Paul Quarrington), Denys Arcand's *Love and Human Remains* (1994; based on the play *Unidentified Human Remains and the True Nature of Love* by Brad Fraser), John Greyson's *Lilies* (1996; based on the play by Michel Marc Bouchard), Mort Ransen's *Margaret's Museum* (1996; based on the short story 'The Glace Bay Miners' Museum' by Sheldon Currie), Lynne Stopkewich's *Kissed* (1997; based on the short story 'We So Seldom Look on Love' by Barbara Gowdy), Sturla Gunnarsson's *Such a Long Journey* (1999; based on the novel by Rohinton Mistry), Rodrigue Jean's *Full Blast* (1999; based on the novel *L'ennemi que je connais* by Martin Pître), Robert Favreau's *Les muses orphelines* (2000; based on the play by Michel Marc Bouchard), Charles Binamé's recent popular remake of *Séraphin* (2002), Wiebke von Carolsfeld's *Marion Bridge* (2002; based on the play by Daniel MacIvor), Bernar Hébert's *The Favourite Game* (2003; based on the novel by Leonard Cohen), and Scott Smith's *Falling Angels* (2003; based on the novel by Barbara Gowdy). But all of these adaptations have resonated only minimally with contemporary movie audiences in this country, largely because they only turn up at the local multiplex for a fleeting few weeks at most, if at all. Indeed, an interesting irony in the specific context of adaptations is that Atom Egoyan's and David Cronenberg's film treatments of works of literature by American and British authors (Rusell Banks's *The Sweet Hereafter*, William Trevor's *Felicia's Journey*, William Burroughs's *Naked Lunch*, J.G. Ballard's *Crash*) are probably better known than any of the titles listed above.

Debates continue to rage among cultural pundits in this country about how our proximity to the American media behemoth has affected local film production and distribution;[39] the fact remains that despite successive multimillion-dollar infusions of cash into Telefilm's Feature Film Fund over the years – $165 million over five years beginning in 1986, and a guaranteed $100 million a year starting in 2001[40] – government and industry policies have consistently failed to address adequately the issue of how to get Canadian films into Canadian theatres. For mega-chains like Famous Players, Cineplex Odeon, and even Alliance Atlantis, which make most of their money from food concessions, and therefore need to maximize the number of bums in seats, programming locally made films is simply bad business. The issue is further complicated by the fact that Canada has acquired – and only somewhat inaccurately – a reputation for making 'art house films' on 'difficult' and often sexually 'inscrutable' themes.[41] Molly Parker making love to a cadaver versus Arnold Schwarzenegger blowing up nasty Arab terrorists: the choice would seem clear to most moviegoers.

However, the situation is slightly more complicated. While the $100 million per year Canadian Feature Film Fund has allocated, for the first time, a portion of its funds to 'distributors to increase their marketing budgets,' it has tied these funds to a 'performance-based' formula, one that 'relies primarily on ongoing success at the box office.'[42] Despite reference in the report to a 'Complementary Activities Program' that will provide funds for 'alternative distribution networks,'[43] no attempt has been made to impose exhibition quotas on theatres – a content-based system akin to the one that has worked so well for the music industry in this country and that has long been employed by the European film industry. As a letter to the editor in the *Globe and Mail* put it, in response to an earlier article by James Adams on the combined two-month run in Canadian movie theatres of 2002's Genie nominees for Best Picture,[44] 'after the Second World War, European nations dealt with the looming dominance of U.S. film culture by imposing quotas on cinemas to guarantee an outlet for their own films. Canada unwisely decided against this policy. The results speak for themselves – the rise of national cinemas in Europe that reach a national audience, the opposite in Canada.'[45] Indeed, despite similar trauma caused to Canadian publishers by the formerly warring, now recently merged, Indigo and Chapters bookstore chains, and their squeezing of industry profits through market share incentives, it is still much easier in Canada to 'read the movie' – as a sign says on one display table in my local Chapters – than it is to 'see the book.'[46]

While the film industry in this country careens back and forth between rather inchoate and poorly defined policy directives and bureaucratic overregulation, I take heart in some modest signs of flexibility and creativity recently demonstrated by the Canadian Radio-television and Telecommunications Commission (CRTC) in the areas of television licensing and programming. Indeed, the CRTC's first wave of specialty channel licensing in 1995 was a godsend to those of us in search of hard-to-find or non-video-transferred Canadian films. To this end, I have become a devotee of the Bravo! and Showcase channels, and am slowly building up an impressive video library of adaptations. Indeed, where would film and literature scholars in this country be without Moses Znaimer? A cultural maverick, he treads a lonely but resolute path between the identitarian hand wringing of Canadian Heritage and the CBC, and the ideological arrogance of the Asper family and CanWest Global. Not only has he taken up, through his Bravo!FACT fund, the mantle of the NFB, by helping fund a series of film shorts – many of them based on works of literature[47] – but who else in Canadian broadcasting would have agreed to Bruce McDonald's crazy scheme of airing a live television adaptation of Michael Turner's *American Whiskey Bar* on CityTV the night of 19 September 1998? In greenlighting the latter project, Znaimer also revealed – as I argue at greater length in chapter 7 – an intuitive understanding both of Turner's novel and of the fluid intertextual, 'intersemiotic,' and 'intermedial'[48] exchanges that characterize the adaptive process, insisting on framing the broadcast with his own taped introduction and, in so doing, turning in an eerily accurate portrait of Klaus 9, the shadowy producer figure from *American Whiskey Bar*.

What is missing from this rather potted history of film adaptation in Canada and Quebec is a concomitant history of the theory behind the adaptive process. For almost as long as film adaptations have been made, literary and film scholars have been arguing about how to talk about them. Since at least the publication of George Bluestone's *Novels into Film* in 1957, the critical model that has tended to dominate is one based on aesthetic formalism and textual fidelity, with a focus on individual case studies and on how narrative translates or 'metamorphoses' (to use Bluestone's term) between verbal and visual signifying systems; and with an implicit prioritization and privileging of the original literary texts (most often canonical novels) as the 'standard of value against which [a film's] success or failure is measured.'[49] Comparatively little effort has been expended on developing a broader base of what constitutes an adaptation in the first place (a movie can be based, for example, on a comic book, a video game, a song, or even an earlier version of the same movie) or on a more generalizable model or theory of the process of adaptation itself.

Gradually, however, the sway that fidelity criticism has for so long exerted over the discipline of film adaptation studies has begun to be challenged. Drawing largely on the work of French theorists – in particular, the structuralist narratology of Roland Barthes and Gérard Genette and the psychoanalytical semiotics of Christian Metz – critics like Christopher Orr, Seymour Chatman, and Brian McFarlane have shifted the focus from fidelity to more 'sophisticated' notions of intertextuality and narrative rhetorics. 'Within this critical context,' Orr writes, 'the issue is not whether the adapted film is faithful to its source, but rather how the choice of a specific source and how the approach to that source serve the film's ideology.'[50] For his part, Chatman rejects the 'notorious and, to [him], hollow issue of "fidelity" to the original' and focuses instead on the interrelationship between an adaptation's aesthetic and ideological rhetorics. The former's function is, in the words of Chatman, 'to suade me to accept the form of the work,' and the latter's, 'to suade me of a certain view of how things are in the real world.'[51] Finally, McFarlane frames the issue as follows:

> The stress on fidelity to the original undervalues other aspects of the film's intertextuality. By this, I mean those non-literary, non-novelistic influences at work on any film, whether or not it is based on a novel … Conditions within the film industry and the prevailing cultural and social climate at the time of the film's making (especially when the film version does not follow hot upon the novel's publication) are two major determinants in shaping any film, adaptation or not. Among the former (i.e. conditions within the industry) one might include the effect of certain star personae, or, in the days of the studios' dominance, a particular studio's 'house style,' or director's predilections or genre conventions, or the prevailing parameters of cinematic practice. As to the latter (i.e. the climate of the times) it is difficult to set up a regular methodology for investigating how far cultural conditions (e.g. the exigencies of wartime or changing sexual mores) might lead to a shift in emphasis in a film as compared with the novel on which it is based. However, it is necessary to make allowance in individual cases of adaptation for the nature of such influences.[52]

For these reasons, argues McFarlane, a theory of film adaptation needs to focus not just on questions of 'narration' and its transferral between semiotic systems, but also on questions of 'enunciation,' by which he means 'the whole expressive apparatus that governs the presentation – and reception – of the narrative.'[53]

McFarlane's enunciative model of film adaptation would seem to be especially relevant to the Canadian context, in which attention must be paid not only to the indeterminate system of narrative borrowings and transformations that occur between and across different media, but also to how those borrowings and transformations are registered by different cultures. Indeed, examining the *differences* that emerge within English-Canadian and Québécois models of literary and film *production*, I would argue, allows for a concomitant analysis of the *dissonance* that often accompanies these models within a framework of cross-cultural *reception*. A case in point would be the process of adapting Gabrielle Roy's acclaimed novel of wartime Montreal, *Bonheur d'occasion/The Tin Flute*, for the screen. The films were shot simultaneously in French and English with the same cast, both for theatrical release as a two-hour feature film and for television broadcast as a five-part miniseries, and were received very differently inside and outside of Quebec. French critics mostly hailed the arrival of a 'classic' to the screen and described Claude Fournier's adaptation as a 'moving' melodrama of a piece with a particular tradition of postwar Québécois films;[54] yet English critics almost universally dismissed the film as a cheesy soap opera and got caught up in picayune debates – for example, over the 'hit-and-miss accents' of the principals.[55] A more contemporary example would be the virtually antithetical notices accorded Robert Lepage's films – all of them adaptations of one sort or another – by Montreal and Toronto critics, each group tending to over- or under-allegorize the material depending on the prevailing political climate.

These issues are even further complicated by the addition of 'other solitudes' into this bicultural equation. For example, during the 1990s there began appearing on television and (albeit briefly) in movie theatres a spate of films focusing on Aboriginal peoples that were adapted from works of literature by white writers. These films included *Clearcut* (Richard Bugajski, 1991; based on the novel *A Dream Like Mine* by M.T. Kelly), *Black Robe* (Bruce Beresford, 1991; based on the novel by Brian Moore), *Dance Me Outside* (Bruce McDonald, 1995; based on the collection of stories by W.P. Kinsella), and *Big Bear* (Gil Cardinal, 1998; based on the novel *The Temptations of Big Bear* by Rudy Wiebe). Not surprisingly, these films were received very differently by Native and non-Native audiences and critics. As I demonstrate at greater length in chapter 3 in connection with *Black Robe* and *Shadow of the Wolf*, any analysis of their adaptive politics must be carried out in the context of a sustained discussion of the debates that arose over Native versus non-Native casting for some of the roles; linguistic, historical, and cultural inaccuracies in the respective narratives; the fraught contemporary political climate in which these historical epics about colonial contact were produced; and the representational, social, and cultural exigencies faced by Aboriginal peoples in the film and publishing industries in this country more generally.[56] Similarly, any intertextual, enunciative discussion of Sturla Gunnarsson's 1999 adaptation of Rohinton Mistry's *Such a Long Journey* would need, I think, to comment on the casting of Anglo-Indian actor Roshan Seth in the lead role, and the extra-Canadian audiences this move might have been designed to attract. And my own discussion of the Hart, Brassard, and Benner films in chapter 4 will need to be contextualized – as Waugh has noted – in terms of the post-Stonewall, post-CFDC climate in which they were made, and also in terms of the 'positive images' debate they sparked upon their release.[57] Again, I submit that in the case of Canada, one must speak of such issues precisely because one *cannot* speak of a monolithic and monological national literature and/or cinema.

Dudley Andrew framed this kind of approach to the literature-into-film phenomenon succinctly when he declared, in 1984, that it was 'time for adaptation studies to take a sociological turn': 'Adaptation is a peculiar form of discourse but not an unthinkable one. Let us use it not to fight battles over the essence of the media or the inviolability of individual artworks. Let us use it as we use all cultural practices, to understand the world from which it comes and the one toward which it points.'[58] Understanding the world from which adaptation comes means paying attention to political, economic, cultural, and ideological issues, including more or less measurable indices such as feature film policy, financing, distribution, and audience and critical reception, but also to more abstract concepts like canonicity and institutionality – especially in terms of which texts are deemed representatively 'Canadian' and how that representation necessarily transfers to the screen. In this country's film industry, which is kept afloat largely through government subsidies and dominated by the fickle whims of Telefilm Canada, name recognition and profile – in terms of who wrote the original text and who is involved (from screenwriter and story editor to director and producer) in adapting it for the screen – count a great deal in terms of which projects get green-lighted for funding.

In this regard, in *Hard Core Roadshow* screenwriter Noel S. Baker provides an hilarious (though often heartbreaking) account of the hoops (from initial development funding to script approval and final production financing) that he, Bruce McDonald, and producer Christine Haebler had to jump through in order to satisfy the cultural docents at Telfilm and the Ontario Film Development Corporation that in adapting Michael Turner's *Hard Core Logo*, they were in fact 'making a Canadian movie! Yeehaa!'[59] Conversely, Patsy Kotsopoulos, in her discussion of the 'exporting' of the television series *Road to Avonlea* to American and other foreign media markets, has carefully documented the lengths that the CBC and Sullivan Entertainment, working in conjunction with Disney in the United States, were willing to go to downplay the regional and national specificity of L.M. Montgomery's texts.[60] The now-defunct NFB Canadian Literature series of filmed shorts is yet another useful example; in terms of the works included in its list, it functions as its own mini-canon, much like McClelland & Stewart's New Canadian Library series.

As influential as the writings of Orr, Chatman, and especially McFarlane have been in film adaptation studies, one persistent weakness in their work – and in the work of many other adaptation theorists – is that it focuses almost exclusively on films derived from novels. By comparison, relatively little attention has been paid to films adapted from plays – and this, despite some obvious and long-standing connections between the two media, including the performative frameworks governing their production and reception, and the frequency and fluency with which most actors, directors, and production crews work in both. This is no doubt related to the fact that a printed play's movement from a verbal to a visual signifying system is governed by a performative framework, both prior and anterior, that further mediates the circuit of translation and reception. Put another way, the stage production(s) that precede the film's projection, and the stage productions that will almost certainly follow it, depending on the artistic vision of individual directors/companies, are likely to be very different from both the original theatrical version and the celluloid adaptation. At the same time, because of the necessarily ephemeral and evanescent nature of live performance, the filmic artefact tends to take on more authority (or 'auteurity,' as I dub this process in chapter 5 in connection with Robert Lepage's ongoing adaptation of his stage work for the screen) as a stable and 'definitive' record of both the play's 'story' and the 'discourse' of its performative telling.

All of which raises important questions of authority, intentionality, interpretation, and spectatorship. In drama and film, where and with whom is meaning invested? With the printed script or the staged/filmed performance? With the individual idea or the collaborative mise-en-scène? With the playwright/screenwriter or with the director? Or with the audience? In theatrespeak, the term 'dramaturge' helps mediate somewhat between such paradoxes. Significantly, Canadian novelist Susan Swan (who herself has a background in theatre) has characterized the collaboration between herself, playwright/screenwriter Judith Thompson, and director Léa Pool on the transformation of Swan's novel *The Wives of Bath* into the film *Lost and Delirious* (which I analyse in greater depth in chapter 6) as largely an exercise in dramaturgy (complete with staged readings and so on).[61] Yet while we are perfectly willing to accept that a theatre director or company can update or radically alter traditional stagings of classic plays by Shakespeare or Ibsen, we often remain intransigently unforgiving of a film director who does the same thing to a cherished work of literature (I will have more to say below on why this might be). In his perspicacious reading of John Greyson's film of Michel Marc Bouchard's *Lilies*, which forms the core of his recent book-length study of cinematic adaptations of Canadian and Québécois plays, André Loiselle frames this paradox in terms of presence and absence. The space of the theatre, even when it is staging death, offers plenitude and the 'living presence' of art. In contrast, cinematic representation by its very nature is as much showing us what *is not* there as what *is* there; the image on the screen, and our identification with it, is contingent not on an actor's bodily presence, for example, but on his or her virtual (or mechanical) reproduction via the camera.[62]

In this, Loiselle is drawing on some key texts in the history of apparatus theory that deal with the intersection between theatre and film, including Steven Shaviro's *The Cinematic Body*, Christian Metz's *The Imaginary Signifier*, André Bazin's *What Is Cinema?* and, perhaps most importantly, Walter Benjamin's 'The Work of Art in the Age of Mechanical Reproduction.'[63] In his classic essay, Benjamin singles out the differences between acting for the stage and acting on film as a representative example of the destruction of the 'aura' of a work of art:

> The artistic performance of a stage actor is definitely presented to the public by the actor in person; that of the screen actor, however, is presented by a camera, with a

twofold consequence. The camera that presents the performance of the film actor to the public need not respect the performance as an integral whole. Guided by the cameraman, the camera continually changes its position with respect to the performance. The sequence of positional views which the editor composes from the material supplied him constitutes the completed film. It comprises certain factors of movement which are in reality those of the camera, not to mention special camera angles, close-ups, etc. Hence, the performance of the actor is subjected to a series of optical tests. This is the first consequence of the fact that the film actor lacks the opportunity of the stage actor to adjust to the audience during his performance, since he does not present his performance to the audience in person. This permits the audience to take the position of a critic, without experiencing any personal contact with the actor. The audience's identification with the actor is really an identification with the camera.[64]

For his part, Bazin contends that the question of presence and absence in theatre and film, respectively, is related to two further considerations. The first of these is what he calls the different 'psychological modalities' of performance governing each medium. That is, audience and actor mutually collude in the creation of an imaginary theatrical world that is wholly circumscribed by the temporal and spatial constraints of the performance itself; in film, this act of imaginative creation takes place only on the part of the audience member, and furthermore, it need not be restricted by or confined to the literal temporal and spatial parameters governing the projection of the film.[65] Related to this psychology of performance, as I've already intimated, is the question of space, or what Bazin (like Benjamin) calls 'decor.' Basically, Bazin's point about the function of space in theatre and film is that it operates centripetally in the former, the architecture of the stage and the decor of the sets 'enclos[ing], limit[ing], circumscrib[ing]' our imaginations and 'framing' our attention inwards to a 'locus dramaticus' or 'privileged spot' of physical presence on stage, where an actor's corporeal body moves through space. By contrast, space in film operates centrifugally, 'masking' a whole universe that lies just beyond the edge of the frame, a universe that encompasses, of course, not only the decor of the film's fictional diegesis, but also the 'real' apparatus of the camera itself, and any number of other spatial identifications we make in the course of viewing a given film.[66] In adapting Bazin for his own study of the dialectical relationship between 'afferent drama' and 'efferent cinema' in the Canadian and Québécois context, Loiselle notes that despite the centrifugal spatial dynamics of cinema, most adaptations of plays in this country continue to be 'stage-bound,' unable to escape completely the locus dramaticus of their source texts.[67] Again, paradigmatic in this regard is *Lilies*, where the anti-naturalist hyper-theatricality of Bouchard's play is deliberately retained by Greyson in order to highlight how an imaginative space of homosexual desire for young lovers Simon (Jason Cadieux) and Vallier (Danny Gilmore) is foreclosed upon by the town of Roberval, panoramic location shots of which Greyson provides in abundance with his 'realist' camera.

In discussing the scopic drive that necessarily governs the 'passion to perceive' in cinema, Christian Metz also distinguishes between the spectacle of theatre and that of film. Specifically, he notes that in film, both what is being represented and the representation itself are imaginary (because both are absent). In theatre, what is being represented is imaginary but, crucially, the representation – and the act of representing – is fully real because it is fully present: we see it happening live before us on stage. This leads Metz to conclude that in theatre, one tends to iden- tify more with the actor (as the person doing the representing), because the authenticity of his/her representation depends more on the quality of his/her technique; in film, one tends to identify more with the character (as the person being represented), because – as Hollywood never ceases to remind us – bad actors can still be film stars, their dearth of skills rescued by other qualitative (and quantitative) measures of the success of a production (such as special effects and box office gross), or by a 'star' persona that makes no distinction between on- and off-screen.[68] Paradoxically, then, because of the 'realness' of the representa- tion (or the act of representation) in the theatre, what Metz calls attempts to 'defi- ctionalize' the spectacle of representation have been more successful (as per Brecht's catalogue of alienation effects);[69] by contrast, narrative cinema, because its fictional signifiers are absent, can largely only escape the constraints of realism through various genre conventions (think of Busby Berkeley–style choreography in a musical, or the revenant killer who is a staple of the slasher flick).

Moreover, in distinguishing between the operation of the gaze in theatre and in film, Metz notes that in the former it is more or less consensual because both spec- tator (seer) and actor (seen) are bodily present, occupying the same space; the cin- ematic gaze, by contrast, is non-consensual, or 'unauthorized' (that is, the person being watched doesn't know he/she is being watched).[70] This in turn leads Metz to speculate on the differences between theatre and cinema audiences; theatrego- ers' general collectivity and cinephiles' relative fragmentation are related to the different material and ideological conditions governing the histories of both arts.[71] To put it crassly, theatre, in spite of some of the more egregious excesses of Broadway, can still lay claim to a cultural economy based on ritual; the economy of film has always been and will remain inextricably tied to financial capital.

Orr, Chatman, and McFarlane contend that they are attuned to how such 'con- ditions' of ideology and cultural materialism play out in the adaptive process. Yet as Lee Parpart has noted, these same critics have 'too often turned a blind eye to the ideological implications of their own analyses.'[72] This is especially apparent where issues of gender are concerned. In a very useful overview of recent struc- turalist narratological studies of film adaptation and feminist narratology more generally, and drawing on adaptive examples ranging from *The Color Purple* to *Kissed*, Parpart notes that film critics would do well to reconsider a wholesale jetti- soning of notions of textual fidelity and mimesis, especially where representa- tions of gender intersect with issues of ideology and emotional affect in what she calls the 'transactional' bonds created between film and reader/viewer.[73] More- over, as Glen Lowry and Gillian Roberts demonstrate in separate readings of *The English Patient*, textual and critical responsibility, performativity, and location are equally determinant considerations when it comes to the representation and – more often than not – the non-representation of racial conflict on screen. For Lowry, the excision of all references to Hiroshima and Nagasaki from Minghella's film, and the failure to dramatize in any way Kip's reactions to the bombings – as well as, according to Roberts, the failure of most critics to note in any significant way this major departure from the book – at once allow Minghella's version of Ondaatje's characters to dwell in a dehistoricized past (hence the weight given to the Katharine/Almásy narrative in the film) and allow us, as viewers, to consume this past within a dehistoricized present (in which other Western powers' – including Canada's – complicity in the bombings is glossed over in ways that adaptations such as Alain Resnais's *Hiroshima, mon amour* and even Lepage's *Nô* simply will not allow).[74]

These issues become even more complicated when certain generic conventions associated, for example, with romance, melodrama, historical epic, and costume drama (all of which *The English Patient* draws upon in equal measure) come in contact with the political and economic exigencies of an industry driven by the need to find new export markets and to satisfy the demands of already existing ones. In the new global economy, in other words, if we are to move our cultural products as easily as we do our wheat, they must be truly 'borderless';[75] they must play as well internationally as they do domestically. In the case of adaptations, this often means de-emphasizing the gender, cultural, regional, and historical specificity of the source texts. Which makes it all the more important to insist on such specificities in our critical readings, both of the film/televisual product and, retrospectively, of its source text.

With fidelity criticism, one of the things that literary and film scholars talk about (although not always in dialogue with one another) is what happens when the author-function comes in conflict with the auteur-function. In theorizing the relationship between literature and film as a form of 'reauthorizing,' Timothy Corrigan notes that especially with the rise of the French *nouvelle vague* directors in the late 1940s and early 1950s (who, in their films, frequently turned to works of literature for source material, and who, in their criticism, invented the concept of the auteur), 'literature began, decisively I believe, to loose [*sic*] its hierarchical control over film, and films began to claim their own rights and powers as an independent way of examining the literary paradigms of the past.'[76] However, Judith Mayne notes that during the classic era of Hollywood filmmaking, often it was the producer as much as the director who was responsible for this reauthorization; she cites David O. Selznick as the 'single individual most responsible for exploiting and refining the connections between novels and films in the 1940s,' not least in his savvy inclusion of the source text as part of his overall marketing of product tie-ins: 'Buy the novel and you recapture the experience of seeing the film.'[77]

But where does this leave the critic? Indeed, despite all the fancy terminological posturing, there remains a fundamental tension in adaptation studies: How are we to perform close textual readings within a poststructuralist theoretical framework often suspicious of such readings? Roland Barthes offered a useful critical paradigm for such intersemiotic theorizing in *Image–Music–Text*, and it is perhaps not surprising that so many theorists of film adaptation (including McFarlane) return to his work.[78] Indeed, adapting slightly Teresa de Lauretis's own reworking of Barthes's primal (that is, Oedipal) scene of nativity/narrativity in her central 'Desire in Narrative' chapter of *Alice Doesn't*,[79] we might say that whereas the death of the author is required in order to enable the birth of the reader, the process of adapting a work of literature for the screen requires that the author – or auteur – die a second time in order to enable the birth of the spectator.

That this doesn't always happen – that an author, in witnessing the transformation of his or her work for the screen, might, as it were, refuse to die and might, moreover, align himself or herself so closely with the auteur's vision as to make resistant readings of the filmic end product almost impossible – is something Roberts has examined in her discussion of the relationship between Ondaatje and Minghella, and the critical dissemination of that relationship during the making and reception of *The English Patient*.[80] Things get even more complicated in this regard when the author of the source text is also the screenwriter for the adaptation. Such is the case with Monique Proulx, who wrote the screenplay for Paule Baillargeon's film version of her 1987 novel, *Le sexe des étoiles*. In a short but focused essay on the Proulx–Baillargeon collaboration, Michael Eberle-Sinatra focuses on this important point and advances a reading of Baillargeon's film as a 'rereading' of the original novel by the author herself.[81] That this rereading results in a more conservative realignment of narrative focus in accord with the heteronormative conventions of the cinematic medium – and patriarchal culture more generally – is of principal concern for Eberle-Sinatra, and is something I will return to at greater length in my own reading of this adaptation in chapter 4. Similarly, Robert Lepage's auteurist 'reauthorizing' of his stage plays – particularly where images of the queer male body are concerned – will be the primary focus of chapter 5.

The act of cinematic birthing (and note how the gendered metaphors persist, even beyond the fidelity model) is a painful process, not least, as Parpart notes, for the reader/viewer, whose emotional investment with/in a given narrative can change dramatically across different signifying systems, and not least because verbal and visual signifying systems, in particular, have different ways of producing what she calls 'affective meaning.'[82] (How else to explain my own violent disapproval of the film version of *Le sexe des étoiles* when I first saw it? Or my use, already in this book, of such emotionally laden words as 'whitewash' and 'egregious' to describe the adaptations of *The English Patient* and *Anne of Green Gables*?) Desire – as it relates to how a narrative unfolds, what a character should look like, how a text should end – is always bound to be thwarted in the process of adaptation because the reader and the spectator identify with and through narrative differently. It is this thwarting or redirection or *translation* of narrative desire that we should be focusing on in our discussions, in order to argue that film adaptation (in general, but perhaps even more so within the cross-cultural Canadian context) not only results in the production of different texts, but also requires a new critical methodology for evaluating and analysing the relations between those texts.

Translation theories, as applied to film adaptations, are widespread, but have also received their share of negative criticism, largely, again, because of the persistence of a model of fidelity in framing such applications. However, if we conceive of translation as an indeterminate and ongoing system of structural, linguistic, cultural, and historical transformations, borrowings, and mediations that occur between and across forms, and if we further examine what these transformations say about the historical context in which texts are produced and received, then translation's critical potential, as applied to the adaptive process, is, I believe, recuperable. Indeed, such a focus on translation between narrative media (where, it must be stressed again, textual *infidelity* as much as textual *fidelity* becomes the key) can, in my experience, have both an *intrinsic* and an *extrinsic* focus, especially in classroom settings. That is, attention can be paid, on the one hand, to close readings of similarities and differences between very specific narratological issues relating to point of view, voice, story/plot, character and narrational functions, discourse and segmentation, and scene/shot analyses; and on the other, to broader contextual and cultural issues like critical reception, canonicity, institutionality, ideology, and nationalism. Adaptation theorists, in other words, need to develop a model of cinematic translation more along the lines of theories developed by feminist theorists of literary translation – one that prioritizes neither source nor target text, neither original nor copy, but rather foregrounds the co-implicatedness of each in the other's production and dissemination *as text*, as always already *a representation*, and, moreover, the situatedness of all such representations within the power structures governing material culture.[83] This is, I believe, partly what Benjamin Rifkin is getting at with his coining of the term 'transcoding' to describe the semiotics of the adaptive process: 'The filmmaker who creates a film based on a work of prose fiction first interprets (decodes) the primary text (the literary text), then encodes information and meaning (some or all of which was derived from the primary text) into a secondary text (the filmic text). The filmmaker, effecting an information transfer from one medium to the other, transcodes meaning from one art form to another.'[84]

Recently, respected film theorist Robert Stam, in a provocative and theoretically sophisticated article that draws on the work of Gérard Genette, Julia Kristeva, and Mikhail Bakhtin, has suggested something of a critical rapprochement in adaptation studies among the terms translation, intertextuality, and – perhaps most importantly – dialogism:

> An adaptation ... is less an attempted resuscitation of an originary word than a turn in an ongoing dialogical process. The concept of intertextual dialogism suggests that every text forms an intersection of textual surfaces. All texts are tissues of anonymous formulae, variations on those formulae, conscious and unconscious quotations, and conflations and inversions of other texts. In the broadest sense, intertextual dialogism refers to the infinite and open-ended possibilities generated by all the discursive practices of culture, the entire matrix of communicative utterances within which the artistic text is situated, which reach the text not only through recognizable influences, but also through a subtle process of dissemination.[85]

In such an 'infinite and open-ended' system of 'discursive practices' and 'communicative utterances,' it is possible to see every literary text, every film, indeed 'every representational artefact' as an adaptation sui generis,[86] and that a film, for example, is perforce incorporating multiple prior texts within its signifying system, only some of which may be expressly 'literary.' This is akin to what May Telmissany, in a discussion of films by Arcand, Lepage, and Lauzon, has called 'filmic citation,' in which the embedding of one textual 'event' (and I am using that term, as I believe she is, in both a Bakhtinian 'iterative' sense and a more conventionally historical sense) within another creates a rupture within the processing and interpretation of narrative temporality.[87] In much the same way that Metz and others have theorized cinematic representation as the presence of absence, Telmissany conceives of filmic citation – whether it be Lepage's carefully crafted quotations of Hitchcock or the crass product placement of Disney – as necessarily 'anachronistic,' because our visual memory in watching a film is always one step behind the actual projection of the film, not to mention potentially completely out of sync with the film's diegesis. In other words, the work of adaptation does not end with the product we see before us on the screen; it continues through our own processing – our own adapting, if you like – of its meaning within a particular cultural moment, which is also always an intercultural moment.

As such, the case studies that follow are in their own ways adaptations – not least in each chapter's appropriation and retooling of gender theory for genre analysis (and vice versa). In 'citing' the multiple and manifold ways that Canada has been 'sighted' on film – refracted through the prism of literature and reflected in the camera's lens – one of the things I want to point out is that this country's cultural mythology is itself the 'site' of constant reinvention and renegotiation. And in terms of the state-sponsored discourse around 'telling our own stories' that has emerged in this country in recent years, especially where government regulation of film and television production are concerned, adaptation studies are of crucial importance, for their examination of what stories are being told, how they are being told, by and for whom they are being told. As Metz has put it: 'Film tells us continuous stories; it "says" things that could be conveyed also in the language of words; yet it says them differently. There is a reason for the possibility as well as for the necessity of adaptations.'[88]

2 Feminism, Fidelity, and the Female Gothic: The Uncanny Art of Adaptation in *Kamouraska*, *Surfacing*, and *Le sourd dans la ville*

In [Jane Eyre's] world ... even the equality of love between true minds leads to the inequalities and minor despotisms of marriage.

Sandra Gilbert and Susan Gubar, *The Madwoman in the Attic*[1]

The great mystery of adaptation is that true fidelity can only be achieved through lavish promiscuity.

David Hare, *The Hours: A Screenplay*[2]

The uncanny is that class of the frightening which leads back to what is known of old and long familiar.

Sigmund Freud, 'The "Uncanny"'[3]

Gothic literature, like adaptation studies, has long been haunted by the equally frightening and familiar spectre of fidelity. On the one hand, marriage represents, for the gothic heroine, the promise of deliverance from the psychic terrors of an orphaned female desire that she has tried to repress since being turned out of her father's house and arriving at that of her new master, and would-be husband. On the other hand, the heroine's faith in the gothic marriage plot is severely tested by the hero's promiscuous attachment to some dark sexual secret from his past – a phantom former wife, perhaps, lurking, be it in body or in spirit, in the shadows of the gothic couple's future domestic happiness. The repetition, however diffusely, ironically, and/or resistantly, of this basic ur-plot over a vast corpus of largely (but by no means exclusively) women's texts spanning four centuries, from such Old World progenitors as Ann Radcliffe's *The Mysteries of Udolpho* (1793) and Charlotte Brontë's *Jane Eyre* (1847) to such New World revenant-reinventions as Isabelle Allende's *The House of Spirits* (1985) and Ann-Marie Mac-Donald's *Fall on Your Knees* (1996), points to how fidelity in gothic literature likewise operates at the level of genre, resulting in what Eve Kosofsky Sedgwick has identified as the remarkable 'coherence of gothic conventions'[4]: the presence of a large and mysterious house, manor, or castle wherein the central action unfolds; a double family secret – relating to her own parentage and her suitor's amorous past – that the heroine works simultaneously to conceal and reveal; the arrival of a mysterious stranger/long-lost relative to help expose one or other of those secrets; requisite instances of pathetic fallacy (storms, fires, floods), connoting the heroine's inner psychic torment; dark hallways that lead to locked doors; portraits and mirrors that stare back at, mock, accuse, or otherwise undermine the heroine's self-image; and so on.

What is more, feminist criticism of gothic literature has, with notable exceptions, by and large faithfully adhered to the notion, advanced by Ellen Moers in her pioneering study *Literary Women* (1977), that the gothic (Horace Walpole, Matthew Lewis, and their imitators notwithstanding) is essentially a female form (that is, in Moers's terms, written *by* women *for* women);[5] and that, following Gilbert and Gubar's influential refinement of Moers's argument in *The Madwoman in the Attic* (1979, 2000), this form is principally autotelic and 'monitory.' Thus, the gothic heroine's 'mad' double becomes a convenient way to represent what remains unrepresentable about so-called hysterical female experience in patriarchal culture, as well as to highlight the personal accommodations and psychic sacrifices that the heroine must make if she is to achieve in the socially sanctioned contract of marriage her longed-for 'equality of love.' As Gilbert and Gubar put it, with reference to *Jane Eyre*, 'while acting out Jane's secret fantasies, Bertha does (to say the least) provide the governess with an example of how not to act': 'the literal and symbolic death of Bertha frees [Jane] from the furies that torment her and makes possible a marriage of equality – makes possible, that is, wholeness within herself.'[6]

And yet while Freud's famous linking of adult female hysteria to the repression and subsequent reminiscence of a trauma in childhood undoubtedly overlaps with the standard female gothic plots,[7] psychologically (as opposed to psychoanalytically) inflected feminist readings of gothic literature have curiously made very little of the fact that Freud, in his most gothic of essays, 'The "Uncanny,"' concludes his 'collection of examples' about the consistency and the constancy with which the frightening leads back to the familiar not with a discussion of female hysteria, but with one of male abjection, not with the female's estrangement from her own body, but with the male's horror of the female body:

> It often happens that neurotic men declare that they feel there is something uncanny about the female genital organs. This *unheimlich* place, however, is the entrance to the former *Heim* [home] of all human beings, to the place where each one of us lived once upon a time and in the beginning. There is a joking saying that 'Love is home-sickness'; and whenever a man dreams of a place or a country and says to himself, while he is still dreaming: 'this place is familiar to me, I've been here before,' we may interpret the place as being his mother's genitals or her body. In this case, too, then, the *unheimlich* is what was once *heimisch*, familiar; the prefix 'un' ['un-] is the token of repression.[8]

Recent gothic criticism, drawing on Julia Kristeva's *Powers of Horror: An Essay in Abjection*, has refocused attention on what Robert Hume identified back in 1969 as the central importance of the 'complex villain-hero,' or what Michelle A. Massé has more recently summarized as the main paradox of most (female) gothic fiction: that 'the narrative is shaped by the mystery the male presents and not by the drama of the supposed protagonist, the Gothic heroine.'[9] In this scenario, then, Rochester's blindness at the end of *Jane Eyre* can be read both as a symbolic castration *and* as a necessary defence against the threat of castration, here figured as the return of the repressed image of none other than Jane herself, Bertha's double (rather than the other way around). I linger over such expressly gendered debates in order to highlight that both gothic literature and psychoanalytic theory, in their respective 'repression-based' genre analyses, share a fidelity to a model of healthy, normative male–female social (and sexual) relations based on the primacy of what Massé calls 'heterosexual genitality,' in which marriage 'is revealed as the reality principle before which the problematic pleasures of the female body yield.'[10] Moreover, this 'rescreening' (Massé's term) of the gothic uncanny, in which the frightening (the female body, and the passions that might abound within it and because of it) is rendered familiar through the familial (the husband replacing the father), means that 'the voice of the heroine as speaking subject is also erased, lost in the epithalamium of the fictional closure.'[11]

It stands to reason, then, that in the epiphenomenon of the filmic adaptation, which – no matter theorists' varied attempts to rework, reconsider, or repudiate altogether the concept of fidelity – still depends for much of its signifying force on an underlying transactional metaphor of marriage (and, for that matter, divorce), 'conveying the integrity of women's voices and representing appropriately the female point of view continues to be a problem … for those contemporary filmmakers who adapt fiction by women.'[12] Certainly this would seem to be the legacy of classic Hollywood adaptations of gothic literature by women. Commenting, for example, on Robert Stevenson's 1944 film version of *Jane Eyre*, starring Joan Fontaine and Orson Welles, Kate Ellis and E. Ann Kaplan lament the picture's 'watered-down' voice-over narration, the elimination of Miss Temple as a character from the Lowood section of the film, the bombast of Orson Welles's performance as Rochester, and the shadowy, noirish marginalization of Bertha's presence, all of which they read as a suppression of the novel's female point of view and as a playing up of traditional male authority. Ellis and Kaplan argue that even in those instances – particularly at Thornfield – where Stevenson's film explicitly engages and foregrounds Jane's desiring gaze, no added female autonomy seems to accrue with the 'reversal' of the traditional Mulveyian schema of looker and looked-at:

> Cinematically, Jane is placed as Rochester's observer: she yearns for him, waits upon him, watches him from the window, the stairwell, a corner of the room, hiding her tears from him behind closed doors. We retain Jane's point of view, but her gaze is fixed on Rochester as object of desire, an odd reversal of the usual situation in film where the male observes the woman as object of desire in such a way that the audience sees her that way too. Interestingly, the reversal of the look does not give Jane any more power: Rochester comes and goes, commands and manages, orders Jane's presence as he wishes. Jane's look is of a yearning, passive kind as against the more usual controlling male look at the woman.[13]

This is consistent with Mary Ann Doane's reading of the paranoid gothic woman's film of the 1940s, a 'miscegenated' genre, much of it adapted from literature (cf., in addition to *Jane Eyre*, Doane's primary examples: *Caught, Rebecca, Gaslight, Dragonwyck, The Two Mrs Carrolls*, and *Suspicion*, all of them adapted from literary works, by Libbie Block, Daphne du Maurier, Patrick Hamilton, Anya Seton, Martin Vale, and Anthony Berkeley, respectively). This genre, which borrows from film noir and horror, in its 'sustained investigation of the woman's relation to the gaze,' and in its testing of 'the very limits of the filmic representation of female subjectivity for a female spectator,' offers a 'metacommentary' on the whole supra-genre of the 'woman's film' more generally.[14] Arguing that female scopophilia is differentiated from male scopophilia in that it is a drive that is 'objectless' and 'free-floating,' Doane rereads Freud via Kristeva to argue that in film adaptations like *Jane Eyre* and *Rebecca*, what we are seeing is the female protagonist *not seeing* her own fear, the madwoman who cannot be shown and whose non-representability reflects back to the female protagonist 'an image of her own lack.'[15] Hence the repetition of narcissistic patterns of looking in such films; the paranoid gothic heroine sees everywhere – in mirrors, fashion magazines, photographs, portraits of wifely predecessors, and projected films within films – the spectre of her own subjective annihilation, a collapsing of the self into non-self that is explicitly figured as a consequence of the estrangement of marriage: 'In the paranoid gothic films, the woman's gaze, free-floating, objectless, and conducive to the phobia, is subjected to a return to its like, a narcissistic folding over upon itself. The women's films as a whole precipitate a narcissism of looking (woman at woman) which is the dilemma of the genre and must be mitigated or concealed. Even here, in the most explicitly phobic of the films, the narcissism is overlaid, deflected by the stress on a violence inhabiting the institutionalized heterosexual relation of marriage.'[16]

In chapter 6 I will have more to say about Doane's own practices of female abjection and estrangement in her 'institutionalized heterosexual' theorization of both the female gaze and the female spectator in relation to classic Hollywood film. For the time being, however, I want to apply her insights to an analysis of the film adaptations of three classic 'neo-gothic' feminist novels from Canada that explicitly foreground marriage not as the fulfilment of the female protagonist's wishful romantic fantasies, but rather as the uncanny source of her horror and alienation – as that which repeats the trauma of sexual difference itself. Here, again, I am following the lead of Massé, who identifies a generic variant of 'marital Gothic,' wherein the figure of the husband, or husband-surrogate, instead of serving 'to lay horror to rest' becomes 'the avatar of horror who strips voice, movement, property, and identity itself from the heroine.'[17]

This description certainly accords with the basic plots of Anne Hébert's *Kamouraska* (1970) and Margaret Atwood's *Surfacing* (1972), two novels that critics have often linked in terms of their narrative experimentation and, more pertinently, their self-conscious appropriation and reworking of various gothic tropes in order to represent a fragmented feminine consciousness.[18] *Kamouraska*, based on actual historical events in nineteenth-century rural Quebec, tells the story of Elisabeth d'Aulinières – of the slow, steady obliteration of self, the 'tel enfer' ('trial by horror') she experiences at the hands of not one but two husbands.[19] Married at sixteen to Antoine Tassy, the dashing squire of Kamouraska, Elisabeth finds her dreams of a fairy-tale life of never-ending romance quickly turn to the nightmare reality of Antoine's violence, alcoholism, constant philandering, and general indifference towards the two male heirs she dutifully provides him. Seeking solace in the arms of George Nelson, an American doctor summoned to treat her nervous disorder, Elisabeth soon discovers herself pregnant by her lover and hatches a plan to kill Antoine. However, things go badly awry when George, tormented by guilt following the murder and newly suspicious of Elisabeth's feminine 'wiles,' absconds to the United States, and when Aurélie Caron, the servant girl who had been in on the murder plot, testifies against Elisabeth at the subsequent trial. Released from prison after two months due to the perjured testimony of her female relatives, Elisabeth quickly marries Jérôme Rolland in order to restore her honour, bearing him eight more children in rapid succession. It is from his deathbed, on the Rue du Parloir in Quebec City, that Elisabeth narrates her story, in the form of a meandering interior monologue that flashes backwards and forwards in time, reflecting at once on how 'La folie de l'amour,' 'L'amour meurtrier. L'amour infâme. L'amour funeste' (11; 'The Madness of love,' 'Murderous love. Treacherous love. Deadly love' [5]), has resulted in her being 'qu'un ventre fidèle' (10; 'nothing but a faithful belly' [4]), a womb for hire, and on how her impending widowhood will secure her freedom once and for all.

Like *Kamouraska*, Atwood's *Surfacing* is set in northern Quebec and is structured as a first-person narrative, one that increasingly starts to fracture and fragment (registering this, quite materially, at the level of language and syntax) as the unnamed narrator gradually develops an uncanny sense of her own split subjectivity – a sense that she had 'allowed [herself] to be cut in two,' one half 'locked away,' the other, 'wrong half, detached terminal.'[20] Negotiating between these two 'victim positions' (for *Surfacing* is nothing if not the fictional elaboration of the famous thesis regarding Canadian literature that Atwood advanced in *Survival* two years earlier), the paranoid gothic heroine is 'terrified' she's being hunted along the forest path by 'a bear, a wolf or some indefinite thing with no name, that was worse' (73); at the same time her hysterical mad double, who knows she 'must have appeared grotesque' (106), sinks beneath the pond scum of repressed memories relating to an earlier 'phantom' marriage and the abortion that issued from it. All of this culminates in the narrator refusing fidelity to patriarchal language altogether and attempting to forge a return to the pre-Symbolic realm of her dead mother. That this refusal is precipitated, on the one hand, by the narrator's search for her father – a research biologist who has gone missing in the field – and on the other, by the implicit threat posed by her brooding boyfriend Joe and his violent and misogynist best friend, David, is no less important in terms of the argument being constructed in this chapter.

The formal experimentation, first-person narration, distinctive regional (and in the case of *Kamouraska*, historical) setting, and overt feminist politics of each novel would seem to make them unlikely candidates for adaptation to film – especially in the tax-shelter era of the 1970s and early 1980s, when (see chapter 1) funding agencies like the CFDC were pushing for popular Hollywood-style genre films (think *Meatballs* and *Porky's*) that would appeal to a broad international market. And yet adapted they were, in both cases by eminent Québécois director Claude Jutra, whose career, in retrospect, shows a distinctive facility with both women's stories and literary adaptations.[21] With *Kamouraska* and *Surfacing*, however, various pre- and post-production exigencies specific to the *medium* of cinema generally, and to the *institution* of a Canadian national cinema more specifically, conspired to hamstring Jutra's attempts to narrativize on film the gothic preoccupation with the obliteration of female selfhood found in the source texts. At the same time, I want to argue, following from Doane, that such exigencies – registered in *Kamouraska*'s promiscuous attempts to represent discursively and/or diegetically (through voice-over, mise-en-scène, shot construction, a thematization of the gaze, music, and so on) the female protagonist's split subjectivity, and in *Surfacing*'s apparent abandonment of all such strategies – actually reveal a fidelity to the exogamy of marriage, which 'institutes a "man/woman strangeness"' and 'a reinforcement of the opposition internal/external at the level of social relations.'[22] That is, just as a full sense of female interiority remains, fundamentally, inaccessible to the camera, so does woman remain invisible under patriarchy.

This is the representational paradox at the heart of Mireille Dansereau's remarkable 1987 adaptation of Marie-Claire Blais's *Le sourd dans la ville*, the third case study to which I turn briefly in this chapter's concluding section. Blais's novel is constructed much like Virginia Woolf's *Mrs Dalloway*, as a long, collective interior monologue; it shifts its stream-of-consciousness point of view among and between various denizens of the Hôtel des Voyageurs, including owner Gloria, her ill son Mike, and, above all, the 'toute bourgeoise et lucide' ('middle class and lucid') Florence, who has sought temporary refuge in the hotel following the collapse of her marriage to her 'powerful' physicist husband.[23] At first glance it would seem that Blais's novel is even more unfilmmable than *Kamouraska* and *Surfacing*, least of all as a gothic thriller. And yet, eschewing voice-over narration, and relying instead on an imaginative use of sound bridges, flashbacks, and a haunting central performance by Béatrice Picard, Dansereau is (as I will demonstrate) able to communicate stylistically an atmosphere of suspense and dread, not to mention something of the (inter)subjective paranoia experienced by Blais's Florence, 'un informe être humain captif des forces mauvaises de la vie' (33; 'a shapeless human being imprisoned by the evil forces of life' [30]), 'hunted' by death, and tormented, in her memories of her husband, by a 'familiar sensation' of fear that lurked 'behind the malicious, enchanting, screen of pleasure' that was their marriage: 'autour de lui la sensation de peur était là mais on ne la voyait, pas sous l'éran malicieux, enchanteur du plaisir, mais la peur était là, partout, sous le ciel pur et tranquille' (32; 'the sensation of fear floated all around him, even if it was something invisible it was there lurking behind the malicious, enchanting screen of pleasure, everywhere, fear beneath the pure, tranquil sky' [29]). In this way, the film version of *Le sourd dans la ville* becomes a form of ghost-writing – a form, moreover, that returns us, via the epigraph from David Hare, to the 'great mystery,' the uncanniness, of both marital gothic as a genre, and adaptation as a gendered construct: in promiscuously reauthorizing what lies repressed in each system, Dansereau faithfully exposes why that which is most frightening is also that which is most familiar.

Following the overwhelming success of Jutra's *Mon oncle Antoine* (1970) – still regarded as the best film ever produced in this country – there were high hopes surrounding the announcement that the director's next project was to be a big-budget adaptation of a critically acclaimed historical novel with a genuine international star. (Geneviève Bujold at the time was a hot Hollywood property, having recently been nominated for an Oscar for *Anne of a Thousand Days* [1969], in which she played opposite Richard Burton, and having even more recently appeared with Katherine Hepburn and Vanessa Redgrave in *The Trojan Women* [1971].) Many hoped that Jutra's *Kamouraska* would be Quebec's answer to *Gone With the Wind*, and that the smoldering intensity which would no doubt be generated between Bujold and her American co-star, the dark and brooding Richard Jordan (see Figure 2.1), would provoke favourable comparisons to Vivien Leigh and Clark Gable.[24] But period authenticity and the chance to reproduce on film elements of Québécois cultural heritage were hardly what most attracted Jutra to Hébert's text. Indeed, as Jim Leach has noted, 'Jutra made no secret of his own attraction to the gothic elements in the novel' and was equally excited about the non-linear, noirish manner in which Hébert narrated Elisabeth's story, which would allow him to create '"a film-mosaic which leaps continually from one place to another."'[25] Jutra admired the dream-like, hallucinatory atmosphere that accompanied Hébert's use of subjective flashbacks within Elisabeth's interior monologue; collaborating closely with the author on the screenplay, he sought to reproduce this effect in his film.

Audiences and critics, however, had expected to see a historical epic, with all of the requisite attention to physical details and exterior visuals that the genre usually entails, so they were by and large confused by Jutra's apparent contradictory and self-cancelling focus on gothic interiority, in terms of both the representation of the female protagonist's inner psychic drama *and* the enclosed domestic spaces to which, as a woman, she perforce was mostly confined.[26] To make things worse, Jutra, even though he was being hailed as the auteur who would rescue Québécois cinema, did not have final cut on the film; thus he could only watch while his three-hours-plus director's version of *Kamouraska* was edited down to 124 minutes for theatrical release. It promptly failed at the box office. In 1983, three years before his suicide, Jutra returned to his original negative and re-edited the film as a 173-minute miniseries. This version was broadcast on Canadian pay television and subsequently sold on video; it was then retransferred to 35 mm film in 1995, prompting a limited run in a handful of cinemas across the country. It is this restored version, and the generic and gendered oppositions operating within it, that I examine below; in so doing, I want to suggest that its commercial failure ironically might have had something to do with the fact that it was *too* faithful to Hébert's source text – that it 'was too close a "copy" of the original literary version.'[27]

In his discussion of E.T.A. Hoffmann as 'the unrivalled master of the uncanny in literature,' Freud notes that 'those themes of uncanniness which are most

2.1   *Kamouraska*: Elisabeth (Genviève Bujold) and George (Richard Jordan) enjoy a secret tryst.

prominent' in the author's work 'are all concerned with the phenomenon of the "double,"' with the 'doubling, dividing and interchanging of the self.'[28] These themes, especially as they become connected 'with reflections in mirrors, with shadows, with guardian spirits, with the belief in the soul and with the fear of death,'[29] are repeatedly played out in – although by no means fully coextensive with – the female gothic, and both the literary and film versions of *Kamouraska* are no exception in this regard. From its opening pages, Hébert's novel sets up a tension between the outward appearance of Madame Rolland, 'soumise et irréprochable' (7; 'dutiful and above reproach' [1]), attending faithfully at the bedside of her dying second husband on the Rue du Parloir in Quebec City, and the inner torment of Elisabeth d'Aulinières, 'veuve d'Antoine Tassy' (8; 'widow of Antoine Tassy' [2]), who walks through the street with 'l'idée que je me fais de ma vertu à deux pas devant moi' (9; 'the image of my virtue just a few steps ahead'

[3]). She is convinced that the townsfolk 'm'observe. On m'épie. On me suit' (7; 'are watching. Spying. Following me' [1]), coming 'closer and closer' to the secret from her youth that she has worked so hard to bury – namely, her role in 'le malheur de Kamouraska' (10; 'the tragedy at Kamouraska' [4]) and the murder of her first husband. Elisabeth struggles in vain to keep these two identities separate – a losing battle she herself adumbrates early on in the novel:

> Rêver au risque de se détruire, à tout instant, comme si on mimait sa mort. Pour voir. Inutile de se leurrer, un jour il y aura coïncidence entre la réalité et son double imaginaire. Tout pressentiment vérifié. Toute marge abolie. Tout alibi éventé. Toute fuite interdite. Le destin collera à mes os. Je serai reconnue coupable, à la face du monde. Il faut sortir de ce marasme tout de suite. Confondre le songe avant qu'il ne soit trop tard. S'ébrouer bien vite dans la lumière. Secouer les fantasmes. (23)[30]

For indeed, the real gothic horror at the heart of Hébert's novel is – as Arnold Davidson has suggested – the female protagonist's discovery that the reality and the dream have always been the same,[31] and that both coalesce around the necessary estrangement that comes with marriage. In this, the physical terror Elisabeth experienced at the hands of Antoine – dodging, while pregnant, not only flying kitchen knives but also the hangman's noose – is equivalent to the psychological torment she suffers under Jérôme, who delights in reminding her of her guilt and of the final judgment (by God) that awaits her. As Elisabeth summarizes her predicament early in the novel, speaking as much of her past life with Antoine as of her present life with Jérôme: 'Pris au piège tous les deux. C'est cela le mariage, la même peur partagée, le même besoin d'être consolé, la même caresse dans le noir' (24; 'Caught in the trap, the two of us. That's what marriage is. One fear shared by two, one need to be consoled, one empty caress in the darkness' [18]).

Here, the female heroine's desire to 'se nommer Elisabeth d'Aulinières à jamais. Habiter toute sa chair intacte, comme le sang libre et joyeux' (23; 'be forever named Elisabeth d'Aulinières. To live to the fullest in your flesh, intact, like blood coursing happy and free' [17]) comes up against the waking nightmare, the death in life, that attends her renaming as Madame Rolland, and before that, Madame Tassy. This inevitable acquiescence on the part of the gothic heroine before the Name/Law of the Father finds a corollary in what Doane has described as the syntagmatic repetition of the name Mrs de Winter in Alfred Hitchcock's classic adaptation of Daphne du Maurier's *Rebecca*. The creepy housekeeper Mrs Danvers (Judith Anderson) repeats it obsessively and possessively with reference to the spectre of the 'first Mrs de Winter' (the Rebecca of the title), forcing the nameless Joan Fontaine character to stake her claim to the identity in an uncanny act of doubling: 'I am Mrs de Winter now,' she boldly asserts as she orders Mrs Danvers to empty the house of all traces of her predecessor. At the same time, as Doane points out, this act of feminine mimesis (compounded by the Fontaine character's later appearance at the masquerade ball wearing a copy of the costume worn by Rebecca) insistently links both Mrs de Winters via their past and present positions as wife – a structural relation of narcissism that results in 'the collapse of the subject/object distinction': 'Within the field of language [and, we might add, the institution of heterosexual marriage] the woman is allowed no access to difference and is consigned to an inevitable repetition of the same.'[32]

This imprisoning paradox is foregrounded early on in Jutra's film when – in a scene transposed only slightly from Hébert's novel – the ghost of Aurélie (Suzie Baillargeon) confronts a restless Elisabeth, who has just awoken from a dream flashback depicting her 'sunny' girlhood in Sorel. In the film, this flashback scene is accentuated by Jutra's use of natural light to flare his shots and imbue Elisabeth's remembrance of the idyll that was her pre-married youth with a fantasy, rainbow-like radiance. Not so the harsh (ir)reality of the present on Rue du Parloir, to which Jutra then cuts – a noticeable shift in mise-en-scène from the novel. Here, artificial backlighting, a shot/reverse-shot sequence of medium close-ups, and a similarly severe Mrs Danvers–like black wardrobe for both principals, together accentuate the pallor of Elisabeth and her uncanny double, Aurélie, both now in mourning for a lost past, a cloistered gender. Pointedly, Aurélie insists on calling her former friend, mistress, and co-accused 'Madame.' In the film, unlike in the novel, Elisabeth responds by pronouncing aloud her full maiden name in a desperate attempt to shore up her flagging sense of self. Even when she succeeds at the end of this scene in turning Aurélie's attention back to the halcyon days when they were 'deux filles innocents' obsessed with clothes and boys, Aurélie (whose sorceress's gifts of prophecy, it should be pointed out, work much better analeptically than proleptically in both the novel and the film) suggests that the repetition of the repressed trauma of Elisabeth's unnaming – figured most obviously in her two marriages – might actually have had a much earlier origin: 'En ce temps-là on vous appelait "Mademoiselle"' ('Back then they called you "Mademoiselle"') is the line, cribbed from Hébert's novel (62; 59), that provides the sound bridge to Jutra's return to the forest path of Elisabeth's flashback.

The dialogue and cutting of this scene, when juxtaposed with that of the flashback scene which brackets it – in which, for instance, Elisabeth and Aurélie, both fifteen years old, are twinned in a series of two-shots – is coextensive with what Freud calls the double's inevitable reversal of 'its aspect,' moving from an initial association with 'primary narcissism' and youthful self-love, where it acts as 'an insurance against the destruction of the ego,' to an eventual dissociation from and self-censoring agency over the ego, where it 'becomes the uncanny harbinger of death,' 'a thing of terror,' forcing a self-critical rehearsal of past traumas and unfulfilled fantasies of the future.[33] As Elisabeth herself puts it near the end of the novel: 'C'est le moment où il faut dédoubler franchement. Accepter cette division définitive de tout mon être' (196; 'The time has come now to split in two. Accept this total, sharp division of my being' [194]). Thus the nightmare realization Elisabeth must inevitably wake to after her long vigil of the soul: that beneath the outward 'image' of 'Madame Rolland' crying for her dying husband lurks the inner 'daemon' of her mad gothic double, buried alive long ago, now exhumed, and quite literally starving for attention:

> Brusquement le cauchemar déferle à nouveau, secoue Elisabeth d'Aulinières dans une
> tempête. Sans que rien n'y paraisse à l'extérieur. L'épouse modèle tient la main de son

mari, posée sur le drap. Et pourtant … Dans un champ aride, sous les pierres, on a déterré une femme noire, vivante, datant d'une époque reculée et sauvage. Étrangement conservée. On l'a lâchée dans la petite ville. Puis on s'est barricadé, chacun chez soi. Tant la peur qu'on a de cette femme est grande et profonde. Chacun se dit que la faim de vivre de cette femme, enterrée vive, il y a si longtemps, doit être si féroce et entière, accumulée sous la terre, depuis les siècles! On n'en a sans doute jamais connu de semblable. Lorsque la femme se présente dans la ville, courant et implorant, le tocsin se met à sonner. Elle ne trouve que des portes fermées et le désert de terre battue dont sont faites les rues. Il ne lui reste sans doute plus qu'à mourir de faim et de solitude. (250)[34]

How to represent this on film without recourse to voice-over or an 'impossible' point of view shot depicting what Doane has referred to as the unrepresentable 'nonobject' of the gothic heroine's fear?[35] While, as we shall shortly see, Jutra employs such techniques elsewhere in the film to foreground Elisabeth's split subjectivity, and to set up, in terms of the film's overall visual semantics, a dialectical relationship between display and concealment, inside and outside, voyeurism and projection, here he opts instead for a final long take, in medium close-up, of Elisabeth crying. Having already been implicated in the act of looking expressly thematized in this particular scene (and throughout the film, more generally) via the shot immediately preceding this one – wherein a servant, speaking directly into the camera, draws our attention to the visible signs of Elisabeth's grief for her husband – we as spectators are suddenly confronted by and forced to assimilate an indexical or 'objective' image of almost pure exteriority (crucially, no extra-diegetic music plays over the film's closing frames[36]) in the context of a filmic discourse and narrative style that has hitherto worked very hard to incorporate iconic or 'subjective' representations of the protagonist's interior consciousness into the diegesis. That fundamentally we are unable to do so – that throughout the course of that long take Elisabeth's tears remain as undecidable to us as they must be to her in terms of their absent on-screen referent, their obscure object of desire (who or what is she crying for, and in connection with which time frame?) – points to the fact that what remains most overdetermined in Jutra's film adaptation (as with all gothic narratives generally) is the very scopic drive itself, the trauma of seeing and not seeing, vision and re-vision. In this, once again Jutra takes his cue from Hébert's novel, which concludes with one of the servants (Elisabeth is pointedly unsure which one) saying 'Voyez donc comme Madame aime Monsieur! Voyez comme elle pleure …' (250; 'Just look how Madame loves Monsieur! You see, she's crying …' [250]; my italics; ellipses in original).

Here, I want to link up Doane's reading of the window as paradigmatic site of the 'specularization' of the female heroine in the paranoid gothic woman's film with Jim Leach's excellent reading of the opening sequence of shots in Jutra's Kamouraska,[37] particularly as they effect, through the act of looking, an interface between two sexually and socially distinct spaces (inside and outside) and temporalities (past and present). This initial rupturing of narrative continuity – repeated throughout the film, which adopts a highly subjective point-of-view structure (mostly via recourse to flashbacks and voice-over) – mirrors not only Elisabeth's increasingly fragmented consciousness, but also her divided conscience.

Hébert's novel opens by emphasizing Elisabeth's imprisonment within the domestic confines of the home – 'Mme Rolland, contre son habitude, ne quitta pas sa maison de la rue du Parloir' (7; 'Unlike other years, Madame Rolland didn't leave her home on Rue du Parloir' [1]) – and by emphasizing the window's symbolic associations with both the desire to look and the dread of looking, of seeing and being seen: 'Mme Rolland, très droite, sans bouger le buste, les mains immobiles sur sa jupe à crinoline, approche son visage de la jalousie, jette un regard vert entre les lattes, prête l'oreille, sous les bandeaux de cheveux lissés' (12; 'Madame Rolland stands erect, hardly breathing, hands poised on her crinoline skirt. Bends her head toward the shutters and takes a sharp look between the slats. Pricks up her ears, hidden by hair pulled tightly back' [6]). Jutra plays up this suspense first by having his highly mobile, voyeuristic, and phantom camera eye penetrate the window, and then by aligning it with the stationary, projective, and haunted inner eye of the gothic heroine who peers out from it. As we fade in on a night shot of some trees being whipped by wind and rain and Maurice Leroux's funerary piano score is introduced, the opening credits begin to roll, and the camera slowly pans left and upwards along the exterior of an imposing stone mansion, lingering over a banging gutter, before finally settling outside a sheerly curtained window. The sound of the banging gutter is replaced by off-camera male shouts, which coincide with Elisabeth's appearance at the window with a lamp, and her pulling back of the curtains. We then cut to a crane shot that approximately mirrors her position, only we are now looking at a sleigh being driven wildly across a snowy field. It comes to rest right before the camera, and a male character whom we will later learn is George Nelson (Richard Jordan) looks up, seeming to return Elisabeth's gaze. As Leach points out, this 'impossible' shot sequence establishes a dialectic between interiority and exteriority, past and present, real and imaginary that will be developed throughout the remainder of the film, suggesting that while Elisabeth's body may be shut up inside the dark, cloistered spaces of the chamber of death associated with her second husband, Jérôme (Marcel Cuvelier), 'her spirit is outside in a snowy landscape that represents both freedom and danger and is associated with her lover and with the violent death of her first husband.' In so doing, 'the film proclaims its ability to show what she sees with her inner eye but also implies that her memories may be distorted by the pressures and desires of the present.'[38]

That these pressures coalesce as much around the repeated trauma of marriage as they do around the repressed trauma of murder is signalled by another sequence of 'distorted' and highly subjective point-of-view shots, among many such examples which punctuate especially the flashbacks of the film. In concluding my discussion of both the uncanny operations of adaptation and the ambivalent approach to fidelity on offer in Jutra's *Kamouraska*, I wish to comment on these very briefly. I am speaking, in particular, of the series of flashbacks that record Elisabeth's betrothal to Antoine (Philippe Léotard). Following the sun-kissed exterior scenes with Aurélie described above, in which Elisabeth pumps her new friend for information about boys, there follows a quick succession of temporally asynchronous and spatially disjunctive scenes that once again fore-ground the act of looking, and that move Elisabeth (and the viewer) inexorably from girlhood to womanhood, and from outside to inside: Elisabeth making her social debut at the Governor's Ball, where she is clearly positioned as the object of the male gaze; Elisabeth meeting Antoine, and sharing the look, while out hunt-ing ducks; Elisabeth spying from the staircase (another paradigmatic site of the specularization of the paranoid gothic heroine, according to Doane, and one to which I will return shortly in my discussions of *Le sourd dans la ville*) as old Madame Tassy (Camille Bernard) arranges with Elisabeth's mother (Huguette Oligny) the match between their children; and finally Elisabeth *refusing* to look at Antoine, whom she claims to have seen carrying on with another woman, while dancing with him at the Cazeaus' ball. However, during the course of this last scene, Elisabeth is very pointedly *made* to look – this time at herself – as Jutra cuts invisibly within the same mise-en-scène from an 'objective' shot of Elisabeth and Antoine dancing to a 'subjective' point-of-view shot of a bewildered (literally out-of-body) Elisabeth now watching herself move, like a 'poupée mécanique' ('little mechanical doll'), down the aisle with her new husband.

Once again, Jutra in this scene reveals an uncanny facility for rendering on film the divided sense of female self that Hébert records in her novel: 'Cette distance même qui devrait me rassurer est pire que tout. Penser à soi à la troisième per-sonne. Feindre le détachement. Ne pas s'identifier à la jeune mariée, toute habillée de velours bleu' (71; 'This distance that ought to be comforting me, this sense of detachment. It's worse than all the rest. Seeing yourself as someone else. Pretend-ing to be objective. Not feeling that you and that young bride dressed in blue vel-vet are one and the same' [67]). Yet just as importantly, it seems to me, the sense of literal déjà vu rendered here and elsewhere in the film suggests that the visual image's indexicality, or fidelity, to a representation of reality is incommensurable with the social symbolic that is marriage – an institution that transforms woman into a 'mechanical doll.' In this regard, Hébert's novel and Jutra's film together serve as an important feminist gloss on Freud's reading of Hoffmann's tale 'The Sand-Man.' Freud suggests that the casting of the female character in that story, Olympia, as an automaton, a 'living doll,' excites less fear than Nathaniel's anxi-ety about losing his eyes to the evil Sand-Man (which, as per our discussion of Rochester, above, Freud reads as evidence of a male castration complex);[39] by con-trast, the adaptive example of *Kamouraska* makes it clear that the real horror for the gothic heroine is precisely that she cannot look away from the spectacle of her own 'mechanical reproduction.' That as per Doane, Jutra seems to be building into his own paranoid gothic film a metacommentary on 'woman's relation to the gaze' is further illuminated if we compare *Kamouraska* with Jutra's next 'failed' foray into the genre: *Surfacing*.

'Atwood Gothic' is the term that Eli Mandel first proposed to describe the links between the diverse range of texts that have resulted from the author's prodi-gious output in a number of different modes[40]: from the emphasis on madness, monstrosity, and mirroring in her early poetry (especially *The Journals of Susanna Moodie*, *You Are Happy*, and *The Animals in That Country*, the latter of which features a suite of poems called 'Speeches for Dr Frankenstein'); to her obsessional dissection of motifs of victimization, haunting, doubling, and death in her criticism (see especially *Survival, Strange Things: The Malevolent North in Canadian Literature,* and *Negotiating with the Dead: A Writer on Writing*); and, of course, to her continued elaboration of the secret inner lives and fears of the typically gothic heroines who populate her fiction (from *The Edible Woman* to *The Blind Assassin*), many of whom are convinced that their husbands or lovers are trying to kill them. Indeed, that Atwood channelled much of her thinking and reading around her abandoned PhD thesis on Victorian sensational fiction into her first three novels has long been noted by critics. Yet while the complicated romantic entanglements of Marian MacAlpin in *The Edible Woman* and Joan Foster in *Lady Oracle* – along with the respective fantasies of being ritually cannibalized and staging one's own death that plague them – have been interpreted in terms of 'an explication of marital and exogamous relations and the constitutive and destructive effect they have upon the protagonist's identity,'[41] the interpretation of *Surfacing* as a species of marital gothic has often lagged behind.

This is in part because the gothic elements in *Surfacing* – especially as they coalesce around the unnamed protagonist's paranoic hatred of Americans and her initial estrangement from and eventual submersion within the primeval landscape of her youth (her 'home ground,' we learn early on in the novel, is simultaneously 'foreign territory' [11]) – have all too frequently been conscripted into a 'sociological' reading of the novel as an allegory of menaced national identity rather than fractured gender identity.[42] At the same time, however, the novel makes it clear that in the narrator's struggle to become human – 'The trouble some people have being German ... I have being human,' she notes at one point (130) – such identity categories not only are co-implicated, but also more often than not are at war with one another. Thus, while the novel ends with the narrator acknowledging that Joe, as a non-American, can be trusted, it also makes clear that as a potential husband 'he may have been sent as a trick,' adopting the guise of 'a mediator, an ambassador, offering me something: captivity in any of its forms, a new freedom?' (192). That the film adaptation of *Surfacing* resolves this ambiguity in favour of a conventional Hollywood ending that effects a clear romantic reconciliation between its two leads is all the more ironic, given that the roles are played by American actors. This in turn suggests the need for a very different ideological approach to questions of feminism and fidelity as they are operating here – in Jutra's first feature-length theatrical release in English – especially when compared to the previous example of *Kamouraska*. That is, in the adaptive context of *Surfacing* the jettisoning of textual fidelity as a discursive strategy inadequate to the transcoding of narrative across different media paradoxically reinscribes sexual fidelity as the internalized institutional or symbolic measure of the female protagonist's sense of her own adequacy as a woman.

Shortly after her second novel was published, Atwood described it as a 'ghost story,'[43] and one suspects that Jutra, having already attempted to convey the impression of female interiority and psychic uncanniness on film in *Kamouraska*, would have responded favourably to *Surfacing*'s highly subjective representation of the familiar, and the familial, as frightening. Indeed, the female protagonist's own particular brand of projection and voyeurism seems especially suited to the elliptical and non-linear flashback/point-of-view structure Jutra developed for his adaptation of Hébert's novel. That is, in *Surfacing* the narrator's need both to remain invisible and to see coalesces around a double structure of 'camouflage' (a word repeated throughout the text) that relates to two different yet interconnected sets of repressed memories. On the one hand, her invented recollection of her brother's drowning – an event that supposedly occurred before she was born, but that she nevertheless claims to have seen (32) – substitutes for the more traumatic (and, we presume, real) memory of the abortion she was pressured into having by a previous older (and married) lover: 'I have to behave as though it doesn't exist, because for me it can't, it was taken away from me, exported, deported. A section of my own life, sliced off from me like a Siamese twin, my own flesh cancelled. Lapse, relapse, I have to forget' (48). On the other hand, the anxiety caused by her present search for her missing father masks a deeper desire to reconnect and speak with (crucially, in a language other than that handed down by patriarchy) her long dead mother, whose story, like her own, is full of unfathomable holes, and whom, in true gothic fashion, she fears becoming: 'The only place left for me is that of my mother; a problem, what she did in the afternoons between the routines of lunch and supper ... on some days she would simply vanish, walk off by herself into the forest. Impossible to be like my mother, it would need a time warp; she was either ten thousand years behind the rest or fifty years ahead of them' (52).

These doubled narrative strains are structured analeptically around two recurring sets of visual images – the frogs that the narrator's brother used to capture in jars, and her mother's leather jacket, which hangs talismanically on a hook in the cabin – and finally come together when the narrator, using the map of underwater petroglyphs her father had been working from, discovers his drowned body pinned underwater by a rock. This is the signal event that unleashes in her the even more fearful realization of her complicity in the abortion, 'the ruin I'd made': 'It wasn't ever my brother I'd been remembering, that had been a disguise ... It wasn't a child but it could have been one, I didn't allow it' (143). This in turn prompts an apparition of her mother standing in front of the cabin, wearing her grey leather jacket, and the realization that her mother's 'gift' to her was allowing her to look, first and foremost at herself as a woman, and at the person 'sitting up inside her gazing out' (158). Not surprisingly, all of this culminates in the narrator – having fled her companions, lest they guess her 'true form, identity' and 'shoot me or bludgeon in my skull and hang me up by the feet from a tree' (183) – confronting that very form herself in an uncanny moment of gothic specularization and terror-inducing dissociation; Atwood's feral 'natural woman' joins Hébert's disinterred 'black woman' and Brontë's escaped 'madwoman' in identifying with her own abominable image as the only defence against a patriarchal, symbolic order that would contain her through language, naming her as monstrous other:

> I turn the mirror around: in it there's a creature neither animal nor human, furless, only a dirty blanket, shoulders huddled over into a crouch, eyes staring blue as ice from the deep sockets; the lips move by themselves. This was the stereotype, straws in

the hair, talking nonsense or not talking at all. To have someone to speak to and words that can be understood: their definition of sanity.

That is the real danger now, the hospital or the zoo, where we are put, species and individual, when we can no longer cope. They would never believe it's only a natural woman, state of nature, they think of that as a tanned body on a beach with washed hair waving like scarves; not this, face dirt-caked and streaked, skin grimed and scabby, hair like a frayed bathmat stuck with leaves and twigs. A new kind of centre-fold.

I laugh, and a noise comes out like something being killed: a mouse, a bird? (190)

Needless to say, this scene is absent from the film, as is the novel's abiding concern, especially in Part III, with presenting the narrator's haunted wilderness journey as an exterior manifestation of her interior psychic descent into madness. Instead, the film tries to build a double sense of suspense by paralleling the mystery surrounding the disappearance of Kate's (as the protagonist, played by the doe-eyed Kathleen Beller, has here been christened) father with the uncertainty that hovers over the future of her relationship with Joe (Joseph Bottoms). Indeed, Kate's failure 'to deal with the situation' of her complicated relationship with her father – as Joe puts it in an early establishing sequence not in the novel – is presented as the major impediment to the successful resolution of the romantic marriage plot that is really at the heart of this film. We see this especially in the ways in which the novel's back stories about the narrator's abortion, the drowning of her brother, and the death of her mother are elided or else eliminated completely from the film. For instance, soon after arriving at the cabin, Kate perfunctorily tells Joe, David (R.H. Thomson), and Anna (Margaret Dragu) about her mother's premature death merely as a preamble to the more important story of her *father* saving *her* from a near-fatal drowning when she was a child. 'He breathed me back to life,' is how she rather dreamily puts it, as the camera pans from the dock to the rippling water of the lake. Kate's abortion, we also learn, is not connected to a previous liaison with an older married man that she is trying to keep secret from Joe, but rather the result of her not being 'careful' with Joe himself. Moreover, the screen Joe cannot understand why Kate has to keep dwelling on the issue, nor why she should care about her father finding out: 'You weren't careful. You got pregnant. You got an abortion. I mean, it's all fine in my mind. It's just, why do we have to keep going back over that again and again? ... Besides, what is so god-damn important about what your father thinks anyway? ... Why are we killing ourselves to bring Daddy back the sad news?'

That Joe is unambiguously positioned in the film, unlike in the source text, as the romantic suitor who will save Kate not only from her haunted past but also from her equally frightening future is emphasized by two further changes from the novel. First, by rescuing David from the humiliating wilderness hazing he receives from the menacing and trigger-happy hunter Wayne (Michael Ironside), Joe is also implicitly rescuing Kate from an attempted rape by David, who prior to the hunters' arrival had interrupted her mushroom collecting and pinned her against a tree, asking 'What else did your father teach you?' In the novel, these events are unconnected; the group's encounter with the American hunters is wholly benign (except in the protagonist's mind), and David's solicitation of sex is completely inept and non-threatening. Finally, in the film it is Joe, not Kate, who finds the petroglyphs her father had been mapping. In the course of doing so, he falls and breaks his arm and has to be ferried to a hospital. Kate stays behind to complete her search for her father's body, the discovery of which prompts not a final frightening descent into the gothic darkness of feminine interiority, but rather her successful emergence out of it, and apparent reintegration into patriarchal society. Ironically, this is conveyed to us in the film's sole instance of voiceover: 'He's dead, Joe. I said good-bye to him. I'm on my own now. I can manage with my hopes and my failures. Why should I be filled with death? Why should I be in mourning? Everything is alive. Everything is waiting to become alive.' As Mary K. Kirtz has argued: 'These last two sentences, taken directly from the novel, underscore the travesty of the transposition – in the novel, the words come after the protagonist's journey into the depths of her psyche is completed. Here [in the film], she's just cleaning up, preparing for departure.'[44]

Not that Jutra should be forced to shoulder all of the blame for this. Hired to direct the film at the last minute after Eric Till left just as shooting was about to begin, having had no say in the casting choices, and unable to make any extensive changes to the pedestrian screenplay cobbled together by Bernard Gordon, Jutra was also working without many of his longtime collaborators (including cinematographer Michel Brault), and faced constant interference from first-time producer Beryl Fox, a documentarian who had wanted to make this her own directorial debut as a feature filmmaker, and who had invested a considerable amount of her own money in the project.[45] The film's image track attests to the constraints Jutra was working under (the soundtrack, featuring original music by Jean Cousineau and Ann Mortifee, is another matter entirely); it also demonstrates how genre and gender are co-implicated in questions of fidelity when it comes to this particular adaptation. That is, hamstrung by a shooting script that relied almost entirely on continuity editing and an exterior mise-en-scène, it was virtually inevitable that the film version of *Surfacing* would see Atwood's highly allegorical gothic narrative being overrriden by the visual codes of a typical – and typically masculine – action-adventure flick. Hence Martin Knelman's famously dismissive assessment of the film as 'a simple-minded feminist equivalent of a woodsy Boy's Own adventure story.'[46] And hence its repeated comparison, in the extant criticism (what little of it exists), to John Boorman's *Deliverance* (1972), especially in descriptions of the aforementioned scene with the psycho hunters, and of an earlier extended sequence – again, nowhere to be found in the novel – when the two couples, having swapped partners, shoot the rapids in their canoes (see Figures 2.2 and 2.3).[47]

Thus, unable to portray what is *frightening* about the subjective interiority of the gothic heroine's fractured mind, Jutra must resort – as per the dictates of the filmic gaze – to the *familiar* objectification of her body. In this, as Florence Jacobwitz has stated, the adaptation sets up 'an interesting tension [around] the uncovering of a female body for the pleasure of the audience.'[48] We see this in the opening shots of the film, when, in what we will later learn is a flashforward (the only break in narrative continuity in the entire film), Jutra cuts from a wide-angle

2.2   *Surfacing*: Kate (played here by stunt double Catherine Leiterman, substituting for lead actress Kathleen Beller) and David (R.H. Thomson) shoot the rapids.

long shot of a small boat floating on the water before a sheer rock face to a low-angle shot (the camera is actually positioned more or less at water level) of Kate in a bathing suit diving head first into the water and, by extension, into our voyeuristic gaze. As the camera tracks her progress underwater, focusing in on the rhythmic strokes of her naked arms and legs, the credits begin to roll, and Mortifee's 'Gypsy Born' begins to play on the soundtrack.

Later, as Kate and Joe prepare for bed their first night at the cabin, in what amounts to the film's most overtly gothic sequence, Kate's self-consciousness about her own body is expressly linked to a return of the repressed – in particular, a fear that her father might suddenly return from his sojourn in the woods and see her in flagrante with Joe. Here, as in *Kamouraska*, Jutra draws our attention to the act of looking by cutting back and forth between Kate undressing in front of the

2.3   *Surfacing*: Anna (Margaret Dragu) and Joe (Joseph Bottoms) follow suit.

window and the reaction shots of Joe, who is watching eagerly from the bed. Perturbed by the intensity of his gaze, Kate asks him if he has 'to stare,' and modestly covers her breasts as Joe chivalrously pretends to bury his face in a pillow. Seconds later, however, he asks her to shake her shirt 'like a flag' above her head and 'be proud of what you've got,' before seizing her and pulling her into the bed. When Kate protests, asking, in reference to her father, 'What if he comes to the window and sees us?' Joe responds, in an ominous echo of Othello, 'I'll put out the light.'

This scene is, of course, filmed mostly in shadow, and we catch only teasing and largely silhouetted glimpses of Kate's nakedness (and, for that matter, Joe's, the gay Jutra taking every opportunity to expose the male body to the camera's voyeuristic gaze as well). Indeed, only after she discovers her father's bloated corpse underwater in the scene that completes the credit sequence described above, and only with Joe safely away seeking medical attention on the mainland, is Kate able to 'expose' herself completely in the full light of day, bathing naked in the lake. In the novel, this cleansing ritual signals a full immersion in the pre-Symbolic state of 'natural woman,' with the narrator 'leaving my false body floated on the surface, a cloth decoy' (178); in the *film*, it is important to remember, this scene precedes Kate's definitive reunion with Joe, and as such is still very much framed within a patriarchal optics. And here, in a montage suggestive of the film's own divided consciousness, the soft-core porn conventions that play up for voyeuristic consumption what Jacobwitz has called Beller's 'very sexual Playboy-centrefold body' (something completely counter to the spirit of Atwood's book) are somewhat at odds with what Leach has called the sense of 'unease' created by Jutra's camera, which seems 'to adopt the point of view of an unknown lurking presence' (something much more in tune with the gothic premises of the source text).[49]

However muddled and painfully uneven the adaptation of *Surfacing* may be, Jutra is still able to effect something of a subtle autocritique not just of the institution of marriage, but of the cinematic apparatus itself. We can see this by considering briefly the representation of the other couple in the film. Anna and David, unlike Kate and Joe, are married, and their quasi-sadomasochistic relationship is framed entirely by the dominant power relations inherent in heteronormative sexuality, and in patriarchal discourse more generally. Thus, when David is not treating Anna like his private sexual plaything – telling her in the opening car ride north, for example, to keep her legs together lest he drive off the road, or later chasing her around the cabin like a caged animal – he delights in verbally insulting her and pointing out her inferiority, as when he reminds a sunbathing Anna that if she wants to fish he will first need to show her how. In this way, the marriage contract – especially when juxtaposed with Kate's reluctance, at least early on in the film, to formalize her own relationship with Joe – is shown to preclude the possibility of reciprocal love because heteronormative desire, like language, is structured around a subject–object split that mimics and institutionalizes, at a symbolic level, male authority and female subordination. That Anna, Kate's uncanny double, has internalized this subordination is shown in countless ways throughout the film, not least in her repeated application of make-up. She explains to Kate, who catches her daubing her worn face in front of the cabin's tiny mirror the morning after their arrival, that 'he [David] doesn't like to see me without it … Neither do I.' This last comment is especially telling, as in an earlier scene the viewer has already learned that David is aware of Anna's morning routine, and simply '[goes] along with the game.'

Yet as significant as these scenes of 'cover-up' are, once again it is a scene that coalesces around 'the uncovering of the female body' that highlights the full extent of Anna's apparent acquiescence to her own objectification, as well as the film's own complicity in 'exposing' this. I am referring to the episode, late in the film, when the four protagonists come across the strewn-up dead heron. In the book, David and Joe – who, as wannabe avant-garde artists, are compiling a film of found footage called *Random Samples* – think this is the perfect image to put next to some previously collected shots of fish guts. They set up the camera while the women wait, the narrator reflecting internally that the purpose of such a 'lynching' could only be as a crude demonstration of power (116). By contrast, in the film the scene becomes yet another example of David's specific power over a humiliated and utterly abject Anna; he forces her to strip naked and dance around the heron 'like Isadora' as he shoots it all with his hand-held camera. When Kate, horrified by what she is witnessing, asks a seemingly unaffected and disinterested Joe to intervene, he responds by telling her, 'If you don't approve, just don't watch.' However, as Leach has perceptively noted, we as spectators, 'unless [we] close [our] eyes, have not only to watch the dance but also to see much of it through David's camera.'[50] It is hard not to read this in part as Jutra's self-reflexive comment on his own camera's complicity in the frame-up that necessarily attends the screening of gender. As such, Kate's subsequent act of protest, in which she opens up David's film canisters and dumps out the contents, exposing everything to the natural light and elements, can be interpreted, within the overlapping generic contexts of adaptation and the marital gothic outlined in this chapter, as a further statement on the double bind of fidelity.

In an extensive oeuvre that 'exhibits a grimly dark and gothic vision of such depth and complexity that she can well be compared to authors like Flannery O'Connor or even Franz Kafka,'[51] most critics have singled out Marie-Claire Blais's first novel, *La belle bête* (1959; translated as *Mad Shadows* in 1971), with its manifold images of death and decay, its doubled Oedipal narratives of rival sibling matricide and patricide, its allegorical allusions to classic fairy tales, its symbolic use of mirrors, and its fiery climax, as her most quintessentially gothic.[52] Yet as Mary Jean Green points out, *La belle bête*'s 'story of a lonely woman [Isabelle-Marie], unloved by her mother and abandoned by her husband, who is finally driven to suicide,' completely overlaps with that of Florence Gray in *Le sourd dans la ville* (1979).[53] In both novels the gothic marriage plot ends tragically, resulting in a familiar 'annihilation' (a favourite word of Blais's) of female selfhood. Thus, near the end of *Le sourd*, mere moments before she will put a gun to her head and take her life, Florence recalls an earlier scene from her marriage: she and her husband, drunk and in love, had gone to bed in what they thought was 'un grand hôtel près de la mer' (190; 'a first-class hotel near the sea' [211]), only to wake up the next morning 'dans un chambre abjecte, tout contre un abattoir' (190; 'in a sordid room beside a slaughterhouse' [211]). In hindsight, Florence, borrowing a page from her gothic predecessor, Isabelle-Marie, interprets this to mean that an 'odeur de la mort' (190; 'smell of death' [211]) had always been present in their relationship: 'la seule abjection qui la tourmetait aujourd'hui, c'était l'inconscience de ces deux amants se livrant aux joies de la vie pendant que les guettait une mort silencieuse, la mort était avec eux, pensait-elle, dans chacun de leurs abandons, ils ne savaient pas que passait sur leurs joues son haleine, lorsqu'ils ne bougaeient pas, lorsqu'ils ne parlaient pas, lorsqu'ils ne fuyaient pas, elle s'enfermait avec eux dans leur maison, elle glissait avec eux sous les draps, le bel été que l'on voyait fleurir à la fenêtre' (190–1).[54]

However, unlike in *La belle bête*, with its conscious allegorical allusions and fantastical rural setting, in *Le sourd*, Blais seeks to contextualize Florence's estrangement from herself within what Green calls a larger 'community of suffering,'[55] where in her seemingly somnambulistic wanderings throughout the city early on in the novel, and in her later silent vigil on the staircase (an important image in Dansereau's film, to which I shall return) of the Hôtel des Voyageurs, Florence is nevertheless able to identify with the pain of others: with old Tim's obvious despair at having to part with his beloved dog, also named Tim, as he prepares to enter an old people's home; with daughter Lucia's complicated jealousy and admiration of her mother Gloria's easy sexuality; and, most importantly, with Mike, plagued by crippling migraines caused by a brain tumour, and by the dawning realization that the dream Gloria repeats for him of a motorcycle trip to San Francisco in search of a cure will remain forever that, a dream. Indeed, Florence, having been eviscerated of the only self-identity she has hitherto known, that of wife and mother, suddenly finds herself newly 'lucid' and 'transparent,' a spectral body that despite the coldness in her heart is suddenly 'aflame' with a new consciousness: 'quand cette lumière de la conscience descendait sur toutes choses, on comprenait, pensait-elle, combien la douleur est transparente, ou plutôt, elle, Florence, devenait transparente, ses mains, ses yeux, son corps ne la défendaient plus contre cette transparence du froid, tout en elle résonnait de cette froideur, de cette solitude, le malheur des autres' (50–1; 'when the light of consciousness suddenly descends upon all things, it was then, she thought, that one understood how transparent pain was, or rather that it was she, Florence, who became transparent, her hands, her eyes, her body no longer defended her against this transparency of the cold, her entire being was vibrant with this coldness, this solitude, with other people's misfortunes' [50]).

Florence, through the counsel of the philosopher Judith Langeais, who seeks to soothe Florence's pain in part by historicizing it, and through her sojourn at Gloria's hotel, thus discovers a model of social relations that can exist outside the bourgeois patriarchal structures of heterosexual marriage. And while this is not enough, in the end, to forestall her suicide, the novel does close with 'un dernier espoir qui apparaissait soudain' (198; 'the sudden apparition of a final hope' [219]); it emerges very briefly as a 'silhouette dans le brouillard' (198; 'silhouette in the fog' [220]), which in true gothic fashion swallows up Florence's dead body.

This empathic connection across difference (not to mention time and space) that I have been positing as counter-discourse to the asymmetrical misunderstandings of the marriage bond is facilitated in Blais's novel through the very structure of its narration – an extended polyphonic, collective, and multifocalized interior monologue in which, despite the occasional marking of point of view (especially in the case of Florence), voice and narrating consciousness pass freely and repeatedly between characters, sometimes within the same sentence or clause. In this, as I have already suggested, and as other critics have likewise noted,[56] *Le sourd* may be productively compared with Virginia Woolf's *Mrs Dalloway*, especially in terms of Woolf's linking of her linguistic syntax to a broader social project of gender equality, wherein, for example, her famous use of the semicolon becomes a way of positing a horizontal system of relation and signification between all parts of her sentence that is reciprocal, connotatively associative, mutually interdependent, and non-hierarchical. Similarly, Mireille Dansereau's remarkable achievement in finding, for her 1987 film, a visual equivalent to the complex structure of interior-

ization at work in Blais's novel may be contrasted with Marleen Gorris's less successful attempt at bringing Woolf's novel to the screen ten years later, not to
mention director Stephen Daldry and screenwriter David Hare's 2002 adaptation
of Michael Cunningham's novel *The Hours*, his own intertextual and structurally
complex homage to Woolf's *Mrs Dalloway*.

To this end, Gorris relies on an extensive – and resolutely monological – use of
voice-over narration, and the star casting of Vanessa Redgrave (who was also a
producer), to anchor her film to Mrs Dalloway's point of view, with the result that
poor Septimus (Rupert Graves) becomes almost an afterthought. By contrast,
Dansereau preserves the complexity of Blais's intersubjective narration; she does
so by folding external observation and interior reflection in on each other, mixing
still close-ups with travelling point-of-view shots, and soliciting from her lead
actress (Béatrice Picard) an almost entirely wordless performance. And where
Daldry employs rapid-fire montage in the form of an ongoing succession of match
cuts, and the relentless through-line of Philip Glass's pounding piano score, to
lend structural coherence to the connections between the three separate time
frames and the three female protagonists of *The Hours*, Dansereau combines
extremely long interior takes (of Florence on the staircase, for example, or of Mike
at the window) and repeated cutaways to exterior landscapes (of the desert, the
forest, the mountains) with a selective use of silence and sound bridges to suggest
something of both the tenuousness and the randomness of the connections
between her characters, and between her image track and her soundtrack.

Dansereau, who had been involved in early talks around a planned adaptation
of *Kamouraska*,[57] has stated that in bringing *Le sourd* to the screen she was determined to remain 'respectful' of the 'spirit' of Blais's novel while at the same time
recognizing that in visual terms, much of its formal experimentation would have
to be simplified, if only to obtain the necessary financing: 'Je ne pouvais pas
respecter la forme trop éclatée du *Sourd dans la ville* qui est une mosaïque, même si
j'aime les collages, les bribes, les gestes. Il fallait simplifier, ne serait-ce pour
obtenir l'accord des subventionneurs.'[58] In this regard, Dansereau has opted to
telescope visually (and the metaphor is wholly appropriate here, given the filmmaker's canny manipulation of depth of field in many of her shots) much of the
multivoicedness of the novel, eliminating, for example, several of the characters
who do not have an immediate spatial connection with the Hôtel des Voyageurs,
including Madame Langeais, Judith's mother, and Berthe, Gloria's older daughter, who is away studying at university.

Yet it seems to me that the resulting adaptation is remarkably faithful not only
to the spirit of its source text, but also to the spectre of the gothic film genre that
haunts many of its central images. In this respect, I am thinking especially of the
long central sequence – it comprises almost all of the final two-thirds of this
ninety-seven-minute film – that depicts Florence seated silently on the hotel staircase gazing intently, and in turn, at the motley denizens of Gloria's (Angèle
Coutu) bar: the despondent Tim (Pierre Thériault); the smouldering Lucia (Sophie
Léger); the hotheaded Charley (Claude Renart), Gloria's erstwhile boyfriend,
with whom Florence herself has just spent a passionless tryst; and above all, the
stoically innocent Mike (Guillaume Lemay-Thivièrge), with whom, it is suggested

2.4   *Le sourd dans la ville*: Mike (Guillaume Lemay-Thivièrge) brings the desolate
Florence (Béatrice Picard) a plate of spaghetti.

– not least through the visual syntagma of expressionist painting, including
repeated references to Edvard Munch's *The Scream* – Florence shares her 'lucid
transparency.' That is, they share an empathic complicity in each other's pain and,
more to the point, in the pain of others (see Figure 2.4).

As Doane has noted, in the paranoid gothic women's films of the 1940s, 'the
staircase is traditionally the locus of specularization of the woman. It is *on the
stairway* that she is displayed as spectacle for the male gaze.'[59] However, in *Le
sourd* Dansereau deliberately reverses this process. Florence is, after all, for the
most part ignored by the other hotel patrons – with the important exception of
Mike, whose own vigil at the bar's front window metonymically links his gaze, in
its desperate search for a 'way out,' including a way outside the self, with that of
Florence (not to mention, as discussed above, a whole host of filmic forebears).
Instead, what we see here is the woman in full possession of the look. Moreover,
in contrast to what Doane has described as the 'objectlessness' of the female gaze
in traditional gothic women's films, Dansereau, through a succession of high-
angle point-of-view shots, deliberately shows us what (or more properly, *who*)
Florence is looking at. Not that I wish to suggest that the director is setting up any
kind of visual hierarchy with her shot patterns; indeed, at several points we are
shown several of the bar patrons, and above all its presiding *animateuse*, Gloria,
returning Florence's gaze. I would argue that this is Dansereau's shorthand
attempt to represent, at the level of the cinematic shot, the shared point of view
that Blais is able to achieve at the level of the novelistic sentence – in this case

visual inter*objectivity* coming to stand in for linguistic intersubjectivity. In this regard, it is important to contextualize these perspectival exchanges with two other thematizations of the look that Dansereau weaves around Florence's occupation of the staircase, both of which have been isolated for analysis by Bill Marshall in a brief yet trenchant discussion of *Le sourd* in his important recent study *Quebec National Cinema*.[60]

The first has to do with what Marshall calls 'the memory-look,' subjective flashbacks meant to represent Florence's painful recollections of moments during her marriage. In none of these flashbacks do we ever see a full image of Florence's husband; however, in two that are repeated – one at the poolside of a resort, the other at a fancy restaurant – we are given glimpses of an extended leg, the back of a head. But mostly what we see in these scenes is Florence watching her husband watching; indeed, so insistently is her gaze tied to the off-screen male subject's point of view that it almost seems to lead to her own 'virtual' disappearance before our eyes, as when, in the restaurant scene, the camera, following her following the look of her husband, pans to another woman, the 'real' object, we're meant to infer, of the patriarchal gaze. The second of these looks is likewise intimately bound to the apparatus of the camera. I am referring to the prolonged use of close-ups to represent Florence's reactions to what she sees in and registers of the interactions of the bar patrons. Drawing on Gilles Deleuze's discussion of the close-up and 'faciality' in *The Movement-Image*, Marshall contends that what we see in the 'affection-images' projected onto Florence's highly mobile and expressive face is a woman who had hitherto been 'deaf' to the humanity around her learning to 'see' it for the first time in all its complexity and suffering.[61] In this, it seems that Dansereau shares with Jutra – as well as with the gothic women's film more generally – a desire to apply the adaptation process to a broader theorization of cinema's historical representation of female subjectivity and feminine spectatorship.

As Anne de Vaucher Gravili has noted, *Le sourd* was brought to the screen by a filmmaking team that was 'essentially feminine.'[62] It is certainly tempting to read the spirit of feminine collaboration that governed the adaptation of this film as a proactive response to what Robert Stam has described as the all too frequent process of 'repatriarchalization' that many women's texts undergo when they are brought to the screen by male directors and screenwriters (even if only by default, as in the case of Jutra's treatment of *Surfacing*).[63] And yet – to paraphrase Elspeth Tulloch, who along with many other critics has sharply critiqued Yves Simoneau's 1986 adaptation of another of Hébert's novels, *Les fous de bassan* – when it comes to 'fidelity to the feminist enterprises of making women's voices heard,'[64] a shared gender is no guarantee of a shared authorial vision between writer and director. For evidence of this we need look no further than Anna Benson Gyles's muddled 1996 adaptation of Carol Shields's *Swann* (1987). A 'literary mystery' in the vein of A.S. Byatt's *Possession*, but with far more comedy and social satire on the often competing pretensions (and interests) of academic inquiry and popular biography, Shields's novel tells the story of four characters – a feminist professor, a lonesome biographer, a small-town librarian, and an aging journalist and small press publisher – who, as they prepare to gather for a symposium on her work (brilliantly presented by Shields in the form of a film script), are haunted by the disappearance of precious artefacts once belonging to their beloved Mary Swann, a minor Canadian poet celebrated as much for her grisly murder by her husband as for her somewhat trite verse about the dailiness of domestic life.

Elements of gothic repetition recur throughout Shields's novel, not least in the descriptions of Sarah Maloney's rambling Chicago house, in her initial ambivalence towards and eventual acquiescence to the institution of marriage, and, above all, in her vexed relationship with sometime boyfriend Brownie, a mysterious dealer in rare books who likes to argue with Sarah 'about the theme of castration in women's books,' whose chief ambition is 'getting rich,' and upon whom Sarah fixates in Jane-like fashion: 'I keep my objectivity about Brownie polished and at the ready, yet again and again it yields to wild unaccountable happiness when in his company ... I don't altogether understand him, but what does understanding between people really mean – only that we like them or don't like them. I adore Brownie. But with reservations. Last night I was close to loving him, even though he dumped my Mary Swann into the same bathtub with Sigmund Freud. He didn't mean a word of it though; I could almost bet on it.'[65]

Unlike Jutra or Dansereau, Benson Gyles makes no attempt to represent this gothic ambivalence in her adaptation, either internally through voice-over or externally through montage and mise-en-scène. Compounding this is an uncharacteristically flat performance as Sarah by British actress Miranda Richardson, who despite subsequent affecting roles as the quasi-gothic heroine in film adaptations of Canadian literature – including her multicharacter, tour de force turn in David Cronenberg's take on Patrick McGrath's *Spider* (2002) and her impressive portrayal of the depressed and alcoholic mother Mary Field in Scott Smith's treatment of Barbara Gowdy's *Falling Angels* (2003) – here seems unable to convey the curious mixture of professional poise and personal panic that characterizes the Sarah of Shields's novel. Brenda Fricker is equally underused as Rose (see Figure 2.5), the repressed local librarian from Nadeau, Ontario, and Mary Swann's former best friend. In their scenes together, the two actresses, when they are not struggling to maintain their accents, project an all too palpable awareness of the turgidness of the proceedings.

However, what I find especially interesting about the narrative infidelities of Benson Gyles's film, and what makes it – in spite of itself – an appropriate example with which to conclude this chapter, is that in contrast to most liberties taken in the adaptation process, Gyles's changes are clearly made in order to advance an explicitly feminist message – one, moreover, that the filmmaker apparently feels under- or inadequately represented in the source text. To this end, Shields's gentle satire of scholarly ambition, literary fame, and social place is jettisoned in favour of a heavy-handed indictment of the violence perpetrated by men against women, both textually and physically. Thus, the director does more than 'solve' the mystery at the heart of Shields's novel, inserting a scene near the end of the film that confirms Brownie's (David Cubitt) hand in the disappearance (and, as we witness, destruction) of Mary Swann's published and unpublished texts and artefacts; she also resorts to flashbacks to depict the harrowing abuse that Mary (Geny Walter) daily endured living with her husband. By making visually manifest that

2.5   *Swann*: The librarian Rose (Brenda Fricker) in the field outside the ruins of Mary Swann's house.

which was only ever – and necessarily – spectral in Shields's text, namely Swann herself (a still photograph of the poet staring mournfully at the camera is the final image of the film), Benson Gyles leaves no doubt that it is the institution of hetero-sexual marriage, and its uncanny ability to mask (in Jane's words) its rather frightening 'despotisms' as familiar 'inequalities,' in which she has the least amount of faith. So too, it would seem, with the often violent marriage between literature and film, where – as we shall see in the next chapter in connection with adaptations of images of the Indigene – the romance of representation in one medium frequently gives way to very real (ethno)graphic exclusions in another.

3 Images of the Indigene: History, Visibility, and Ethnographic Romance in Four Adaptations from the 1990s

Because he appears in such broken and partial forms, the Indian remains allusive, often little more than part of an inferred and deferred whole.

Armando José Prats, *Invisible Natives*[1]

It is ... impossible to view the 'native' with fresh eyes ... The exotic is always already known.

Fatimah Rony, *The Third Eye*[2]

As Terry Goldie suggests in *Fear and Temptation*, his semiotic analysis of representations of the Indigene in the settler-colony literatures of Canada, Australia, and New Zealand, said representations have historically come to be reified into a transcendental signified or pure 'Image' (it is Goldie who uses the majuscule) – one that has no 'real world' referent in indigenous tribal cultures from either country, but that only signifies, in a 'pervasive autogenesis,' in terms of those textual images which have preceded it.[3] This would appear to be even more the case with visual images of the Indigene reproduced by/in the cinema, a circuit of signification caught within its own feedback loop of remediated primitivism, a white fantasy of the spectacle Indigene wherein D.W. Griffith's *Birth of a Nation* (1915) is of a piece with Disney's *Pocahontas* (1995). For confirmation of this, one need only look at various images of 'Indianness' recycled by Hollywood (a settler-colony within a settler-colony, after all) throughout the eighty-year span separating these two titles. From the five screen versions of James Fenimore Cooper's *The Last of the Mohicans*[4] to Native Canadian actors Chief Dan George and Graham Greene's respective turns as Old Lodge Skins and Kicking Bird in Arthur Penn's *Little Big Man* (1970) and Kevin Costner's *Dances with Wolves* (1991); from any number of John Ford's classic westerns (including *Stagecoach* [1939], *Fort Apache* [1948], *She Wore a Yellow Ribbon* [1949], *Rio Grande* [1950], *The Searchers* [1956], *Two Rode Together* [1961], and *Cheyenne Autumn* [1964]) to Clint Eastwood's revisionist ones (especially *High Plains Drifter* [1973], *The Outlaw Josey Wales* [1976], *Pale Rider* [1985], and *Unforgiven* [1992]); from the mute Bromden (Will Sampson) in Milos Forman's *One Flew Over the Cuckoo's Nest* (1975) to the highly voluble Nobody (Gary Farmer, another Canadian) in Jim Jarmusch's *Dead Man* (1996): what we see on screen repeatedly (with the notable exception, from the above list, of Jarmusch's *Dead Man*, a postmodern western made outside of the studio system, and with lots of in-jokes aimed specifically at an indigenous audience) are images of stark Manichean duality. Offered over and over again to viewers for voyeuristic consumption are the wild savage, or the noble savage; the sage counsel, or the comic relief; the white man's arch nemesis, or his loyal but inscrutable sidekick.

And yet, as Fatimah Rony has pointed out, owing to the pervasive ethnographic bias that has historically governed representations of the 'Native' on film – from early documentaries like Robert Flaherty's *Nanook of the North* (1922) to any of the more contemporary narrative features listed above – one might also say that 'the distance between the signifier and the referent in the construction of Native peoples [on screen] collapses': 'Landscaped as part of the jungle mise-en-scène, or viewed as the faithful Man Friday to a white Robinson Crusoe, or perhaps romanticized as the Noble Savage struggling to survive in the wild, the individual "native" is often not even "seen" by the viewer but is taken for real: as when the barker outside the fair tent calls potential spectators to come in and "see real Indians," or the excitement over Kevin Costner's recent *Dances with Wolves* (1991) as a film employing "real Lakota Indians."'[5]

As the presence of Native Canadian actors Graham Greene (a Mohawk) and Tantoo Cardinal (Métis) in the latter film attests, regardless of whether he or she is viewed as a fantasy image (of the cigar store variety most usually) or as the real thing (confirming in white spectators' minds what they knew all along, that Native peoples are in fact like 'that'), the point is that the screen Indigene is only ever *not seen* – or at the very most, *seen through*. Figured within the white cinematic imaginary as the paradoxically invisible – because always already in the process of vanishing – sign of Otherness, the Indigene's pose is fixed and unchanging, and thus interchangeable. Lakota or Mohawk: it makes little difference when historical and ethnographic verisimilitude devolves, fundamentally, into the romantic spectacle of brown skins in buckskin.

This becomes all the more apparent (if I may be forgiven for using that word) when one considers the adaptive context that subtends many such representations. What is especially interesting about the above-listed titles, for my purposes, is how many of them are based on works of literature.[6] To the extent that these films are cultural texts that participate – however knowingly, obliquely, or even oppositionally – in a reinscription of a narrative of Conquest founded upon a teleology of the vanishing Indigene, focusing on the process of adaptation is of crucial importance. Indeed, what these texts reveal, when examined specifically for how they are transcoded from a verbal to a visual signifying system, is how film participates in a process of what Christopher Gittings calls, in the specific Canadian context, 'whiting-out the Indigene' – that is, constructing 'spectacle screen Aboriginals from the materials of white fantasy' that have no material basis in the socio-historical record, let alone in the source texts from which they are derived,[7] but that nevertheless come to serve as 'evidence,' aesthetically and ideologically, of a racialized Other's necessary (and historically unchanging) difference. That gender should be a corollary axis along which this process of cinematic Othering is carried out should come as no surprise, given the camera's long historical romance with the Indigene as object of an exoticized and explicitly sexualized ethnographic gaze – a point to which I will return.

For the moment, however, let me attempt to clarify the invisibility of the screen Indigene by considering, very briefly, the adaptive example of *One Flew Over the Cuckoo's Nest*. Few people familiar with Forman's Oscar-winning movie, and Jack Nicholson's powerhouse performance as protagonist Randle McMurphy, would likely see it as a logical place to begin a discussion of cinematic depictions of Native peoples. This is because while the role of Bromden – or Chief Broom, as he is called by his fellow asylum inmates – is an important one (he comes to be McMurphy's most important ally among the motley crew of patients committed to Nurse Ratched's care, and crucially completes the journey of heroic resistance initiated by McMurphy against her), it is almost entirely non-verbal. Thus, despite actor Will Sampson's imposing seven-foot frame, and despite the uses to which that frame is put in the classic sequence which shows the basketball game organized by McMurphy between the inmates and the male orderlies, Bromden largely fades into the background of Forman's film, a mostly mute witness to a white masculine striving against institutional authority.

To this end, in his one extended conversation with the pre-lobotomized McMurphy, who is planning to end his sojourn on Ratched's ward once and for all by breaking out that night, the Chief – who is immobilized and in some senses disembodied not only by the straps confining him to his hospital bed, but also by the composition of Forman's shots, which focus only on Bromden's affectless face in tight close-ups – talks about how he is not as strong as McMurphy and, predictably, about his alcoholic father. As Jacquelyn Kilpatrick puts it in her study *Celluloid Indians*, Forman's Bromden 'is much like the stoic, silent Indians of the earliest movies, and perhaps for many of the same reasons.' She continues: 'In the early days, most American audiences had little or no actual experience of Native Americans, and the nonverbal dime-novel Indian filled the experiential gap. In the seventies many audiences still had little experience, but now they had too much information, some of it contradictory. Chief Bromden's imposing, silent, noble demeanor was perfect for an audience who felt more sympathetic toward Native Americans but didn't want to think too much about them.'[8]

Discursively, however, this represents a major departure from Ken Kesey's novel, which is narrated from the first-person point of view of the Chief, who, having 'been silent so long now,' finally lets the 'telling' of his story 'roar out of [him] like floodwaters': 'about all this, about the hospital, and her, and the guys – and about McMurphy.'[9] Denied this voice in the screen adaptation, Bromden is thus rendered by the clinical gaze of the camera an anthropological specimen, (in)visibly out of place in the white hospital ward, and recognizable only when the mise-en-scène returns him to his 'natural' environment, as in the film's final frames. Having smothered the lobotomized McMurphy, the Chief proceeds to perform a surrogate escape for his dead friend, tearing from its moorings the tub room control panel, which McMurphy had earlier tried to lift in a symbolic display of effort to the other men, and hurling it through the window. The camera follows Bromden as he breaks free of the imprisoning hospital and heads off into the distance 'across a wide meadow toward some trees – going back to nature in a literal as well as figurative sense.'[10]

The natural environment for which the screen Indigene apparently yearns, and against which in some senses he can only ever be revealed, is explicitly associated with Canada in both Forman's film and Kesey's book. This is significant, given the argument I wish to advance in this chapter. That is, I want to suggest that all too often in the visual economy of recent film adaptations of Canadian literature, a quasi-ethnographic focus on the Indigene in his 'natural environment' becomes a way of *not focusing* on the Indigene in a socially material and politically proximate cultural context – of, instead, figuratively abstracting the Indigene, through the repetition of synecdochic images of habitation, social organization, ceremonial ritual, and so on, as recognizably and romantically Other, as someone occupying 'an earlier evolutionary stage in the overall history of humankind.'[11]

Here, I want to link up what Rony, in her discussion of *Nanook of the North*, calls the 'taxidermic' impulse of romantic ethnography – the scopic desire to possess, preserve, and endlessly repeat, in a timeless 'ethnographic present,' images of a past culture already presumed to have vanished[12] – with Armando José Prats's recent discussion of the 'defining synecdoche' that determines 'the Indian's *representational destiny*' in so many classic and revisionist American westerns produced by Hollywood: the visual sign – an arrowhead, a slaughtered buffalo, a footprint in the snow – that '*originates* his presence even as it *foretokens* his doom.'[13] What Rony and Prats are separately pointing to is the white cinematic imaginary's tendency to '*detemporalize*' the Indigene, to place him outside both the progress of historical time and the process of filmic narration: 'To exclude the Indian from temporality has become an inherent feature of mythic "history," a fundamental strategy of figuration. History becomes tableau, and nothing happens that is not therein prefigured. The Myth of Conquest "emplots" the Indian only to *disemplot* him. Otherness implies timelessness.'[14] This is related, as well, to what Victor Li has recently described as the 'chronopolitics' at the heart of the 'neo-primitivist turn' in much contemporary cultural theory, in which an apparently politically progressive 'critical repudiation of earlier primitivist discourses paradoxically enables their re-introduction, under different names and configurations to be sure, as cultural, political, ethical, and aesthetic alternatives to Western modernity.'[15]

Thus, in the case of two notable adaptations produced in the early 1990s focusing on colonial contact in Quebec in the seventeenth and early twentieth centuries – *Black Robe* (1991, based on Brian Moore's 1985 novel) and *Shadow of the Wolf* (1993, based on Yves Thériault's 1958 novel *Agaguk, l'homme du loup*) – various generic tropes of ethnographic romance are mobilized on screen that arguably *immobilize* the Indigene in a historical past in order to *demobilize* off-screen protests in the political present, where First Nations and Inuit organizing about land claims and control of regional resources culminated in the armed standoff at Oka in 1990 and in the decision by Jacques Parizeau's provincial government to cancel the Great Whale hydroelectric expansion at James Bay in 1994. A comparison of these two adaptations is revealing for a number of additional reasons. Both were based on immensely popular works of historical fiction by two of this country's best-selling and most prolific authors, who nevertheless attracted a great deal of scrutiny as well as their share of criticism for their methods of historical research. For example, David Leahy has rebuked Moore for, among other things, dissociating 'the Jesuits' *mission civilisatrice* ... from the economic imperatives of the fur trade' and for failing to contextualize the 'political-economical reasons' behind the Hurons' and Iroquois' historical enmity in terms of their competitive roles as 'middlemen' for the French and Dutch, respectively; and Ben-Z. Shek has convincingly established 'the inauthenticity of [Thériault's] so-called documentary portrait of the Inuit' by demonstrating that the author's strategy in '[passing] himself off as a great expert on the Canadian North' – a place he had never visited prior to the publication of *Agaguk* – was based in part on false claims of Native blood in his family.[16]

Also, both films were big-budget co-productions helmed by foreign directors (the Australian Bruce Beresford and the Frenchman Jacques Dorfmann). *Shadow of the Wolf* likewise starred foreign actors (Hollywood B-celebrities Lou Diamond Phillips and Jennifer Tilly), and both films were touted, in advance of their respective releases, as the kind of grand epic that would finally place Canada on the cinematic map. However, while *Black Robe* became the highest-grossing Canadian film of 1991 and won a slew of Genie Awards and mostly very positive reviews (at least among non-Aboriginal critics), *Shadow of the Wolf*, made for a bloated $32 million, foundered at the box office when it opened to uniformly lacerating reviews.[17] Moreover, as Toronto film reviewer Geoff Pevere has perceptively noted, in 'simultaneously appealing to and appeasing a presumably white, liberal audience's sense of cumulative historical shame,' both films repeatedly romanticize fraught issues of colonialism and cultural genocide 'in softening layers of immaculate pictorialism and comforting moral relativism.'[18] Finally – and what will be the main focus of my ensuing discussion – both films, in adapting the generic tropes of romantic ethnography, adapt as well, via their literary source texts, various gender binaries that help constitute the genre, including Western Oedipal notions of an embattled and superannuated masculinity and a mysteriously threatening and potentially monstrous femininity mapped picturesquely and voyeuristically onto various tableaux of indigenous family, community, and sexual relations.

I follow my analysis of *Black Robe* and *Shadow of the Wolf* with a brief discussion of two other adaptations from the same period that ostensibly offer a more socially realistic – and expressly political – portrait of indigenous cultures in the historical present. Richard Bugajski's *Clearcut*, based on M.T. Kelly's 1987 novel *A Dream Like Mine* (which won the Governor General's Award), features Graham Greene, fresh from his Oscar-nominated performance in *Dances with Wolves*, as Arthur. A Native avenger of a piece with the masked and gun-toting Mohawk Warriors from Oka,[19] Arthur kidnaps and leads on a frightening wilderness journey the white liberal lawyer who has just lost his band's court battle to halt logging on their ancestral lands, as well as the owner of the mill doing the logging. Bruce McDonald's third feature film, *Dance Me Outside*, was released in 1995, the year Dudley George was shot and killed by a policeman's bullet during a Native protest at Ipperwash, Ontario; a loose adaptation of a handful of stories from W.P.

Kinsella's controversial 1977 short story collection of the same name, this film centres around a young Native slacker's experience of life on a fictional reserve in Ontario, whose decidedly less than ambitious desires to get into mechanics' school, party with his best friend, and make it with his girlfriend are suddenly put on hold when a young Native woman is murdered by a white thug. And yet for all their social, political, and cultural contemporaneity – highlighted once again by Pevere, whose reviews during this period serve as an important cultural bellwether on representations of Aboriginality in Canadian cinema – these two films also betray, I would argue, a familiar ethnographic sensibility and unrepentant romanticism, particularly in their respective representations of abject masculinities (both Native and non-Native). I will thus conclude this chapter by analysing, again very briefly, how the gendered ethnographic gaze is self-reflexively subverted and returned in Zacharias Kunuk's award-winning Inuit epic *Atanarjuat: The Fast Runner* (2001). That such an analysis should coextensively trouble the very literate foundations on which I have so far built my theory of cinematic adaptation in this book is only fitting.

Published to great acclaim in 1985, *Black Robe* was the third novel by Brian Moore to be adapted for the big screen, following *The Luck of Ginger Coffey* (1964) and *The Lonely Passion of Judith Hearne* (1987). A fourth film based on one of his novels, *Cold Heaven*, appeared the same year as *Black Robe*, and Norman Jewison's recent adaptation of Moore's *The Statement* appeared in 2003 after Moore's death.[20] Of these, however, *Black Robe* was the only film for which Moore also wrote the screenplay; he also served as executive producer. Clearly, he felt close to the material. Based on Moore's reading of the Jesuit *Relations*, as well as Francis Parkman's celebrated work of nineteenth-century historiography, *The Jesuits in North America*, *Black Robe* is a fictional recreation of the physical and spiritual journey undertaken by a naive and idealistic young priest in New France, Father Laforgue, who has volunteered to travel from Samuel de Champlain's settlement at Québec to a Jesuit mission far to the west, deep in the heart of Huronia, in order to check on the fate of the two priests stationed there, as well as to investigate rumours of a mysterious fever afflicting the Huron people in their charge. Laforgue is accompanied by a group of Algonkin, led by the cocky Neehatin and the more sober Chomina, who agree to take the priest as far as the Ottawa River on their way to their winter hunting grounds. Also joining them is a young French colonial named Daniel Davost, who has convinced the Jesuits that he wants to make the trip as a sign of his commitment to God, but who secretly only wants to be near Annuka, Chomina's beautiful daughter, with whom he is conducting a clandestine affair.

When, shortly after their journey begins, Neehatin has a dream that his wife interprets as meaning that Laforgue will bring them danger, and when, subsequently, the sorcerer Mestigoit confirms this, Neehatin orders his people to abandon the two white men and proceed on their own to their winter hunting grounds. Daniel, refusing to be parted from Annuka, gives chase. When Neehatin threatens to kill him, Chomina intervenes, saying that he and his family will return with Daniel to where they left Laforgue, and accompany the two men to just beyond the Ottawa rapids as promised, before rejoining the group. Arriving back at Laforgue's camp, Chomina and his family are ambushed by a party of Iroquois, who kill Chomina's wife and, eventually, his young son, and take everyone else prisoner, torturing them prior to a planned ritual cannibalization of their victims. This plan – and, incidentally, Laforgue's desired martyrdom – is thwarted when Annuka dupes the guard assigned to watch them and helps the others escape, leading her dying father to his final meeting with the She Manitou before accompanying Daniel and Laforgue into the fever-ravaged mission at Ihonatiria.

As can only partially be deduced from the above plot summary, Moore's novel is something of a generic hybrid – half historical thriller, half novel of ideas, an attempt to morally philosophize and to contextualize for a contemporary audience the clash of two different cultures and two different faiths, each of which has a radically antithetical view of the afterlife. Not surprisingly, the genre codes of the historical thriller translate more easily to the screen, and as an adventure epic cum costume drama, Beresford's film adaptation mostly succeeds. But how to convey on screen an ideational tone of doubt, blame, suspicion, outrage, and despair, especially when much of that tone is rendered novelistically through the use of interior monologues divided equally between Laforgue, Daniel, Annuka, Chomina, and Neehatin? There is no equivalent discursive representation of subjective agency in Beresford's film, and furthermore, the camera's gaze, in repeated scenes of quasi-anthropological inquiry and corporeal alienation (the white priest watching the Algonkin eat, or staring down Mestigoit, or spying on Annuka and Daniel having sex), is tied resolutely to Laforgue's (Lothaire Bluteau); as a consequence, the indigenous characters in particular are positioned as objects of ethnographic spectacle, all the more so because of the subtitles that necessarily attend their speech (which has been noticeably cleaned up in the film from the salty and scatological demotic that Moore invented for his 'Savages' in the novel; that the Jesuit priests and French traders should all speak perfect English is, of course, taken for granted). What is most interesting – but perhaps to be expected, given the erotics of looking that subtend romantic ethnography and cinematic viewing in general – is that the spectacle of the Indigene on offer in the film version of *Black Robe* coalesces around various representational fault lines of gender and sexuality.

Neehatin is present as a character in the film (played by Lawrence Bayne); however, Moore's screenplay focuses our attention mostly on Chomina (August Schellenberg), who is accorded the dream given to Neehatin in the novel, and who is shown, at the start of the film, meeting and conducting negotiations with Champlain (Jean Brousseau) on behalf of the Algonkin. This scene, in particular, is shot by Beresford as pure ethnographic spectacle: it is preceded by parallel montage showing Chomina and Champlain donning their respective ceremonial costumes; then an extended shot/reverse shot sequence of cuts shows Champlain making an elaborate speech about the coming together of their two cultures and the supplicant Algonkin waiting for the translation. The indigenous bodies are presented here as mostly uncovered and as sitting on the ground; the white bodies are elaborately overdressed and are standing or seated on chairs. All of this is in keeping with standard tableaux from the genre, both print and cinematic.

Likewise the paternalistic politics of the film as a whole. While Chomina may

3.1   *Black Robe*: Laforgue (Lothaire Bluteau, r) teaches Chomina (August Schellenberg) and a fellow Algonkin the 'sorcery' of writing.

be a reluctant conscript in his role as surrogate father to the besotted Daniel (Aden Young), Laforgue is more than eager to bear the burden of moral instruction and Christian salvation for the entire tribe solely upon his shoulders. Thus, for example, in another scene overdetermined by signifiers of romantic ethnography, Laforgue attempts to bridge the orality/literacy divide between himself and the Natives by demonstrating to Chomina – who is presented as suitably child-like in his awe – the 'sorcery' of writing (see Figure 3.1). Responding to Laforgue's injunction to tell him something he does not know, Chomina says, in halting English: 'My woman's mother dies in snow last winter.' Laforgue proceeds to write this down in his notebook, which he then presents to a bewildered Daniel (who had not been witness to its initial inscription) to read aloud to Chomina. To Chomina's angry demand for an explanation for the magic, Laforgue responds triumphantly: 'I have still other greater things I can teach you.'

In terms of the operations of gender in the film, the phrase Chomina chooses to have Laforgue write down is significant, in that it reminds those viewers who are attentive to the quasi-Oedipal framework governing the various relationships in *Black Robe* that both men are linked syntagmatically – especially via the use of flash-forwards and flashbacks respectively – to an overidentification with the feminine. That is, just as in the novel Neehatin hides from the male members of his tribal council the fact that he relies on his wife's 'gift of sight,'[21] so in the film is Chomina presented as covertly seeking out the interpretive skills of his wife (played by Tantoo Cardinal) following his dream, which turns out to be a presentiment of his own death. Similarly, we learn through a series of flashbacks to scenes of Laforgue's pre-Jesuit days in France that the priest seems to have had an extremely close relationship with his mother. Indeed, it is following one such flashback, in which mother and son debate the marriageable merits of a local young lass, that Laforgue, waking up in the night after a fit of coughing and seeking some air outside the Algonkin's communal tent, stumbles upon Daniel and Annuka (Sandrine Holt) having sex. Adopting Laforgue's point of view, the camera lingers voyeuristically on the lithe young bodies copulating vigorously under the moonlight, before cutting to a shot of Laforgue, stripped to the waist, flagellating himself with some branches. Read in the context of the flashbacks that bracket it (shortly after we are transported once again back to France, where we see Laforgue's mother praying to a statue of Saint Joan before explicitly instructing her newly ordained son to remember her in his prayers in New France), this scene presents us with an explicit pose of what Freud would term 'feminine masochism' – a reminder that behind Laforgue's appeal for forgiveness from the Father he loves (indeed, behind all the 'in nomine patris' he utters throughout the film), it is his mother who is symbolically guiding the lash of the whip.[22]

In this respect, and fully congruent with romantic ethnography's enlisting of the twin discourses of racialization and eroticization to present the indigenous female as absolute Other, it is the sexually voracious Annuka who emerges – especially in the film version of *Black Robe* – as the most serious threat to traditional phallic power, and to the patriarchal/homosocial bonds that underwrite that power. She openly defies her father, and consequently drives a wedge between him and his fellow tribesmen, in carrying on with Daniel; not only that, but she insists, following the death of Chomina, that Daniel choose between setting off with her in search of the other members of the tribe, or accompanying Laforgue on the final leg of his journey to the Huron mission. This is a notable departure from Moore's novel, which depicts Laforgue, Daniel, and Annuka all eventually arriving at the mission.

Moreover, it is worth pointing out that in facilitating their escape from the Iroquois, Annuka is, quite literally, depicted as a *vagina dentata*, luring the guard assigned to watch over them with the promise of sex before clubbing him over the head when he is not looking. In the novel, this scene is filtered through one of her father's interior monologues, with Chomina speaking 'to the wolf, his reigning spirit,' for guidance in aiding a terrified Annuka to accomplish her task.[23] By contrast, Beresford's film eschews voice-over (indeed, any extra-diegetic sound whatsoever) and focuses the camera's gaze resolutely on the actions of Annuka, with minimal cutaways to show the reaction shots of Chomina and the other male captives; thus he presents Annuka as a cooly impassive and emotionally duplicitous femme fatale figure, one who is fully prepared to use her body as a weapon to save her father and her lover and who is equally determined that Laforgue be left to the martyrdom he so desperately craves (in the novel it is Annuka who convinces her father that both Daniel and Laforgue should be saved; in the film it is Chomina who argues that if they rescue Daniel then they cannot simply leave the priest).

Not surprisingly, the scenes of torture and implied ritual cannibalism among the Iroquois emerged as a source of ethnographic controversy among Native and non-Native reviewers of the film, with gender in particular a key focus of the debates. Thus, while Jay Scott, reviewing the film in the *Globe and Mail*, commended the film for portraying indigenous peoples with 'sensitivity, sympathy, and some ethnographic accuracy,'[24] Ward Churchill, in an article published in *Z Magazine* a year after its release, slammed the film – and the white liberal reviewers (including Scott) who greeted it so enthusiastically as the Canadian antidote to *Dances with Wolves* – equating it with anti-Semitic propaganda films made under the Nazis and indicting its elision of the politics of cultural genocide, in the sense that it chose to play up the spectacle of indigenous savagery and to play down the savagery of evangelical Christian indoctrination.

Noting in particular the matriarchal foundations of Iroquois society, which have been well documented in the anthropological record (something that Moore himself highlights in his source text[25]), Churchill argues that the execution of Chomina's son is narratively and historically uncreditable, and 'very far from the sort of "anthropological" accuracy, distance, and integrity attributed to [the film] by most reviewers,' because Mohawk women would have been involved in the 'disposition of captives, a circumstance which led invariably to children being adopted and raised as Mohawks rather than gratuitously slaughtered.'[26] In this regard, ethnographic spectacle is coextensive with historiographic exceptionalism, with gender once again the absent presence in white culture's selective accounting of its own deracination. For as Marilyn Dumont has pointed out, if the film of *Black Robe* wished to present a historically balanced perspective on the clash of New and Old World cultures, it might have attempted to 'provide more than a superficial and sensationalized treatment of torture as practiced by the Indians. For the Old world, 17th century Europe, was also the scene of torture in the form of witches being burnt at the stake. However, the treatment of torture in this film only serves to single out the Indian forms of torture, thereby embellishing the Jesuit perspective.'[27]

Of course, as Pevere noted in his own measured assessment of the *Black Robe* adaptation, 'the sense of keen historical hindsight' that inevitably governs such enterprises, and that confronts 'largely white audiences with the grim spectacle of their ancestral involvement in the decimation of Native culture in North America' – never mind the decimation of heretical religious, ethnic, and working-class cultures in Europe – 'would have represented commercial suicide.'[28] Which perhaps explains why, two years later, the producers of *Shadow of the Wolf* threw all pretenses towards historical and cultural verisimilitude out the window, starting with the casting of its lead roles. When we find ourselves confronted with the spectacle of breathless Hollywood sexpot Jennifer Tilly – fresh from her cameo as a Jim Morrison groupie in Oliver Stone's *The Doors* – attempting traditional Inuit throat singing on screen, the self-cancelling genre codes of historical and ethnographic romance are laid utterly bare. As are the gender codes of the Oedipal romance, which arguably constitutes the key story line of both the film and the novel on which it is based.

Published in 1958, and winner of the Prix de la Province de Québec, Yves Thériault's *Agaguk* was an immediate and resounding success. Never out of print, the novel, which on first reading appears to be the most depoliticized and ideologically uninflected of texts, was one of the most widely read and taught in Quebec during the Quiet Revolution of the 1960s,[29] and has been translated internationally into some ten different languages, including Arabic, Chinese, Czech, Japanese, Polish, and Serbo-Croat. As a tale of father–son rivalry, in many respects it conforms to the basic structural and sociocultural paradigms that Patricia Smart has identified as constitutive of the patriarchal plot of the classic *roman de la fidelité* in Quebec.[30] In a brief author's note, Thériault makes it clear that in some senses he is also writing an ethnography of a culturally estranged and rapidly vanishing way of life: 'L'action de ce roman se déroule chez les Esquimaux tels qu'ils étaient dans les années quarante. Que leur vie soit aujourd'hui modifiée par l'invasion du progès dans l'Arctique est indéniable' ('The action of this novel takes place among the Eskimos, as they were about twenty years ago. It is undeniable that their life today has been modified by the invasion of progress').[31]

In an attempt to forestall this invasion of progress, Agaguk, Thériault's headstrong hero, abandons his father Ramook's village, which he views as overrun by the corrupting influences of alcohol and white traders, and sets off alone across the tundra with Iriook, his new bride. However, needing supplies, Agaguk soon returns, hoping to barter his furs. When the white trader Brown attempts to cheat the hunter, Agaguk responds by dousing him in kerosene and setting him on fire. Thereafter, the narrative alternates back and forth between describing Agaguk's life on the tundra with the newly pregnant Iriook (to whom he says nothing about the death of Brown) and Ramook and the villagers' attempts to cover up Brown's murder to an investigating RCMP officer named Henderson. The parallel plot lines reach their respective climaxes when Agaguk is attacked and mauled by a white wolf that has been stalking their encampment, and when Henderson, on Ramook's order, is murdered and ritually cannibalized by the villagers. As Iriook nurses Agaguk back to health and gradually assumes more and more responsibility for the welfare of their son Tayaout and the unborn girl she believes she is now carrying (whom Agaguk insists they cannot afford to keep), Ramook is faced with a further dilemma: another policeman, named Scott, has arrived, this time with reinforcements, and is demanding an explanation for the disappearances of Henderson and Brown. Ramook decides to betray his son, but when he leads Scott to Agaguk's encampment he cannot make a positive identification because of Agaguk's facial disfigurement. Eventually the villagers turn on their demagogic chief, denouncing him and his accomplice Ghorok as Henderson's murderers. With Ramook taken away to be tried and hanged, the villagers approach Agaguk to become their chief. Under pressure from Iriook (who by now has learned that he murdered Brown), and desiring to remain on his own, Agaguk refuses, and the novel ends with Iriook giving birth to twins: a girl, whom Agaguk, after much soul-searching, decides to let live, and another boy.

Jacques Dorfmann's film adaptation, shot in English as *Shadow of the Wolf*, and then dubbed into French and released under the title *Agaguk*, retains the novel's basic plot; however, some notable changes have been made that affect the

3.2   *Shadow of the Wolf*: Lou Diamond Phillips as Agaguk.

transcoding of representations of gender in particular. In this respect, *Shadow of the Wolf* merits attention both for the scenes of pseudo-ethnography from Thériault's novel that it chooses to omit (there are no images of ritual disembowelment and flesh eating, for example) and for the scenes of romantic spectacle (imported from a familiar genealogy of Hollywood adventure films) that it chooses to add or embellish. In terms of the latter, the film opens with a scene not found in the novel and meant solely to establish for the audience the male protagonist's virility via a demonstration of his prowess as a hunter. Alone on the tundra in the middle of a fierce blizzard, a raging Agaguk (Lou Diamond Phillips; see Figure 3.2) seeks revenge on the polar bear that destroyed his igloo, wrestling and then killing the massive animal with only a small hunting knife. Similarly, a scene in the novel in which Agaguk and Iriook travel to the 'Top of the World' to hunt seals is changed in the film into an unintentionally hilarious sequence depicting the tracking and killing of a marauding whale, with the film summoning up the ghosts of adaptations past (specifically Gregory Peck in *Moby-Dick* and Roy Scheider in *Jaws*) by having Phillips ride the mechanical beast like a latter-day Captain Ahab or an Inuit Martin Brody.

By contrast, scenes from the novel that might undermine our identification with Agaguk as screen hero or highlight in any way a self-abnegating questioning of his worth as a man are either jettisoned completely or significantly altered. Thus, for example, Agaguk's killing of Brown (Bernard-Pierre Donnadieu) is presented as an accident in the film, the result of an overturned kerosene lamp during a struggle between the two men over Agaguk's furs, which Brown refuses to return. And when Agaguk is subsequently bilked out of his just recompense for these same furs by the Scottish clerk McTavish (Harry Hill) at the Hudson's Bay Company trading post, he does not go off on a two-day drunk, as in the novel, but rather swallows his pride and returns home promptly to the missus, renamed Igiyook for the movie version, and played by a pouty Tilly, who is obviously perplexed as to how to look alluring in sealskin. Moreover, the film resolves questions of Oedipal rivalry and patriarchal inheritance left open in the novel (which is the first part of a trilogy that subsequently tracks the adventures of Agaguk's son and grandson in 1969's *Tayaout, fils d'Agaguk* and 1975's *Agoak, l'héritage d'Agaguk*) by having Kroomak (Toshiro Mifune), as he is called in the film, take responsibility for the deaths of Henderson (Donald Sutherland) and Brown. Thus, father and son have suddenly been (re)united in opposing 'traditional' Inuit justice and the 'laws of the earth' to the law of the white man.

However, where *Shadow of the Wolf* most differs from its source text is in its representation of the gender politics underscoring the relationship between Agaguk and Iriook/Igiyook. In the novel, Thériault somewhat awkwardly maps a Western psychoanalytical framework of sexual identity formation (especially the fear of castration induced by the 'law of the father') onto a highly romanticized ethnographic portrait of Inuit customs regarding sex role differentiation. The film, in this regard, resorts to the more generically familiar – if ahistorical and likewise culturally flawed – late-twentieth-century romantic formula of the emancipated woman helping her wild man discover his sensitive side. In the novel, for example, Agaguk is presented as a case study in masculine abjection, simultaneously fascinated and repelled by Iriook's body, which at the beginning he is shown beating and raping on more than one occasion. This is nowhere more evident than in the scene depicting the birth of their son, Tayaout. The cries of pain that accompany the onset of labour in Iriook throw Agaguk into an inexplicable rage:

Alors, lentement, du fond de son subconscient Agaguk sentit sourdre la rage. Non pas en un brusque jaillissement de sang à la tête, mais en une colère lente, implacable, qui monta de ses entrailles pour l'habiter tout entier. Une force nouvelle existait en lui, une puissance extraordinaire qui déciderait des événements. Les mains appuyés contre la paroi de glace, les muscles des jambes bandés, tendus, les genoux à peine ployés, il haletait, sa rage accordée au rhythme des plaintes d'Iriook, à la fureur des cris de la femme … À cet instant-là le vagin s'ouvrait comme une gueule, sorte d'orifice sombre: monstruosité taillée dans le bas-ventre. Les cris de la femme remplissaient l'abri et se répercutaient en échos terrifiants le long des parois et jusqu'au dôme de glace. Toujours appuyé, Agaguk était devenu une bête plutôt qu'un homme. (104–5)[32]

By contrast, in the film a genuinely concerned Agaguk greets the onset of Igiyook's labour pains with a query about whether she wants tea, before switching into action and assisting – as any sexually liberated man of course would – with the birth.

When, later in the novel, following a discussion of how the Inuit tradition of the 'suprématie de l'homme et sa domination restreignent la femme à un rôle de complète passivité' (144; 'male supremacy and his domination limit the woman to a passive role' [84]), Iriook is presented as taking the lead in sex for the first time, this prompts in Agaguk some crude Oedipal musings on his sudden overidentification with the feminine, and his inability to distinguish his wife, as love object, from her role as mother: 'Depuis qu'Iriook avait conçu, jamais il ne l'avait possédée qu'il n'eût, en même temps, la pensée de l'enfant. D'abord, l'être inconnu, le mystérieux anonyme qui gîtait dans le flanc de la femme, puis après, Tayaout. Ce Tayaout en qui il mettait toutes ses complaisances. L'instinct en lui liait les deux choses, se refusait à cloisonner le plaisir du sexe et le plaisir tiré de cet être procrée qui vit près de soi par la suite. Sans le savoir, Agaguk atteignait à la philosophie originelle de l'homme, la pensée première' (144).[33]

Iriook's usurpation of traditional male power is effectively completed after Agaguk is wounded by the white wolf, when she must assume the duties of hunting and providing shelter for her family, and when she shames Agaguk into regaining his strength by straddling him and revirilizing him through sex. However, that the power dynamics in the household have fundamentally shifted, and that Agaguk, despite his physical restoration, nevertheless feels emasculated by the newly emancipated Iriook, is signalled by Iriook's desire for another child, a girl, which in defiance of custom she insists Agaguk let her keep. Save for the requisite sex scene, all of this is absent from Dorfmann's film, whose concern with restoring Agaguk to full masculine plenitude finds its visual corollary in the physical wound on Agaguk's face, which is miraculously healed by the time Lou Diamond Phillips and his impressive cheekbones are due for their final close-up. Not so in Thériault's novel, where the 'horror' of Agaguk's face – 'les dents à découvert,' 'l'oreille gauche mutilée,' 'le trou qui se creusait à la place du nez' (247; 'the exposed teeth,' the 'mutilated ear,' the 'gap where the nose should have been' [153]) – remains as a constant reminder of the once fearsome hunter's wounded pride.

Ironically, these changes have less to do with a sensitivity on the filmmakers' part to the gendered politics of ethnographic representation in the collective cinematic imaginary than with a cynical capitulation to the economics of distribution. Indeed, as Pevere has noted, the non-indigenous casting choices, the egregious plot alterations, and the three million dollars spent on the mechanical whale were among 'no less than sixteen changes suggested by the American distributors' of the film, all of which Dorfmann and producer Claude Léger agreed to. The result, as Pevere goes on to summarize, is a concrete example of what happens when the taxidermic impulse of romantic ethnography collides with the synecdochic strategies of the Hollywood western, wherein the screen Indigene is an absent presence diegetically and an invisible sign of racialization extra-diegetically:

Widely hyped by its makers as an authentic depiction of Inuit life for the period it depicts (the mid-1930s), Dorfmann's film instead commits some of the most retrograde representational crimes imaginable ... Seeing the principal Inuit characters rendered by non-Inuit movie stars, with the real Inuit consigned literally to the background and margins of what is allegedly their own story ... I knew exactly what it must have been like to watch all those clumsily pro-Indian Hollywood movies of the '50s, the kind that featured actors such as Rock Hudson (*Taza, Son of Cochise*), Jeff Chandler (*Broken Arrow*), and Burt Lancaster (*Apache*) as Natives ... How accepting of Native culture and traditions, how convinced of the viability of those cultures and traditions is one likely to be as long as one is looking at a bewigged Burt Lancaster? Or Lou Diamond Phillips in sealskin?[34]

Noting that Beresford's *Black Robe* premiered at the 1991 Toronto Festival of Festivals alongside Bugajski's *Clearcut* – another similarly themed movie about relations between whites and Native people adapted by another emigré director from another award-winning work of literature – Pevere attempts to explain why the former film met with near universal praise from the Canadian cultural establishment and why the latter received only scorn. He suggests, among other things, that the socially realist and resolutely presentist mise-en-scène of *Clearcut* perhaps jolted audiences a little too sharply from the fantasy spectacle of an anachronistic historical past (made over into a timeless 'ethnographic present') on offer in *Black Robe*: 'While the pictorial qualities of *Black Robe* evoke Romantic painting of first wilderness encounters, *Clearcut* conjures a set of far more disturbing and recent images: the 1990 crisis at Oka and the fearsome, masked visages of the militant Mohawk Warriors.'[35]

Clearcut opens with Peter McGuire (Ron Lea), a white liberal lawyer, returning to the Northern Ontario reserve he is currently representing, having failed in his attempts to get an injunction to halt further logging of reserve lands. A biplane deposits Peter at the edge of the island community, and as the camera tracks his uncertain progress through the forest in his Gucci shoes and leather briefcase from a point-of-view angle, we hear off-screen sounds of increasing clamour. Suddenly the branches part and we are thrust into the middle of a frenzied protest: angry band members are clashing with white loggers and with the RCMP officers who are there to keep the peace. All of this Bugajski captures with a hand-held camera; this lends the scene a 'ripped from the headlines' authenticity that would no doubt resonate with audiences already saturated with media images of violent stand-offs over indigenous land claims. However, starting with the scene at the sweat lodge, where band elder Wilf (Floyd Red Crow Westerman) takes Peter to purify himself of his guilt, anger, and wounded pride, Bugajski trades this social documentary impulse for a romantically ethnographic one, filming Peter's 'vision' as a pedestrian dioramic display of superimposed images of Native spirituality: petroglyphs, bleeding rocks, and, most importantly, the angry face of Arthur (Graham Greene).

This scene is meant to suggest that Arthur – a mysterious figure whom Peter first glimpses on the edge of the protest, and whom Wilf subsequently introduces him to simply as a fellow band member needing to be ferried to the mainland – is

3.3   *Clearcut*: An angry Arthur (Graham Greene, l) confronts the white liberal lawyer Peter (Ron Lea) about his knowledge of Native people.

a product of Peter's overactive and guilt-laden imagination, an avenging angel or trickster figure summoned because, in the words of Wilf, 'someone has to pay' (see Figure 3.3). That someone is, most immediately, Bud Rickets (Michael Hogan), the pompous owner of the logging company that is ravaging the band's land, whom Arthur conscripts a bewildered Peter into kidnapping. Arthur then leads both white men on a terrifying wilderness journey that culminates in the Native man – by now pathologized by Bugajski's camera as the embodiment of ethnic otherness – extracting his payment, Shylock-like, in flesh, flaying and cauterizing Rickets's leg. While, as Pevere suggests, Arthur might be 'resolutely unromantic,'[36] the film nevertheless romanticizes his rage (not to mention its Manichean opposite, Wilf's stoic placidity), framing it – within a spectacular wilderness setting that could have been imported from *Black Robe* – as the simultaneously pre- and post-historical, ethnographic subject's 'natural' atavistic response to the unwelcome onslaught of cultural progress, here symbolized as those vexed coevals, industry (the money-grubbing capitalist) and education (the paternalistic lawyer).

All of this represents something of a departure from M.T. Kelly's novel, *A Dream Like Mine*, which maintains the ambiguity about whether Arthur is a 'real' person or simply the white narrator's fantasy creation. It does this in several ways. First, the novel refuses to tie Arthur's appearance and the 'chain reaction of disconcerting omens' that ensue definitively to the narrator's sweat. Second, Wilf is depicted as maintaining a wary distance from and healthy scepticism towards this non-Ojibway interloper from the west (in the movie, he seems tacitly to endorse Arthur's actions via cryptic proverb-like bits of dialogue delivered during a series of 'magical' visits to the terrified white men lost in the wilderness). Third, the novel depicts Arthur's death by drowning as a real event, a suicide that punctuates the end of the narrator's ordeal.[37] In the film version this death is presented, via the metonymy of water (from the film's opening underwater shots, to Peter wading ashore from the biplane in his Gucci loafers, to Peter undergoing his sweat, to Peter staring down Arthur in Wilf's motorboat), a little too obviously as a plunge back into the depths of Peter's unconscious. What is more, the narrator in Kelly's novel is a journalist rather than a lawyer; he has come to research a story on the use of traditional indigenous healing techniques, such as sweat ceremonies, to combat alcoholism. As a writer, the novel's narrator is the first to admit that his identification with Native peoples is overly romantic, the result of a childhood steeped in the classics of ethnographic literature (including the Jesuit *Relations*) and an adulthood newly nostalgic for an autochthonous connection to a pre-urbanized landscape he never knew:

My reading of anthropology, in fact my fascination with Indian culture, was both an obsession and an escape, the equivalent of some people's addiction to science fiction, or fantasy, or mystery novels. But behind it there was a search for a way out, a different way of life. For years, for most of my life, I'd romanticized Indians. As a child I'm sure that I had an inarticulate sense that other people, somehow, somewhere, had felt as I did. I grew up in a city, but when I was a kid and I saw a road-widening smash through the trees where I used to hide it felt as if part of me was destroyed. The empty space, then the street, which replaced those trees left me desolate; all privacy and quiet and shelter were gone. Always I had that awareness of whatever was wild, whatever was being left, being killed. And for no reason. It would have been just as easy to leave it alone. To leave something. Later, as I grew older and my neighbourhood was cut off from sterile, stinking Lake Ontario by an expressway I could still feel loss in the damp air off the lake on summer nights. There were ghosts and stories and hauntings in my city that no one had ever given voice to. Something, part of the lake, was still alive and demanded attention. During a Catholic education, a book I was given about savages and the sweet, glorious martyrdom of Jesuit priests by the Iroquois made me sympathetic to the Indians. In spite of all the doctrine I was being fed the Jesuits seemed insane. I couldn't have been more than ten.[38]

As this passage subtly suggests, Kelly's novel does a better job of underscoring the interdependence of gender and genre in fuelling the narrator's identification with indigenous peoples, by making it clear that the narrator's past sympathy towards the Iroquois and his present attraction/repulsion towards Arthur are both the result of a certain compensatory anxiety about white masculinity and male sexuality. In other words, a vicarious experiencing of and participation in the male Indigene's stylistics of violent rage helps the white man fill the void of a perceived loss of phallic power, which has been displaced here onto the sense of impotence the narrator feels about the rape of his childhood neighbourhood. To this end, it is also worth pointing out that *A Dream Like Mine* is bracketed by two casually relayed – but nevertheless important – revelations relating to the narrator's masculinity: first, the narrator's determination to endure the entire sweat ceremony and, presumably, the sexual fantasies that come to him at the end, are in part motivated by jealousy over the fact that a former girlfriend in the Ministry of Health had 'lasted' through the whole thing; and, second, during his time spent in jail following his ordeal with Arthur (a denouement omitted from Bugajski's film) he witnessed an accused child molester and a fellow gay inmate being assaulted.[39]

By contrast, Bugajski obfuscates the latent homoerotic tension that exists between Peter and Arthur by tipping the performances of Lea and Greene too far in the direction of earnest moral rectitude and broad comedy, respectively, and by suggesting that Peter's unconscious male masochist fantasies of being loved/beaten by Arthur – again as per Freud's dictates in 'A Child Is Being Beaten' – can be consciously explained within a framework of the monstrous feminine.[40] I am referring to the fact that among the characters added to the film *Clearcut* is a young Native girl named Polly (Tia Smith). The first person Peter meets after being dropped off on the island, she leads him through the forest to the protest, rescues the briefcase he loses there, and greets him with it (now laden with various natural symbols of Native mysticism and spirituality – pine cones, eagle feathers, beaded necklaces, and so on) when he is returned to the reserve by Wilf following his ordeal. Whereupon Peter discovers that she is wearing around her neck the same magical emblem that Arthur wore. As in *Black Robe*, and following the dictates of ethnographic cinema more generally, the body of the indigenous female, in combining racial *and* gender difference, scopically reproduces – whether through mother or child – an originary Otherness.

We see this as well, albeit more obliquely, in Bruce McDonald's *Dance Me Outside*, a comedy-melodrama released in 1995 that seems to eschew any overt political or social agenda, conveying instead, via its young, photogenic cast and hip soundtrack, what Pevere sees as a new 'kind of post-MTV native chic': 'McDonald makes sure [his Native characters] are the funkiest, funniest and most drop-dead gorgeous … we've ever seen: Dressed in leather, astride motorcycles and usually scored to pile-driving R & R, they're irresistible pop confections … Moreover, he pays painstaking attention to the rhythms and rituals of daily life on "the rez," so that we acquire a reasonable (if admittedly undespairing) sense of what life there might be like.'[41] Indeed, it's a formula that seems especially suited to the small screen, so it should come as no surprise that a spin-off television series called *The Rez*, executive produced by McDonald and starring many actors from the film's original cast, aired briefly on the CBC in 1996.[42] Yet in attempting to update representations of the screen Indigene for a late-twentieth-century multicultural audience avid to consume and appropriate signifiers of racial difference, McDonald arguably trades one ethnographic gaze for another. As Terry Lusty, reviewing the movie in the Native magazine *Windspeaker*, puts it: 'There is hardly a scene throughout the entire 87-minute run of this flick which does not set apart Indians and their homeland as drinking, cheating, poverty-stricken, pool-playing racist people who have nothing better to do than tear around in old beat-up clunkers.'[43]

This is a reminder, as well, of the original ethnographic impulse that governed the source text by W.P. Kinsella, on which McDonald's film is based. That is, Kinsella wrote *Dance Me Outside*, set on the real Alberta reserve of Hobbema, after listening to the stories of various Hobbema residents, many of which he incorporated into his own collection, often without even bothering to change the names of the 'characters.'[44] In the film adaptation, McDonald attempts to steer clear of this controversy by setting his narrative on the fictional Ontario reserve of Kidiabinesse. Yet by containing the action entirely within this space (unlike Kinsella's text, which shows narrator Silas and his buddy Frank travelling to the big city of Calgary on more than one occasion), he also ensures, to a certain extent, that his Native characters are racially recognizable to a white audience's fantasy projections of ethnographic Aboriginality only because those characters are immediately locatable within their proper 'mise-en-scène.'

Lusty's comments also allude to what Pevere has similarly identified as the potential reverse racism encoded in the scopic epistemology of McDonald's film. Both note that the film's plot hinges on the actions (or inactions, as the case may be) of two white male characters, and the respective responses these actions prompt among the Native characters. In the first and most important instance, a white thug named Clarence Gaskill (Hugh Dillon) receives a minimal sentence for manslaughter after he kills a young Native woman, Little Margaret (Tamara Podemski), during a dance on the reserve one night. This prompts Silas (Ryan Black) and his buddy Frank Fencepost (Adam Beach) to organize a posse of young men from the reserve to seek revenge on Gaskill when he is released from jail.

In the second instance, Silas and Frank have stolen and souped up the car of Silas's white brother-in-law, Robert McVey (Kevin Hicks), during his first visit to the reserve following his marriage to Silas's older sister, Illiana (Lisa LaCroix). On a subsequent visit by the couple, the two initiate Robert into the band with a fake naming ceremony. In this way, they keep the hapless and apparently sterile white man occupied while Illiana hooks up with a former Native boyfriend, Gooch (Michael Greyeyes), in order to conceive a child. This sequence intercuts shots of a drunken, naked, and face-painted Robert running through the woods shouting his new 'Indian' name, Wolverine, with a series of increasingly steamy close-ups of Illiana and Gooch having sex. Whether we read this sequence as signifying, in Christopher Gittings's estimation, the 'sterility of a white fantasy of Aboriginality,'[45] or whether we agree with Pevere and see it as evidence of an equally disturbing 'tendency among liberal white dramatists to equate fair racial representation with self-loathing,'[46] I would argue that the issue of race in McDonald's film is really something of a 'McGuffin' (to borrow the title from one of the stories in Kinsella's collection that does not make it into the screen adaptation).[47] The more compelling issue is the representation of gender.

Indeed, McDonald's film, unlike Kinsella's story collection, is arguably more concerned with documenting the social dynamics of male–female relations than it is with commenting on the politics of white-Native relations, in the sense that it constructs, under the generic guise of a romantic comedy, a quasi-ethnography of late-twentieth-century masculinity that would seem to transcend race and specific (sub)cultural affiliation. To this end, in numerous scenes in which Silas and Frank are berated and lambasted for their lack of ambition by girlfriends Sadie (Jennifer Podemski) and Poppie (Sandrine Holt, in another Native role), McDonald suggests that his indigenous male characters are as emasculated as white city slicker Robert (or, for that matter, the punk protagonists of his next film, *Hard Core Logo*, an adaptation whose particular dynamics of masculine abjection I explore at greater length in chapter 7). However, unlike in *Hard Core Logo*, McDonald links the crisis of masculinity on offer in *Dance Me Outside* directly to a succession of castrating women, who are repeatedly represented as appropriating phallic power in scenes both comic and melodramatic. Thus, for example, it is Silas's mother (Rose Marie Trudeau) and the medicine woman Mad Etta (Gloria May Eshibok) who take charge of arranging Illiana's insemination by Gooch. And even more importantly, it is Sadie and Poppie and the other young women of the reserve who pre-empt Silas and Frank and their male cohorts from exacting revenge on Gaskill by beating them to it, murdering and in this case literally castrating the killer of Little Margaret.

In considering gender and genre in McDonald's film, it is important to note that *Dance Me Outside*, alone among the adaptations I have been discussing in this chapter, employs a voice-over. On the one hand, this is a mere stylistic expedience, a way of transferring to the screen something of the first-person narrative voice that dominates Kinsella's text (which hinges self-reflexively on a familiar oral/literate semiotic within representations of the Indigene, making it clear that Silas is writing down his 'funny' stories at the suggestion of his teacher, Mr Nichols – who corrects his spelling and punctuation, but not his syntax – in order to practise for the entrance essay he 'got to write' to get into mechanics' school[48]). And to be sure, McDonald (who co-wrote the film's script with Don McKellar and John Frizzell), much more than Kinsella, does his best to link this discursive strategy to a sense of self-empowerment within his indigenous male protagonist by tying its appearance – at the beginning and end of the film, in particular – to a specific symbol from native mythology: the opening and closing shots of the raven that Silas attempts to communicate with provide a visual syntagma for his evolution as a storyteller and as a man.

Yet voice-over, by virtue of its retrospective temporality, is inherently elegiac in tone; it is frequently at odds with the forward-moving cuts of a film's image track, and it signals what Prats, for example, sees as an inherent aporia at the heart of revisionist representations of the screen Indigene. Noting that voice-over narration is a discursive strategy common to both classic Hollywood westerns like John Ford's *Stagecoach* and more contemporary 'pro-Indian' westerns like Costner's *Dances with Wolves*, Prats suggests that its use always 'implies the passing of the Indian'; thus it functions 'not only as a strategy of authentication and censure but of exemption and self-othering as well.'[49] To this end, as Silas prepares to leave the reserve for mechanics' school in Toronto at the end of McDonald's film, the voice-over finds him reflecting on 'the events of three months ago' (that is,

3.4   *Dance Me Outside*: Sadie (Jennifer Podemski, l) and Silas (Ryan Black) share an intimate moment as they prepare to leave the Kidiabinesse reserve.

Gaskill's murder) and wondering 'how long [he'll] be gone.' Especially when juxtaposed with the visual montage of Silas climbing on the back of a motorcycle being driven by Sadie and speeding away from the reserve where he has spent his entire life (see Figure 3.4), this suggests that his future identity as a man requires, in some senses, a cathecting of his identity as an Indigene.

Here, it is instructive to compare McDonald's film with *Smoke Signals* (1998), Chris Eyre's acclaimed adaptation of several stories from Native American author Sherman Alexie's 1993 collection *The Lone Ranger and Tonto Fistfight in Heaven*. Like *Dance Me Outside*, *Smoke Signals* is 'partially the story of a storyteller telling stories.'[50] As such, it employs a voice-over to foreground self-reflexively the first-person narration of Thomas Builds-the-Fire (Evan Adams). It is also a film – again like *Dance Me Outside* – about masculine redemption, using a genre favoured by McDonald, the road movie, to document the reconnection of Victor (Adam Beach) with his estranged father (Gary Farmer), whom we learn via flashbacks abandoned Victor and his mother (Tantoo Cardinal) and moved to Arizona following a descent into alcoholism. Eyre's film differs from McDonald's in that it combines image track and soundtrack in a way that presupposes not the inevitable disappearance of the Indigene, but rather his *reappearance*; *Smoke Signals* visually locates Native culture in a temporality that is not focused exclusively, and ethno-graphically, on a vanishing past; rather, to quote Alexie on his own screenplay, it materializes that culture in a way that 'is a lot more circular, so that the past, the present, and the future are all the same thing.'[51]

In January 1998, *Smoke Signals* became the darling of the Sundance Film Festival, receiving the Audience Award, the Filmmakers Trophy, and a nomination for the Grand Jury Prize. Quickly snapped up by Miramax and widely released on screens across North America, the film's gentle humour and winning perfor-mances from Native-Canadian leads Adam Beach (Saulteaux) and Evan Adams (Coast Salish) struck an immediate chord with audiences. The movie easily recouped its initial investment and then some, becoming the first narrative fea-ture written, directed, and co-produced (by Roger Baerwolf and Randy Suhr for Shadowcatcher Entertainment) by Native Americans to achieve such popular and critical success. Four years later, the first narrative feature written, directed, and co-produced by Aboriginal Canadians[52] followed suit when Zacharias Kunuk's *Atanarjuat: The Fast Runner*, fresh from winning the Camera d'Or at Cannes and a host of other awards from international film festivals, opened across North Amer-ica, eventually playing on fifty-six screens in the United States alone – an astound-ing feat for a Canadian film, let alone a 172-minute subtitled Inuktitut-language Arctic epic. Together with the success of Niki Caro's recent *Whale Rider*, based on New Zealand Maori author Witi Ihimaera's 1987 novel – which earned a Best Actress Oscar nomination for its young lead, Keisha Castle Hughes – these films suggest that indigenous filmmakers and storytellers are beginning to assert con-trol over the representation, distribution, and commodification of images of them-selves, their land, and their way of life.

Working once again within a predominantly adaptive context, however, these filmmakers largely avoid the trap of ethnographic romance's atemporal and arti-factual framing of the Indigene as always already knowable, because always already locatable within a static landscape and generic language of racialization specific to Western cinema's 'camera-eye' realism. Instead, films like *Smoke Sig-nals*, *Whale Rider*, and *Atanarjuat* arguably deploy what Rony, in her discussion of the performative and technical strategies of resistance used by Josephine Baker and Zora Neale Hurston in films from the 1920s and 1930s, calls a 'third eye' – a way of seeing and being seen within the cinematic imaginary's 'circulating econ-omy' of representation that acknowledges 'the process of being visualized as an object' and simultaneously 'returns the glance.'[53] In so doing, these films also highlight the co-imbricatedness of gender in racialized representations of the Indigene on screen. Let me try to explain by concluding this chapter with a brief discussion of *Atanarjuat*.

Kunuk is a former senior producer and station manager (from 1982 to 1990) at Canada's Inuit Broadcasting Corporation, and co-founder of Igloolik Isuma Pro-ductions, the first independent Inuit production company in the country (and co-producers, along with the NFB, of *Atanarjuat*). He has stated that he sees his film and video practice as a way of materially and archeologically reclaiming living Inuit history from its museumification at the hands of earlier ethnographic filmmakers: 'We are saying that we are recording history because it has never been recorded. It's been recorded by southern film makers from Toronto, but we want our input, to show history from our point of view. We know it best because we live it.'[54] To this end, in videos like *Qaggiq/The Gathering Place* (1989), *Nunaqpa/ Going Inland* (1991), *Saputi/Fish Traps* (1993), and the thirteen-part television drama *Nunavut/Our Land* (1994–95), Kunuk has reconstructed the recent (pre–Second World War) past of communal Inuit life in his hometown of Igloolik and the surrounding regions of Nunavut 'in order to share it with the future.' In these productions, he depicts a seal or caribou hunt, the laying of fish traps, and the building of community dwellings as culturally, geographically, and historically specific activities; moreover, he eschews (as Rony notes) any taxonomic (and, presumably, taxidermic) translation devices such as superimposed maps, voice-over narration, and subtitles to orient the non-Inuit viewer: we are simply 'plunged immediately into the scene.'[55] Ditto *Atanarjuat*, which despite the passing sop towards linear exposition offered by its English subtitles, from its opening frames immerses the viewer in a complicated five-thousand-year-old story – equal parts myth and historical epic – about sexual jealousy, murder, revenge, and, ultimately, forgiveness set in pre-colonial Igloolik.

For twenty years the nomadic descendants of the chief and shaman Kumaglak (Apayata Kotierk) and his wife Panikpak (Madeline Ivalu) have been plagued by a curse laid upon them by a rival shaman from Aivilik, Tuurngarjuaq (Abraham Ulayuruluk). It has divided the community, pitting the ne'er-do-well children of Sauri (Eugene Ipkarnak) – the unscrupulous Uqi (Peter-Henry Arnatsiaq) and his lazy and sexually promiscuous sister Puja (Lucy Tulugarjuk) – against the children of Tulimaq (Felix Alaralak) – the brothers Aamarjuaq (Pakkak Innuksuk) and Atanarjuat (Natar Ungalaak), who are the tribe's strongest and fastest men, respectively (see Figure 3.5). When Atanarjuat takes the comely Atuat (Sylvia Ivalu), who had previously been betrothed to Uqi, as his bride, Uqi becomes his sworn enemy, cleverly installing Puja within the brothers' household as Atanarjuat's second wife and biding his time for revenge. When Puja returns from the brothers' summer hunting camp shamed for having sex with Aamarjuaq, Uqi at last has his motive. He and his cohorts attack the brothers while they are sleeping, killing Aamarjuaq and sending the naked Atanarjuat fleeing across the tundra. Atanarjuat escapes and is nursed back to health by the family of Qulitalik (Pauloosie Qulitalik), Panikpak's older brother, who lives away from the tribe in the north and discovers the unconscious Atanarjuat on an ice flow. Atanarjuat returns to Igloolik, is reunited with Atuat, and at first plans to take his own revenge on his attackers by killing them while they feast on some caribou meat he has offered them. Instead, he declares that the violence must end. At a ceremony led by Panikpak and the newly returned Quilitalik, the ghost of Tuurngarjuaq is summoned and ultimately defeated, and Uqi and Puja and their followers are forever banished from the tribe.

As an adaptation, *Atanarjuat* is especially complex and explicitly challenges the standard model of semiotic transmission that has so far dominated my discussion of the literature-to-film phenomenon in this chapter – indeed, in this book as a whole. That is, Kunuk's film is based on an oral legend that, in its initial recon-

3.5   *Atanarjuat*: Brothers Atanarjuat (Natar Ungalaak, l) and Aamarjuaq (Pakkak Innuksuk).

struction by Inuit elders and eventual collaborative retelling by scenarists Paul Apak and Norman Cohn and director Kunuk, is also of a piece with a genre of cultural production in this country that Sophie McCall has identified as the 'told-to tale,' which refers to the collective and often asymmetrical process of rendering into written discourse indigenous oral texts.[56] In the case of *Atanarjuat*, this process involved Apak interviewing and recording eight Inuit elders to collect their versions of the oral story, collating and writing an initial treatment of this story in English (in order to attract funding from the Canada Council), and then collaborating with the only non-Inuit partner in Igloolik Isuma Productions, Norman Cohn, to produce simultaneously two different screenplays for the film. Cohn describes the process as follows:

> We met every day for three months around a table either at the office in Igloolik or in a tent a few miles out of town at a place we called Ham Bay … We discussed every scene, every gesture, every line of dialogue, and wrote two scripts at the same time, arguing and acting things out around the table. Apak wrote the scenes down on one laptop in the old Inuktitut font we got from the school, while I wrote the same scene in English on our second laptop, from the same discussions. We had to do this. The

actors would learn their characters and lines from the Inuktitut script, but we had to finance the film from the English script, since no one in the Canadian film industry could read Inuktitut or think like Inuit ... At the same time Apak consulted with other elders, like Emile Immaroitok, a language specialist, or George Aggiak, who knew a lot about shamanism, to make sure the dialogue was right, especially for the olden times when Inuit spoke a more formal, poetic and complex Inuktitut than today. And I consulted in the evenings by telephone with our script editor, Anne Frank, 3000 miles away in Toronto, who was helping us shape the screenplay to work as a film. This whole process was amazing and as I write about it here I can hardly believe how we did it.[57]

I would argue that the resulting film – in this case a tertiary medium of transmission – far from being representationally at odds with the 'original' oral form of the story, actually appears to facilitate its remediation. Indeed, Kunuk has gone on record as saying that he finds the space–time collapses enabled by film and video most closely approximate Inuit oral traditions,[58] which are all about sharing past memories with present and future generations (and in this he has much in common with the cinematic aesthetic of Robert Lepage, as we shall see in chapter 5). Hence the film narrative's deviations from some of the key plot points of the oral legend. For example, in most versions of the story Atanarjuat does indeed exact bloody revenge on Uqi and his cohorts; however, the ending of Kunuk's film must not be viewed, within the lens of fidelity criticism, as a corruption of the original story, but rather as a necessary concession to the theme of community reconciliation and rebuilding that Kunuk, for various extra-diegetic reasons, wishes to stress in this version of the telling. Hence, as well, what McCall has identified as the strategies of 'partial' and 'incomplete' translation in the subtitles to the movie, particularly where the performative representation of song is concerned. According to McCall, by exploring 'the uneven relations of address both within Inuit audiences and between Inuit and non-Inuit audiences' in this manner, Kunuk, Apak, and Cohn highlight 'the space of cultural contact and difference in acts of textualizing orature and orality. The filmmakers thus resist the powerful explanatory impetus of the genre of the ethnographic film, which presumes to elucidate the roles and purposes of cultural practices for outsiders.'[59]

A similar strategy of cross-cultural address, it seems to me, informs the circular structure of *Atanarjuat*, which is framed by sequences outside of the real/reel time of the diegesis proper, showing in a slow-motion dream time the initial conjuring and eventual banishment of the evil rival shaman Tuurngarjuaq. This relates to a characteristic feature of the film's cinematography (not to mention Kunuk's overall style): the repetition of extremely long takes. These function, I would argue, as the visual equivalent of oral pauses in storytelling, in that they force the listener/viewer to acknowledge his/her participation in the performative event of the film's elaboration, to reflect on the very act of looking, or else to look away. And here, in the 'denaturalized' time-space of these visual pauses,[60] the marvellous Inuit actors whom Kunuk has assembled for his film refuse to pose picturesquely for us as romanticized objects of ethnographic spectacle. To be sure, we see them in their traditional sealskin clothing, framed against the seemingly endless expanse of Arctic tundra, performing what we assume (via Flaherty's *Nanook* or some National Geographic special we might have seen) to be 'traditional' Inuit tasks, such as cutting up caribou meat and building an igloo. But they also see us seeing. That is, unlike in most conventional Western cinema, the actors make no attempt to disguise their awareness of the apparatus of the camera; often they look directly into it, returning our gaze with a bright smile, a sidelong wink, or a defiant stare.

This is particularly the case among the women actors, especially Sylvia and Madeline Ivalu, the impish Tulugarjuk, and the wonderfully wall-eyed Neeve Irngaut (who plays Ulluriaq, Aamarjuaq's wife). Despite in many respects being relegated, within the story's narrative, to the status of sexual pawns, these women refuse absolutely to be seen, within a Mulveyesque framework, solely as objects of erotic display. After all, it is Atanarjuat who in the film's most famous set piece is forced to run naked across the tundra. And it is Panikpak, with her shaman's 'third eye,' who at the end of the film exorcizes the ghosts of scopic possession that would fix the ethnographic subject in a timeless past, and who thus completes a circle of looking that once again aligns past, present, and future in an affirmation of cultural identity that makes visible the invisible lines of its living history, its genealogy. To this end, Apak and Cohn's published screenplay concludes with Panikpak staring for *'a long moment'* at the young son of Atanarjuat and Atuat, who is named after her dead husband, Kumaglak, and who has just spoken to her in his voice, before turning *'first to Atanarjuat ... then Atuat ... and finally Qulitalik, who returns her gaze with a thoughtful smile.'*[61] As this sequence appears on film, Panikpak's extended gaze upon baby Kumaglak (Bernice Ivalu, in a nice bit of cross-gender casting) is followed by an exchange of looks between Atanarjuat and Atuat, before a cut – as together they look down at their son – to a tight close-up of the preternatural child looking directly into the camera.

An ancillary goal for Kunuk in making *Atanarjuat* was thus surely to foreground more generally the representational politics of film as an adaptive medium. This can be surmised from the series of production out-takes documenting the shoot that accompany the film's closing credits. Here we learn, among other things, that the film was shot using a handheld digital camera (it was subsequently transferred to 35 mm film for its theatrical release);[62] that camera and cameraman (Cohn) were placed on a makeshift sled pulled by six crew members in order to track Atanarjuat's run across the ice and snow; that the actor playing Uqi spent his downtime listening to music on a portable disc player; that most of the town of Igloolik seemed to be involved in the production in one way or another; and so on. By making visible the various 'technologies' of race and gender behind the screen images we have just consumed – by showing us the whole (the movie) and then the parts that make up that whole (the production out-takes), rather than the other way around – Kunuk is reinscribing what Prats sees as the hegemonic 'representational destiny' of cinematic depictions of Native peoples, (con)temporalizing the Indigene, and emplotting him firmly inside the history of cultural identity production. This is akin to what Stuart Hall, in his discussion of theories of 'Third Cinema,' has described as the cultural 'play' of difference in much contemporary film from the Afro-Caribbean diaspora, a necessary 're-siting' of the binary oppositions between 'past/present,' 'us/them,' and, we might add, 'ethnography/history.'[63] Indeed, as Hall has argued, and as Kunuk's film so abundantly demonstrates: 'Identity is not as transparent or unproblematic as we think. Perhaps, instead of thinking of identity as an already accomplished historical fact, which the new cinematic discourses then represent, we should think, instead, of identity as a "production," which is never complete, always in process, and always constituted within, not outside, representation.'[64]

Of course, this is precisely what the discourse of adaptation forces us to confront: that we cannot theorize gender, for example, outside of the form/context/ medium of its representation/communication/transmission. As we shall see at greater depth in the next chapter, this lesson about life 'on the inside' of representation is one that the men in the prison drama *Fortune and Men's Eyes* find themselves having to adapt to, some more easily than others.

4 Critically Queenie, or, *Trans*-Figuring the Prison-House of Gender: *Fortune and Men's Eyes* and After

QUEENIE: [to the tune of 'A Good Man is Hard to Find']
A hard man is good to find
I always get the other kind
Just when I think that he's my pal
I turn around an' find him actin' like somebody's gal ...

John Herbert, Fortune and Men's Eyes[1]

While today we may take for granted the subversive possibilities of drag, it nevertheless remains true that actual representations of drag in film have reinforced conventional ideas of gender more often than they have challenged them.

Andrew Grossman, 'Transvestism in Film'[2]

Canadian playwright John Herbert died in June 2001 at the age of seventy-four. Although he wrote more than twenty-five plays in a career spanning five decades, was a respected teacher and dramaturge, and enlivened the Toronto gay scene with his drag artistry and activism, he is best known for writing *Fortune and Men's Eyes*, his exploration of the dynamics of sex and power in a men's prison that premiered off-Broadway in 1967. The play would go on to receive more than one hundred productions worldwide, and would be translated into some forty languages. In 1971 it was turned into a film by director Harvey Hart, based on Herbert's own screenplay. Given the acclaim that Tom Fontana's now defunct television series *Oz* garnered for its frank depiction of life on the inside – including sexual life on the inside[3] – it now seems timely, thirty-five years after its initial release, to reconsider Hart's film in light of its own equally complex interrogation of the prison system's queer subculture. Dismissed at the time of its release by several openly gay critics writing in the mainstream press (and later by noted film historian Vito Russo) as retrograde in its depiction of heteronormative role playing among the inmates it portrayed, in retrospect the film's situational politics offer productive ways to think through some of the binary codes of representation that adhere to the regulation of gender and sexuality in most institutional spaces, as well as some of the ways those codes might be resisted within the particular space of the prison.

In this regard, as a representational artefact, *Fortune and Men's Eyes*'s status as a film adaptation highlights the fact that the transformative process undergone by literary texts when they are brought to the screen is, in effect, one of 'queering,' in which one narrative form is disassembled and reordered as another. In this chapter I turn to this latter process, not in order to leave the discussion of queer representation in *Fortune* by the wayside, but rather in order to examine how the adaptation process *specifically impacts on queer representation*, in both the play and the film. A detailed explication of theories of cinematic adaptation as they relate to the theatre is beyond the scope of this book – beyond the scope, that is, of my summary of such theories in chapter 1. Even so, it is important to note, along with André Loiselle, that *Fortune*'s movement from a verbal to a visual signifying system is for the most part typical of the 'stage-bound' performative framework that has tended to govern the process of adapting Canadian plays to the cinema since the 1940s.

Loiselle refers to the works that result from this process as 'film-mediated drama' and notes that they necessarily remain 'haunted by [their] theatrical past'; this haunting is, however, 'crucial to our understanding of the relationship between the original and the screen version.'[4] Loiselle further notes that the Canadian auteur tradition, which has historically tended to favour independently developed projects by writer-directors, means that 'adapting a play for a Canadian filmmaker is thus a struggle wherein independent creativity clashes with the rigid parameters of the pre-existing text.'[5] In the case of *Fortune* these considerations are especially pertinent. Back-to-back stagings of the play in New York in the 1960s resulted in wildly different interpretations (and critical reactions); not only that, but the film adaptation (which several reviewers have found 'confusing' and schizophrenic, not least in its depiction of homosexuality) was itself the product of two different directorial visions.

For these and other reasons, it is crucial to situate *Fortune*'s successive adaptations – both on stage and on screen – within the increasing proliferation and politicization of queer cultural references post-Stonewall. In this context, I contend, the changes made between the 'original' source text and the film version of *Fortune* can be seen as having resulted not only in the production of a different narrative epistemology in each case, but in a different sexual epistemology as well, one in which the compulsory institution of heterosexuality, and the traditional gender roles ascribed and inscribed therein, are more openly – one might even say flagrantly – challenged and undermined, if only by virtue of the *visualization* of important queer counter-images on screen. My remarks, in this regard, will focus mainly on the pivotal, and highly visual, role played by the drag queen and cell 'mother,' Queenie, in the play and the film. I argue that her centrality as a figure of both gender *and* narrative ambivalence refuses to allow the viewer to foreclose on her in the spectatorial production of desire on and off screen; she exceeds the parameters of the film's closing frames – quite literally, as we shall see.

Besides examining *Fortune*'s further 'queering' of the sexual politics of its source text, in what follows I provide some of the background to the original production and reception of the play, and discuss the initial impetus for turning it into a film. As I have already intimated, I will scrutinize the process of reception, particularly in terms of the national and sexual differences that emerged among American and Canadian reviews of the play and among straight and gay critiques of the film. Contemporary gay reviewers' responses to the film version of *Fortune*, and Vito Russo's more extended consideration of it in *The Celluloid Closet* ten years after its release,[6] were thoughtful, impassioned, complex, and on the whole negative.

This chapter ends with a coda that contextualizes these responses in relation to the shifts over the past three decades in the politics of representation and reception vis-à-vis queer images on screen, particularly drag and transgenderism. Here, I move from a close reading of *Fortune*'s gender and sexual politics to a more expansive and generalized survey of some of the films that might be said to have either absorbed or rejected *Fortune*'s queer tutelage. First, in terms of both narrative structure and reception, I briefly compare *Fortune* to two other film adaptations of Canadian literature from the period: *Il était une fois dans l'est* (1974), André Brassard's miraculous cinematic amalgam of six of the plays in Michel Tremblay's 'Belles Soeurs' cycle; and Richard Benner's *Outrageous!* (1977), the Craig Russell vehicle based on the short story 'Making It' by Russell's friend, Margaret Gibson. I then catalogue the antics of some famous drag queens in recent Hollywood film, to show how drag has been elevated in queer theoretical circles to become the privileged episteme from, by, and through which to challenge traditional cultural norms of gender and sexuality.

I conclude by suggesting that the transsexual may fast be eclipsing the drag queen in terms of undermining gender and narrative coherence on screen. Here my remarks centre first on the complex representational politics on display in John Cameron Mitchell's iconic *Hedwig and the Angry Inch* (2001), and then on several further cinematic examples from Canada, including Brad Fraser's *Leaving Metropolis* (2002; based on his play *Poor Super Man*) and Paule Baillargeon's *Le sexe des étoiles* (1993; adapted from the novel of the same name by Monique Proulx). In *Leaving Metropolis*, Shannon arguably performs a similar (albeit greatly reduced) role to that of Queenie in *Fortune*, heroically seeking to liberate others from their gender and sexual fixity through the comedic barb, while at the same time managing to transcend comic book caricature in her own right. In *Le sexe des étoiles*, by contrast, protagonist Marie-Pierre's *trans*formation from page to screen is, as we shall see, decidedly unheroic, suggesting that when it comes to representing the limits – and liminalities – of gender, cinema still has some lessons to learn.

Fortune and Men's Eyes is based on Herbert's own six-month stay in a Guelph, Ontario, reformatory in 1946.[7] Having been sexually and physically harassed by a group of local homophobes, Herbert, the victim, ended up doing time when his victimizers accused him of coming on to them – this at a time when homosexuality was still illegal in Canada. Interestingly, Herbert would use this as the basis for the incarceration of Mona's character, who reveals to Smitty at the end of the play and film that he ended up in prison after having been similarly accused of propositioning the group of men who had gang-raped him. That Mona's sexual exploitation continues at the hands of his fellow inmates reveals much about Herbert's comment on how closely inside mirrors outside in this case, particularly in the replication of hierarchies of power.

To this end, the play follows new inmate Smitty, a clean-cut teenager who has been convicted of marijuana possession, as he gradually becomes acculturated to these hierarchies. Smitty is educated, in this regard, by his three cellmates. Tough guy Rocky first outlines to him the specific rules of the prison system: every new 'boy' needs an 'old man' to look after him, to protect him from being 'gang splashed' in the storeroom, among other brutal indignities; in exchange, the boy (in this case, Smitty) agrees to supply his old man (Rocky) with a little one-on-one action in the showers. 'It's me or a gang splash,' is how Rocky presents Smitty's options at the end of Act 1, Scene 1, 'Now move your ass fast. I'm not used to punks tellin' me what they want' (F 35–6). Next, Queenie savvily – and swishily – demonstrates how this system can be subverted, how Smitty can 'play it' so that he ends up 'on top': 'Rocky's nowhere near the top dog in this joint …,' Queenie instructs Smitty sagely at the end of Act 1, 'just a hard crap disturber who gets a wide berth from everybody … If you get out from under Rocky, and I spread the news you're boss in this block, they'll listen' (F 51; first ellipsis in original). Finally, Mona, the sensitive 'punk,' in refusing to let Smitty become his old man at the end of the play, reveals that Smitty, far from subverting the system in his toppling of Rocky, has merely reinscribed its power dynamics: 'Now you've flexed your muscles and found power, I'm an easy convenience' (F 89).

The film adaptation, which fleshes out the play's deliberately close and cramped mise-en-scène with additional scenes of prison life and activity, and which adds a few minor characters, mostly follows Smitty along the same narrative trajectory. Noticeable plot differences do occur, however, which will be discussed at more length below. That the prison system, in both the play and the film, is clearly a metonym for the broader sex/gender system and its own binaristic rules of identification and role playing invites critical interrogation. Interestingly, this interrogation – what little there is of it – has tended to coalesce around the 1971 film adaptation rather than around successive stagings of the play.

The play premiered off-Broadway, at the Actors' Playhouse, in 1967, in a production directed by Michael Nestor. Given one's particular point of view, it is either sadly ironic or wholly appropriate that the beginnings of modern gay drama in Canada – indeed, one might say modern Canadian drama *tout court*[8] – should have happened elsewhere. While the play had been workshopped at the Stratford Festival in 1965, it did not receive a full-scale, commercial production in Canada until 1975. Significantly, this production occurred only after a wildly successful 1969 remounting of the play in New York (by an increasingly out Sal Mineo), only after several other acclaimed productions around the world, *and* only after the play had been turned into a motion picture with the financial backing of a major Hollywood studio, MGM.[9]

However, the 1967 premiere of *Fortune* was covered by at least two prominent Toronto theatre critics – Nathan Cohen and Herbert Whittaker – and their enthusiasm for the play is worth noting, if only for how spectacularly it contrasted with the overwhelmingly negative response of most New York critics. Both Dan Sullivan, in dismissing *Fortune* in the *New York Times* as 'distressing,' 'self-pitying,' and 'monotonous,' and Edith Oliver, in panning the show in *The New Yorker* as 'histrionic' and 'repulsive,' made explicit reference to the Canadian setting of the play, as if this could explain the poor quality of the production.[10] Perhaps to compensate for this slight by his American counterparts, Whittaker began his *Globe and Mail* review of Herbert's play as follows: 'But if success in Canadian theatre continues to be measured by approval in the United States the Toronto playwright may find his purposes best served by the taut, lively production Mitchell [*sic*] Nestor has directed here. The praise Brundage wins under his pen-name, John Herbert, and the art of washing our dirty linen in the neighbor's yard may indeed bring him the recognition in Canada he deserves.'[11]

For his part, in noting that *Fortune*'s critical reception in New York had been 'mixed,' and that the 'resistance of the entertainment departments of the press and other media to the play' bordered on 'active hostility,' Cohen, a long-time supporter of Herbert, maintained that such reaction proved that *Fortune and Men's Eyes* 'poses a truly critical challenge. It asks deeply disturbing questions about long-established personal and social assumptions. It does not enrich our vision. It undermines it.'[12] Thanks in large measure to Cohen's active endorsement of the play, and his ongoing tracking of successive productions, cultural impresarios in Canada started to take notice. Cinemex Canada eventually joined MGM as co-producers of the film version of *Fortune*, and the Canadian Film Development Corporation (CFDC) put up some of the money for financing; also, the movie was filmed on location at a penitentiary in Quebec City.

Belated interest in a native son who achieved success south of the border helps explain the CFDC's involvement in so controversial a project (all the more surprising when we consider how cautious it was in its early days). To understand how MGM attached itself to a film based on a 'queer-themed' play by a little-known Canadian, it is important to place the play's second New York production in context. Recall that 28 June 1969 was a watershed moment in North American gay liberation: the impact of the riots at the Stonewall Inn, where queers fought back against their police oppressors, cannot be underestimated. Moreover, in the context of the argument outlined in this chapter, it is also worth stressing that it was the drag queens who were at the front lines of this revolt. The increased political visibility in the media that resulted from Stonewall was accompanied by an increased artistic visibility on stage.

For example, the landmark production of Mart Crowley's *The Boys in the Band* had opened off-Broadway only a year earlier. Its depiction of nine self-absorbed (and self-hating) gay men gathering at a surprise birthday party for one of the characters received mostly rave reviews from the straight press, evoking numerous comparisons to Edward Albee's *Who's Afraid of Virginia Woolf* (itself a closet gay drama) and prompting *New York Times* critic Clive Barnes to philosophize as follows: 'We are a long way from "Tea and Sympathy" here. The point is that this is not a play about a homosexual, but a play that takes the homosexual milieu, and the homosexual way of life, totally for granted and uses this as a valid basis of human experience. Thus it is a homosexual play, not a play about homosexuality.'[13] Although gay audiences were much more mixed in their reactions, the play quickly became a phenomenon: it opened in London in 1969, was immortalized in an A&M cast recording, and was eventually adapted for the screen (with the same original off-Broadway cast) in 1970 by director William Friedkin, who ten years later would gain infamy in the gay community for making the Al Pacino vehicle *Cruising* (1980), about a 'gay' serial killer and the cop who goes 'undercover' to catch him.

A year after *The Boys in the Band* opened in New York, and only four short months after the Stonewall riots, Sal Mineo, the former Hollywood ingenue turned theatrical risk taker, directed a controversial revival of *Fortune and Men's Eyes* at Stage 73, with Michael Greer in the pivotal role of Queenie (Greer would reprise that role in the screen version – a fortunate bit of casting that I will return to momentarily). The remount involved a significant 'gaying up' of the material, with lots of nudity and a specific focus on the scenes of male–male sex, both consensual and non-consensual. This time around, the estimable Clive Barnes was not amused. Edith Oliver had noted in her otherwise damning review of the 1967 production that one of *Fortune*'s few virtues was that it gave 'no evidence ... of pornographic intent';[14] Barnes felt that he could not say the same thing of the 1969 staging of the show. 'I consider that the changes Mr. Mineo has made in this play have been in the interest of sexual titillation – chiefly of the sado-masochistic variety – rather than in the interest of drama,' he opined in the *Times*. 'There is no objection to sexual titillation (although I strongly believe that pornography of a sado-masochistic nature is the one thing that should be outlawed) but I resent very much when it poses as raw and vital art.'[15] Despite Barnes's and other reviewers' protests, the remounting of the play was a hit.[16] Given this sudden craze for 'homosexual images,' is it any wonder that MGM wanted its own 'gay movie' to do business alongside that of its rival, CBS Films, which produced *The Boys in the Band*?

According to Vito Russo, however, MGM's interest in *Fortune* – and particularly that of co-producer Lester Persky – was the kiss of death for the film. Persky actually sacked the original director, Jules Schwerin, who had presided over the first thirty-one days of the film's shoot in Quebec City, and who was apparently interested in using the film to make a plea for prison reform. In replacing Schwerin with Harvey Hart, according to Russo, Persky sought to change 'the basis of ... Herbert's play (seemingly with the cooperation of the author) from a comment on sex as power to an exploitation of sex as a matter of gender identification.'[17]

Russo's main objection to the film version finished by Hart is that it fails to adequately stress that the heteronormative roles of 'old man' and 'wife,' 'politician' and 'mother,' that Smitty, Rocky, Mona, and Queenie alternately find themselves acquiescing to and resisting, overturning and displacing, are situationally contingent, engendered (Russo's term) by the institution of the prison itself, within which sex as an eroto-genital act – as opposed to sexuality as an identity category – is a commodity to be traded, like cigarettes, drugs, cushy work details, and freshly pressed linen. Russo contends that the movie version, instead of critiquing 'a society that demands we play one sexual role and one sexual role only,' turns *Fortune* into a 'sexual peep show' – one that plays up 'a covert homoeroticism for a burgeoning "gay market"' by having the camera linger, for example, over scenes of male nudity and gang rape, and that internalizes homosexual stereotypes of the active, masculine, straight-identified top and the passive, feminine, bottom.[18] The coup de grâce, according to Russo, is the fact that in the movie, unlike in the play, Rocky commits suicide after he is successively humiliated by Smitty in front of their fellow inmates and the prison guards, the implication being that death is preferable to submitting to this reversal of dominant roles.

Russo's condemnation of the film adaptation of *Fortune* was presaged by several other contemporary gay reviewers, whose chorus of disapproval stood in contrast to the generally favourable notices the film received from straight critics.[19] Writing in the *New York Times*, Stuart Byron noted that the film is 'unbearably confusing in its treatment of homosexuality. Near the end, in a tender scene between Smitty and Mona, it seems to be saying that homosexuality is as valid a form of love as any other kind, and even that, by being a prisoner, Smitty found out something which would have been denied him otherwise. Yet everything else in the film, intensified by the leering, overwrought direction of Harvey Hart, screams and yells that prison is bad because it causes homosexuality.'[20] *Village Voice* critic Richard McGuiness declared that 'the film has an unliberated, craven homosexual personality ... the fabulous, epic bitchiness of the institutionalized faggot. Gay and proud it is not. Elusive, self-destructive and cruel it is.'[21] And Jack Babuscio compared *Fortune* unfavourably to Jean Genet's classic prison-set film of homoerotic sexual fantasy, *Un chant d'amour*, contending that Genet's 1947 film 'goes far further than the sadly compromised film version of John Herbert's play. Genet ... challenges the morality of his audiences. The real prison, he seems to be saying, is within.'[22]

While I sympathize to a certain degree with some of the criticisms made by Russo and other critics, and while I do think that MGM and Persky's interest in *Fortune* was very cynically motivated (something that backfired on them, as the film performed poorly at the box office), I also think that Russo, in particular, errs greatly in trying to separate 'sex as power' from 'sex as a matter of gender identification.' Both the play and the film question the rigid gender roles imposed on men in our society, demonstrating how sex *becomes* or is *acquired* as an instrument of power: Smitty learns from Rocky what it means to rape, from Mona what it means to be raped, and from Queenie how one negotiates between these two extremes. That Smitty by the end of the play and the film displaces Rocky as the cell's 'old man' indicates just how well he has absorbed the brutal lessons of masculine identity formation. Moreover, while I agree that Rocky's death in the film is somewhat problematic in terms of what Russo calls its 'equation between homosexual discovery and suicide,'[23] I think that Russo retrospectively misreads key aspects of the play, particularly with regard to the changes made in adapting it for the screen.

Finally, I think that Russo's failure to discuss in any substantive way the two self-identified queer characters in the film, Mona and Queenie, is rather puzzling. Queenie, in particular, has undergone substantial revision between play and film; Herbert's screenplay moves her from the peripheries to the centre of the action. As played by Michael Greer, these changes to Queenie's character are arguably even more iconically – and iconographically – rendered. For not only did Greer play the role on stage two years earlier in Mineo's controversial revival of *Fortune*, but that same year he appeared as the flamboyant queen Malcolm in Bruce Kessler's *The Gay Deceivers* (1969), a performance Russo effusively praises in *The*

Celluloid Closet – which makes his glossing over of Greer's performance as Queenie in Hart's film all the more curious. In her reclaiming and embracing of the epithet 'faggot,' in her promiscuous switching of allegiances between and among her cellmates, and especially in her tour de force drag performance and the specific gender (dis)identifications it prompts in her audience, Queenie would seem to be destabilizing the proscribed social norms that Russo rails against at every turn. Indeed, from a late-1990s, Judith Butler–inspired perspective, we might say that Queenie is among the most 'critically queer' characters in the film.[24]

In this regard, Queenie, the self-declared 'mother' of the cell, ironically seems to disrupt heterosexual role playing in prison every chance she gets. A close examination of individual scenes within the film reveals that whenever couples re-form along old man/wife lines, she renders these liaisons asunder. It is Queenie, for example, who first reveals to Smitty Rocky's gender hypocrisy, noting that Rocky essentially played the role of 'wife' on the outside, being kept by a wealthy sugar daddy. (Rocky himself reveals to Smitty that the reason he ended up in jail was that, during an S/M scene with his lover, he refused to reverse roles and allow himself to be topped; in a fit of rage, Rocky stole his lover's car and a bunch of jewellery.) Queenie also reminds Rocky, in front of Smitty, of his 'first semester' at the prison, when Rocky came in for some special attention of his own from an older inmate named Screwdriver: 'Wasn't it Screwdriver who gave you your coming out party? I believe he made you debutante of the year.' The implication of Queenie's comments, supported by other scenes in the film, is that this relationship between Rocky and Screwdriver continues – that every cell's old man plays boy to another politician higher up the ladder. It is after this scene that Queenie counsels Smitty to turn the tables on Rocky by fighting him in the showers.

At the end of the film, Queenie, newly returned from solitary following her drag show at the Christmas pageant, disrupts Smitty and Mona just as Mona says 'I love you' to Smitty, because the same heteronormative paradigm is once again re-establishing itself. Although it *is* possible to read Queenie's actions throughout as motivated by her own jealousy and unrequited love for Rocky – she does seem, at the end of the film, to be visibly upset by Rocky's suicide, and the sight of Smitty and Mona in a clinch on what used to be Rocky's bunk might be read as 'setting her off' – her subsequent remarks to Mona after Smitty is led away to solitary do seem to contextualize her actions in terms of a defiantly oppositional queer stance: 'There'll be other Smitties,' she says to an upset Mona, adding that 'if you weren't such a goddamn martyr … well, honey, I could almost like you.'

It is worth spending a bit more time on the ending of the film, because it subtly revises the play's narrative closing and in so doing radically shifts its dominant sexual epistemology. In the play, as in the film, Mona and Smitty are alone in the cell. After Mona reveals how he ended up in prison – by being falsely accused of opportuning his homophobic assailants – Smitty tries to put the make on his young cellmate, offering to become his old man. Mona rejects the overture, recognizing that it is motivated only by 'circumstance' and that he is being offered 'indifference,' not love. 'I separate things in order to live with others and myself,' he tells Smitty. 'What my body does and feels is one thing, and what I think and feel apart from that is something else … It's to the world I dream in you belong. It endures better. I won't let you move over, into the other, where I would become worthless to you – and myself. I have a right to save something' (*F* 89). The rejection, because it directly assails the sexual and gender hierarchies he has so recently internalized, provokes a violent reaction in Smitty, who first verbally assaults Mona and then turns on him physically: 'Did you think I wanted your body? You make me sick. I wanted some kind of reaction to me, and only because I'm caught in this hellhole, you filthy fairy! You cocksucker!' (*F* 90).

The film makes it very clear that Smitty does indeed want Mona's body, by having actors Wendell Burton and Danny Freedman mime a struggle over Smitty's desire to have Mona go down on him. Moreover, the camera's close-up makes it clear that their reconciliation – effected by Mona's admission of love for Smitty (something less explicitly articulated in the play) – will likely be sealed with a kiss, which is interrupted only by the untimely (or timely, depending on one's point of view) return of Queenie to the cell. In the play, by contrast, it is the poetry of Shakespeare that brings Mona and Smitty back together, specifically sonnet twenty-nine, which also furnishes Herbert with his title. (In the movie, the sonnet is visible as a fragment of text above Mona's bunk, but its enunciation is displaced onto a pop song that plays over the opening and closing credits; I will have more to say later about the film's deliberate marginalization of Shakespeare.)

It is at this point in the play that Queenie and the still very much alive Rocky return to the cell. Queenie, who we learned only moments before has been sleeping with Smitty (a plot revelation notably absent from the film), flies, in true bitch-queen fashion, at Mona. Rocky and Smitty join the fray, and a full-scale brawl ensues. When the guard breaks up the melee and demands an explanation, Queenie and Rocky claim that Mona had been making a pass at Smitty. Despite Smitty's denials of this claim, and despite his offer of a fifty-dollar bribe to the guard, Mona is 'not going to get off so easy': 'Up off your ass, you little pansy!' the guard yells at him. 'You know what you got the last time this happened, don't you? You can bend over all you want, in the kitchen' (*F* 94). Mona is led away screaming, with Smitty vainly trying to retroactively claim responsibility for making the pass (which is, of course, the way it happened in the first place). Smitty then turns on Rocky and Queenie, laying the ground rules for their immediate and future submission to his dominance as top dog of the cell. Having fully usurped Rocky's position, in the closing tableau of the play Smitty lights a cigarette with Rocky's lighter and stretches out on Rocky's bunk, '*a slight, twisted smile that is somehow cold, sadistic and menacing*' – as the stage directions read – playing across his face as he speaks his final line: 'I'll pay you all back' (*F* 96).

The quid pro quo of the sex/gender and prison systems thus remains intact at the end of the play, but can we really say this of the ending to the film adaptation? When Queenie returns to the cell in the film – alone this time – she again flies into a rage when she discovers Smitty and Mona in what appears to be an intimate embrace. But this time, when the guards are called, it is Smitty who is led away kicking and screaming. Above the clamour of voices – Smitty's pleas of innocence, Mona's screams, fellow prisoners' incitements to violence – the word 'faggot' is clearly audible, repeated at least twice (by whom it is unclear) as Smitty is hauled out of the cell and down the prison corridor. In this scene, Smitty's vehement denunciation of the charge (both of starting the fight with Queenie and, presumably, of being queer) ironically constitutes an active avowal of just the sort of role reversal he had hitherto been unable (or unwilling) to acknowledge in his reconstituting of heternormative power dynamics within explicitly homosocial and homosexual contexts. As such, he discovers that while his 'gender melancholia' (the process, according to Butler, 'by which heterosexualized genders form themselves through the renunciation of the *possibility* of homosexuality')[25] entrenches a certain proscribed position of dominance in most situations, it can also deny him the space to manouevre when this position forecloses on him.

In other words, Smitty is denied queer agency – something that mobilizes Queenie's political resistance to all forms of institutionalized coupling within the space of the prison, and that mobilizes as well her open mocking of the heteronormative roles underpinning such coupling in her drag act. In its own way, queer agency also mobilizes Mona's separation of what goes on in the kitchen and storerooms from what goes on in the showers. That these two 'queer' characters remain in the cell while Smitty is carted off to solitary at the end of the film strikes me as a powerfully heroic statement (however unintentional) to make about the regulation of desire, and about resistance to that regulation; it also contrasts sharply with the opening tableau of the film, which features Smitty, handcuffed to another male prisoner, being loaded onto a bus as his girlfriend gazes after him mournfully through a chain link fence.

However, Queenie's most heroic assault against the 'gender melancholia' inherent in the compulsory regime of heterosexuality comes in her triumphant drag performance at the prison's annual Christmas pageant. Performed offstage in the play (we glimpse only an impromptu rehearsal that Queenie gives for Rocky, Mona, Smitty, and the Guard), in the film a full eight minutes are devoted to the spectacle and to the frenzied chaos that ensues when the Warden calls an abrupt halt to the proceedings. Indeed, this scene is the most visually stylized in the entire film, with the camera at its most carnivalesque, miming the handheld spotlights trained upon Queenie by her fellow inmates as it swoops around her from all angles, first catching her from down below, then from up above, then from side to side. This is parody, to be sure, but of a highly sophisticated and critical nature, with heteronormative canonicity being displaced in much the same way as the canon of Shakespeare. When Mona attempts to recite Portia's 'quality of mercy' speech from *The Merchant of Venice* (which is nothing if not a plea for the maintenance of a certain dominant, that is, Christian, status quo or world view), he is booed off the stage; when Queenie offers her own queerly redistributive (but no less retributive) take on Shylock's 'craving of the law,' it's eaten up.

Clearly, for these prisoners, there's drag and then there's drag. While the critical crossings inherent in Mona's performance are no less complex than in Queenie's – a boy playing a woman playing a man – they work to obscure the body's legibility through concealment and disguise, through an absence of signification. Recently, Robert Wallace has convincingly argued that 'Mona's drag performance, while less stereotypical than Queenie's, is more sophisticated in its technique. Replacing the obvious parody of Queenie's act with complex intertextual ironies, Mona's performance politicises role-playing by eliciting negative reactions.' Moreover, Wallace suggests that 'metonymically, the performance of Mona, like Queenie's performance, initiates a crisis of category that more than subverts stable classifications of Herbert's play' and that has led to ongoing 'academic confusion' about its generic status as either gay drama or social problem play.[26] But it is important to note here that Wallace is specifically talking about the play version of *Fortune*, not the film version.

Crucially, in the play, unlike in the film, Mona's recitation *follows* Queenie's act rather than proceeds it, and he is able, with Smitty's encouragement, to get through the whole speech – although he is later discouraged from delivering it at the Christmas concert itself. Either way, Mona's/Portia's speech depends for its effect on affect, on the solicitation of certain desired emotions in his/her audience. But Mona's fellow prisoners – as both the film and play have up to this point made abundantly clear – lack a context both for Shakespearean quotation and for any virtues of mercy extolled therein. Like Shylock, they want their pound of flesh. And Queenie happily obliges, bumping and grinding her way to a money shot that, Russo's and other reviewers' criticisms notwithstanding, is neither so narrativistically nor ideologically gratuitous as at first it might seem. When the Warden, repulsed by the excess of femininity on display before him, calls a halt to her act, Queenie responds by stripping off her remaining undergarments, exposing the one signifier whose meaning even the Warden cannot fail to grasp.

Indeed, the climactic revelation that – as one of the reviewers of an earlier version of this chapter felicitously phrased it – 'Queenie has a weenie' (not to mention the fact that actor Michael Greer is a natural blond), reminds us that Queenie is performing her act for two different albeit simultaneously present audiences: the prison officials and their wives; and the prisoners. If, in performing the '*sexually* unperformable,' Queenie allegorizes or exposes what Butler calls 'heterosexual melancholy' (the assumption of a masculine or feminine gender identification based on the renunciation of – or refusal to grieve – that same gender as a 'possibility of love'),[27] it must be remembered that she is doing so within a profoundly homosocial environment, one in which such melancholic gender identifications are even more precariously maintained. Arguably this is something that John Greyson has also intuited in retaining the prison as his outer frame setting in the film adaptation of Michel Marc Bouchard's play *Lilies* (*Les feluettes*). Whereas Bouchard has the adult Simon Doucet and his fellow ex-cons perform their play-within-a-play for Bishop Bilodeau in an abandoned theatre, Greyson has the still incarcerated Simon and the other inmates make do with the prison chapel for their play-within-a-film (the high school auditorium will find its way instead into Robert Favreau's film adaptation of another Bouchard play, *Les muses orphelines* – a text that, given Luc's cross-dressing, is not without relevance to this chapter). In so doing, Greyson highlights how the prison, in its queer 'mimicry' of the institution of hetero-patriarchy, remains a prime space for the theatricalization of gender, and for the rehearsal of normative and non-normative identities alike.

Thus, while Queenie's lascivious song and dance, her gaudily painted face and light-up nipples, occasion in the Warden and his screws more than a little discomfort by avowing as possible what they have disavowed as impossible – and therefore prohibitive – they have their wives beside them to pre-empt the full expression of their grief. Not so for the prisoners, and for Rocky in particular, who, just prior to the start of Queenie's performance, is bumped from his seat beside Smitty by Screwdriver. The implication is clear: word has gotten out about Smitty's besting, or topping, of Rocky in the showers (indeed, this scene immediately follows the fight between Rocky and Smitty), and Screwdriver has shifted his political (and no doubt sexual) allegiances accordingly. Rocky is banished to the back of the room, there to mourn, or 'beweep,' his newly 'outcast state,' as Shakespeare's sonnet would have it. That Queenie, the prison's 'good fairy,' is playing as much to Rocky's personal anxiety over the possibility that he has just been publicly outed as 'queer,' as she is to the collective heterosexual melancholy of the assembled audience, is made clear through specific codings in the lyrics of her song: she taunts Rocky during one of her sashays to the back of the room by singing 'I'll be glad to give your bed a test – remember, Rocky?'; and, on passing the bench where Screwdriver and Smitty are sitting, she croons 'He's free, Driver, he's free.' The song itself, 'It's Free' (written by Michael Greer, who also composed most of his own dialogue for *The Gay Deceivers*), queers the pitch even further by parodying the economics of exchange that characterize heteronormative relations in both the sex/gender and prison systems:

> When you're out with me, you're out on bail.
> My hips are tripped to take you out of jail.
> And, as you can see,
> There's quite a lot of me.
> And it's free, Daddy,
> It's free.

The prison officials cannot contain the cross-gender identifications unleashed by Queenie's tour de force striptease: a riot erupts when the Warden calls a halt to the performance and orders the naked 'pervert' to spend a week in the hole (see Figure 4.1). Neither can the film itself contain Queenie. And I mean this quite literally. She, alone among the other characters in *Fortune and Men's Eyes*, turns up in another of Herbert's later plays. 'Pearl Divers,' one of four short works that make up *Some Angry Summer Songs*, premiered in Toronto in 1974. It features Queenie, newly released from prison, applying for a waitstaff position as part of a government-sponsored rehabilitation program. She announces her presence on stage by singing the last few bars of Helen Kane's 'I Wanna Be Loved By You,' and, in typical fashion, proceeds to offend both the restaurant's gruff hostess and its harried assistant manager. Only the working-class Irish dishwasher, Mary, recognizes in Queenie a fellow foot soldier in the ongoing war against normative bourgeois culture; and since Mary really runs the joint, she hires Queenie on the spot.

This aspect of the drag queen exceeding the parameters of the final frame of the film is also a constitutive feature of two other film adaptations that emerged from Canada during this period. La Duchesse de Langeais and Hosanna had already had individual plays devoted to them, in 1969 and 1973 respectively, when Michel

4.1   *Fortune and Men's Eyes*: Queenie (Michael Greer) is led away to solitary following her performance at the Christmas pageant.

Tremblay's long-time director, André Brassard, brought them together on screen in *Il était une fois dans l'est* in 1974. But Sandra, arguably the film's most pivotal queen in terms of her destabilization of the narrative and sexual epistemologies of Tremblay's previously published dramatic corpus – and especially those of the play that immediately preceded the release of the film, that is, *Hosanna* – would have to wait until 1977 for her own moment in the theatrical spotlight with *Damnée Manon, sacrée Sandra*, the final instalment of the 'Belles Soeurs' cycle. In the meantime the celluloid Sandra, at the club that bears her name, stages the scene of Hosanna's humiliation that we only hear about in the 1973 play; furthermore, in so doing she shifts the focus on identity inherent in both works away from questions of national authenticity towards a more explicit engagement with questions of gender and sexual ambivalence.[28]

On stage, Claude/Hosanna's dispensing of his Elizabeth Taylor as Cleopatra costume is meant to signify, according to the playwright, that he has 'kill[ed] all the ghosts around him as Quebec did';[29] in Brassard's film, by contrast, the proliferation of Cleopatras on screen, each more resplendent and beautiful than Hosanna, visually reinforces for the viewer what Butler has called the 'imitative structure' and 'radical contingency' of gender itself,[30] exposing what's real as a

4.2   *Il était une fois dans l'est*: Sandra (André Montmorency, l) leads her fellow denizens of The Main on an outing.

copy, and the copy as what's real. Like Queenie, Sandra is motivated primarily by self-interest (she has designs on Hosanna's boyfriend, Cuirette), but she is also critically aware of the heteronormative presumption that underscores life both on and off the Main, including Hosanna's relationship with Cuirette (see Figure 4.2). And also like Queenie, Sandra gets the last word, her monologue in *Damnée Manon, sacrée Sandra* being a summation not only of her own personal philosophy of sex, gender, and selfhood, but also, arguably, of Tremblay's.

Likewise, Craig Russell was simply 'too outrageous' in his first screen outing as Robin (see Figure 4.3), drag star on the rise and soulmate to Hollis McLaren's schizophrenic Liza, not to have a sequel of that very name eventually devoted to his outsized talents in 1987. (More recently, Brad Fraser made a morbid attempt to revive Robin/Russell's divaesque spirit in a musical version of *Outrageous!*, which played briefly on Toronto's Canadian Stage in September and October 2000.) The process of bringing *Outrageous!* in its initial incarnation to the screen involved not so much changing Margaret Gibson's original narrative, as elaborating it or filling it in, the short story upon which the film is based having been written as a series of letters between Liza and Robin.[31] But the epistolary genre is historically based on certain normative romantic conventions; it should come as no surprise, then, that as much as Gibson queers those conventions in her story, reproductive sexuality looms large throughout.

4.3   *Outrageous!*: Robin (Craig Russell) as Carol Channing.

Liza's pregnancy remains a significant focalizing event in the film, but it is not the only one, and both the gay male and the straight female main characters are depicted as happily non-monogamous and sexually promiscuous. Moreover, the film's narrative does not end with the stillbirth of Liza's child, as it does in the story. Rather, Robin – who in Gibson's text cannot bring himself to reply to Liza's news that 'Vanessa was born dead'[32] – reanimates Liza's thirst for life by bringing her to New York and by demonstrating that they can make their own queer family without replicating the structures of heteronormative domesticity. 'I've never known anyone worth knowing who wasn't a positive fruitcake,' Robin, dressed as Tallulah Bankhead, tells Liza in the film's closing frames. 'You and me are here to love and look after each other.'

At one point early in *Outrageous!* Robin's boss at the hair salon where he works is reluctant to give Robin time off to practise his 'tacky drag.' Worried about losing the 'straight edge' he has cultivated among his women clients, the boss vows that he will never have 'a drag queen working in my shop.' And true to his word, he eventually fires Robin after the gay son of one of his clients mentions having caught Robin's night-time act. The reaction of Robin's boss accords with similar sentiments expressed by many gays and lesbians who were active politically and socially in the decade after Stonewall. As Esther Newton, writing in 1972, puts it at one point in her classic study, *Mother Camp: Female Impersonators in America*:

> The drag queen is an ambivalent figure in the gay world. The drag queen symbolizes all that homosexuals say they fear the most in themselves, all that they say they feel guilty about; he symbolizes, in fact, *the* stigma. In this way, the term 'drag queen' is comparable to 'nigger.' And like that word, it may be all right in an ingroup context but not in an outgroup one. Those who do not want to think of themselves or be identified as drag queens under any circumstances attempt to disassociate themselves from 'drag' completely. These homosexuals deplore drag shows and profess total lack of interest in them. Their attitude toward drag queens is one of condemnation combined with the expression of vast social distance between themselves and the drag queen.[33]

The drag queen didn't parody society's gender roles; she internalized the worst of its sex-affective stereotypes. Her hyperfemininity did not constitute a subversion of the patriarchal system; rather, it reconstituted a culturally inherited misogyny. Such views perhaps go a distance towards contextualizing the fact that another constitutive feature of the reception of *Il était une fois* and *Outrageous!* is that, like *Fortune*, they too attracted their share of negative criticism from the gay press. Thus Robert Trow, in the July–August 1975 issue of *The Body Politic*, lamented the 'uncritical way' that Tremblay and Brassard presented the 'shattered lives' of their protagonists, and Michael Riordon, in the October 1977 issue of the same magazine, questioned Richard Benner's motives in pitching the gay stereotype of a hairdresser/drag queen to a mostly straight audience: 'Will one heterosexual be changed by it – not comforted but changed, challenged, moved to original thought?'[34]

What a difference a few decades make – and a few thousand pounds of pancake, eyeliner, and sequins. Whereas in the 'gay '70s,' the drag queen was quite often someone to denigrate and/or pity, in the 'queer '90s and '00s,' she's someone to celebrate and even emulate. Once hidden away within a closed circuit of bars in the gay ghettos of major urban centres (think of Chez Sandra in *Il était une fois*, or the cramped Jack Rabbit Club, where Robin first plays when he finally goes off to 'make it' in New York in *Outrageous!*), the drag queen is now being 'exported' to mainstream, heteronormative culture as a metonym for virtually the whole spectrum of queer culture. As a result of this process of exportation, which has been greatly facilitated by Hollywood, performers like Divine, RuPaul, Lypsinka, and Lady Bunny can become major celebrities in ways that Queenie, Robin, Hosanna, and Sandra could only dream of (and, interestingly, they can do it by creating their own female personas instead of mimicking icons like Mae West, Bette Davis, Barbra Streisand, or Elizabeth Taylor).

What gay-themed, studio-produced movie of the past decade hasn't featured a drag queen in a prominent – and prominently heroic – role? *To Wong Foo...*, *The Birdcage*, and *Flawless* are just three examples where Hollywood actors like Patrick Swayze, Wesley Snipes, Philip Seymour Hoffman, and the oh-so-butch Nathan Lane have camped it up in crinolined chiffon and shiny taffeta. Independent films produced within the gay community also frequently contain a requisite scene featuring a larger-than-life drag queen.[35] In fact, so synonymous has drag become with queerness in the twenty-first century – especially as represented on film – that the Showcase channel in Canada has run, for the past several years, a series of ads promoting its June Pride Film Festival that feature three drag queens (Toronto's B-Girlz; see Figure 4.4) and three drag kings dancing and spouting famous lines from movies like *On the Waterfront* and *Taxi Driver*. At the end of each ad, in a parody of the Gap clothing company's ubiquitous consumer rhetoric, and in a subtle critique of gender as commodity fetish, the copy reads: 'Everyone in drag.'

The popular dissemination of drag in film and other media coincided, in the 1990s, with its critical rehabilitation in queer theory as the sine qua non of gender 'performativity' (Butler) and 'undecidability' (Garber). Critics like Butler, Marjorie Garber, Carole-Anne Tyler, and John Champagne, among others, saw drag as a powerful deconstructive tool of normative culture.[36] (And I should note that I am not exempt, especially in this chapter, from this list.) As Chris Straayer summarizes, in discussing what she calls 'the temporary transvestite film' (a subgenre where, as in *Some Like It Hot* or *Victor/Victoria*, a character cross-dresses in order to adopt a necessary, and presumably momentary, disguise), 'one measure of the radicalness' of the 'drag element' in such films 'is its relative ability to dismantle viewer assumptions about gender fixity and sex-role stereotypes': 'The rebellious effect of a drag queen depends on a disguise that appropriates and manipulates gender conventions and on the purposeful breakdown of that disguise into essentially contradictory levels of information. This leaves the viewer unsure about sexual identification and rules for sexual determination, and thereby offers the most radical conclusions.'[37] Indeed, according to Butler, 'drag fully subverts the distinction between inner and outer psychic space and effectively mocks both the expressive model of gender and the notion of a true gender identity.'[38] While Butler would later disavow, in *Bodies That Matter*, any notion of drag as unproblematically '*exemplary* of performativity' or of putting on a gender the way one puts on clothes,[39] she did so, interestingly, by citing (repeatedly) Jennie Livingston's 1991 film *Paris Is Burning*, a documentary about the drag balls put on by rival 'houses' of gay and transgendered Latinos and African Americans in Harlem.

Livingston's film has received a lot of ink from queer critics, including Garber and Champagne, for the way its subjects parody the normative 'realness' of various identity categories such as gender, race, sexuality, and class. In so doing, several of these critics seem to be implying that transvestism and transsexualism are coextensive terms, subsumed equally under the drag ball participants' resistance to 'a normalized, gendered subjectivity.'[40] This elision is particularly apparent in discussions of the fate of Venus Xtravaganza, the petite and light-skinned transgendered ball walker and sex worker who can presumably pass as white, but not completely as a woman, as her subsequent murder (by a trick, perhaps) implies.

4.4   The B-Girlz

While I do not have the space in this chapter to offer an extended critique of such elisions,[41] I would point out that if both the drag queen and the transsexual form part of Garber's 'transvestite continuum' (and this would appear so, as her encyclopedic study of 'cross-dressing' also includes separate analyses of such famous male-to-female transsexuals as Jan Morris, Renée Richards, and Christine Jorgensen), then their uneasy occupation of this continuum is a resistance as much to the conflation of the critical crossings of queer theory as it is to a 'normalized, gen-dered subjectivity.'

This tendency to conflate the drag queen with the transgendered person as oppositional hero/heroine is also replicated in several recent feature films. In Stephen Elliott's *The Adventures of Priscilla, Queen of the Desert*, many reviewers conveniently overlooked that Terrence Stamp's Bernadette, unlike her fellow ABBA-loving divas on tour through the Australian outback, is actually transgen-dered. And in *Flawless*, Philip Seymour Hoffman's Rusty, besides tinkling the ivo-ries for Robert De Niro, is saving up for sex reassignment surgery. Recently, of course, the transsexual (at least the male-to-female transsexual) has emerged in popular film and television as a fully fledged hero/heroine in his/her own right, and one who even more radically and subversively 'troubles' gender and sexual norms. Think of the Lady Chablis, playing herself, counselling bewildered jurors on the status of her 'toolbox' in Clint Eastwood's otherwise forgettable *Midnight in the Garden of Good and Evil*; or of awkward 'dads' Henrietta and Bree reconnect-ing with their new sons in *The Adventures of Sebastian Cole* and *Transamerica*, respectively; or of any of Pedro Almodóvar's beloved trannies, including those featured most recently in the award-winning *All About My Mother* and *Bad Educa-tion*; or even of little Ludovic's reorientation of his family's gender politics in Alain Berliner's *Ma vie en rose*; or, most spectacularly, of John Cameron Mitchell's star turn in his adaptation of his and Steven Trask's hit off-Broadway musical, *Hedwig and the Angry Inch*.

And here, let me digress for a moment to comment on how Mitchell's much dis-cussed and critically debated film consciously trades on and mobilizes both a genre-specific and a gender-theoretical conception of what I am calling 'transgen-der drag' as a masquerading of identity and a troubling of categories of the origi-nal and the copy. As the title of the rock musical indicates – and as Hedwig subsequently makes clear to her diegetic *and* extra-diegetic audiences via the nar-rative commentary with which she brackets her songs – a botched sex change operation has left her with no discernable masculine or feminine genitalia, only an 'angry inch.' As such, Hedwig's gender presentment neither completely con-tradicts nor completely agrees with her biological sex. It is, rather, what constructs her internal comprehension of the world's external *in*comprehension of her iden-tity (and note, in this regard, how all the shots of Hansel/Hedwig's 'bishop in a turtleneck' – or what remains of it – are deliberately obscured in the film, from the cartoon drawings that appear during Hansel's initial meeting with Luther to the shot of the rear end of a newly naked, and very masculine-looking, Hedwig at the end of the film).

In this, I am adapting Judith Halberstam's discussion of the 'transgender gaze,' which she sees operating in Kimberley Pierce's *Boys Don't Cry*, the acclaimed nar-rative film about Brandon Teena, a twenty-one-year-old preoperative transgen-dered male from Lincoln, Nebraska, who, along with Lisa Lambert and Philip DeVine, was murdered on New Year's Eve 1993 by former friends Thomas Nissen and John Lotter after it was discovered 'she' was not the man 'he' had pretended to be. Specifically, Halberstam analyses the slow motion POV shot/reverse shot sequence that interrupts the climactic examination of Brandon's body by Nissen and Lotter, wherein it is revealed that among the crowd of onlookers observing the stripping and 'castrating' of Brandon is none other than a fully clothed Brandon, a 'split transgender subject' whose 'divided look' actually 'works to highlight the *sufficiency* of the transgender subject' by undermining 'the spectator's sense of gender stability and also [confirming] Brandon's manhood at the very moment that he has been exposed as female/castrated.'[42]

I would argue that something similar happens in *Hedwig*. During a performance of her signature song 'Angry Inch' at one of the Bilgewater Restaurants that she and her band are playing on their shadow tour of former lover/protégé-turned-plagiarist rock superstar Tommy Gnosis, Hedwig begins to receive a torrent of homophobic and transphobic abuse from the audience. At which point Hedwig's back-up singer and 'husband,' Yitzhak, jumps into the crowd and starts a fight. He is soon followed by the rest of the band members, and a full-scale brawl ensues. Hedwig is eventually lifted out of the fray and transported magically to the ceiling, where she flies in slow motion above the action like a vigilant and all-seeing superhero. Following from Halberstam, then, we could say that in *Hedwig* – especially in scenes of the sort I have just described – an 'empowered' transgender gaze is enjoined to another transgendered gaze (that is, Yitzhak's) seeking empowerment,[43] or perhaps more properly, a transgender *voice* is linked to another transgender voice via Yitzhak's backing vocals. In the two characters' relationship on and off stage, we are likewise exposed to the gravity of their respective gender embodiments.

However, as in Halberstam's reading of *Boys Don't Cry*, one could say that John Cameron Mitchell ultimately betrays this transgender gaze, converting it in the end to a gay and therefore primarily masculine gaze, one in which the 'truth' of Hedwig's (gender) identity 'becomes sutured to nakedness.'[44] Hence Hedwig's crucial final confrontation with Tommy Gnosis at the end of the film, during which the hitherto transgender woman and her equally gender and sexually ambiguous boy lover (who up until this point has been unable to 'learn to love the front' of Hedwig) finally become recognizable and readable as gay men, down to the familiar homological and homo-narcissistic employment of the trope of identification with the same (via the painted crucifixes on Hedwig's and Tommy's foreheads). This would seem to accord with the particularly gay-masculinist reading of Plato's *Symposium* that Mitchell seems to want to emphasize in his film – in this regard, note the reprise of *The Origin of Love* song and the closing close-up of the tattooed sun-and-moon icon on Hedwig's exposed flank. Indeed, as we read in the afterword to the published text of the stage play, 'the healing of man' after the division of the three sexes will occur not through heteronormative gender relations, nor through an emphasis on transgenderism or androgyny – rather, it will take place through a version of pederastic mentorship, whereby the most manly in our society embrace 'that which is like them.'[45]

This somewhat problematic vision of gay politics once again shifts the burdens of masquerade and gender performance back onto femininity, specifically via Yitzhak's own transformation at the end of the film. That is, Yitzhak, with the aid of a makeover and Hedwig's blonde wig, seems to move from a hitherto FTM gender identification to discovering her hidden femme within. To Mitchell's credit, in the stage version of *Hedwig*, Yitzak (who is meant to be played by a female actress) was typed much more overtly as a gay-identified character, a frustrated drag diva in her own right. Miriam Shor's reprising of the greatly expanded role in the film version necessarily complicates such a reading. Nevertheless, however we read – or read through – Yitzak's/Shor's body, Mitchell's representation of gender identification and presentment in this film remains muddled, to say the least. And this points to both the representational and the real violence that continues to be visited upon trans bodies in our culture. For every fictional Henrietta or Hedwig, for every Anna Madrigal and Roberta Muldoon, for every Dil and Heaven and Kim Foyle, there is always the embodied life (and death) of a Venus Xtravaganza, or a Robert Eads, or a Brandon Teena – Hillary Swank's Oscar-winning turn in *Boys Don't Cry* notwithstanding.[46] Here, let us not forget the fate that befalls Robert Lepage's Jacques/Jennifer in Peter Mettler's 1992 film adaptation of *Tectonic Plates*, the play collectively created by Lepage and Théâtre Repère in the late 1980s. When the hopelessly naive and linguistically challenged Kevin discovers the truth about Jennifer's sexual identity, he strangles her.

That the transsexual may in fact be eclipsing the drag queen in film as the ambivalent sign of gender instability, on the one hand, and of narrative coherence, on the other, can be seen in several recent films to emerge from Canada. For example, in Anne Wheeler's frothy *Better Than Chocolate* (1998), based on Peggy Thompson and Sharon McGowan's liberal romp through recent Vancouver queer history, Peter Outerbridge plays Judy Squires, a male-to-female transsexual who self-identifies as a lesbian and is in love with Ann-Marie MacDonald's uptight bookseller, Frances. Judy is made to suffer the grossest indignities in the film (renunciation by her parents, harassment by gender-policing dykes); she also emerges as the film's wise moral centre, helping reconcile baby dyke Maggie (Karyn Dwyer) with her mother Lila (Wendy Crewson), and so on. And she is given a bravura scene in which she sings, at the local Cat's Ass dyke bar, the show-stopping number 'I Am Not a Fucking Drag Queen,' composed by the late and much lamented local diva Star Maris (see Figure 4.5).

In Brad Fraser's *Leaving Metropolis* (2002), based on his play *Poor Super Man*, Shannon (Thom Alliton), a pre-operative transgender woman and former sex trade worker whose HIV-positive status precludes her from undergoing complete sex reassignment surgery, performs a similar mediating function. That is, it is Shannon, who has 'always been something else – in between,'[47] around whom other characters' identities either cohere or begin to unravel, as the case may be. Thus, that Shannon is able to pass as a beautiful woman in the eyes of Matt (Vincent Corazza) – made all the more improbable in the film version by the heavy five o'clock shadow that shows through actor Alliton's make-up – serves to highlight not only Matt's sexual naivety, but also how his recourse to a presumptively heteronormative visual hermeneutics serves to buttress his increasing attraction to David (Troy Ruptash). Moreover, Shannon reminds Kryla (Lynda Boyd) that her railing against the inherent misogyny of patriarchal culture is laden with its own essentialist rhetoric; to Kryla's claim that 'if you're born with a cunt you're fucked,' Shannon retorts acerbically: 'I've always thought a vagina was the true

4.5   *Better Than Chocolate*: Judy (Peter Outerbridge) performs her signature tune at the Cat's Ass bar.

test. Anyone can buy breasts.'[48] And finally, Shannon's death awakens in David the realization that he has been living in the past – taking a job as a waiter despite his fame as an artist and chasing after straight boys – as a way to avoid a far more uncertain future.

Significantly, in the film version, apart from some deft cross-cutting and parallel montage in an earlier sex scene, this is one of the few sequences that Fraser shoots in a way that fully exploits the visual potential of his new medium and (as with Queenie's drag number in *Fortune*) the full diva-ness of Shannon's character. After a close-up on a now bald and haggard-looking Shannon's face at the moment she loses consciousness, we cut to a long shot of David alone at the bathhouse. The white walls, David's white towel, and the steam slowly filling the frame lend a spectral luminosity to the proceedings. A red gel is added to signal a change in tense, temporality, and tone, and as the camera pans from a bewildered and grief-stricken David towards the door, the brush-stroked names of dead friends and lovers we had previously glimpsed as part of a simple canvas hanging on the wall of David's apartment are superimposed over the image of a dozen male bodies rising from the steam, each clad in a similar white towel. Into this gathering walks Shannon, wig and make-up back in place, and clad in what appears to be a shimmering white ball gown. She blows David a farewell kiss and then disappears along with the other men. It's a quietly moving scene, and one that rescues not only David but arguably the entire movie from the comic book clichés into which, despite the irony with which the genre is treated in Fraser's source text, the adaptation has repeatedly threatened to dissolve.

A decade earlier, Paule Baillargeon's film adaptation of Monique Proulx's 1987 novel *Le sexe des étoiles* had surfaced briefly on the film festival circuit and in Canadian theatres. In Proulx's sexually polymorphous and narratively polyphonic novel, Marie-Pierre Deslauriers, a former award-winning microbiologist, returns to Montreal following a successful sex change operation in order to reconcile with her young daughter, Camille, a budding astronomer. Woven into this story are those of several other Montrealers, including a blousy but efficient female radio researcher and a blocked male writer, who cross paths with Marie-Pierre and become fascinated by her complicated sexuality, as well as by the apparent ease with which she inhabits this sexuality. Marie-Pierre, whose excesses (in dress, in food and drink, and in the recounting of her own life story) are wonderfully matched by the hyperbolic expressiveness of Proulx's prose, delights in confounding the normative assumptions of these 'biologiques,' as she calls them, suggesting that Gaby, the researcher, must learn to get more in touch with her male 'yang' side, and telling Dominique, the newly unblocked writer, that he is not really in love with her, but rather with 'l'idée que je représente, tu aimes en moi la Femme avec un F majuscule, justement … Tu es très énormément excité, mon chou, par mon F majuscule. Ne compte pas sur moi pour régler tes problèmes.'[49] The genderfuck that Marie-Pierre so revels in is replicated in the narrative construction of the novel. The authorial/authoritative representation of the male and female writing subject merges at least twice: once when the text of the final paragraph of Proulx's novel mirrors that of the final paragraph of Dominique's; and again when Gaby, sent a copy of Dominique's manuscript following his untimely death in a traffic accident, crosses out Dominique's name on the title page and appends her own.

All of this is absent from the film version. Proulx, adapting her own work in the screenplay, chooses to cut Gaby and Dominique. She focuses instead on the family triangle between Marie-Pierre, Camille, and Michèle (Camille's mother and Marie-Pierre's estranged wife), and on Camille's blossoming romance with Lucky Poitras, a classmate who moonlights as a young male prostitute. The novel is structured almost entirely around Marie-Pierre, and around the shifts in thinking and ways of being that the frank celebration of her gender ambiguity occasions in others; by contrast, the film is focalized (quite literally, given how often her gaze is reflexively foregrounded) almost exclusively through the perspective of Camille, who refuses to accept her father as a woman. In a recent article, Michael Eberle-Sinatra, quoting extensively from published interviews with both Proulx and Baillargeon, demonstrates how their mutual endorsement of the resulting film, and its shift in narrative and ideological focus, betrays the author's gradual estrangement from her own text, as well as the director's role in this process. For Baillargeon only agreed to direct the film after being assured that the 'heroine' of the story was going to be a 'little girl' and not a transsexual.[50]

Thus we once again have produced, in a film adaptation, a radically different

4.6   *Le sexe des étoiles*: Marie-Pierre (Denis Mercier, l) and Camille (Marianne Coquelicot Mercier) contemplate the heavens.

sexual epistemology to accompany the narrative changes made to the source text. This time, however, the results offer no great challenge to heteronormative culture; rather, they reinscribe some of its most entrenched clichés regarding masculinity and femininity. As with the club scenes featuring Sandra and Robin in *Il était une fois* and *Outrageous!* – and in the vein of Queenie's climactic performance at the Christmas pageant in *Fortune* – we witness a specific hyper-theatricalization of gender in *Le sexe des étoiles* when Lucky drags Camille to the Nefertiti, a local trans hangout with a rotating line-up of talent. Instead of being pulled out of her melancholia, however, Camille is driven deeper into it, especially after she spies her father, in a slinky red dress, kissing a person of colour who is of indeterminate gender. This is compounded by the fact that the club's name – in its metonymical associations with the Café Cléopâtra, an actual bar in Montreal's red light district that caters to 'a transsexual/transvestite clientele' – locates 'transsexuals within the system-associated commonplaces of prostitution: corruption, drug use, sexual exploitation, vileness.'[51]

For her part, Marie-Pierre, instead of heroically celebrating her new identity, as she does in the novel, must sublimate and repress that identity in order to ease Camille through the transition into young womanhood (see Figure 4.6). Indeed, as the film nears its conclusion, Marie-Pierre, in straight male drag, says goodbye to Camille, having just been bribed by Michèle to leave for New York and never see Camille again. There follows a cut to a scene a few months later. Camille, up until this point a rather androgynous-looking young girl, is in the bathroom, applying make-up and fixing her hair; after kissing her mother goodbye, she dons a helmet and hops aboard Lucky's scooter, wrapping her arms around him. Camille, who earlier in the film (and book) railed against the 'coupling' of the universe and ruminated on the fact that – among the stars at any rate – such couples are the product of a 'paradoxe le plus fantasque: les Trous noirs et les Quasars,'[52] is now effectively – and very heterosexually – coupled.

The black hole that often accrues around our understanding of gender (a space of identification from which no body that matters can escape) insists that in order to be read legibly, there must be some sort of correspondence or coherence between one's interior, psychic identification as one or another gender, and the exterior expression of that gender; and that 'if one identifies *as* a given gender, one must desire a different gender.'[53] Queenie and her drag and trans successors in film do not automatically free us from such imprisoning logic. But the figure (an 'iconographic' or 'hyberbolic' figure, in the words of Butler) s/he represents on screen does help expose the limits of a theory of gender and sexual identity (or any identity, for that matter) based on causality or equivalence. Moreover, as both a seasoned performer *and* a seasoned prisoner, Queenie understands better than most that any role is situationally contingent, dependent equally on who is taking it on, where it is being played out, and who is receiving it. As such, in the next chapter we shall see that the policing of queer bodies as they move from stage to screen requires a concomitant adapting of how we think about time and space.

5 Space, Time, Auteurity, and the Queer Male Body: Policing the Image in the Film Adaptations of Robert Lepage

What constitutes the crystal-image is the most fundamental operation of time: since the past is constituted not after the present that it was but at the same time, time has to split itself in two at each moment as present and past, which differ from each other in nature, or, what amounts to the same thing, it has split the present in two heterogeneous directions, one of which is launched towards the future while the other falls into the past ... In fact the crystal constantly exchanges the two distinct images which constitute it, the actual image of the present which passes and the virtual image of the past which is preserved: distinct and yet indiscernible, and all the more indiscernible because distinct, because we do not know which is one and which is the other. This is unequal exchange, or the point of indiscernibility, the mutual image.

Gilles Deleuze, *Cinema 2: The Time-Image*[1]

In the growing body of scholarship on the theatre of internationally renowned Quebec director Robert Lepage, a dominant critical paradigm has emerged to describe the global/local interfaces at work both in the subject matter of his plays and in the methods of their production/reception. Drawing on the work of Patrice Pavis, and focusing primarily on *The Dragons' Trilogy* and *The Seven Streams of the River Ota* – the epic dramatic cycles collectively created with Théâtre Repère and Ex Machina in 1985–7 and 1994–6 respectively – critics have pointed out the 'intercultural' nature of Lepage's work.[2] That is, employing the metaphors of translation and travel foregrounded in the plays themselves, these critics have analysed the mixing of histories, geographies, languages, and performance traditions in Lepage's dramatic universe, as well as their transnational communication and significations in different production contexts around the world. For some critics, like Sherry Simon, Lepage's cultural and linguistic 'code switching' enacts a 'vision of "cosmopolitan globalism" as a dialogue among differences.'[3] For others, like Jennifer Harvie, Lepage's dramaturgy all too often practises a cultural relativism and a 'recidivist exoticism,' with its 'tourist gaze' fixing an interchangeable Oriental other, in particular, as the commodified site of difference against which Western (read Québécois) fantasies of 'autonomy and self-determination' can be measured.[4] A similar sort of 'intermedial' code switching is at work in Lepage's films (all of them fundamentally adaptations). I would argue that the results are equally paradoxical, particularly when it comes to representations of the queer male body – its absent presence and its present absence.

Before I explain more fully what I mean by this, it is vital to understand that in the critical work being done on Lepage's cinematic universe, a dominant theme seems likewise to be emerging. The focus here is again on an interface (both diegetic and extra-diegetic) – in this case between the functions of time and those of space in Lepage's films. Drawing primarily on the work of Gilles Deleuze, and making frequent comparisons to the cinema of Alain Resnais and Alfred Hitchcock, critics like Bill Marshall, Henry A. Garrity, Martin Lefebvre, May Telmissany, and Aleksandar Dundjerovic have elaborated an entire taxonomy of space–time collapses – from parallel montage, flashbacks, and films within films – that work to absorb and sustain the past within the present in Lepage's cinematic representations of memory.[5] Such effects are, in turn, often linked to questions of authority or the lack thereof. For, as Garrity in particular points out, the reconstructed past in Lepage's films is essentially a *de-* or *un-*authorized one; it lacks an identifiable narrator, in the sense that the edits used to evoke the past temporally and spatially on screen are more often than not the result of Deleuzean 'irrational' cuts, which cannot be tied to a diegetic character's actual sensory-motor recognition but only to extra-diegetic or virtual representation – what Deleuze calls the 'recollection-image.'[6] Neither can these recollection-images be tied to a stable point of view – other, that is, than what is provided by the omniscient camera.[7] Which is another way of saying that if Lepage's films, by virtue of their status as mediated texts generally, and as 'adaptations' (however broadly defined) more specifically, lack an author (in the Barthesian sense), they do at least have an auteur.

In this chapter I want to examine the intersection of auteurism and adaptation in Lepage's cinema by focusing very specifically on the temporal and spatial transposition of images of the queer male body from his theatrical source texts to their filmed adaptations.[8] While perhaps not as visibly or politically 'out' as fellow Québécois theatre contemporaries René-Daniel Dubois and Michel Marc Bouchard, both of whom have seen their most famous (and famously gay) plays adapted memorably for the screen (see below), Lepage makes no secret of his homosexuality. Moreover, his theatrical creations are filled with all manner of queer characters and images of same-sex eroticism. Curiously, however, in Lepage's first four films, such characters and images are either largely absent, or else – in the case of his first and most celebrated film, *Le confessionnal* – so overlain with the symbolic weight of internalized guilt and dysfunction as to be borderline homophobic. It is possible to interpret such changes as Lepage's required concession to the pressures of commercial pragmatism and mainstream audience tastes that govern the film industry – a consideration I return to at the end of this chapter. Likewise, one can see this as a necessary consequence of what, after Deleuze, we might call the collision of 'two distinct images' of the Quebec cinematic imaginary, in which past memories of political, social, and religious repression continue to haunt present representations of gender and sexuality. At the same time, however, I would argue that they also point significantly to Lepage's own *self*-adaptation from theatre to film director.

What is at stake here is that, as a film auteur (and one very much depicted by the popular press as being in the classic Hitchcockian all-seeing, all-knowing, all-controlling mould), Lepage is arguably able to police his cinematic narratives more vigilantly than his theatrical ones, most of which were created collaboratively with his Théâtre Repère and Ex Machina troupes, or with co-writers like Marie Brassard, and which Lepage has famously argued are never 'finished,' because they are always evolving and being adapted in the necessarily evanescent and non-repeatable context of the performance moment. However, when it comes to the filmic artefact, and representations of the queer male body recorded (or not recorded) therein, a degree of auteurity necessarily accrues, by virtue of each film's temporal positioning after – and thus definitive recording of – each play's constitutive images. In terms of the weight that Western culture assigns the visual as a means to produce space and thereby knowledge, these images necessarily take on added authority and permanence when captured on film.

Or, to put this in the terms outlined by Gilles Deleuze in this chapter's epigraph, the image moves from the 'virtuality' of the past (those once fleeting and now lost moments of theatrical inspiration, rehearsal, and performance) to the 'actuality' of the present, where it can be ceaselessly and unchangeably replayed in the temporal and spatial moment of apprehension that constitutes the film's projection. What I want to explore in this chapter, then, is the 'unequal exchange,' the 'point of indiscernibility' that arises from the 'crystallization' of images of the queer male body in Lepage's translation of and surveillance over his (and others') stage narratives as they are adapted into screen narratives. Because many of these images reflect a highly ambivalent – and atemporal – intersection of the religious and the secular, the political and the personal, the social and the familial in Lepage's work, attention must also be paid to how this surveillance extends to and encompasses both the sexual symbolic and the national symbolic in much Québécois cinema.

My use of the word surveillance is deliberate, and alludes not only to what I see as the visual and narrative policing of the queer male body in Lepage's films, but also to how that policing is generically inflected, each of his films – with the notable exception of his most recent one, *La face cachée de la lune* – falling at least partially into the overlapping categories of thriller/mystery/detective story/whodunit/film noir, or what, for my purposes, is more accurately summed up by the French term *policier*. As Richard Dyer and Robert Corber have each shown, besides formal elements such as low key lighting, unusual camera angles, flashbacks, and voice-over narration, one of the things that distinguishes classic Hollywood film noir narratives is the preponderance of 'characters [usually villains] who are explicitly marked as gay,'[9] from Sidney Greenstreet and Peter Lorre's Gutman and Cairo in *The Maltese Falcon* to Clifton Webb's Lydecker in *Laura*. Moreover, as Corber also notes, the gay male of film noir, in being linked iconographically with the femme fatale, is seen as a threat not only to the stability of the bourgeois family, but also to national security, because his conspicuous consumption and commodity fetishism undermine the Fordist model of production and 'capital accumulation,' which at the time the films were produced was in the process of establishing itself in postwar America.[10] In drawing from some of the genre's stylistic devices in his films, Lepage also reproduces some of film noir's most entrenched clichés regarding gender and sexuality. Thus, in *Le confessionnal* we are told that Marc (Patrick Goyette), the rent boy, is failing to provide adequate financial support for his estranged girlfriend, Manon (Anne-Marie Cadieux), and their son. At the same time, we witness Marc accepting expensive gifts of clothes and travel from one of his clients, Massicotte (Jean-Louis Millette); and in another memorable shot we see him standing aloofly off to the side in his leather jacket, blazer, designer jeans, and boots, smoking while Pierre (Lothaire Bluteau) works to get the old family Dodge running.

Dundjerovic has argued, somewhat unconvincingly, that *Le confessionnal* represents Lepage's contribution to the international New Queer Cinema, which was just coming into vogue in the 1990s.[11] Lefebvre has, I think, better examined how the film's queer significations are more intranationally delimited. So before going on to my own queer reading of Lepage's filmography, I think it important to note how any such reading is inherently governed by a broader, and largely psychoanalytic, cultural discourse in Quebec. This discourse has repeatedly recuperated filmic (and other media) representations of homosexuality within a 'symbolic' framework of that province's arrested development and English Canada's social dominance. Here, I am alluding to a very influential 1987 article by Gilles Thérien, which argues that representations of same-sexuality in films by Micheline Lanctôt (*Sonatine*), Jean Beaudin (*Mario*), Léa Pool (*Anne Trister*), and Yves Simoneau (*Pouvoir intime*), among others, are in fact restagings of Quebec's permanent identity crisis, wherein the child of the Quiet Revolution, alienated from a patriarchal family environment, yet unable to completely cathect him/herself from that environment, displaces this power dynamic onto a 'falsely feminine' idealization of a person of the same sex (who cannot but be read as standing in for English Canada).[12]

Thérien's argument and the homophobic presuppositions underpinning it have been succinctly and efficiently deconstructed by critics such as Robert Schwartzwald and Bill Marshall,[13] but this has not stopped others from applying its analytical paradigms to an endless catalogue of films not discussed by Thérien – including, in Lefebvre's case, *Le confessionnal*. As Lefebvre notes, the scenario described by Thérien 'completely overlaps with Marc's situation in Lepage's film.'[14] That is, Marc, unable to reconcile his feelings of bitterness for his recently deceased 'adoptive' father, allows himself to fall back into a homosexual relationship with the ex-priest turned federal diplomat Massicotte, who drags Marc to Japan on government business. Significantly, it is here, in this foreign country, that Marc commits suicide, death being 'the only possible outcome for he [that is, the sexual deviant, the passive homosexual] who can't accept domination yet refuses to challenge it.'[15]

While I find much in Lefebvre's reading of *Le confessionnal* to be convincing, this last point is less so. Indeed, the problem with conscripting the queer male body as a signifier of failed or unrealized national identity in Québécois cultural production generally, and in the corpus of Lepage's films more specifically, is that that signifier very often ends up a corpse. In an illuminating article on Hitchcock's frequent film adaptations of drama (including *The Secret Agent*, *Rope*, *Dial M for Murder*, and *I Confess*), Alenka Zupančič notes that '*every time cinematic and theatre realities coincide*, every time cinematic and theatre narratives overlap, *there is a corpse*.'[16] Recently, in a series of articles to which I shall return at the end of this chapter, André Loiselle has explored the pertinence of this insight to Jean Beaudin's 1992 adaptation of Dubois's play *Being at home with Claude* and John Greyson's 1996 adaptation of Bouchard's play *Lilies* (*Les feluettes*).[17] One could just as easily apply this insight to the films of Lepage, each of which is an adaptation of a theatrical narrative in some fundamental way, and each of which features, however obliquely (as in the case of *Nô*), a corpse. My argument in the rest of this chapter, then, is that the corpse as signifier in Lepage's films, even when not literally embodied/discarnated by the queer male, is nevertheless all too often tied to the 'death' of certain important homosexual significations in Lepage's source texts, and that such auteurial revisionism has important implications for the gendered reception of his cinematic *and* his theatrical narratives.

Le confessionnal: Framing the Body

As an adaptation, *Le confessionnal* is quintuply complex. Not only does it contain characters from Lepage's first great theatrical triumph, *The Dragons' Trilogy* (chief among them protagonist Pierre Lamontagne); but it also consciously quotes and incorporates scenes from Hitchcock's *I Confess*, which is itself an adaptation of a 1902 stage play, *Nos deux consciences*, by French playwright Paul Anthelme. Moreover, as Dominique Lafon and Michael Vaïs have separately pointed out, Anthelme's play received its own *québécisation* prior to Hitchcock's film treatment via Quebec playwright Julien Daoust's theatrical adaptation, *La conscience d'un prêtre*, which premiered in Montreal in 1903. According to Lafon, Hitchcock and his scenarists (George Tambori and William Archibald) must have known about Daoust's play, as the script for *I Confess* 'présente de singulières similitudes avec l'oeuvre de Daoust, indépendamment de leur source commune, la pièce d'Anthelme.'[18] Lafon argues that Daoust's influence on Hitchcock's film extends beyond the director's retention of the Quebec City setting; Daoust gives Anthelme's melodramatic plot a particular Québécois inflection, which Hitchcock then incorporates into *I Confess*, and which Lepage exploits and expands on in *Le confessionnal*. Finally, *Le confessionnal* must also be considered, in some senses, an anachronistic and anamorphic sequel to Lepage's next great theatrical project, *The Seven Streams of the River Ota*, which concludes by placing the Eastern-identified Pierre in Japan.

In conversation with Rémy Charest, Lepage has described the character of Pierre Lamontagne as his '*alter ego*,' a 'linking character' who makes connections between the various threads of Lepage's theatrical and cinematic narratives, and between those narratives and the audience: 'He's all-purpose because he is relatively young and an artist, which allows us to place him almost anywhere, in almost any circumstances. He's a very flexible, very mobile character – a blank character, in a way. He provides the link between the story and the audience. His naive approach towards the events he encounters reflects the spectator's position.'[19] However, Lepage also goes on to admit that 'over the course of his incarnations, the character [of Pierre] developed a few inconsistencies.'[20]

Thus, for example, *Le confessionnal* begins with Pierre returning from China, where he had gone to study calligraphy, in 1989 (news coverage of the Tiananmen Square massacre accompanies clips from *I Confess* as a parallel intratext throughout the film). *Seven Streams*, however, ends with the character (here renamed Pierre Maltais) arriving in Japan in 1995 to study *butoh* dance – an Orientalist elision that makes one question Lepage's statement, elsewhere in *Connecting Flights*, that his 'fascination with Japan began when I was sufficiently mature to be able to distinguish it from China.'[21] Similarly, within the framework of the present analysis, it is worth noting that the fluidly bisexual Pierre of *Seven Streams* (who seduces not only David Yamashita but also, it's implied, David's mother, Hanako) is in some senses straightened out, or at least *desexualized*, in *Le confessionnal*: in the sequence early in the film where he searches for Marc at a gay sauna, Pierre's nervousness and discomfort are visibly apparent; this sequence concludes with Marc telling him he doesn't belong there.[22] Pierre and his fluid sexuality do not survive at all the screen transposition of *Seven Streams* into *Nô*.

Le confessionnal opens with a Hitchcockian establishing shot of the same Pont de Québec that will appear in the film's closing frames, along with a voice-over by Pierre that gestures towards that ending and that establishes the disjunctive spatio-temporal poetics that govern the film as a whole, including its multiple diegetic frames: 'Dans la ville où je suis né, le passé porte le présent comme un enfant sure ses épaules.'[23] Immediately bearing this out, there is a cut to shots of the 1953 premiere of Hitchcock's *I Confess* at Quebec City's grand Capitol cinema. Here, the space of our 'real' present-tense viewing of *Le confessionnal* starts to merge with the spatio-temporality of Lepage's fictional intradiegetic spectators' viewing of Hitchcock's film. This is enhanced by Pierre's voice-over, which recalls – as the camera focuses first on his aunt, Jeanne d'Arc (Lynda Lepage-Beaulieu, the director's sister), then on the swollen belly of his mother, Françoise (Marie Gignac) – that there were actually three Lamontagnes attending the screening that night. In the next scene, the now-adult Pierre is shown arriving home to attend the funeral of his father, Paul-Émile (François Papineau), who recently died after a long battle with diabetes. Thereafter, the film cuts back and forth between the 'present' diegesis of 1989 and the 'past' diegesis of 1952.

The outer frame narrative concerns Pierre's attempts to reconnect with his estranged adopted brother Marc. Having secured a job as a bellboy at the Chateau Frontenac courtesy of his cousin, André (Richard Fréchette), Pierre one day spies his brother by chance exiting in a fury from the room of an older diplomat, Monsieur Massicotte. Inveigling his way into Massicotte's room, Pierre learns that Marc is working as a male prostitute, and eventually tracks him down at a local gay sauna. Over drinks, the brothers discuss their complicated family history, including Marc's unhappy relationship with their father and the suicide of his unmarried birth mother, Rachel (Suzanne Clément), who was Françoise's sister and thus Pierre's aunt. Pierre resolves to help Marc track down the identity of his biological father, which leads to a trip to the suburb of Charny in order to recover an important photo album from Manon, who works as a stripper with her First Nations partner Moose (Billy Merasty) in order to support her son by Marc, a child whom Pierre later learns is, like his father, diabetic.

However, it is Massicotte who holds the key to the identity of Marc's 'real' father; furthermore, he provides the link between the film's past and present narratives. In flashbacks to 1952, we learn that a much younger Massicotte (Normand Daneau) actually began his working life as a priest, serving the church in Quebec City where Hitchcock (Ron Burrage) and his crew are preparing to shoot scenes for *I Confess* under the distressed guidance of Hitchcock's harried female assistant (Kristin Scott Thomas), and where Rachel also works as a *femme de ménage*. No longer able to hide her pregnancy, Rachel is dismissed from her job, but not before confessing to the young Massicotte the identity of her unborn baby's father. Unable to break the seal of confession, and with Rachel unwilling to confirm otherwise, Massicotte is removed from his post after suspicions are aroused in the congregation that he may be Rachel's lover. Meanwhile, an increasingly withdrawn and abject Rachel moves into the cramped home that her sister and brother-in-law – who are themselves trying to have a baby after several miscarriages – share with Paule-Émile's sister, Jeanne d'Arc, and her family.

The two story lines converge in a double denouement that features several cuts between parallel scenes in both time frames: Massicotte revealing to Marc in 1989 that his adopted father is in fact his biological father while they are in a limousine on their way to the airport, where the two men will board a plane for Japan, juxtaposed with Paul-Émile obliquely confessing as much to Hitchcock in February 1953 in his synopsis of a 'suspense story' that he pitches to the director as he drives him back to the Chateau Frontenac following the premiere of *I Confess*; Rachel's suicidal leap off the Pont de Québec in 1952 following the birth of her son, Marc, cuing that son's suicide thirty-seven years later in a bathtub in Japan; and the closing titles and final shot of the Chateau Frontenac at the end of *I Confess* signalling to Hitchcock's 1953 audience that the mystery at the centre of that film has definitely been solved, mirroring Pierre's similar apprehension of the final 'truth' in Massicotte's room at the same hotel at the end of *Le confessionnal*. Bringing his spectators full circle, Lepage's film, like Hitchcock's, closes with a reframed shot of the iconographic landmark with which it opened, the camera tracking Pierre as he places Marc's son on his shoulders and leads him on a vertiginous walk across the lip of the pedestrian guardrail of the Pont de Québec.

I have already demonstrated, via my discussion of Lefebvre and Thérien, how this narrative can be recuperated allegorically into the broader heternormative story of Quebec's national identity crisis. What I want to focus on now is how the queer male character's key symbolic role as the 'fall guy' within that plot – that is, as someone unable to reconcile competing false claims to the 'truth' of his identity, and by extension Quebec's – is policed imagistically by Lepage's camera, how, in other words, the queer male body is framed and disciplined by the quasi-panoptical composition of several of the director's shots. In this regard, it is important to note that the two queer characters in Lepage's film (I will discuss the imaging of the actor Montgomery Clift momentarily) are introduced to the spectator via their positioning within lofty spaces. Massicotte occupies a grand suite in one of the turrets of the Chateau Frontenac (its sweeping marble staircase features prominently in one scene), outside of which Pierre first spies his brother. And when the brothers finally get together to talk properly face to face, following their encounter at the sauna (where, significantly, Marc's body is obscured to Pierre by steam), the meeting takes place in the revolving restaurant at the top of the Quebec City Hilton, which has a 360-degree view of the city and its environs.

These associations, ironically, far from signalling the queer character's reverse panopticism – that is, his ability to return and thereby subvert the minoritizing gaze of heteronormativity – actually position him metonymically even further as the disciplined object of that gaze. In order to understand this, we need to examine more carefully one of the scenes that bridges the two I have just described – namely, the one that takes place at the gay sauna where Pierre finally tracks down Marc. The scene begins at dusk with an exterior shot of the nondescript, opaquely windowed building, which stands isolated on a lonely and deserted street; it is dusk. Pierre enters the frame, pausing to look sideways along the street before crossing it to enter the building. Except for the absence of the requisitely suspenseful music and perhaps some lower key lighting, this is a classic detective story/film noir sequence, one usually meant to bestir anxiety in the viewer for the detective-hero who has come to investigate a mysterious lead: Who on earth would come here? Whatever for? What dangers lurk behind those doors?

In the lobby, Pierre is greeted by a wary front desk clerk, who with mild disdain ('Do you want a room, or are you just here to look at our Christmas decorations?') surveys Pierre's scrutiny of the Tom of Finland wall drawings and the sign-in list. He comments to Pierre that no one in their right mind would use their real name at a gay sauna – a reminder of the continued need for anonymity in a community whose sexual spaces are still subject to routine raids by the police. Hence, as well, the double coding of the goldfish bowl on the clerk's counter, into which Pierre peers upon entering the sauna: placing oneself on display inside such a space is potentially subject to exterior surveillance as well. As if to bear this out, once Pierre has found his room and changed into his towel, Lepage's camera begins to track his search for Marc from an overhead angle, pulling back panoptically to reveal, through the wire mesh atop their cubicles, all that the men are getting up to inside of them (which isn't much, admittedly) (see Figure 5.1). The guarantee of anonymity – long a constituent feature of public gay sex – no longer holds in this space. The queer male body, even when it does not want to be found out, will be exposed and put on display by Lepage's all-seeing camera, as when, at the end of this scene, the outline of Marc's naked body emerges from the steam to be framed alongside his brother's towelled one in the doorway to the shower area.

Lepage's panoptical framing of this gay sauna scene might not seem so significant were it not for the fact that he employs a similar overhead camera angle three more times in the film. Each time it is Marc's body being framed by the shot (see Figures 5.2, 5.3, and 5.4). The first instance again takes place at the sauna, and again the camera is looking down through the grille atop a cubicle; this time it captures a naked Marc – to whom Pierre has just disclosed that, according to Jeanne d'Arc, Rachel killed herself because her baby's father was a priest – curled up in the fetal position. The second instance occurs in the limousine that will take Marc and Massicotte from the motel in Charny to the airport and their flight to Japan; there, in the back seat, with the camera looking down through the open sun roof, Massicotte prepares to correct Pierre's previous misinformation, by tell-

5.1   *Le confessionnal*: Overhead shot of the gay sauna where Pierre tracks down Marc.

ing Marc the truth about his parentage. The last of these overhead shots records Marc's suicide in Japan; standing up in the sunken bathtub, the blood from his slashed wrists trickling down his body, Marc falls backwards into the water, and the camera tracks back quickly to reveal a top shot of his submersion. Just as the jacuzzi jets begin, the water starts turning red. All three shots occur just after or just before Marc receives crucial information about his family and about his own place within that sphere. Here I am suggesting that their combined imagistic weight adds up to a policing of the queer male body as forever outside – *even when inside* – the bourgeois family, to the point of Marc's ultimate self-disciplining of his own body through the act of suicide.

Arguably, something similar happens in terms of Massicotte's association with another Foucauldian space of sexual self-disciplining – namely, the confession box.[24] Early in the film, during one of the 1952 flashback scenes, Massicotte is shown hearing Rachel's confession. The young priest is visibly nervous; he is clearly receiving news he does not want to hear – news that, like that received by Montgomery Clift's Father Logan from the killer, Keller, in *I Confess*, he must keep secret because of the seal of the confessional, but that, paradoxically, will have the effect of framing him (like Logan) for a crime he did not commit. This points to how the confessional, far from being a space that disciplines the congregation (as

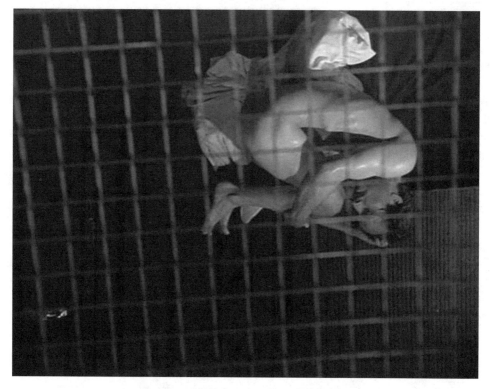

5.2   *Le confessionnal*: Overhead shot of Marc (Patrick Goyette) in the gay sauna.

its prominent presence within the nave of most churches is meant to), in this case serves to frame and discipline Massicotte. His extended time within its confines with a now visibly pregnant Rachel later in the film comes to serve as evidence, in the congregation's mind, of his guilt by association. In this regard, I would argue that the grille that separates Rachel from Father Massicotte in the confessional box in the 1952 flashback scene described above, like the grille above the cubicles in the gay sauna, becomes a symbol of the social constraints faced by the queer male when placed in the context of a later flashback scene. Massicotte, now facing pressure from the congregation and his clerical superiors to resign, visits Rachel at home to beg her to reveal to all that he is not the father of her child. Rachel refuses to let him in, and he is forced to speak to her through the grille of the doorframe. This is a striking visual representation of Massicotte's own imprisonment and a reminder, in the context of what the audience knows about him from the 1989 frame narrative, that there would be another way for him to prove to the congregation that he is not Rachel's lover: by declaring that he is homosexual.

Of course, it's really no choice at all – either way, Massicotte would be forced to leave the priesthood. In this respect, Lepage's film represents, as Garrity suggests (drawing on the work of French film critics Raymond Durgnat and André Bazin), a far more 'ruthless' updating of Hitchcock's film, in which 'the self-contained

5.3   *Le confessionnal*: Overhead shot of Marc (l) and Massicotte (Jean-Louis Millette) in the limousine that will take them to the airport.

Jansenistic priest of *I Confess* who escapes punishment despite his own inaction is transformed by Lepage into one who suffers humiliation and degradation, never succeeding in rehabilitating himself with his church or parishioners.'[25] This is a reminder that there is another queer male 'framed' within Lepage's film: Montgomery Clift. Although he appears as Father Logan only in one brief excerpted scene from *I Confess* (significantly, the one where he first discovers Keller hiding at the back of his church), the flashing of his name on the screen-within-the-screen at the start of Lepage's film necessarily interpolates him as a crucial absent presence throughout *Le confessionnal*, and one even more crucially tied to policed and disciplined images of the queer male body. As Deleuze notes at one point in his discussion of the crystal-image, the film-within-the-film 'has often been linked to the consideration of a surveillance, an investigation, a revenge, a conspiracy, a plot.'[26] In the case of Clift's role as the tortured priest in *I Confess*, who not only is unable to declare his innocence of murder but who also is unable to return the love of the female protagonist, Anne Baxter, one site of surveillance must necessarily be the actor's own sexuality. Indeed, Clift's equally tortured life off screen is a reminder that the closet is as powerful a space of self-disciplining as the confessional.

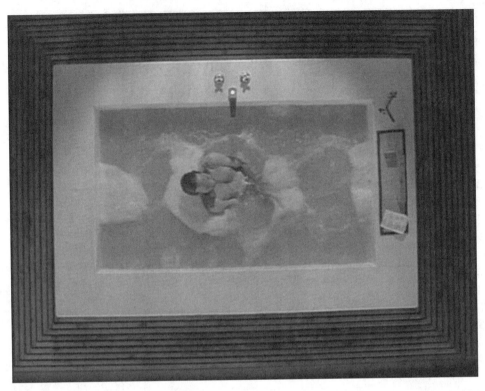

5.4 *Le confessionnal*: Overhead shot of Marc committing suicide in the bath in Japan.

Le polygraphe: Hiding the Body

Lepage's second film, *Le polygraphe*, is based on the play of the same name that he conceived of, co-wrote, and co-starred in alongside long-time friend and collaborator Marie Brassard. It premiered in Quebec City in May 1988 in a French-language production directed by Lepage for Théâtre Repère. The play was subsequently produced in an English translation (by Gyllian Raby) at Toronto's Harbourfront in February 1990, again with Lepage directing, and with Lepage and Brassard playing the roles of David and Lucie alongside Pierre Philippe Guay's François. It is this latter version that Lepage chose to have tour the world, as well as to be published – first in a 1990 issue of *Canadian Theatre Review*, and then in several anthologies of modern Canadian drama that have appeared since.[27] For the film version, however, Lepage reverted to French dialogue, although not without first radically revisioning the original script.

The play begins with a prologue: against the backdrop of a brick wall that runs the entire length of the stage, and on which – à la film's opening credit sequences – are projected slides flashing various titles and cast and crew names, Lucie Champagne reads from an autopsy report of a female murder victim and David Haussman talks about the construction of the Berlin Wall. The two characters, oblivious to each other's presence, speak in counterpoint, their dialogue occasionally over-lapping and even synchronizing. As if caught in a film loop, the scene, once ended, repeats itself, only this time at a faster pace, culminating in the appearance of the naked body of François Tremblay above and behind the wall, with anatomical slides of '*bones, muscles and organs superimposed on his flesh*' (P 652). The prologue is called 'The Filter,' and the rest of the play slowly brings into sharper focus the complex interrelationships among these three characters by juxtaposing, among other things, the weight of the past with the terror of the present, the inability to forget with the inability to remember, a policing from without by the state with a policing from within by the self, performative effect with embodied affect.

David, we learn, is a criminologist who escaped from East Berlin and now works at a forensics institute in Montreal. He meets Lucie when they witness a suicide in a Metro station and they slowly begin a relationship. Lucie, an actress from Quebec City, has just been cast as the murder victim in a film based on an actual unsolved case, for which François, her gay neighbour, remains the prime suspect. François maintains that he is innocent and has even taken a lie detector test to prove it, but the police assert that the results were inconclusive, and their continued harassment, together with their failure to find the real murderer, begins to take its toll on him physically and mentally. At the end of the play, no longer able to remember with any certainty where he was or what he was doing on the night of the murder, François takes his own life (by also jumping in front of a sub-way train) rather than live with the imagined guilt. Meanwhile, the audience learns that David has his own secrets: he left a former lover behind when he escaped to the West, and in the play's penultimate scene it is revealed that he not only administered the lie detector test to François but also planted the seeds of doubt in him about the validity of his testimony – in order, paradoxically, 'to use the spontaneous emotional reaction of the witness as the ultimate proof of his innocence' (P 682). At this point, the stage directions indicate, 'François *leaps to his feet, tearing off the electrodes, beside himself with rage and panic. He is screaming and crying that he has told the truth, again and again and again, he has told the truth, and that the truth will never be enough for them but it's all that he has … he breaks down and stumbles out of view*' (P 682; ellipsis in original).

Early on in the play, David boldly states that 'the body never lies' (P 652), although what Michael Sidnell has identified as the 'instrumental' operations of 'somatic truth' in this play relate as much – if not more – to what sexual acts François voluntarily chooses to have performed upon his own body as they do to what was involuntarily visited upon the body of the murder victim, Marie-Claude Légaré, whom we are told was raped before being stabbed repeatedly.[28] That is, the play version of *Le polygraphe* makes it clear that François, who is a gay masochist, is the subject of a police investigation in part because of his perceived 'criminal' sexuality; and that his feelings of guilt and self-doubt derive in no small measure from the shame he is made to feel in confessing to the police – and, tangentially, to Lucie – the pleasure he gets from pain. This autocritique is largely absent from Lepage's film adaptation, which, in its narrative and imagistic polic-ing of the play, shifts the hermeneutics of truth, as applied to the queer male body, from detection to cover-up.

5.5   *Le polygraphe*: François (Patrick Goyette, l) is hooked up to the polygraph machine by Hans (James Hyndman).

To this end, the all-important polygraph scene, which closes the play, opens the film, a temporal relocation that spatially abstracts the forensic thrust of the action that follows. Specifically, Lepage uses the opening credit sequence to capture with diagnostic precision the head, torso, arms, and fingers of François (Patrick Goyette) as they are being hooked up to all manner of wires, straps, electrodes, and patches (see Figure 5.5), as well as, through time lapse dissolves, the prosthetic record of his responses to the questions put to him by the technician Hans (James Hyndman), whom we later learn is an old friend of Christof (Peter Stormare), the film's reworked version of the David character from the play.

What is significant about how this scene has been adapted for film – apart from who is asking the questions this time around and the fact that Lepage once again employs a series of top shots to frame François's body – is that the audience not only witnesses François's self-declaration of innocence at the start of the film's narrative diegesis (rather than at the close of the play's), but also in effect has 'objective' corroboration of this in the form of the polygraph needle's steady and unwavering movement over the course of Hans's endless stream of printout pages. Whereas in the play the audience is left to wonder about the *othered* François's innocence or guilt until the very end, Lepage's film works to solicit spectators' identification with the character from its opening frames, thereby transferring the weight of narrative suspense to the question of who *other than*

François is responsible for the murder of Marie-Claire (Marie-Christine Le Huu), and what exactly the police might be trying to cover up in fudging the truth to François about the results of his polygraph test. Here, again, the presence of a film within a film serves as an important 'mode of the crystal-image.'[29] Yet while the scenes documenting the making, editing, and broadcast of Judith's (Josée Deschênes) film about Marie-Claire's murder do, in the end, resolve the generic conspiracy at the heart of Lepage's crime drama – by revealing, eventually, the identity of the murderer – they also perpetuate further conspiracies relating to gender by confirming that the only alibi François ever needed was his heterosexuality.

I am referring to the fact that among the changes made in the film version of *Le polygraphe*, one is the addition of a back story (absent from the play) which informs the spectator not only that François and Marie-Claire were lovers who had had a quarrel the night of her murder, but also that while she was seeking comfort from her best friend, Judith, he was getting drunk in a bar, allowing himself to be picked up by Marie-Claire's sister, Claude (Maria de Medeiros), with whom François had had a previous affair. In scenes of double parallel montage near its conclusion, the film cuts temporally and spatially from Judith and François talking about the night of the murder in her Montreal editing studio to Lucie (Marie Brassard) showing Claude the empty apartment of François in Quebec City; and from shots of Judith's film's in-the-end false intra-diegetic reconstruction of the murder (she blames the cops because, as she tells Lucie in an earlier scene, they made her doubt, for a time, François's innocence) to Claude's flashbacks of what really happened – namely, that she, in a fit of jealousy, had stabbed her sister and set fire to her apartment. In other words, in the film it is François's relative gender normativity that, as it were, gets him off.

I say relative because the film does at the very least indicate that the erotic basis of François and Marie-Claire's relationship was partially informed by S/M sexual practices. In a scene just prior to François's departure for Montreal, Lucie confronts him in his bathroom about what she has learned about his relationship with Marie-Claire during the making of Judith's film; he tells her that she does not know everything, and proceeds to blindfold her and tie her hands to the washbasin with a leather belt (see Figure 5.6). Then, before hitting and breaking the bathroom mirror in rage, he says that he sometimes tied up Marie-Claire when they made love. Yet even here, the scene is a relatively sanitized version (complete with a well-scrubbed white tile floor) of the one from the play on which it is based, not least because the queer male body is hidden – or covered up – and because the belt is transferred from a signifier of male masochism to one of male sadism.

In the play, when Lucie stops by François's apartment to return a book on male orgasm that he had loaned her, he explains to her that one of the functions of the belt is as a device for auto-asphyxiation during masturbation: 'Quand je me masturbe, j'me sers de ça. J'tire pis j'lâche, j'tire pis j'lâche. Pis, juste avant de venir, j'tire de plus en plus fort … Mais un moment donné, y faut qu'tu lâches–si tu veux pas venir pour la dernière fois' (*P* 677; ellipsis in original).[30] He then demonstrates another of the belt's applications, blindfolding Lucie and tying her, like his screen

5.6   *Le polygraphe*: Lucie (Marie Brassard, l) and François in François's bathroom.

surrogate, to the washbasin. However, in the ensuing dialogue he informs Lucie that in the case of his own sexual practices, he is invariably the person being tied up rather than the one doing the tying. Furthermore, this confession to Lucie, delivered in French, is simultaneously translated for the audience into English by David, who – it soon becomes clear – is actually reading from a transcript of François's police interrogation in connection with the murder of Marie-Claude. By contrast, in Lepage's film version of *Le polygraphe*, we never witness François divulging his sexual secrets to anyone other than Lucie, and even then those secrets serve not so much to demonstrate his vulnerability as to confirm his power.

In the end, the queer male body in *Le polygraphe* is most hidden when it is most exposed. In order to understand what I mean by this, it is important to note that in addition to the insertion of the crucial back story mentioned above, there are several key shots of actor Patrick Goyette's back in the film. Here, *Le polygraphe* is linked metonymically to *Le confessionnal* not only through the casting of Goyette in the respective roles of François and Marc, but also in terms of how, in both films, the actor's naked body is framed by the camera. That is, just as in *Le confessionnal* Lepage uses a series of panoptical top shots during key scenes featuring Marc, so does he shoot François from above not only during the opening polygraph/credit sequence, but also during another scene early on in *Le polygraphe*.

François is in the bath, bent forward with his head between his knees, so that all

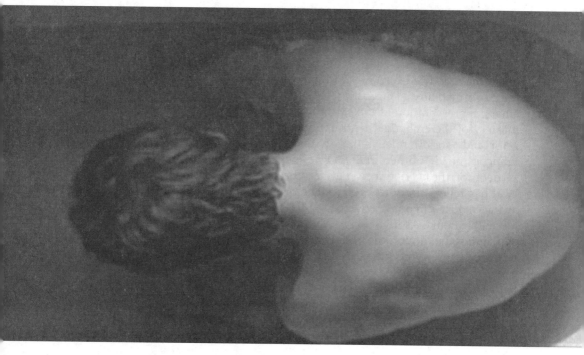

5.7   *Le polygraphe*: François in the bath.

we see of his body is the smooth and unblemished expanse of his naked back (see Figure 5.7). The camera lingers clinically, forensically, as if searching for some tell-tale sign embedded in the skin, a scratch or bump or bruise that might betray a secret that somehow evaded detection by the polygraph machine in the film's opening scene. But there is nothing, no mark of Cain: not in this scene, nor in subsequent ones when François, again fresh from the bath, parades about his apartment shirtless. The François of Lepage's film has nothing to hide. Unlike, say, Christof, who is made to bear the burden of guilt in the film vis-à-vis a betrayal of heteronormativity when it is learned that the wife he left behind in East Berlin has committed suicide now that the Wall has come down. And unlike the François of Lepage's play, whom we witness in a scene titled 'The Flesh' entering a '*crowded gay bar*,' being '*propositioned to have sex in a private room*,' kneeling against a wall, removing '*his shirt ... his belt ... which he gives away*': '*He turns his back, and unzips his pants. As he is beaten, with each sound of the whiplash,* François *physically recoils against the wall. La petite mort and collapse, finally, the exchange is finished. Satisfied, soul weary,* François *gathers his clothes and his shreds of self-esteem*' (P 657–58; ellipses in original). After which, in a follow-up scene, we see François examining the evidence of his night of debauchery and self-abasement in his bathroom mirror, peeling off his leather jacket and T-shirt, and '*craning to see the weals on his back reflected in the small mirror*' (P 661).

A comparison of the play and film versions of *Le polygraphe* yields two very different images of François. Both solicit the (male) viewer's gaze, but whereas the screen François invites identification (including erotic identification), the stage François effects only alienation. How to explain this phenomenon? One way, as I have been suggesting, is in terms of gender: the theatrical representation of the queer male body's excessive 'anti-naturalness' and of its passive acquiescence to the performed lie distances the (stage) actor from the (stage) role; whereas the cinematic representation of the straight male body's proximate 'realism' and active mastery of the embodied truth renders obsolete the distinction between (social) actor and (social) role. (Note, in this regard, the film's concluding image of François, newly minted PhD and no longer a murder suspect, expatiating to his students on the need for trust between East and West Germans now that the Berlin Wall has fallen.) In other words, heterosexuality does not depend on illusion or artifice: it just *is* (a point to which I will return in my reading of *Possible Worlds*). So too with cinema. As my previous language was meant to intimate, another way of explaining the differences between the stage François and the film François is in terms of genre – or, rather, in terms of the *form* or *medium* of representation of each's body. That is, as Steven Shaviro has noted in discussing the differences between theatre and film, whereas theatrical spectatorship depends for its effect on 'the physical presence of the actors' bodies in space,' cinematic spectatorship replaces bodies with images, physical space with virtual space, presence with absence:

> Film's virtual images do not correspond to anything actually present, but *as* images, or *as* sensations, they affect me in a manner that does not leave room for any suspension of my response. I have already been touched and altered by these sensations, even before I have had the chance to become conscious of them. The world I see through the movie camera is one that violently impinges upon me, one that I can no longer regard, unaffected, from a safe distance … The cinematic image, in its violent more-than-presence, is at the same time immediately an absence: a distance too great to allow for dialectical interchange or for any sort of possession.[31]

In this equation, passivity shifts from the actor to the viewer. Which is another way of saying that if in my policing of images of the male body on offer in Lepage's *Le polygraphe*, I am seeking in part to 'uncover' specific representations of the gay masochist, perhaps I need look no further than myself. In this regard, Shaviro, drawing on the work of Kaja Silverman, Leo Bersani, and especially Gilles Deleuze, has argued that film viewing is itself inherently masochistic, and that the ambivalence and abjection and implicit violence I see hidden in Lepage's body-to-image transposition of François from stage to screen are things I myself willingly submit to in choosing to watch the spectacle: 'The aggressive act of filming is only a detour en route to the passivity and self-abandonment of spectatorship. And violence against the Other is finally just an inadequate substitute for the dispossession of oneself. The reflections of masochistic spectacle create a space of superfluity, of violently heightened ambivalence, in which every exercise of power gets lost.'[32]

Nô: Disposing the Body

In an important article examining the 'tragic resiliency' of various homophobic tropes that have helped fuel 'a profound sexual anxiety in Québec's anti-colonial discourse' from the early days of foment during the Quiet Revolution of the 1960s to the post-referendum malaise of the 1980s, Robert Schwartzwald has demonstrated how the queer male body has repeatedly been invoked as a signifer of 'fatal mimicry' in Quebec popular culture, from the jokes about *fédérastes* that routinely appeared in the back pages of the journal *parti pris* in the former era to the representation of the character of Claude in Denys Arcand's *Le déclin de l'empire américain*, which became Quebec's defining film of the latter era.[33] As Schwartzwald explains, *parti pris*'s punning link between federalism and pederasty implies that Quebec's national self-interests have been perverted and corrupted by a predatory and ultimately non-productive English-Canadian system. By contrast, Arcand's apparently innocuous depiction of both the gay Claude's happily non-monogamous pursuit of sexual pleasure and the potentially fatal price he seems to have paid for that pursuit (scenes of him cruising Mont Royal are presented alongside scenes of him pissing blood) in the end suggests that such behaviour is symptomatic of Quebec intellectualism's trading in of its communitarian ideals for American-style individualism, which in turn threatens the future 'propagation' of the community as a whole:

> The theatricalization of homosexuality in the *Déclin* ... betrays the silencing gesture behind a repressive tolerance that seems willing to admit the depiction of homosexuality as something 'normal.' ... In the 1960s, homosexuality for Arcand only exists in relation to a normative dialectic of ALIENATION-REVOLT-REVOLUTION, in which it is appropriately admissible only at the intermediate stage, as something 'in between.' In the 1980s, when Revolution and the question of national independence seem off the agenda and the materialism of the Quiet Revolution triumphant, gay men serve as beacons in whose shadows an entire society's dislocation may be discovered.[34]

In this section I suggest that Lepage's third film, *Nô*, traces a similar representational trajectory over the ten years of its diegesis. I further contend that a reading of the shifting representations of the queer male body within the film requires us to look at how that body has been fatally disposed of in the process of its adaptation from stage to screen.

Shot with super-16 millimetre film in seventeen days on a series of soundstages at Lepage's creative headquarters in Quebec City, La Caserne, for only a million dollars, *Nô* came together as a film almost by accident. When funding for a planned television adaptation of *The Dragons' Trilogy* fell through at the last minute, Lepage and his Ex Machina team found themselves with a two-month hole in their otherwise hectic work schedule. Having already collaborated with Francis Leclerc on the script for Leclerc's sixty-two-minute television condensation of *The Seven Streams of the River Ota*, and nursing perhaps ambivalent memories of what happened the last time he entrusted the adaptation of one of his theatrical works to another filmmaker (as, for example, with Peter Mettler's hit-and-miss take on *Tectonic Plates*), Lepage decided to try his own hand at bringing a portion of this material to the screen.[35]

Nô, the film that resulted, is based on Section 5 ('The Words') of *Seven Streams*. The play, which in its epic entirety comprises seven parts staged over seven successive hours, was developed collaboratively over a three-year period with the members of Ex Machina, and subsequently toured to more than twenty-five different stages around the world. Its plot, which spans fifty years, moves back and forth in time and space between Japan, the United States, and Europe. It incorporates more than fifty speaking roles in four different languages (English, French, Japanese, and German) and employs all manner of metatheatrical and metarepresentational devices (including still photographic and moving video projections, plays-within-plays, opera, dance, magic, puppetry, mirrors and moving screens, simultaneous translation, and supertitles) to foreground the processes of spectatorship and cultural mediation. Even more boldly, *Seven Streams* also attempts to make political and historical sense of such cataclysmic world events as the Holocaust, the bombing of Hiroshima, and AIDS in terms of a recurring set of aesthetic oppositions: between East and West, life and death, tragedy and comedy, masculinity and femininity.

Wisely, Lepage narrowed his scope for the eighty-five-minute *Nô*. In the film he has chosen to focus on the story of Sophie (Anne-Marie Cadieux), a Québécoise actress starring in a production of Georges Feydeau's nineteenth-century French farce *Dame de chez Maxim* as part of Canada's cultural program at the 1970 World's Fair in Osaka, Japan. Sophie, with the aid of Hanako (Marie Brassard), a blind Japanese translator attached to the show, has just learned that she is pregnant, and she is not sure if the father is her co-star, François-Xavier (Éric Bernier) or her boyfriend, Michel (Alexis Martin), a writer who, back in Montreal, has suddenly been thrust into the thick of the October Crisis thanks to an unexpected visit by radical but technically inept friends intent on planting a bomb. After the concluding performance of the Feydeau play, Sophie finds herself at dinner with the cultural attaché from the Canadian embassy in Tokyo, Walter (Richard Fréchette), and his annoyingly superior wife, Patricia (Marie Gignac). With Patricia supposedly on her way back to Tokyo and Sophie desperate to avoid a confrontation with François-Xavier, Walter ends up escorting an increasingly drunk Sophie back to her hotel and, we eventually discover, sleeping with her. When both Patricia, who has missed her train, and François-Xavier wind up in her hotel room shouting accusations and mutual recriminations, life and art start to overlap as Sophie finds herself an unwilling participant in her own bedroom farce.

Meanwhile, back in Montreal, Michel has been labouring over the wording of the political message that will be attached to his friends' bomb, as well as under the misapprehension that the clock being used to set the bomb's detonator is telling the local time, as opposed to the time in Japan, which Michel has also been keeping track of in order to gauge Sophie's periodic phone calls. Realizing their mistake, the would-be anarchists beat a hasty retreat from the apartment; the inevitable explosion that follows coincides with Sophie's return from Japan. The

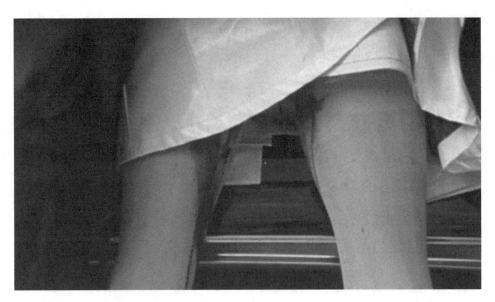

5.8 *Nô*: Sophie (Anne-Marie Cadieux) suffers a miscarriage as she is being arrested.

two narratives, whose temporal and spatial distinctiveness has to this point been signposted by the scenes in Montreal being filmed in black and white and the scenes in Japan in colour, merge in a key scene where Sophie is arrested by Bélanger (Tony Conte) and Ménard (Jules Philip), plainclothes detectives who have been keeping her and Michel's apartment under surveillance all along. The shift from black and white to colour that occurs near the midpoint of this scene chromatically connects the intra-diegetic media footage of the 1980 Quebec referendum results that follows in the film's epilogue with similar intra-diegetic footage of Pierre Trudeau being interviewed about introducing the War Measures Act to deal with the FLQ in the 1970s, which was used at the start of the film. Furthermore, this scene's focalization of the spectator's gaze on the blood flowing down Sophie's legs as a result of the miscarriage brought on by her arrest serves as a syntagma that connects the various overlapping discourses of nationalism and sexuality throughout the film (see Figure 5.8).

In this regard, it is first of all important to note that in an earlier scene in the film, the police officers arresting Sophie are explicitly depicted as *fédérastes* of the sort derided in the pages of *parti pris* (as described above) – that is, as duplicitous not only in terms of their collaboration with the state in that they are spying on their nationalist brothers, but also in terms of their attempts to hide the true nature of their domestic *ménage*. I am referring here to an especially hilarious scene in which the police officers, while staking out Michel and Sophie's apartment from what they believe to be an unoccupied apartment across the street, are interrupted by the landlady, who is attempting to show the place to a pair of prospective renters. While Agent Bélanger attempts to keep her at bay by blocking the door, Agent Ménard quickly hides their surveillance equipment on the floor,

5.9   *Nô*: Agent Ménard (Jules Philip, l) tries to play it cool in front of the landlady (Nathalie D'Anjou).

covering it with the roll-out cot from the hide-a-bed sofa, on which he promptly installs himself in a languorous pose (see Figure 5.9). This is how Lepage and André Morency's script describes the ensuing shot: '*Poussant son interlocuteur, la concierge entre énergiquement et s'immobilise aussi-tôt en voyant l'autre policier étendu nonchalamment sur le divan-lit. Outrée, croyant avoir affaire à un couple homosexuel, elle les foudroie du regard. Se méprenant également sur l'identité sexuelle des policiers, les visiteurs, eux-mêmes homosexuels, leur jettent des regards entendus, tentant d'établir une connivence qui embarrasse singulièrement les représentants des forces de l'ordre.*'[36]

This scene, like most in the film, is played for laughs. In a social satire of the sort directed here by Lepage, one should no doubt be cautious about taking grave personal offence over broad stereotypes employed for comic effect. Still, in the context of the long-entrenched symbolic associations of homosexuality in Québécois culture that I have been sketching throughout this chapter, it is hard not to take away a wearisomely familiar message. That the queer male body is being overwritten with/by the 'forces of order' in this scene means, concomitantly, that it cannot also be linked with the forces of revolution and change. Hence the gay couple blithely out shopping for an apartment while all around them the world is exploding. And hence the queer 'self-abortion' that in some senses constitutes Sophie's miscarriage at the hands of these same *fédéraste* police officers.[37]

Let me be clear: I do not wish to indict Lepage for his failure to produce positive images of queerness here, or elsewhere in his cinema. Rather, to come back to the ambivalent heterogeneity of Deleuze's time-image, I want to suggest that the virtual traces of national memory in Lepage's films, and in Québécois cinema generally, are in part sustained by a willed sexual amnesia in the actual present, whereby a teleological vision of progress paradoxically preserves a heteronormative link between past repression and future liberation. Here it is worth examining more closely the conclusion of *Nô*, which flashes forward from October 1970 to 20 May 1980, the night of Quebec's first referendum on sovereignty-association.

As Sophie and a newly yuppified Michel watch dispiritedly the television results confirming a victory for the 'No' side, Michel expounds on his theory to explain the loss: 'Les gens qui ont un project collectif sont toujours un peu désavantagés par rapport aux gens qui ont pas de project. Dans le sens où les gens qui ont pas de projet ont toujours la force d'inertie avec eux. L'idée, c'est que ça prend toujours plus d'énergie pour changer les formes politiques, les formes sociales, que ... que rien faire.'[38] To Sophie's response that the 'common project' of the No side in the referendum must surely be the idea of a unified Canada, Michel scoffs: 'C'est un peu immobile comme projet, non?'[39] He then suggests that perhaps he and Sophie need a common project – beyond, that is, living together – something that looks to 'posterity,' something, for example, like a child. Incredulous, Sophie asks him whether he would have considered that a worthy 'common project' ten years earlier, at the start of their relationship. To which Michel replies that it wouldn't have been the same thing ten years ago: 'Y'a dix ans, on était occupé à changer le monde ... Les temps ont changé.'[40] The scene ends with Sophie – who clearly intends not to tell Michel about her earlier failed pregnancy – gradually acceding to Michel's increasingly amorous arguments, assenting to the idea of a baby in an escalating series of percentages – she goes from being 40.5 per cent sure, to 49 per cent, to 50 per cent, and then finally 50.5 per cent – that mirror the closeness of the numbers for and against sovereignty in Quebec's second referendum.

Indeed, it is impossible not to read this scene in light of the events of 1995. The film's release date of 1998, combined with the appearance of Jean Chrétien as a talking head in some of the television footage shown of the 1980 referendum, ensures that Sophie and Michel's conversation will resonate with both Québécois and English-Canadian audiences. Not least because of the discourse surrounding reproduction that emerged over the course of the 1995 campaign, with sovereigntist leaders like Lucien Bouchard and Jacques Parizeau urging *pure laîne* Québécois to do their bit to reverse the plummeting provincial birth rate (among the lowest in North America) in order to offset, among other things, the inevitable anti-nationalist consequences of 'les votes ethniques' and, by extension, 'les votes *fédérastes*.' This confluence of discourses of racial and sexual difference in the context of Quebec self-determination, as encoded by the ending of Lepage's *Nô*, leads us back to *The Seven Streams of the River Ota* and explains, paradoxically, why Sophie's miscarriage is, in some respects, absolutely necessary.

In the narrative universe of the play, Pierre – the son that results from Sophie's drunken liaison with the Canadian diplomatic toady Walter – is both a born *fédéraste* and a future gay libertine. He is voracious in his pursuit of new experiences and pleasures, and equally opportunistic in his consumption of different cultures and different genders. Indeed, when he should be back in Quebec performing his nationalist duty by voting in the referendum, the Pierre of *Seven Streams* is actually in Japan learning to dance like a woman: one of the last images we see in the play is of him dressed in a Japanese wedding kimono, his face covered in white make-up, '[performing] a butoh dance in which a woman moves gracefully, then experiences a moment of terror and pain.'[41] Is it any wonder that such an image is excised from the film version of *Nô*? In the 'common project' that is the Quebec national imaginary, the queer male body is, fundamentally, disposable. Like the Oriental body, it functions as an arrested Other against which to measure the normative progress of an autonomous selfhood; but, also like the Oriental body, it is in the end unassimilable.[42]

Possible Worlds: Ransacking the Body

Lepage's *Possible Worlds* opens, in classic crime genre style, with another familiar overhead shot of a corpse. The camera focuses, from the inside, on a window cleaner (Griffith Brewer), who is busy washing, from the outside, the curtainless floor-to-ceiling windows of a trendy condominium loft. As he gradually wipes away the soap suds with deft strokes of his squeegee, he is able to see inside the condo, whereupon he makes a shocking discovery: the dead body of its owner splayed across the sofa. We then cut to the arrival on the scene of Detective Berkley (Sean McCann), who learns from his partner, Williams (Rick Miller), the identity of the murder victim – George Barber (Tom McCamus), a successful stockbroker. He also learns what makes this particular crime so gruesome: the killer has neatly sawn off the top part of his victim's skull and absconded with the brain. Lepage's fourth film, *Possible Worlds* represents a departure from the director's previous work in a number of significant ways. First, it is Lepage's cinematic debut in English. Second, the film's cast is largely composed of non-Théâtre Repère and Ex Machina actors (with whom Lepage was working for the first time). And finally, while the film is based on a previously staged dramatic work, it is not, this time, one by Lepage. Instead, he is adapting John Mighton's 1992 Governor General's Award-winning play of the same name. However, a brief analysis of the plot and structure of Mighton's play reveals some familiar Lepage themes, including the parallelling and overlapping of different temporal and spatial realms, the repetition and replaying of scenes of personal connection and disconnection between characters, the mourning of a lost love object, and the unravelling of a mystery whose solution is in some fundamental sense beyond imagination.

   In the case of *Possible Worlds*, this mystery concerns not just who stole George's brain, and why, but also the exact nature of his relationship with his wife, Joyce (played in the film by British actress Tilda Swinton). To summarize, both the play and the film – like all of Lepage's films – follow two (at the very least, as we shall soon see) separate narrative temporalities, flashing back from the opening scene described above to trace the initial meeting, the falling in love, and (it's briefly suggested) the subsequent estrangement of George and Joyce. But even here, in the flashback narrative, there are further diegetic layers. In one version of events, George and Joyce meet in the cafeteria of the hospital where she works as a research biologist – or rather re-meet, as it soon becomes clear that they are from the same small town in Northern Ontario. George is fascinated by this coinci-

dence and sees it as a sign that they are meant to be together, while Joyce is initially sceptical of George's motives and remains deliberately aloof. In another
possible scenario that both theatre and film audiences witness, the couple meet in
a crowded downtown bar, with a coquettish Joyce, who now seems to be working
as a stockbroker in the same office as George, this time aggressively pursuing a
liaison.

These scenes, and others documenting further stages in the couple's twin relationships, are repeated throughout the play and film, dramatizing what George
describes to Joyce at one point as the metaphysical romance of human intercon-
nection – that 'Each of us exists in an infinite number of possible worlds. In one
world I'm talking to you right now but your arm is a little to the left, in another
world you're interested in that man over there with the glasses, in another you
stood me up two days ago – and that's how I know your name.'[43] Meanwhile, in
the present tense of the crime narrative, the play and film's other couple, Berkley
and Williams, who kibitz, cajole, and generally annoy each other as if they've
been married for several years, trace the theft of George's brain to a Doctor Penfield, renamed Doctor Keiber in the film (and creepily played by Gabriel Gascon).
Penfield is a neurologist who has been stockpiling the cerebella of very intelligent
and powerful people (in one scene we learn that George's success as a stockbroker
is due in no small measure to his superior math skills) as a way of 'extracting
information from them' (PW 27). As Penfield puts it to Berkley early on in the
play, before he is even a suspect: 'The question is why do we have imaginations?'
(PW 26). And what possible futures do we imagine for ourselves, and with who
else? Again to quote Penfield: 'Everything you think, Inspector, even the most
trivial fantasy, leaves a trace, a disturbance in that field. I'm trying to learn how to
control those disturbances' (PW 26).

What, one might well ask, has any of this to do with representations of the
queer male body? Arguably nothing and everything. That is, George's fantasies of
heterosexual happiness with Joyce – who may or may not be the same 'wife'
whom George repeatedly claims died three years ago in another of his possible
lives – would depend, as we've seen from my applications of Judith Butler's theories of gender melancholia to Fortune and Men's Eyes in the previous chapter, on
the trace signs of another 'disturbing' fantasy that he has repudiated – namely,
homosexuality. In other words, Doctor Penfield/Keiber might not be the only one
trying to 'control' George's imagination. George's own obsessive replaying of his
life with Joyce – which, remember, is only ever presented as but one of a number
of possible scenarios – might betray certain anxieties around the equally possible
'fictiveness' of his presumed heterosexual gender. But what images of the queer
male body are there in Lepage's film to support such a claim? None other, I would
argue, than that of George's corpse itself. Let me conclude my reading of Possible
Worlds by trying to explain.

Monique Wittig has argued that 'the straight mind continues to affirm that
incest, and not homosexuality, represents its major interdiction. Thus, when
thought by the straight mind, homosexuality is nothing but heterosexuality.'[44]
Likewise, Butler has theorized normative heterosexual gender identification as a
kind of melancholia in which unresolved same-sex desire is internalized as a pro-

5.10   *Possible Worlds*: Detective Berkley (Sean McCann, centre) surveys the blood from George's (Tom McCamus) corpse.

hibition that precedes the incest taboo.[45] Homosexuality, in other words, is – to use terminology borrowed from two other classic essays by Wittig – nothing more than a 'fiction,' but a necessary one, whose symbolic otherness helps constitute and maintain the 'heterosexual contract.'[46] Thus, structuring the various versions of George and Joyce's marriage contract that we witness throughout the course of Lepage's film is, I would argue, another 'possible world,' another window of gender identification, one that is made available to the spectator in its opening minutes.

As Detectives Berkley and Williams and their fellow boys in blue circle George's corpse looking for evidence and a motive for the crime, and thus policing to a certain extent our generic reading of the scene, Lepage's camera swoops down from the upper reaches of the loft, lingering almost pornographically over the body of actor Tom McCamus, who is splayed across the back of his sofa, shirt front open to the waist, a look of absolute ecstasy on his face (see Figure 5.10). In short, George is made into an object of desire for the viewer, even if only clinical desire, *and regardless of the gender of that viewer*. And here our screen surrogates are none other than the homothetical couple of Berkley and Williams; as the camera makes clear, their close inspection of George's body, like the surveillance of Sophie and Michel's apartment by Agents Bélanger and Ménard in *Nô*, is lovingly professional. As Loiselle has perceptively noted, by opening his film with an image of George's corpse, 'Lepage transforms every scene into a clinical examina-

tion of the body of George to understand his lives': 'The whole film, with its blu-
ish hues and its clinical, distant, static, impersonal camera work, can be seen as
adopting an autopsic mode of observation, as perusing the bodies of the actors to
understand the cause of their devolution.'[47] If, in Butler's and Wittig's readings of
Freudian and Lacanian psychoanalysis, homosexual cathexis must precede ego
identification and the successful resolution of the Oedipal complex, then this is
the scene in Lepage's film which performs most spectacularly that rupture, and
which perforce haunts our reading of all subsequent images in the film, especially
those involving George.

To this end, it is important to note that the opening image of George's body
draped provocatively across his sofa is repeated at a later point in the film; this
time, however, George wakes up to the realization that he is merely suffering
from a massive hangover and that he has just slept with Joyce #2, the stockbroker.
Moreover, consider the opening scene as I have discussed it in relation to the
speech by Joyce #1 that closes both the play and the film: 'The word "not" is really
magical. I could describe something and say – "But it's *not* that, it's something
more" – and you'd know what I meant. It's a way of getting around our ignorance. That's how they used to describe God. Everything we can't conceive of. We
say "Things might not have been the way they are," and feel free or uneasy. But
there's really nothing behind it. Just a bunch of ghostly possibilities. Because, in
the end, everything simply is' (*PW* 74).

My argument about the absent presence of images of the queer male body in
Lepage's film adaptation of *Possible Worlds* likewise coalesces around this inter-
dictive word. Homosexuality is what is 'not' in our culture; it's the ghost in the
machine, of the 'heterosexual matrix' generally,[48] but also of the matrix of cinema
more specifically – a point to which I will return in more detail in the next chapter.
In other words, take away the straight mind and what you are left with is the
queer body.

La face cachée de la lune: Body Doubles

Commenting on the 'recurring appearance of death and suicide in [his] plays,'
Lepage has said that

> there is in death – it may seem terrible to say, but it's nevertheless true – a deep sensu-
> ality, a profound fulfilment of carnal reality. That's why *The Seven Streams of the River
> Ota* is a project about sexuality, a play in which sexuality is omnipresent … In *Poly-
> graph*, death is also an important theme that is constantly linked to sexuality. One of
> the characters is a forensic surgeon. While dissecting a corpse, he explains how the
> flesh is made, how the blood circulates, how the various organs function or no longer
> function. The details are insignificant. What's important is that he has both his hands
> physically immersed in a body.[49]

What is equally important, I would argue – and this significant detail is glossed
over by Lepage – is that the body from *Le polygraphe* that he is here referring to is,
in fact, a queer body, a version of the scene with David and the anonymous

cadaver described above, which appears near the start of the play, repeating itself at the end, this time with 'François' *naked corpse [lying] on the gurney'* (P 683). According to criminologist David, 'the body never lies ... [it] has nothing, whatsoever, to do with your cinematic realism, or fiction' (P 652). But, of course, both narrative film and the theatre depend for much of their impact on a body positioned, necessarily, on the edge of fiction and realism, both in the general terms of actors convincingly embodying characters who are different from their 'real' selves and, for example, in specific cases where an actor might have to 'play dead' on stage or screen. André Loiselle has examined the latter paradox in both separate and comparative analyses of the gay male corpses that lie at the intersection of stage and screen in films adapted from the work of two other Québécois playwrights, René-Daniel Dubois and Michel Marc Bouchard. I want to conclude my reading of Lepage's work by discussing each of those films briefly here, before turning to an examination of Lepage's most recent film adaptation, *La face cachée de la lune* – specifically, how the presence of Lepage's own body within *La face* revises the patterns of queer male signification in his preceding films.

In Jean Beaudin's taut and kinetic film of Dubois's 1985 play *Being at home with Claude*, a young male hustler named Yves (Roy Dupuis) kills his lover, Claude (Jean-François Pichette), while making love to him, and then barricades himself into the office of a prominent Montreal judge with a police inspector (Jacques Godin) for the purpose of explaining why he committed the crime. In John Greyson's heavily stylized English-language adaptation of Michel Marc Bouchard's celebrated 1987 play *Lilies* (*Les feluettes*), a band of convicts in 1952 Quebec, headed by Simon Doucet (Aubert Pallascio), have summoned a Catholic bishop, Bilodeau (Marcel Sabourin), to their prison block under the pretext of having their confessions heard, but really in order to get Bilodeau to confess his role in the death of a teenaged Simon's (Jason Cadieux) lover, Vallier (Danny Gilmore), forty years earlier at a small Catholic boys' college in northern Quebec where all three were students. Both film adaptations have much in common with those of Lepage. For example, both are 'crime dramas' in a broad sense, and both use multiple time frames while maintaining an overall spatial coherence in terms of mise-en-scène (particularly in the outer, 'present tense' frames, which in both films take place in a single room). Also, both have what one might call an especially 'Catholic' intertwining of church and state via the trope of confession; and in *Lilies* at any rate, we are presented with the *mise-en-abîme* of a work of art being produced within a work of art (the convicts stage for Bishop Bilodeau not only the events of 1912, but also a play by Gabriele D'Annunzio – *The Martyrdom of Saint Sebastian* – which the boys were rehearsing at the time). The presence of a queer corpse in each film might suggest further connections with Lepage in terms of a fundamentally abject linking of *homo*sexuality with death, yet I would argue that Beaudin's and Greyson's own narrative policing of their source texts reveals a radical rethinking of the symbolic association of images of the queer male body in both intra- and extra-Québécois cultural production.

In Loiselle's perceptive reading, the corpse that 'lies' at the heart of each film comes to stand for certain formal tensions and performative differences that exist between live theatre and recorded cinema, by foregrounding 'the ambiguous relationship between the stage and the screen as the latter provides the realistic receptacle within which the former's artificiality is acted out'; it also comes to represent 'the diverse levels of betrayal generated by the process of adaptation' itself.[50] Here, Loiselle focuses on a significant change that Greyson makes in the film version of *Lilies* – one that relates to the events that result in Vallier's queer body turning into a corpse. In Bouchard's *play*, Simon sets the fire that ultimately kills Vallier, but their planned double suicide is thwarted by Simon's rescue, at the last minute, by Bilodeau, who is himself in love with Simon. In Greyson's *film*, it is young Bilodeau (Matthew Ferguson) who deliberately starts the blaze, by breaking a kerosene lamp on the floor of the church belfry in which Simon and Vallier are hiding and then locking the door. He then has second thoughts and rushes back (as in the play) to save Simon, but not Vallier.

According to Loiselle, Bouchard has stated that 'the change was made at Greyson's request to avoid the rather pessimistic conclusion that suicide is the only option for young gay lovers.'[51] This might seem like an unnecessary capitulation of a historical narrative to the contemporary whims of political correctness; yet the change – as Loiselle rightly suggests – also serves other functions, one of which, I would argue, is to free imagistically the queer male body – even when in drag – from the burdens of a prescribed nationalist inscription in the ongoing cultural narrative of Quebec's identity crisis. Thus, in the play, Simon is unable to reconcile the opprobrium of his *gen de souche* father, Timothée (played in the film by Gary Farmer), with his love for Vallier, the son of a French countess (played in the film by Brent Carver), and chooses suicide as the only apparent way out of this impasse; whereas in the film it is made very clear that he is able to envision a life lived on his own terms with the man he loves.

While arguably not as politically motivated as Greyson's policing of Bouchard's text, Beaudin's updating of the setting of Dubois's play from July 1967 to July 1991 Montreal, with the Jazz Festival rather than Canada's centenary and Expo celebrations serving as backdrop, serves a similar function. As I have argued in my reading of *Being at home with Claude*, this change sunders to a certain extent the uneasy allegorical alliance between nationalism and homosexuality in Quebec social discourse, by forestalling the institutionalization of this alliance within the historical animus of one stock character (the queer male), and by forcing audiences to assess Yves's murder of Claude (who in the play, we are told, is a 'card-carrying separatist'[52]) in terms other than those of either's sexuality.[53] The film's 'universalizing' and normalizing of Yves's alterity and 'excess of alienation' via a discourse of romanticism that (in the words of Bill Marshall) 'invites *identification*' with the homosexual and his '*amour fou*' is highly problematical on one level; but on another level it reveals that in the Québécois context 'the nationalist master narrative is unable to soak up all these issues, notably homosexuality and human intimacy.'[54]

Another crucial difference between film and play is that Beaudin actually dramatizes Yves's murder of Claude – an event that in Dubois's play occurs offstage, before the action starts. This ten-minute opening sequence, filmed in black and white, cuts back and forth frenetically between wide-angle tracking shots of the teeming city of Montreal and tightly framed close-ups of Claude and Yves making love, before zooming in on the lovers' naked bodies and Yves's slitting of Claude's throat just as they are reaching mutual orgasm. In Loiselle's estimation, this scene serves as a prolegomenon to the subsequent action in the judge's office, in that it visually encodes not only the *how* of Yves's act but also the *why*; in particular, the colourized bright red blood operates as a chromatic and syntagmatic signifier that 'not only encapsulates the antecedents and content of the play but also analogizes the transpositional process' of theatre-to-film adaptation as, in some senses, a death.[55]

Arguably, the blood we see trickling down Marc's wrists in *Le confessionnal*, or pooling on the floor around George's well-appointed sofa in *Possible Worlds*, or running down Sophie's leg as she miscarries in *Nô*, serves a similar function. Significantly, however, in the case of *Le confessionnal* and *Nô*, these scenes of blood emerging from bodies occur at the end of Lepage's films, just prior to black-screen-bracketed epilogues that move the action ahead temporally (in the case of *Le confessionnal* by several months, in the case of *Nô* by a whole decade).[56] Moreover, in the case of *Nô* (which, like Beaudin's *Being at home with Claude*, mixes black-and-white with colour footage), the viewer's chromatic registration of the blood as a syntagma that not only synchronically, or spatially, links Sophie's narrative in Japan with Michel's narrative in Montreal, but also diachronically, or temporally, links both these dieseges from 1970 with the coda set in 1980 that immediately follows, occurs not as a selective bit of colourization within individual frames, but rather as a complete switch of the film stock from black and white to colour for the last time. What this means, among other things, is that unlike Beaudin's prologue, Lepage's epilogue contains no visual trace – no memory-image, to put it in Deleuzean terminology – of Sophie and Michel's virtual past within their actual present that we are witnessing on the screen. Similarly, as I have argued, Lepage's film works hard – particularly in its final few frames – to sever ties with several of the significations proposed by its source text, including that of the (virtual) queer body.

Of course, I am all too aware, in my own gendered and generic policing of Lepage's film images in this chapter, that to a certain extent I am guilty of producing my own corpse, sacrificing the body of the author/auteur on my interpretive altar. As Lepage is the first to admit, in artistic production 'there can be a huge gap between intention and result,'[57] and my assessment of his cinematic corpus must, in the end, remain ambivalent. As much as I question the ideology of many of Lepage's images – including his images of death – I remain in awe of their aesthetic delivery. Zupančič argues that the corpse in Hitchcock's film adaptations of theatrical narratives, the presence of 'this death, is as much a punishment for erasing some fundamental difference between both "fictions" [i.e., cinema and theatre] as it is the price for the re-establishment of this difference.'[58] His comments are a reminder that the self-disciplining aspects inherent in the adaptive process – which, in bridging different narrative media, relies on a telescoping of certain elements and a protracting of others – must not be elided; neither must be the extra-market forces inherent in the film industry, a milieu in which the pressure to recoup an initial outlay of capital might lead to majoritarian, audience-friendly compromises not normally associated with the more esoteric world of the theatre. Deleuze has written perceptively on this, linking the cinema's crystal-image –

which, in its endless reconstitution of the past within the present is as apt a metaphor as any for the phenomenon of adaptation – not only to an initial investment
of time, but also to the unequal space of exchange that is money:

> This is the old curse which undermines the cinema: time is money. If it is true that
> movement maintains a set of exchanges or an equivalence, a symmetry as an invari-
> ant, time is by nature the conspiracy of unequal change or the impossibility of equiva-
> lence ... The crystal-image thus receives the principle which is its foundation:
> endlessly relaunching exchange which is dissymmetrical, unequal and without equiv-
> alence, giving image for money, giving time for images, converting time, the transpar-
> ent side, and money, the opaque side, like a spinning top on its end. And the film will
> be finished when there is no more money left.[59]

In Canada, unfortunately, a lack of money all too often translates into poor distribution and limited theatrical release, even for films made by such internationally respected artists as Lepage. Indeed, his fifth film, *La face cachée de la lune*,
despite having won the FIPRESCI International Critics Prize in the Panorama
Series at the Berlin International Film Festival and a Canadian Genie Award for
Best Adapted Screenplay, played for a scant two weeks in the spring of 2004 at
one art house cinema in Vancouver. Shot in high-definition video, the film is an
adaptation of Lepage's award-winning solo play of the same name, and is set
against the backdrop of the American–Soviet space race and current investiga-
tions into extraterrestrial life. Jumping back and forth in time between the 1950s
and the present day, the film's narrative through-line concerns the complicated
relationship between two Quebec City brothers, Philippe and André (both played
by Lepage himself), and their different responses to the death of their mother
(played in flashbacks by a mute Anne-Marie Cadieux). Not only is *La face* Lepage's most personally memorial film to date (the impetus for the source play came
from the death of Lepage's own mother); not only does it mark his debut as an
actor in one of his own films; but it also sees Lepage, as director, consciously quoting from his previous work. Indeed, I contend that at least one important scene
crucially revises and reorients the scopic regime of queer male images on offer in
Lepage's previous films. Let me conclude this chapter by very briefly trying to
explain what I mean.

The theme of narcissism runs throughout *La face*. Most prominently, it serves as
the theoretical cornerstone of Philippe's twice-rejected PhD thesis in the philosophy of science, which argues that the competition between the American and
Soviet space programs was fuelled not by the desire to seek out and explore new
worlds, but rather by the desire to claim and remake those worlds in each country's national and ideological image. As for Philippe's own self-image, it has been
shaped by childhood memories and battered by adult failures. Still living in the
old family apartment, surrounded by his dead mother's clothes and shoes, he is
unkempt and socially inept. Reduced to taking on a series of menial and under-
paid jobs while he revises his thesis, Philippe is eventually fired as a telemarketer
for the local newspaper for having too many personal conversations. Even his one
shot at academic stardom he manages to sabotage: having been invited to present
his research at a conference in Moscow, he sleeps through his scheduled panel.

5.11   *La face cachée de la lune*: Carl (Marco Poulin) checks out Philippe (Robert Lepage) in the sauna.

Younger brother André could not be more different. A self-absorbed and pompous weatherman on a local television station, he lives in a trendy and well-appointed new condo overlooking the harbour with his equally well-appointed boyfriend, Carl (Marco Poulin). André is the stereotyped embodiment of gay male narcissism, obsessed with surface appearances, both his own and others'. However, just when it looks like Lepage is in danger of once again recycling classic homophobic tropes from Hollywood cinema, he inverts this process by exposing his own body to the minoritizing gaze of the camera.

In a very funny scene midway through the film, Philippe, having put in a desultory workout at a local gym, suddenly finds himself sharing a sauna with Carl. Never having met his brother's boyfriend, Philippe misinterprets Carl's friendly grin and casually provocative legs-splayed pose as a cruise, and rapidly rushes to declare his heterosexual credentials. It is only at this point that Carl reveals his own identity, noting that he immediately recognized Philippe as André's brother owing to the family resemblance. Thereafter, the two men fall into a casual conversation about work, with Philippe evincing surprise at Carl's apparent interest in his research. What I find most interesting about this scene is how it subtly revises the epistemology of surveillance that governs the sauna scene in *Le confessionnal*. Not only is it the straight male who is required to out himself in this space, but it is his body that is subjected to both Carl's and the camera's voyeuristic gaze (see Figure 5.11). That that body is here framed in medium close-ups and a shot–reverse shot sequence of edits rather than via the overhead tracking shots used in *Le confessionnal* also forces us to consider exactly who is policing whom in *La face*. That is, in the necessarily sexualized space of the sauna, Philippe's over-weight, out-of-shape, and pale straight body, when juxtaposed against Carl's tau-ter, tanned, tattooed, and pierced queer one, cannot help but be found wanting.

Moreover, that Philippe's semi-naked, bedraggled, and vulnerable straight body and André's overly clothed, coiffed, and made-up one are both played by Lepage himself, who has openly acknowledged his at times painful alienation from his own body (he suffers from alopecia, resulting in a complete hair loss), would seem to authorize a re-evaluation of all of his screen images of the male body. In this regard, consider *La face*'s memorable closing shot. In it, Philippe's/ Lepage's body 'floats,' courtesy of blue-screen technology and the director's own surprising physical agility, up out of the Moscow airport lounge where he awaits his return flight to Canada, and into the stratosphere. For me, its orbit, like Deleuze's crystal-image, splits time in two (in terms of both the temporality of my viewing experience and the temporality of my writing of this chapter), launching Lepage's queer male body into a future as yet indiscernible, but one fundamen-tally free – at least in my estimation – of the weight of its hitherto overdetermined nationalist significations.

Perhaps it was just such a representational weightlessness that Léa Pool was hoping to achieve in launching her queer female body into space at the end of *Lost and Delirious*, her adaptation of Susan Swan's novel, *The Wives of Bath*, to which I turn in the next chapter. However, as I demonstrate there, the citational chain of signification that attaches itself to that body as it moves from text to screen, and beyond, also makes available to the lesbian spectator, in particular, further lines of gendered and generic identification.

6 Ghosts In and Out of the Machine: Sighting/Citing Lesbianism in Susan Swan's *The Wives of Bath* and Léa Pool's *Lost and Delirious*

Why is it so difficult to see the lesbian – even when she is there, quite plainly, in front of us? In part because she has been 'ghosted' – or made to seem invisible – by culture itself.

Terry Castle, *The Apparitional Lesbian*[1]

The best of Hollywood lesbian movies are always in some sense 'ghost' movies ... Lesbianism is the ghost in the machine, a sign of the body, desire, the other woman.

Patricia White, *Uninvited*[2]

During its formative years in the 1970s and 1980s, mainstream Anglo-American feminist film theory performed a double critical manoeuvre when it came to analyses of cinematic spectatorship, simultaneously critiquing and reinscribing the orthodox construction of the female spectator as a viewing subject defined by lack, negativity, absence, deficiency, and failure. Writing in 1975, in her groundbreaking essay 'Visual Pleasure and Narrative Cinema,' Laura Mulvey outlined the parameters of this construction by arguing that narrative cinema splits ego identification and object recognition on the screen between the active, male gaze and the passive, female image, between the projected male fantasy and the displayed female spectacle, between the act of looking and the state of '*to-be-looked-at-ness.*'[3] Expanding on this distinction six years later, Mulvey argued that the only way the female spectator could assume an active identification and engagement with narrative cinema was through 'the metaphor of masculinity'[4] – that is, by adopting one of the two psychical positions traditionally accorded the male viewer: voyeur, or fetishist. For her part, in analysing the 'social/psychological construction of female spectatorship' and the 'apparent blockage at the level of theory' around this construction, Mary Ann Doane, writing in 1984, insisted that voyeurism and fetishism are 'inaccessible' to the woman spectator and that the only subjective viewing position available to her is, paradoxically, objectifying because it depends on a narcissistic overidentification with her own image.[5] As Doane put it: 'Situating the woman [spectator] in relation to a desiring subjectivity seems to effect a *perversion* of the very notion of agency' (my emphasis).[6]

Numerous other feminist film critics, from E. Ann Kaplan and Annette Kuhn to Kaja Silverman and Jackie Stacey,[7] have offered – usually through recourse to similar pyschoanlaytical/semiotic paradigms – their own thoughts on what Teresa de Lauretis has characterized as the female spectator 'stranded between two incommensurable entities, the gaze and the image.'[8] What is striking about most of these analyses is that, with very few exceptions (from the above list, Stacey is a name that stands out[9]), they base their conclusions on a universal, undifferentiated, and remarkably stable conception of the female spectator as someone who, once the lights go down, seems to view narrative cinema in essentially the same way regardless of fundamental differences in the social and material conditions mediating that viewing experience. That this universal female spectator is presumed to be white, middle-class, and heterosexual is an unstated but no less powerful axiom in much of the critical discourse on women's relations to narrative cinema and the filmic apparatus. Nowhere, for example, does Doane conceive that the lesbian spectator – let alone the female spectator of colour – might desire differently in identifying with (or without) her own projected image in women's films from the 1940s. And this even though, as Patricia White has recently noted, 'a lesbian specter can be said to have haunted feminist film theory as it developed in the 1980s, in particular to stalk the female spectator as she was posited and contested in that discourse.'[10]

Thus, we have Mulvey blithely stating in 'Afterthoughts on "Visual Pleasure and Narrative Cinema"' that with respect to what prompted the writing of her earlier influential essay: 'I was interested in the relationship between the image of woman on the screen and the "masculinization" of the spectator position, regardless of the actual sex (*or possible deviance*) of any real live movie-goer' (my emphasis).[11] And we have Doane noting, as one consequence of the 'perversion' of female subjectivity in narrative cinema, a certain 'bisexuality' in terms of spectatorial orientation, but only insofar as the female spectator must identify, or 'think' like a man, not in acknowledgment of the possibility of her desiring another woman.[12] As White notes, Mulvey and Doane, in separately aiming to broaden the discourse around female spectatorship, each end up advancing a 'profoundly disempowering proposition,' one in which 'the very possibility of female desire as well as spectatorship is relinquished in the retreat from the ghost of lesbian desire.'[13]

Building on the work of White and other film theorists, in this chapter I begin to reconceive – and potentially re-empower – the acts of looking and being looked at as they relate to film viewing; in so doing, I hope to bring about a kind of critical rapprochement between lesbian desire and female spectatorship in feminist theories of narrative cinema. And I hope to do so, paradoxically, by positing a degree of subjective agency and representational plenitude within absence. Here I am drawing from Gilberto Perez's formulation of the spectral contract enacted between film and viewer. In *The Material Ghost: Films and Their Medium*, Perez argues that cinema's 'convention of the shot entails our agreement not only to look at what is being shown on the screen but also not to look at what is not being shown.'[14] Contra Christian Metz and dominant feminist film theory, which equates the movie camera with the Lacanian mirror, and which posits ego identification as a kind of transcendental act of self-perception with/in the 'imaginary signifier' on screen,[15] Perez argues that 'cinematic representation depends on our acceptance of absence,' that there is 'an indefinitely larger space extending unseen beyond the boundaries of the image' being projected before us on the screen.[16] And it is precisely in the space of this absence, I suggest, in the 'beyond' of the image (and the gaze), in what Mulvey has called 'the extra-diegetic tendencies represented by woman as spectacle,'[17] that we can locate both a resistant viewing position for the female spectator and a supplemental signifying chain of lesbian desire. If, in other words, the male subject, as 'bearer of the look,' 'controls the film phantasy,' both in terms of how the male protagonist advances the plot and in terms of how the male spectator identifies with his 'screen surrogate,'[18] then it would seem that the female subject, in attempting to negotiate her own meanings from and identifications with the representations she is consuming, is forced to look elsewhere: to other films she might have previously viewed, or to the actors who may have starred in those films, or to events she may have witnessed or experienced in 'real life.'[19]

This points to the fact that a lesbian-feminist textual analysis of narrative cinema needs to heed not only the formal and structural properties of an individual film, but also *intertextual* connections between films and *contextual* considerations mediating the production, exhibition, and reception of cinematic representations as a whole. In *Cinema and Spectatorship*, Judith Mayne examines various '[inter]textual strategies of address' used by films to hail an audience economically, politically, and emotionally. These strategies range from certain generic conventions and historical quotations that position a film within a particular canon (the maternal melodrama, for example, or the buddy action flick) to the personas of movie stars that help make a film instantly recognizable and attractive to a particular fan base.[20] 'Star-gazing,' as Mayne puts it, has been a particularly important identificatory strategy for gay and lesbian audiences, and 'suggests the importance of the cinematic public sphere in the shaping of marginal communities.'[21]

Indeed, from Hollywood legends like Greta Garbo, Marlene Dietrich, Agnes Moorehead, and Bette Davis to contemporary stars like Jodie Foster, Catherine Deneuve, Tilda Swinton, and Sandra Bernhard, dyke-icons abound in Western cinema,[22] although Shameem Kabir would argue that their various celluloid sightings across a range of narratives constitute an 'extratextual' rather than an 'intertextual' chain of lesbian filmic citation. Kabir uses the term extratextual in much the same way that Mulvey and other film theorists use the term 'extra-diegetic' – that is, to signal a range of 'secondary cinematic identification[s]'[23] that are neither intrinsic to the story's plot nor bound by specific rules of genre and narrative, but that instead frequently alert viewers to the arbitrariness of such rules.[24] Examples of a film's multiple extratexts thus include its cast, its director, its screenwriter, its source material (if any), its musical score, audience reactions, and so on. As Kabir demonstrates, and as I hope to illustrate further in this chapter, all of these elements are of crucial importance for the 'lesbian spectator of mainstream film,' who is 'usually denied any direct representation of lesbian desire.'[25]

However, for the purposes of this chapter, and to avoid further confusion, I will use the term 'citationality' to refer to the complex web of signifying practices encompassed by the terms intertext, extratext, and context, and to discuss their roles in marking a supplemental space of cinematic identification for both the female spectator and the desiring lesbian subject. This referential circuit of indirection, as I have been arguing, requires the viewer to look both at and beyond the image bounded by the screen, and to pay attention to ghosts that lurk both inside and outside the machine – to in effect see double.[26] White describes a similar process in the final pages of *Uninvited*, and I will be returning to her concept of 'retrospectatorship' at the end of this chapter. However, I prefer the term citationality, in part because my prior literary training continues to inform my reading of the cinema – especially as I see the chain of discursive effects that marks a space for lesbian spectatorship in what follows as necessarily moving beyond the realm of the purely visual. In adopting the term for this chapter, I also have in mind Judith Butler's reformulation of her influential theory of gender performativity in *Bodies That Matter* as 'a kind of citationality,' whereby the 'acquisition' of subjectivity or the 'assumption' of identity is seen to be complicit with the 'conventions of authority' and the operations of power.[27]

I develop this theory of cinematic ghosting and lesbian citationality in the context of Canadian film adaptation primarily through a discussion of *Lost and Delirious*, director Léa Pool's treatment of Susan Swan's novel *The Wives of Bath*, about the relationship between three teenage girls at a female boarding school. Before that, however, I take a short detour through two narrative films that while not adaptations strictly speaking, and while not even all that 'Canadian,' nevertheless establish a citational circuit of lesbian cinematic representations and identifications on which to build. I begin with a brief analysis of *Salmonberries*, Percy Adlon's 1991 film about cross-cultural bonding and female homosociality that marked the screen debut of the Canadian lesbian singing icon k.d. lang. Then I discuss, also very briefly, *Fire*, Indo-Canadian director Deepa Mehta's controversial film about lesbian awakening among two sisters-in-law in New Delhi trapped in loveless marriages. The representation of lesbianism in both these films is, as Kabir notes, somewhat problematic. Using Kabir as my starting point, I will examine how the lesbian spectator is additionally – and perhaps even more hospitably – hailed by referencing other work by both directors as well as, in the case of lang, one of the stars. With *Fire*, I also consider how spectatorial identifications can take place across gender and culture.

When we move on to *Lost and Delirious*, we discover quickly that the specific operations of lesbian citationality and spectatorial identification are a little more complex. That is, not only is that film framed by the context of director Pool's broader cinematic oeuvre (particularly her 1986 film *Anne Trister* and her 1999 masterpiece, *Emporte-moi*), but it also needs to be further sited/cited within the specifically *adaptive* history of lesbian cinematic representation with which *Lost and Delirious* is necessarily in dialogue (just as Swan's novel draws on its own set of literary intertexts, most notably Radclyffe Hall's *The Well of Loneliness*). From *Mädchen in Uniform* and *Olivia* to *The Children's Hour*, *Picnic at Hanging Rock*, and *The Prime of Miss Jean Brodie*: haunting Pool's film is less the ghost of Swan's original 'written' text than the combined spectre of these cinematic *inter*texts, each of which analyses the continuum of affective relationships between girls and women in the context of the boarding/day school, and each of which is also an adaptation

of a work of literature (by Christa Winsloe, Dorothy Strachey Bussy, Lillian Hellman, Joan Lindsay, and Muriel Spark, respectively). I thus conclude this chapter
by commenting briefly on some of the possible applications of a citational
approach to lesbian representation in the specific context of film adaptation.

In *Salmonberries*, k.d. lang plays Kotzebue, an androgynous-looking, part–Native
American woman who is named after the Alaskan mining town in which she was
abandoned as a baby. On a visit to the town library to learn more about her possible origins, she meets Roswitha (Rosel Zech), an older East German woman who
came to Alaska two decades earlier and who is still mourning the death of her
husband during a botched escape under the Berlin Wall. Unable to learn more
about her own past, Kotzebue resolves to help Roswitha come to terms with hers.
After witnessing a television news report about the collapse of the Berlin Wall,
Kotzebue buys two tickets for Berlin, where Roswitha works through her grief
over her husband's death by confronting her brother about his role in alerting the
East German authorities to their planned escape, and by visiting her husband's
grave. The events in Berlin bring the two women closer, and as a sign of their new
affection they bestow on each other new names: Kotzebue calls Roswitha 'Swita'
('because you're so sweet'), and Roswitha nicknames Kotzebue 'Babu.' However,
Kotzebue misinterprets the extent of Roswitha's affection for her, and when she
tries to seduce the older woman (see Figure 6.1), her advances are rebuffed.
Roswitha then goes into a long explanation about why she cannot reciprocate
Kotzebue's feelings for her sexually. As Kabir notes, this scene 'is cut so that its
duration appears to be over a long night,' with multiple fade-outs interrupting
Roswitha's monologue, as if 'to suggest that there can be no hope for lesbian
desire at the gaps, that there is no space, no room, for such desire, as reasons for
its rejection are so unremitting.'[28] At the end of this scene, Kotzebue says she can
no longer stay in the hotel room with Roswitha, and promptly faints. On the plane
ride home, they sit in opposite rows.

   While the unspooling of Roswitha's heterosexual panic is a distressing denouement to say the least, perhaps even more problematic is the way the film maps lesbianism onto racial otherness, '(re)producing racial and gender (in terms of butch
and femme) hierarchies.'[29] Louise Allen has convincingly documented how the
differences between the masculine- and ethnic-looking Kotzebue and Roswitha's
feminine white European identity are visually compounded by the play of light
and dark in the film, with lang's character often filmed in shadow and Zech's in a
superabundance of white light. Moreover, Kotzebue's sexual desire for Roswitha
is partially framed as a concomitant desire for the whitening of her racial identity.
Kotzebue declares to a barroom full of Berliners that she is 'Eskimo,' only to have
one English-speaking patron tell her that they are also all Eskimos. Later, at the
hotel, while they are standing together in the bathroom doorway, which is backlit
with white light, Kotzebue declares her love to Roswitha by stating: 'I was in the
dark, Swita, you're bright.' And while the full expression of Kotzebue's sexual
desire is abruptly arrested when Roswitha rejects her advances, Kotzebue's whitening continues. Her 'illumination' about the extent of Roswitha's feelings for her
is presented as a movement from darkness to light, with the scene's temporal

6.1   *Salmonberries*: Kotzebue (k.d. lang, top) and Roswitha (Rosel Zech) share a moment of connection in their Berlin hotel room.

edits tracking a slow progression from night to dawn. On returning home to Alaska, Kotzebue discovers that her father is white, the town's bingo caller, Chuck, having been profligate not only in his affection for young Native girls, but also in the gifts he bestowed on them.

If, as Allen has suggested, the 'look' of lesbianism in *Salmonberries* is presented as a process of 'passing' – of moving from an emphasis on 'visible' signs of difference (both racial and gender) to the invisibilizing of those differences through the privileging of a normalized subjectivity predicated on white heterosexuality – where is the lesbian spectator (and especially the lesbian spectator of colour) to look for representations of desire with which she can identify? One place might be director Adlon's previous film, *Bagdad Café*, his first English-language feature and an unexpected crossover hit in North America. Like *Salmonberries*, *Bagdad Café* focuses on a displaced German woman, Jasmin (Marianne Sägebrecht), who has been 'abandoned' by her husband and who, in the course of getting on with her life in an alien and alienating America, forges a homosocial relationship with a woman of colour, in this case the harried African-American owner of a road stop motel and diner, and newly single mother, Brenda (CCH Pounder). Each film is set in an extreme and hostile landscape: *Bagdad* in the Nevada desert, *Salmonberries* on the Alaskan tundra. Kabir further notes that the two films share a similar film language or authorial style, with Adlon employing 'uncertain first images, unusual angles, disjuncture in temporal editing, intercutting, slow motion merging into real-time, and a pleasing play with lighting to suggest the uncanny.'[30] Finally, each film's soundtrack is overlain with a haunting central song – for *Bagdad*, 'Calling You' (written by long-time Adlon collaborator Bob Telson and sung by Jevetta Steele) and for *Salmonberries*, 'Barefoot' (co-written by Telson and lang and sung by lang) – that recurs at key moments and seems to comment on the film's diegesis.

A citational chain of lesbian spectatorial positions is thus made available to the viewer of *Salmonberries* from the moment 'A Film by Percy Adlon' appears in the opening credits, the 'subtextual suggestion of lesbian desire'[31] in the director's earlier film receiving a more explicit – if wholly confused – treatment in this 'outing.' Moreover, a comparison of the two films' endings demonstrates how in many respects the visual pleasure on offer to both the female spectator and the lesbian spectator in the earlier film is more appealing in terms of emotional and political affect. Whereas *Salmonberries* ends, as I have suggested, by reinscribing a normative subject position of white heterosexuality, *Bagdad Café* actually ends with a subtle critique of heteronormative patriarchy, and of the ways in which that institution refuses to accommodate single white working women and women of colour. Jasmin has to return briefly to Germany once her tourist visa expires, but is reunited with Brenda at the end of the film, although it is not clear for how long. In the film's closing scene, a long-time male resident of the hotel (played by Jack Palance) offers to marry Jasmin so that she can stay in the country permanently; instead of immediately accepting the proposal, Jasmin says: 'I'll talk it over with Brenda.' As Kabir puts it, with this response 'we can read that any marriage that takes place will be one of convenience under patriarchal law, and that the real marriage is the mergence of the women, not as sexual partners necessarily, but as two women who mutually recognize and support each other's presence and autonomy.'[32]

Yet lesbian citationality in *Salmonberries* circulates not only at the level of auteur, but also at the level of star. Indeed, all sorts of further identifications suddenly become possible when k.d. lang's name appears on screen (above the title and above that of Adlon and her co-star Zech, it should be noted). These identifications have to do both with how her on-screen persona necessarily starts to merge with her off-screen persona throughout the course of the film, and with how lang the movie actor starts to merge with lang the pop singer.

The construction of Kotzebue as androgynous and sexually ambiguous consciously trades on lang's own celebrity image as a singer then famous almost as much for her cropped hair and fondness for wearing men's suits as for her silken voice. Combine this with the fact that the film's North American release more or less coincided with lang's own public coming out as a lesbian in the pages of *The*

Advocate, and a spectatorial signifying chain of art imitating life imitating art starts to spiral out at the audience exponentially. This chain is further extended by the song, 'Barefoot,' that lang sings in the film. The lyrics are specifically crafted to invite multiply coded readings of both the film and its star ('You hear the howling of dogs and wind / stirring up the secrets that are frozen within'; 'The ice will haunt you, it lays so deep / locking up inside you the dreams that you keep'); not only that, but the song's soft pop-musical style signalled a major departure from lang's country and western roots – something that lang herself would confirm a few months later with the release of her fourth album, *Ingenue*. That album's title can further be read as a playful nod not only to lang's 'new' lesbian identity, but also to her new role as a screen goddess – a doubled persona that the video for the first single, 'Miss Chatelaine,' had fun with by shooting a hyper-femmed lang in a yellow organza gown and chenilled hairdo frolicking about a cardboard set of 1940s furniture. That *Chatelaine* is the name of a venerable women's magazine in Canada – one that named lang its 'Woman of the Year' in 1988, and one whose particular brand of domestic advice is not without certain lesbian subtexts[33] – only adds to the proliferation of possible identifications prompted by the overlapping of lang the movie star and lang the singer.

As one final citation in this regard, it needs to be noted that two years after she appeared in *Salmonberries*, lang composed the soundtrack to *Even Cowgirls Get the Blues*, Gus van Sant's film adaptation of the Tom Robbins novel about Sissy Hankshaw, a female-identified rancher with expert thumbs.[34] In multiple ways, then, *Salmonberries* 'invites' the lesbian gaze (see White), soliciting a look and holding that look through what we might call the 'double takes' of director and star.

A similar process of lesbian citationality is enacted by Mehta's film, except that in the case of *Fire* spectatorial identifications are further multiplied across gender (and culture). The film, a Canadian–Indian co-production, tells the story of Radha (Shabana Azmi) and Sita (Nandita Das), two contemporary women in New Delhi who are married, respectively, to Ashok (Kulbushan Kharbanda) and Jatin (Jaaved Jaaferi), brothers who share both cramped living quarters and the family business, a busy takeout food and video emporium. Also part of this menage are Biji (Kushal Rekhi), the brothers' aging mute mother, and Mundu (Ranjit Chowdhry), their servant and employee. Despite being newly wed to Sita, Jatin continues a torrid affair with girlfriend Julie (Alice Poon), the daughter of a Chinese immigrant family from Hong Kong; Ashok, learning that Radha cannot have children, has forsworn desire and sexual intimacy for a life of celibacy based on the advice of his local swami. Thus rejected by their husbands, the two women turn to each other for friendship and, eventually, sexual solace (see Figure 6.2).

The younger Sita, who thinks 'the concept of duty is overrated,' initiates the affair, but soon enough, a shocked Radha returns her passion unreservedly. When Mundu, under threat of expulsion for masturbating in front of Biji to one of the pornos illicitly stocked by Jatin, betrays the women to Ashok, Radha responds to her husband's fury by stating: 'Without desire I was dead ... I desire to live again. I desire Sita. I desire her warmth, her compassion, her body.' The film consciously draws from the Hindu epic *The Ramayana*, in which the heroine Sita proves her

6.2   *Fire*: Radha (Shabana Azmi, l) and Sita (Nandita Das) share a laugh.

chastity to her husband, Ram, by setting herself aflame; specifically, it ends with Radha (in Hindu mythology, the long-suffering wife of the womanizing god Krishna) enduring her own trial by fire when her sari is accidentally set ablaze, before choosing voluntary exile in the arms of her sister-in-law.

The representation of lesbian desire in Mehta's film is not without its problems. First, in presenting lesbian sex as a kind of fallback position in the face of an absent phallus and the preferred option of normal heterosex, *Fire* reinforces certain unfortunate sexual stereotypes and gender hierarchies. Second, as Kabir notes, the paralleling of Radha's discovery of Mundu masturbating with Ashok's later discovery of her in bed with Sita suggests a somewhat disturbing conflation of 'perversions,' 'where the illicit pleasures of [straight] pornography are equated with the pleasures of lesbian desire.'[35] Even so, read in the broader context of India's colonial history and the rise of post-partition religious fundamentalism, there can be no doubt that *Fire* has set itself a revolutionary agenda – to break down taboos and document multiple liberation struggles. This is confirmed not only by the subsequent instalments in Mehta's elemental film trilogy (the historical epic *Earth* [1998] and the recently completed *Water* [2005]), but also by the reception accorded *Fire* when it first premiered in India.

That reception – specifically, the protests mounted against the film by religious fundamentalists (particularly in the state of Maharashtra, which happens to be both the centre of India's multibillion-dollar movie industry *and* the centre of Hindu extremism in the country) – has been well documented, so I won't rehearse it here.[36] Nor will I tackle in any depth what Gayatri Gopinath has rightly critiqued as Western critics' own 'foreclosure' on the 'complex model of queer female desire suggested by the film' – except to highlight Gopinath's key point that the mainstream recuperation of *Fire*'s lesbian images within a 'developmental narrative' of queer Western modernity and visibility ignores completely the source text on which the film is based. According to Gopinath, Urdu writer Ismat Chughtai's 1942 short story 'The Quilt' is an intertext that, 'in its representation of the complicated and wild desiring relations between women in the seemingly traditional space of the home,' foregrounds how 'queer desire in the film functions (albeit obliquely) as a modality through which women resist a complicity with the project of Hindu nationalism and its attendant gender and sexual hierarchies.'[37] My focus is somewhat different. That is, I am chiefly interested in how a movie that has been violently condemned, on the one hand, for making available to Indian audiences scandalous Western spectating positions and cinematic identifications, and politely dismissed, on the other hand, for its supposed 'illegibility' to non-Indian audiences, simultaneously doubles (and even triples) both the possibilities and the directions of those positions and identifications by hailing the cross-cultural/diasporic/queer spectator (who may or may not be watching the film in the 'West') through instances of self-referentiality and self-citation.

Filmic quotation abounds in *Fire*. First, there is Jatin's thriving video rental business and the disguised pornos that Mundu borrows from his stock and surreptitiously watches. Next, Bollywood is directly referenced at least twice: through an elaborately stylized fantasy sequence dramatizing a story that Radha tells Sita, and that Mundu, overhearing, casts in his mind with members of the household; and through a scene in which Sita (cross-dressed as a man) and Radha dance and lip-sync to an Indian pop song of the sort that often serves as the backdrop to one of the elaborate musical numbers on offer in most Bollywood epics. The dance scene, coming soon after the women first go to bed together, is especially important. Sita's cross-dressing sets up an extra context of gender transgression and identification, opening up a more inviting space of lesbian spectatorship than the polarized positions on offer through the intra-cinematic representations of female sexuality elsewhere in the film (that is, Mundu's pornos [woman as wanton sex object] and Bollywood fantasies [woman as chaste sex object]); furthermore, it sets in motion, both intra- and intertextually, a citational chain of queer address, one that signifies across gender and that has an important Canadian connection.

Specifically, Sita's dance outfit reminds the viewer of an earlier scene in the film in which she also cross-dressed. Soon after arriving at her new home, Sita is shown by Radha to her bedroom. There she goes through her husband's clothes, selects a pair of jeans, hikes up her sari, and puts them on. Then, having turned on some music, she lights a cigarette and dances around the room in gleeful abandon until she is interrupted by a disapproving Radha. At first glance, there would seem to be nothing terribly remarkable going on in this scene. However, once the careful viewer recognizes that in both this scene and the subsequent scene of Sita's cross-dressing Mehta is consciously quoting herself, a further layer of meaning is added and an additional spectatorial position is opened up. I am referring here to the fact that the actor who plays Sita's husband in *Fire*, noted Indian comic and DJ Jaaved

Jaaferi, performed his own cross-dressed Bollywood-style musical number in *Sam and Me* (1991), Mehta's Canadian feature film debut. In *Sam and Me*, Jaaferi plays Xavier, one of a group of recent male immigrants to Toronto who has a fondness for cricket, hot-oil massages, and dressing up in saris. Other members of this 'bachelor' household include *Fire*'s Kulbushan Kharbanda and Ranjit Chowdhry, who plays Nikhil, the 'me' of the film's title. Nikhil is forced to take a job babysitting Sam (Peter Boretsky), the crotchety Jewish father of his uncle's boss.

Against all odds, and across both generational and cultural differences, Sam and Nikhil, like *Bagdad Café*'s Jasmin and Brenda, end up forging an affective bond that, although non-sexual, is nevertheless profoundly homosocial *and* deeply troubling of traditional patterns of cultural and familial affiliation. At the beginning of the film, both Sam and Nikhil, as diasporic subjects, long to be repatriated as soon as possible to the countries they regard as their homelands, Israel and India, respectively. However, by the end of *Sam and Me* – a film in which, as in Mehta's *Bollywood/Hollywood*, Toronto is given a starring role as local metonym for the global national and sexual diaspora – such artificial borders have been effectively 'queered,' with Mehta disentangling 'habitation' from 'nation' in the same way that lesbian-feminist critics of both the social and the cinema have likewise dismantled the barrier-slash between sex and gender, identification and desire, the (masculine) gaze and the (feminine) look. In other words, Mehta brings to her cinematic portraits of the lives of marginalized subjects a decidedly transitive angle of vision, a process of reinscribing both the local and the global.

In this, Mehta is the first to acknowledge the important role played by her adopted country. At the premiere of *Bollywood/Hollywood* at the 2002 Vancouver International Film Festival, Mehta, in her opening remarks, drew explicit attention to the slash mark in the title, thanked her distribution company, Mongrel Films, and claimed that the film, in its unabashed celebration and performance of formal, cultural, and sexual hybridity, could only have been made in Canada. While Mehta was undoubtedly playing to a partisan crowd (one filled, moreover, with docents from Telefilm, the country's national funding body for films), I could not help but reflect afterwards that in all of her films – including her recent adaptation of Carol Shields's *The Republic of Love*, where Winnipeg gets to stand in for London, England – Canada contributes, to a greater or lesser extent, a continuum of subversive spectating positions that invite identifications *across* multiple subjectivities, rather than exclusively *with* one or another. Above all, what Mehta's films show is that the nature of fantasy is that it crosses borders – that it links individually and differently sexed bodies in an intersubjective, affiliative, and performative production of shared identity and/or desire. A being-in-the-world that is also a becoming-of-the-world. A turning of the one into many and the many into one, what Judith Butler calls, at the end of *Bodies That Matter*, 'the unstable and continuing condition of the "one" and the "we," the ambivalent condition of the power that binds.'[38] Which is as apt a description as any of the theory of lesbian citationality as it is operating in this chapter.

Fans of Susan Swan's novel *The Wives of Bath* might be forgiven for failing to recognize it as the basis for Léa Pool's recent film, *Lost and Delirious* (2001), so radically have Pool and screenwriter Judith Thompson altered key aspects of Swan's

6.3   *Lost and Delirious*: Tory (Jessica Paré, l), Paulie (Piper Perabo), and Mouse
(Mischa Barton) pose for the camera.

original narrative about the complicated relationships among three friends –
Pauline 'Paulie' Sykes, Victoria 'Tory' Quinn, and narrator Mary Beatrice 'Mouse'
Bradford (see Figure 6.3) – at Bath Ladies College, a boarding school for girls in
1960s Ontario. The setting has been updated to the present, and narrator Mouse's
(Mischa Barton) physical deformity is nowhere in sight on screen (in the book she
has a sunken chest, a curved spine, and a hump on her back she calls Alice); not
only that, but subplots involving Mouse's relationship with her father and stepmother and the love affair between the school's headmistress, Miss Vaughan
(played in the film by Jackie Burroughs), and one of the other female teachers,
Mrs Peddie, are either jettisoned completely or deeply sublimated. Perhaps most
dramatic, however, is the fact that in the film, the basis for Paulie's devotion to
Tory has been changed from a complicated case of gender dysphoria to what we
might call a more straightforward (and, given the audience being targeted with
the casting of pouty actresses Piper Perabo and Jessica Paré in the roles of Paulie
and Tory respectively, the word is wholly appropriate) presentation of teenage
lesbian desire and internalized homophobia. In the novel, Paulie masquerades as
'Lewis,' Paulie's caretaker brother and erstwhile boyfriend to Tory, and leads
Mouse on a frightening odyssey of disavowing their biological sex and the gender
ideologies inscribed upon it. All of this leads to a major difference in the way that
Paulie desperately and climactically declares her love for Tory: murder in the
novel versus suicide in the film.

Yet as Swan herself puts it in the preface to a new edition of her novel published to coincide with the film's release, textual fidelity is perhaps the least serviceable model with which to assess a film adapted from a work of literature. Pronouncing herself 'shamelessly satisfied with [her] book's journey into film,' Swan instead highlights the extra layers of meaning brought to her novel by Thompson and Pool: 'I feel as if my story about boarding school girls has passed through the imaginations of three women sitting around a campfire, each one adding their unique knowledge to my tale of female rebellion and adolescent love.'[39] In other words, a citational chain of lesbian desire is enacted expressly within *Lost and Delirious*'s adaptative framework, with the spectator invited to make certain connections and identifications not only across different narrative genres (that is, novel to film and back again) but also within a specific genre. Here, I argue, *Lost and Delirious*'s iconographic status as a 'boarding school film' is especially important, in that it signifies spectatorially in terms of how screenwriter and director both site their film and cite other films within this tradition. Moreover, I suggest that the model for such an intertextual mode of address can be found in Swan's 'boarding school novel,' which finds itself in dialogue not only with other examples – from Diderot's *La religieuse* (1796) and Colette's *Claudine à l'école* (1900) to Charlotte Brontë's *Jane Eyre* (1847) and Rosamund Lehmann's *Dusty Answer* (1927) – of what Diana Fuss, in her reading of Bussy's *Olivia*, has called 'an identifiable subgenre in modernist literature,' but also with what Fuss has likewise called perhaps the most 'representative lesbian novel of the modern period,' Radclyffe Hall's *The Well of Loneliness*.[40]

Swan has stated that she based the 'weird, Napoleonic act of self-assertion' (*WB* 5) that serves as her novel's gothic climax – in which Paulie/Lewis murders and castrates the school's dwarf janitor, Sergeant, clumsily appending his penis to her own genitalia in a desperate bid to prove to Tory's suspicious brother that 'she' is in fact a 'he' – on a similar real-life crime that took place in Toronto in the late 1970s (*WB* ix). Excerpts from Paulie's trial, in which various lawyers and psychologists argue about the correct clinical diagnosis for her cross-gender identifications and about her criminal responsibility for the crime, are woven throughout the novel. Thus Paulie's defence lawyer, Miss Whitlaw, in response to the Crown's expert testimony on Paulie's 'gender disorder' and 'sexual deviation,' at one point notes Karen Horney's claims that 'Freud himself exaggerated the importance of penis envy among little girls. She believed that both sexes envy each other, and that just as little girls wish for penises, little boys wish for breasts' (*WB* 115–16).

This subtle feminist revisioning of dominant psychoanalytic theory is in keeping with Mouse's own later conclusions about the social construction of masculinity: 'It did seem unfair that Paulie needed a penis to be a man. John Wayne would still be John Wayne if he had a vagina, wouldn't he? … If the world didn't give boys so many advantages, Paulie wouldn't want to be one. At least, that's how I saw it then. Paulie saw it differently, because as far as she was concerned, she was a boy, period' (*WB* 213). And it is also in keeping with a minor tradition in the modern schoolgirl novel: near the end of Muriel Spark's *The Prime of Miss Jean Brodie*, psychologist turned nun Sandy reflects that 'many theories from the books of psychology categorized Miss Brodie, but failed to obliterate her image'[41]; and

Dorothy Bussy, older sister of James Strachey (Freud's English translator) objected at the outset of *Olivia* to 'the psychologists, the physiologists, the psycho-analysts, the Prousts and the Freuds' who would 'poison the sources of emotion,' turning the 'vital experience' of a sixteen-year-old girl's love for her teacher into 'something to be ashamed of, something to hide desperately.'[42]

Arguably, however, it was Hall's *The Well of Loneliness*, first published in 1928, and immediately the subject of its own highly publicized trial for obscenity, that inaugurated the tradition of the 'lesbian' novel (however broadly defined) being in dialogue – if not always in agreement – with the prevailing psychological and sexological theories of the day. Indeed, Hall's tale of the tortured life of the 'congenital invert' Stephen Gordon is very much influenced by her own reading of Edward Carpenter's *The Intermediate Sex* (1908); Richard von Krafft-Ebing's *Psychopathia Sexualis* (1886), a text that Stephen stumbles upon in her dead father's study and that, discovering her own name among its marginalia, she reads avidly, eventually realizing that she is one of the 'thousands of miserable, unwanted people, who have no right to love, no right to compassion because they're maimed, hideously maimed and ugly'[43]; and especially Havelock Ellis's 'Sexual Inversion in Women' (1895), whose case studies and 'ascending scale of inversion' from the 'womanly' or feminine-identified invert to the 'mannish' or 'actively inverted woman,' provided Hall with much of the raw material for her novel.[44] Later, Ellis would provide a 'scholarly' preface to Hall's novel when it was published. In Hall's novel, Stephen Gordon is educated at home by a series of governesses, including the devoted Puddle, who becomes a loyal companion in London and Paris after Stephen is banished from her beloved Morton by her mother. But no doubt the author would have been familiar with Ellis's musings on 'the ardent attachments which girls in schools and colleges form to each other and to their teachers': 'These girlish devotions, on the borderland between friendship and sexual passion, are found in all countries where girls are segregated for educational purposes, and their symptoms are, on the whole, singularly uniform, though they vary in intensity and character to some extent, from time to time and from place to place, sometimes assuming an epidemic form.'[45]

It is Virginia Woolf who is the Sapphically identified author referenced by name in Swan's novel – her *Orlando* arguably serves as an important intertext with respect to Paulie/Lewis's multiple cross-gender *trans*formations. Yet there are also many significant overlaps between *The Wives of Bath* and *The Well of Loneliness*. Not least of these are the complicated family triangles at the heart of each novel; Mouse's adoration of her father, Morley, and her uneasy and often acrimonious relationship with her stepmother, Sal, find their corollaries in Stephen's feelings for her own parents, Sir Philip and Anna. Indeed, the unspoken (because deeply repellent) accusation that Anna Gordon harbours towards her daughter throughout Hall's novel (but even more so after her husband's untimely death) – that she should have been and yet will never be the son her parents wished for – is echoed at the end of *The Wives of Bath*, in recriminations traded by Sal and Mouse in the aftermath of Morley's funeral, with Sal assuring Mouse that she 'never heard Morley say he wished you were a boy, even if you didn't play baseball or know how to throw a football,' and with Mouse responding: 'I guess you wish you'd given Morley a son. That way, he might have stayed home with us more' (*WB* 194–5).

At the outset of the novel, when describing how she came to be sent to Bath Ladies College in the first place, Mouse claims that she can sympathize with her father's 'unfortunate inferiority complex about bringing up girls' because girls – or 'mock boys' as she calls them –are her own 'least favourite gender' (*WB* 14–15). In part it is this alienation from her own body – exacerbated by her obvious physical deformity and by the fact that having skipped two grades, she is younger than the other girls and so has not yet begun to menstruate – that leads Mouse to join Paulie in donning male attire. Both girls are attempting to achieve 'mastery' not only over nature, men, and women, as Paulie explains the tests that Mouse must pass (*WB* 92), but also, arguably, over the whole vexed issue of embodiment itself, and of the necessarily asymmetrical relationships between embodiment, identification, and desire.

In this respect, I argue that, as with Judith Halberstam's reading of Hall's novel, in *The Wives of Bath* 'a sartorial semiotic provides this novel with its system of knowing and unknowing, concealment and disclosure, and the trace of secrecy in this text involves not secret desires but the secret female body ... which of necessity remains covered.'[46] That is, just as Stephen Gordon's increasingly masculine apparel as she is growing up comes to signify the 'open warfare, the inevitable clash of two opposing natures' within her (*WL* 71), so Paulie's passing as Lewis reflects her deep-seated conviction that 'being a woman [is] bad' (*WB* 142). As Mouse – who, significantly, when dressed as 'Nick the Greek,' fails to pass completely – puts it at one point in the novel: 'Paulie looked so much like a boy in Lewis's clothes that only the masculine pronoun will do' (*WB* 142). Yet while for both Lewis and Stephen masculinity is no mere masquerade, the specific operations and effects of cross-dressing in each novel must not be conflated. For Lewis, as a 'passing woman,' secretly cross-dressing as a male represents access to a masculine economy of power and erotic exchange from which women perforce are exempt. For Stephen, the 'masculine invert' trapped in 'the no-man's-land of sex' (*WL* 77), wearing men's clothes becomes the visible expression of reconciling publicly her private torment over a female 'body' in which her male 'spirit' cannot feel at home:

> That night she stared at herself in the glass; and even as she did so she hated her body with its muscular shoulders, its small compact breasts, and its slender flanks of an athlete. All her life she must drag this body of hers like a monstrous fetter imposed on her spirit. This strangely ardent yet sterile body that must worship yet never be worshiped in return by the creature of its adoration. She longed to maim it; for it made her feel cruel; it was so white so strong and so self-sufficient; yet withal so poor and unhappy a thing that her eyes filled with tears and hate and turned to pity. She began to grieve over it, touching her breasts with pitiful fingers, stroking her shoulders, letting her hands slip along her straight thighs – Oh poor and most desolate body! (*WL* 187–88)

This famous mirror scene, in which, in a belated version of Lacanian *méconnaissance*,[47] Stephen confronts the image of her alienated and (literally) inverted self –

and over which much lesbian-feminist and queer theoretical ink has been spilt[48] – is arguably split between *two* selves in *The Wives of Bath*. Shortly after arriving at Bath Ladies College, Mouse stands in front of her bedroom mirror and offers the following assessment of what she sees: 'Mouse, you are grotesque, I told myself in the drafty bedroom. I stood staring in the mirror, hating the sly, wise face that stared solemnly back at me. The lips of its thin, lopsided mouth didn't move. See, it agrees with you, I thought' (*WB* 31). Immediately afterwards, in search of a washroom, Mouse stumbles upon Lewis (she doesn't yet know he's Paulie) shaving 'in front of the bathroom mirror, a cigarette dangling from his lips': 'He wasn't making a sound, although he was obviously enjoying his masculine ritual. He was lost in it, daydreaming' (*WB* 32). That the images both Mouse and Lewis/ Paulie see reflected in their respective mirrors are fictional or imaginary ones – in the Lacanian sense – will be borne out by events later in the novel when the symbolic order of patriarchal culture (represented most obviously by the boys school, Kings College, which wants to merge with Bath) exposes in Mouse a femininity she could not or would not see (asked to the school dance by Jack O'Malley, a Kings boy, Mouse 'checks herself out' in the rearview mirror of the school bus, noting with satisfaction the 'short strapless taffeta formal' she is wearing and the glitter she has sprinkled in her hair [*WB* 209]) and, furthermore, exposes in Lewis a failed, fake, and fantasmatic masculinity that others can see through (Lewis is prevented from taking Tory to the same dance by Tory's brother and father, headmaster of Kings, unless he can prove that he is a 'real' man).

The film adaptation of *The Wives of Bath* condenses the 'sartorial semiotic' operating in the novel into one brief scene in which Paulie, dressed in pants, dress shirt, and a purloined Kings jacket, crashes the school dance and attempts to cut in on Tory while she is waltzing with her father. However, director Pool does incorporate scenes with mirrors to great effect throughout *Lost and Delirious*. For example, during the opening establishing sequence, as Mouse is being driven to her new school, mirrors are used to reflect – and refract – very economically the complicated triangulated relationship between Mouse, her father, and her new stepmother. First we see a sullen Mouse opening a small compact in the back seat as a voice-over intones: 'When I looked in her compact and saw my face, I remembered hers … my mother.' Next, the camera cuts to a POV shot of Mouse watching her new stepmother adjusting her make-up in the mirror on the car's passenger-side sun visor. This is followed by a quick cut to a second POV shot of Mouse catching her father's gaze reflected in close-up in the rearview mirror.

Pool also uses mirrors to comment on the masquerade of hyperfemininity that Tory hides behind in the wake of rumours circulating around the school about her relationship with Paulie. While Tory is preparing for a date with her brother's friend midway through the film, we see her plucking her eyebrows and applying rouge in front of a handheld make-up mirror, Paulie's accusing face reflected behind her; and near the climax of the film, in a montage of slow pans, we see Tory and several of her fellow classmates primping in front of large, multiwatted theatrical mirrors as they prepare for the school dance. This is preceded by perhaps the most direct allusion to the mirror scenes in both *The Wives of Bath* and *The Well of Loneliness*: a long take of Paulie, alone in the room she shares with Mouse

6.4   *Lost and Delirious*: Paulie (Piper Perabo, l) makes Mouse (Mischa Barton) swear an oath of loyalty.

and Tory, staring fiercely into the mirror, at one point pinning back her hair in an attempt to look more masculine. When this doesn't seem to work, she hoists the mirror off the wall, smashes it on the floor, and picks up a shard, eventually asking a startled Mouse, who has happened upon the chaos, to cut off her hair 'because [she's] going to war.' When Mouse refuses, Paulie slashes each of their palms, forcing Mouse to declare her loyalty to Paulie as 'blood brother' (see Figure 6.4).

Paulie's preparations to do battle for the heart of Tory echo the 'curious warfare' that erupts between Stephen and her old friend Martin Hallam (a Canadian, no less!) over Mary Llewellyn at the end of *The Well of Loneliness* (*WL* 436). Indeed, if – as I've been suggesting – Swan's novel can be read 'citationally' alongside Hall's, so too can Pool's film; the many scenes of Paulie fencing remind attentive audiences of Stephen Gordon's own prowess at the same sport. However, as I now wish to demonstrate, Pool's citational chain of address extends to other texts as well.

Judith Thompson, who wrote the screenplay for *Lost and Delirious*, says she eliminated both the murder and the trial from her adaptation, in part because she feared a backlash from contemporary queer audiences, who would likely object to '[representing] a young lesbian woman as a raving psycho.'[49] No doubt Thompson and Pool also worried that if they kept the original narrative's transgender elements, their film would be compared unfavourably by critics to Kimberley

Pierce's Oscar-winning *Boys Don't Cry*, about the life and murder of Brandon Teena, a trans woman who almost passed as a straight man.[50] Yet in consciously removing one intertext from her script, Thompson is careful to insert another. And she does so by cleverly combining literary quotation and filmic quotation to form a citational chain of lesbian signification that leads the spectator, metonymically, to another 'true crime' story about 'sexual deviance,' this one from 1810.

Several commentators on the film have noted the extensive references to Shakespeare throughout.[51] And while Paulie's overidentification with Lady Macbeth's desire to 'unsex herself' in the film's closing frames can be seen as Thompson's somewhat clumsy attempt to make an allusion to the novel's more complicated reading of female masculinity (not to mention feminist film theory's reading of cinematic spectatorship),[52] it is important to remember that Lady Macbeth is not the only Shakespearean heroine with whom Paulie identifies in the film. Indeed, in one scene, Paulie, having been rejected by a newly sexually conformist Tory, and clothed in her fencing costume, confronts her former lover in the library, quoting from the Act I, Scene v speech in *Twelfth Night* in which Viola, disguised as a man, pretends to woo Olivia: 'Make me a willow cabin at your gate, / And call upon my soul within the house' – a line that Paulie repeats just prior to her climactic leap from the school's roof.[53] And the text that Miss Vaughan's English class spends the most time unpacking together is *Antony and Cleopatra*, with Paulie alone among the students in siding with Miss Vaughan – and Cleopatra – in defending love, even to the point of dying for it. Here, in front of her fellow students, and later, in private conference with Miss Vaughan, Paulie quotes fervently from Cleopatra's Act IV, Scene xiii speech to a dying Antony: 'shall I abide / In this dull world, which in thy absence is / No better than a sty?'[54]

The Cleopatra references provide a double literary and cinematic link to another key text in the boarding school genre. I am referring to *The Children's Hour*, Lillian Hellman's 1934 play about two girls' school teachers, Karen Wright and Martha Dobie, accused of lesbianism by a spiteful pupil, Mary Tilford. This play served as the basis of two films by William Wyler: *These Three* (1936; starring Merle Oberon and Miriam Hopkins), which altered the plot's central situation (to a charge of heterosexual adultery and potential child abuse) in a direct attempt to placate film censors of the day, and which was forbidden to mention directly Hellman's source material in any publicity associated with the film[55]; and *The Children's Hour* (1962; starring Audrey Hepburn and Shirley MacLaine), which restored both Hellman's original plot and her name to the screen version of the material, and which added a further self-referential layer to the intertext with Wyler's earlier film by casting Miriam Hopkins in the pivotal role of Mrs Mortar. Hellman's play is in turn based on a chapter in William Roughead's book *Bad Companions* (1930), a compendium of famous criminal scandals and trials from nineteenth-century Scotland, one of which was 'The Great Drumsheugh Case,' where two Edinburgh headmistresses, Marianne Woods and Jane Pirie, were accused by one of their pupils, Jane Cumming, of sharing 'an inordinate affection' for each other.[56]

Hellman's version of the story (at least the 1953 'acting edition' published to coincide with the play's first Broadway revival)[57] opens with Mrs Mortar, a former stage actress, coaching the schoolgirls in their elocution lessons; the text she has them read from is *Antony and Cleopatra* – specifically, Cleopatra's suicide speech to the asp in Act V, Scene ii. Wyler retains this scene in his 1962 film adaptation of the play, although he defers its temporal placement in the diegesis until after a long establishing sequence in which we are introduced to the narrative's main characters through a recital and garden party thrown for the schoolgirls' parents. That a similar welcoming scene – in which Paulie spikes the punch and replaces the sedate classical music with her own bootleg tape of the Violent Femmes – finds its way into the opening minutes of *Lost and Delirious*, and that a Mary Tilford-style character seems to have been reborn in Alison, Tory's gossip-mongering sister, only brings this chain of filmic citations full circle.

My point here is that these conscious references to previous lesbian representations in literary and cinematic history (however tortured and anachronistic they might be) open up a further space of spectatorial identification for the viewer beyond the rather restrictive (and highly gendered) space of textual fidelity to Swan's source material. Of equal importance in this regard is the casting of actress Jackie Burroughs in the role of Miss Vaughan. Burroughs's exuberant performance as the free-spirited and only nominally closeted headmistress recalls Hopkins's over-the-top turn as the spinster aunt Mrs Mortar (who pines for a return both to the stage and to the warm embrace of her great friend, Delia Lampert) in Wyler's 1962 film; she also seems to be channelling the ghost of Maggie Smith in Ronald Neame's 1969 film adaptation of Muriel Spark's *The Prime of Miss Jean Brodie*, another classic entry in the schoolgirl genre. As with Smith's Brodie, whose sexual and political contradictions are eventually exposed by a savvy student, Sandy (Pamela Franklin), Miss Vaughan's attempts at uncloseted empathy – particularly as they are refracted through literature – are scorned by Paulie, who favours physical action and the bold gesture. Add to this the fact that Burroughs brings to the role her own prior – and uniquely Canadian – set of queer significations (including a huge following among gay men)[58] via her long-time role as the spinster aunt Hettie King on the television series *Road to Avonlea* (based on the fiction of Lucy Maud Montgomery), and a further series of lesbian spectatorial identifications are made available to the viewer of *Lost and Delirious*.

Also lurking behind Burroughs's performance are the ghosts of two other famous celluloid schoolteachers: Mademoiselle Julie (Simone Simon), adored co-director of the French finishing school Les Avons in Jacqueline Audry's 1950 adaptation of Bussy's novel, which (significantly) was retitled *The Pit of Loneliness* for its North American release; and, even more importantly, Fräulein von Bernburg (Dorothea Wieck), the beautiful and beneficent surrogate mother beloved by all the girls – but particularly by new arrival Manuela (Hertha Thiele) – at the militaristic Prussian boarding school featured in Leontine Sagan's landmark 1931 film *Mädchen in Uniform*, adapted 'proleptically' from Christa Winsloe's novel *The Child Manuela*. I say proleptically because while Winsloe originally conceived Manuela's story as a novel, 'and so wrote it,' the text did not actually appear in print (in an English translation, no less) until 1933, and even then only after the success of Sagan's film and an earlier stage production titled *Yesterday and Today*. Moreover, the novel, unlike the play and the film, goes into much more detail about Manuela's life prior to the death of her mother and her arrival at the dreaded boarding school known as 'Princess Helene's Seminary.'[59] Sagan's film, which has been hailed by B. Ruby Rich as both a powerful anti-Fascist statement and the 'first truly radical lesbian film,'[60] and which has been remade twice,[61] haunts the entire boarding school genre, and arguably lesbian melodrama more generally. *Lost and Delirious* acknowledges this spectral presence, explicitly citing – both visually and narratively – *Mädchen* on numerous occasions.

Not that director Pool doesn't bring to the film her own authorial significations as a renowned lesbian auteur. Having directed such classic portraits of female desire and sexual identity confusion as *La femme de l'hotel, La demoiselle sauvage, Mouvements du désir, Rispondetemi* (also known as 'Urgence' in the 1991 *Montréal vu par …* compilation film), and especially *Anne Trister* and the miraculous *Emporte-moi*, Pool's name attaches to *Lost and Delirious* certain spectatorial associations and expectations. One of these is a visual style and narrative texture steeped more in European art house than in Hollywood cinematic traditions. In *Emporte-moi*, for example, Pool sets up a citational chain of (lesbian) identification with female iconicity that leads all the way back to the *nouvelle vague*. To this end, she concludes with a *cinéma vérité* homage to such auteurs as François Truffaut (*Emporte-moi* shares many affinities with *The 400 Blows*) and Jean-Luc Godard, and she actually has her teenage heroine, Hanna (Karine Vanasse), sneak into a local screening of Godard's *Vivre sa vie*, in which Godard's long-time muse, Anna Karina, plays an unhappy housewife who turns to prostitution. Cut off from her depressed mother (played by Quebec actress Pascale Bussières, who achieved her own iconic status among dyke cinephiles when she starred in Patricia Rozema's *When Night Is Falling*), Hanna starts to form a Manuela-like attachment to her teacher (played by Canadian author Nancy Huston), in whom she sees Karina's free-spirited image.

All of this provides fertile ground for the treatment of lesbian desire in *Lost and Delirious*. However, working both in English *and* from someone else's script for the first time, it's almost as if Pool felt she needed to import a new film language as well. Her camera is less emotionally distant here (as are the performances of the lead actors), and the angles and editing are more languorous and involving. Indeed, in *Lost and Delirious* Pool seems to have discovered, mid-career, a fondness for the close-up and for slow motion. Here, she is following in the best melodramatic tradition of the boarding school genre, which always teeters precariously between sentimentality and symbolism. In this regard, Sagan's *Mädchen in Uniform* set the stylistic tone by employing close-ups, slow dissolves, lots of shadows, Soviet-style montage, and a contiguous use of sound both within and between scenes (an Altmanesque technique used to great effect by Pool in *Lost and Delirious* as well) in order to heighten the affective experience of the spectator. Pool accomplishes something similar in *Lost and Delirious*, and she does so, arguably, through an extended cinematic homage to Sagan's film.

While it is possible to point to numerous parallel scenes in both films – from the 'motherless' girls in each talking about what they would put in letters home if only they were allowed (or could bring themselves) to send them, to Manuela's and Paulie's respective 'breechless' declarations of love before their classmates, and the social and sexual dissidence witnessed in similar choir scenes – what is most striking in the context of the argument outlined in this chapter is the way in which both Sagan and Pool use their cameras to frame architectural space, with interior and exterior shots of the boarding school itself coming to represent the inside/outside dialectic of female sexuality and lesbian desire. Sagan, who before making *Mädchen* apprenticed with legendary German stage director Max Reinhardt, puts her training in theatrical expressionism to great use in the film, particularly in the opening exterior montage, where the school's imposing stone façade, gothic archways, and threateningly phallic steeples are juxtaposed with shots of girls in striped uniforms marching in military-like formations. According to lesbian filmmaker and historian Andrea Weiss: 'As the prevalence of these symbols suggests, what is unusual about this boarding-school film is its militaristic, authoritarian, absolutely non-feminine atmosphere; it stands in for the girls' absent Prussian officer fathers, literally the absent patriarchy, rather than a loving female-defined space.'[62] Although far less intimidating architecturally, Bishop's University in Lennoxville, Quebec, where *Lost and Delirious* was filmed, functions in much the same way in the opening shots of Pool's film, particularly as the buildings are initially viewed by Mouse from the backseat of her father's car, their brick façades reflected impassively in the window. Note here that Mouse's father (who will later renege on a promised visit to her) registers his daughter's departure with barely the slightest trace of emotion.

Dominating the inside of the boarding school in *Mädchen*, and framing many of Sagan's most important shots, is a massive iron staircase. It is on this staircase that Manuela first meets Fräulein von Bernburg and – perhaps not so coincidentally – it is from its upper reaches that she threatens to throw herself when she faces expulsion over her public declaration of love for her teacher (see Figure 6.5). (A magnificent double staircase also dominates the foyer of Les Avons in Audry's film; Mademoiselle Julie makes her first appearance from the top of it, the camera quickly cutting to a close-up of Olivia down below as she gazes rapturously on the teacher who will very quickly come to occupy all her thoughts.) As a liminal space, a transitional space, a space leading from the regimentation and regulation of the classrooms and common areas down below to the more unruly and expressly sexualized zone of the girls' dormitory up above (where they eagerly receive their nightly kiss from Fräulein von Bernburg), the staircase represents the psychological contradictions and identity confusion experienced by Manuela, who is struggling to come to terms with her desires.

Here, it is important to consider Fräulein von Bernburg's own metonymical associations with the staircase, particularly as they relate to her ambivalent role in the film. That is, if Fräulein von Bernburg, as a woman, in some senses licenses – and even encourages – the devotion that her students, particularly Manuela, feel for her (at one point she tells Manuela that she often thinks of her), she also, as a teacher (and therefore authority figure), in some senses 'functions as an agent of repressive [control] for such feelings.'[63] As Rich puts it: 'If the girls focus their sexual desires upon her – where they can never be realized – then the danger of such desires being refocused on each other (where they *could* be realized) is averted.'[64] Which makes all the more interesting the fact that in the end, it is Manuela's fellow students, and not Fräulein von Bernburg, who rescue her. As a first step in

6.5   *Mädchen in Uniform*: Manuela (Hertha Thiele, in black) surrounded by her new classmates on the school's main staircase.

her (self)liberation, both erotically and politically, Manuela learns a painful but nonetheless immensely important lesson about (collective) identity – namely, that as a cross-dressed Mouse puts it when she and Paulie visit the tavern at Old Mill in Swan's novel, identity is 'what makes you different from the rest of the world … And it's also what you have in common with others – i.e., the way I have something in common with girls' (*WB* 128).

By contrast, in *Lost and Delirious*, in much the same way that Stephen surveys 'the most miserable of all those who comprised the miserable army' of queers in Alec's bar at the end of *The Well of Loneliness* (*WL* 393), Paulie chooses to stand (and fall) on her own – to position herself defiantly outside the bounds of both institutionalized patriarchal space and any potential female or lesbian counter-environment to that space. 'I'm not a lesbian,' she tells a bewildered Mouse at one point. 'I'm Paulie, and I'm in love with Tory.' Like Sagan, Pool reinforces Paulie's progressive sense of isolation visually. Already, at the outset of the film, Paulie, Tory, and Mouse, the self-declared 'lost girls,' occupy a room that is represented as somehow separate from the rest of the boarding school, tucked away in a turret and accessible only by a long, winding staircase that Pool shoots just as vertiginously as Sagan does hers. Easy access to the rooftop is provided from the room's windows, and it is here that Mouse first sees Paulie and Tory kissing. Gradually, as she is shunned by Tory and increasingly ostracized by the other schoolgirls, Paulie will abandon the interior spaces of the school – and the entreaties of Miss Vaughan to help – almost altogether, preferring to commune with the injured raptor she has nursed back to health in the school's adjoining forest. This process of self-isolation reaches its inevitable conclusion in the film's closing frames, when – in a direct reversal of Sagan – Pool has Paulie, holding the raptor, jump from the rooftop of the school as her classmates and Miss Vaughan look on helplessly, unable to save her.

That the citational effect of *Lost and Delirious*'s ending may in fact be one of spectatorial *dis*identification, rather than identification, is a risk that Pool is prepared to take. Consider here the long tracking shots that close both films. In *Mädchen*, Sagan's camera, adopting what can be read as the collective POV shot of the schoolgirls, follows a chastened Frau Oberin (Emilia Unda), the school's fascistic headmistress and merciless persecutor of Manuela, as she begins a slow, silent descent down the stairs, retreating along an empty hallway as the screen slowly fades to black. In *Lost and Delirious*, Pool follows not the arc of Paulie's fall, but rather that of the raptor's flight, tracking the bird as it circles the school before freezing the frame just as it appears to be flying directly into the camera. On the one hand, we see the agent of repressive authority being vanquished by a resistant minority gaze; on the other, we arguably witness the self-martyrdom of a free spirit who refuses to be looked at, affixed, and judged in any terms other than those she sets for herself. Without repudiating the defiant tone of *Mädchen*'s ending, Pool reminds her viewers that the liberation of lesbian desire is a process that is far from complete, both representationally in terms of the cinema and materially in terms of culture at large, and that, moreover, building a collective identitarian chain of citational address does not come without individual costs to self-expression.

In the final chapter of *Uninvited*, Patricia White states that 'all spectatorship, insofar as it engages subjective fantasy, revises memory traces and experiences, some of which are memories and experiences of other movies.'[65] She labels this process 'retrospectatorship,' whereby the reception of a given film 'is transformed by unconscious and conscious past viewing experience.'[66] In the specific context of *lesbian* retrospectatorship, we might also need to consider cinematic transformations enacted by past *reading* experiences, so frequently have both classic and contemporary 'lesbian' films been adaptations of works of literature, from *Rebecca* and *All About Eve* (both analysed by White) to *Fried Green Tomatoes* and *The Color Purple*.

Indeed, within the framework of film adaptation, White's theory of retrospectatorship fits well with the citational model outlined in this chapter, particularly as questions of narrative fidelity and lesbian representability overlap. In this regard, much has been written about the continued ghosting of images of lesbian desire in mainstream cinema, to the point of movies like *Fried Green Tomatoes* and *The Color Purple* radically rewriting their source material. However, I would argue that a citational approach to lesbian cinematic representation shifts the focus away from questions of narrative fidelity and the content of a given production to spectatorial infidelity and the contexts of its reception. That is, rather than concerning ourselves with abject discussions of what has been 'lost' in the adaptation of a novel by Susan Swan or a play by Lillian Hellman or (looking ahead to the next chapter) a book of poetry by Michael Turner, why not reinvest agency with the spectator by discussing what can be 'found' within the space of the film's viewing? Here, it seems to me that the lesbian/queer/feminist spectator is at a strategic advantage: as the slash fiction adaptations of *Hard Core Logo* briefly discussed in the next chapter attest, she is necessarily more promiscuous in her cinematic identifications, both on and off screen. In the films discussed in this chapter, and in others too numerous to mention, the lesbian spectator does not have to look hard to find much to see; she just needs to know where to look.

7 Adapting Masculinity: Michael Turner, Bruce McDonald, and Others

> The male's seeming exemption from visual representation may work very hard to preserve the cultural fiction that masculinity is not a social construction, but ... movies have always served as one of the primary sites through which the culture, in the process of promulgating that fiction, has also exposed its workings as a mythology.
>
> Steven Cohan and Ina Rae Hark, *Screening the Male*[1]

> P
>
> Say, you said that you guys have adapted books. Which ones?
>
> B
>
> *Catcher in the Rye, On the Road, Breakfast of Champions, American Psycho* – Oh, and some letters to these fag magazines that my boss said he found on our route once.
>
> Michael Turner, *American Whiskey Bar*[2]

In an article published in *Screen* in 1983, Steve Neale lamented the paucity of critical scholarship on representations of (heterosexual) masculinity in mainstream cinema, and attempted to open up a space for further dialogue on the subject by applying Laura Mulvey's then still relatively recent insights on identification, looking, and spectacle in 'Visual Pleasure and Narrative Cinema' to 'images of men, on the one hand, and to the male spectator on the other.'[3] While much has been published in the past twenty years to fill this void – including important edited collections by Peter Lehman, by Steven Cohan and Ina Rae Hark (who reprint Neale's essay as a prologue to and 'historical referent' for their contributors' ensuing analyses of both classic and contemporary Hollywood cinema), and, in the Canadian context, an excellent special issue of the *Canadian Journal of Film Studies* on 'Cinemas, Nations, Masculinities'[4] – discussions of the sort sought by Neale remain underrepresented in film studies discourse, as in culture at large. This is because of the abiding perception that theories relating to masculinity, unlike those relating to femininity, do not require (in the words of Neale) investigation, but merely testing, and that 'masculinity, as an ideal, at least, is [always already] implicitly known.'[5] In the Canadian context, and the English-Canadian filmic context more specifically, what has come to be implicitly and often unquestioningly known about masculinity, according to Thomas Waugh, is that representations of heterosexual male crisis on the screen are necessarily symptomatic of larger crises of national self-definition.[6]

In this final chapter, unlike in many of the preceding ones (most notably in my discussion of Robert Lepage in chapter 5), I will heed Waugh's advice and for the time being 'bracket the national-sexual that has prematurely and problematically been the animus of Canadian film studies.'[7] I will further adopt both the structural model and one of the examples outlined by Waugh in his article, 'que(e)rying' what is known and not known about canonical representations of masculinity in contemporary Canadian cinematic and literary culture by investigating the work of Michael Turner as it has intersected with and been adapted by different male filmmakers and video artists in this country. In the first, and most comprehensive, part of the chapter I will look at Bruce McDonald's highly successful 1996 film adaptation of *Hard Core Logo*, a 'novel in verse' about four male members of a once legendary Vancouver punk band reuniting for a tour of Western Canada and 'one last shot' at fame and glory, first published by Turner in 1993. Of special importance to my analysis is how the *invisible* (or understated) crisis of gender in the novel is rendered *visible* in the film via a concomitant crisis in genre.

To be sure, the theorization of masculinity in cinema studies has most often followed a genre analysis; Neale himself cites the western, the historical epic, the musical, and the women's melodrama as potential productive sites for investigating spectacularized representations of both normative and non-normative masculinities (here one thinks as well of the pioneering work of Joan Mellen).[8] Most scholarship in this field has looked at how the resiliency and stability of various genre conventions compel a similar conformity in terms of representations of a masculine ideal; I approach this question of representation from a slightly different direction, arguing that the generic *in*stability of McDonald's film helps expose the lack of wholeness and plenitude – indeed, the gaping abjection and melancholic disavowal – that constitutes the performative 'non-performance' of heteronormative masculine gender identification. My remarks, in this regard, will focus on the relationship between the band's two front men, lead singer Joe Dick (Hugh Dillon) and lead guitarist Billy Tallent (Callum Keith Rennie), as it is framed by the competing formal impulses of McDonald's documentary realist and melodramatic road movie cameras, and how this finds its corollary in the competing narrative claims of Turner's equally hybrid book, which can itself be read as at once a documentary poem and a picaresque novel.

In a coda to this chapter I will also trace Turner's subsequent collaborations with McDonald: on the 1998 live television broadcast of Turner's novel, *American Whiskey Bar*; and on the 1998 short film *Elimination Dance*, based on Michael Ondaatje's book of poetry, and in which Turner appears in the pivotal role of the caller. This will lead to a short digression on some of the filmic intertexts referenced in Turner's 1999 novel, *The Pornographer's Poem*. Finally, a few remarks about Turner's work with celebrated Vancouver photographer and video artist Stan Douglas on the 2001 video installation *Journey into Fear* will allow me to return to the visible/invisible dialectics of masculinity, and to conclude by offering a set of axioms on the shifting representations of masculinity in contemporary culture, as well as the ways in which such representations shift still further across different media.

It is Turner himself who best sums up the filmic potential of his text when, in *American Whiskey Bar*, he has his fictional Hungarian director, Monika Herendy, comment as follows: '*Hard Core Logo* has a visual sensibility, a cinematic quality that suggests it could have been written as much with a channel-changer as a pen and paper' (*AWB* 14). As Herendy goes on to note: 'When Bruce [McDonald] told me he was going to be making a movie based on *Hard Core Logo* I was shocked: <<But Bruce,>> I said, <<the book is a movie. It's a movie with pages>>' (*AWB* 14). Before *Hard Core Logo* became a movie, however, it was first transformed into a radio play and then a stage play. Indeed, one of the fascinating things about *Hard Core Logo* as a culturally embedded text is its status as an ongoing adaptive phenomenon, one that is – since the book's publication in 1993 – remarkably resilient and, well, adaptable: besides Michael Turner's novel, the aforementioned radio and stage plays, and McDonald's film, we have Danny Salerno's documentary about the making of McDonald's film, Noel S. Baker's screenwriter's diary, *Hard Core Roadshow*, Nick Craine's comic book, *Portrait of a Thousand Punks*,[9] the tribute CD, the now defunct website (www.hardcorelogo.ca), the 1997 VHS cassette of McDonald's film, and the 2003 DVD re-release (which includes lots of bonus material).

There began appearing that same year in Vancouver ads for a local band named Edmonton Block Heater, the title of one of Hard Core Logo's more popular songs; no doubt they are hoping to emulate the recent success of Juno-nominated rockers Billy Talent. Finally, all of these textual productions have become a rich source of material for an abiding and ongoing proliferation of *Hard Core Logo* slash fan fiction posted on the Internet, most of it foregrounding and making sexually explicit the sublimated romance between Joe and Billy that forms the absent centre of Turner's and McDonald's respective texts. I will have a bit more to say about this last adaptation of masculinity in *Hard Core Logo* later on in this chapter; but first let me outline more concretely the connections between novel and film.

Hard Core Logo, based in part on Turner's own experience fronting the Vancouver-based punk/rockabilly band The Hard Rock Miners in the late 1980s, documents the aspirant fortunes and increasingly diminishing returns of band members Joe Dick (lead vocals and guitar), Billy Tallent (guitar), John Oxenburger (bass), and Pipefitter (drums), who together achieved local punk superstardom in the late 1970s and early 1980s, before exploding in a series of mutual recriminations over drug and alcohol abuse, money, egos, wanting and not wanting fame, and the shadowy, implicitly nefarious influence of manager Ed Festus. The book opens with the band re-forming itself for a one-off benefit gig in aid of the Green World Coalition; the success of this gig prompts them to consider – especially following Joe's overly confident projections of a net profit of between $2,000 and $2,500 each – an acoustic reunion tour of old haunts in Calgary, Regina, Winnipeg, Saskatoon, Edmonton, and Vancouver. However, following escalating tensions – over poorly attended and/or cancelled concerts, Joe's renewed drug use and the effect this has on his already controlling personality, Pipe's slovenly habits, Billy's secret telephone communication with Ed Festus, John's recording of all of this in his tour diary, and, most crucially, the unstated fallout from the band's impromptu visit with their bitter and washed-up punk hero and musical inspiration, Bucky Haight – history repeats itself. This time the band implodes on stage in Edmonton following Billy's revelation that he's quitting what he calls *'this retro shit hayride'* tour to take up a *'lead guitar gig in a grunge-metal super-band'* being put together by Festus in Seattle.[10]

As Bart Beaty has recently argued in 'Imagining the Written Word: Adaptation in the Work of Bruce McDonald and Nick Craine': 'While the central characters of the band and their idol, fictitious punk legend Bucky Haight, have been retained in the film, along with the structure of the reunion tour,' McDonald and screenwriter Noel S. Baker alter 'the origin, relevance and resolution' of said tour, 'as well as fundamentally shifting the proximate cause of the band's eventual dissolution.'[11] This shift is accomplished through a double masquerade: first, via McDonald's decision to shoot his narrative fiction film in a faux-documentary style (à la Rob Reiner's *This Is Spinal Tap*, a crucial intertext to which I will return); and, second, again mimicking Reiner, via the conflation of McDonald, the extra-diegetic filmmaker, with McDonald, the diegetic character. In this way, I want to argue, the film self-consciously highlights the inherent narrative compromises and infidelities of both adaptation as a generic cultural process *and* masculinity as a gendered cultural product. That is, what McDonald's on-screen orchestrations and manipulations of his subjects and what his editor, Reg Harkema's, off-screen cutting of their recorded words and actions make visible is that the affective relationship between presumably (or presumptively?) straight men in our society is as tenuous and fragile as the relationship between a film and the book on which it is based.

Turner has stated that his early writing – *Company Town*, *Hard Core Logo*, and *Kingsway* (which has itself been adapted as a short film by Clancy Dennehy) – constitutes 'experiments in crossbreeding the ethnography with the poetry collection.'[12] (The author's undergraduate training in anthropology would seem to have been a formidable influence, as his next two novels – *American Whiskey Bar* and *The Pornographer's Poem* – can also be read as experiments in mixing ethnography with the screenplay.) Moreover, in defending his work to the faux filmmaker Herendy in the preface to *American Whiskey Bar*, Turner has argued 'that literary genres bring with them certain constraints, certain expectations; and that these expectations limit the readings of those texts by rendering them conventional, predictable' (*AWB* 2). Noting that *Hard Core Logo* 'could just as easily have been written as [a] banal realist [novel],' he states that he chose to write it 'in verse in order to subvert the varying misconceptions poetry carries,' to 'contrast the boredom of a touring punk rock band with a heroic – or even epic – form' (*AWB* 2). *Hard Core Logo*, the book, then, is The Sex Pistols' 'Anarchy in the UK' by way of Alexander Pope's *The Rape of the Lock*, The Gang of Four's 'Return the Gift' as dissected by Greil Marcus, The Buzzcocks' 'Boredom' rendered into Boccaccio's *Decameron*.

It is a tribute to Noel S. Baker's intuitiveness as a screenwriter that in adapting *Hard Core Logo* for the cinema, he was able to convey some of Turner's parodying of genre on screen. This was accomplished, I would argue, not only by tapping into something of the gritty handy-cam aesthetic that informed McDonald's first two features, *Roadkill* (1989) and *Highway 61* (1991), but also by drawing on McDonald's even earlier apprenticeship as a pseudo-documentarian (see his 1985 *Knock! Knock!*).[13] By transforming what could very easily have been just another 'road movie' into a mock documentary, Baker and McDonald achieve in filmic terms the parodic equivalent of Turner's poetic subversion of genre. *Hard Core Logo*, the film, is Julien Temple's *The Great Rock 'n' Swindle* by way of the NFB, Rob Reiner's *This Is Spinal Tap* as funded by Telefilm, Penelope Spheeris's *Decline of Western Civilization, Part I* as it might have looked on the CBC. And, indeed (if I can bring back questions of the national for a moment here), as Baker makes clear in his published production diary, *Hard Core Roadshow*, the completed movie is a document as much to the institutional, economic, and political constraints that bedevil the Canadian film industry as it is to those contraints which bedevil the Canadian music industry, which is allegorized both in the film's diegetic account of the band's struggles to make ends meet on their do-it-themselves 'Western Canadian Reunion Tour' and in Baker's extra-diegetic account of McDonald's struggles to fund, shoot, and distribute his film, as well as in both texts' aligning of material success in the arts with a necessary flight south of the border. As Baker comments near the end of *Hard Core Roadshow*:

> It's a fact of life that just when people become viable as writers and filmmakers they must weigh the personal cost of remaining in Canada versus the advantages of a career Stateside. The dilemma is dramatized in brutal terms in *Hard Core Logo*: Joe Dick wants to stay put and have a band that does things its own (independent, marginal) way; Billy Tallent does what loads of talented Canadians in music and film have been doing for years and heads south. It occurs to me, in light of the choices faced by many screenwriters and filmmakers, that *Hard Core Logo* (the film, not the book) can be read as an inverted and ironic Atwoodian survival fable.[14]

In his 1997 limited edition chapbook, *Survival*, his 'strobic guide' to Margaret Atwood's famous 1972 literary-nationalist treatise, Turner cannibalizes and reconstitutes as poems the various quotations chosen by Atwood as epigraphs to her chapters. Given this, Baker's assessment is not so far off the mark. And, here, paying attention to how questions of gender would seem to 'invert' questions of nationality is particularly important. That is, in the various 'games' played by Joe and Billy throughout the film of *Hard Core Logo* (not least the disappearing game and the 'Cool Film Game,' to which I will momentarily return), we are witness to a 'kicking against the pricks' (as it were) that has as much (if not more) to do with each's rehearsal, repudiation, and renegotiation of their perceived victimization as men as it does with any similar enactments of other possible victim positions associated with being Canadian (or even punk musicians) that they may have internalized.[15]

Earlier in *Hardcore Roadshow*, in discussing how he prepared to adapt Turner's novel, Baker addressed the text's generic hybridity as follows:

Read *Hard Core Logo* twice more last night, bringing the number of read throughs to five. Question remains: what the hell is it? Not a novel. Not exactly a poetry collection and not precisely a prose poem. It's more of a collage of fragments that conspire to form an absorbing narrative about this defunct Vancouver punk band ... The fragments are composed of song lyrics, letters, answering machine messages, diary entries, press release copy, confessions, interview excerpts, receipts and invoices, the odd picture. It's lean and spare, full of gaps and silences, the eloquence of things left unsaid.[16]

As Beaty has noted, this tension between what is said (or represented) in the book, and what is left unsaid (or un[der]represented), crucially overlaps with issues of adaptability;[17] just as crucially, it also overlaps with issues of masculinity. That is, just as most of the implied meaning of Turner's text remains either *below* or else resolutely inseparable *from* the surface typography/topography of the printed page, so does white heteronormative masculinity construct itself as the visible ground of culture precisely by rendering invisible its figurative operations, by refusing to say what it *is*, only what it *is not* (a point to which I will return at the end of this chapter). Before I discuss how the mixing of these visual and verbal taxonomies relates to the spectacle of masculinity on offer in the film, let me first address its unspoken presence in the novel by zeroing in briefly on questions of narrative voice.

While Joe is certainly the dominant character in the novel and, not so coincidentally, the lead singer of the band, and while most of the narrative seems to be focalized through his perspective, other voices intrude (John's, Pipe's, and Billy's most obviously, but also Bucky's, new manager Bruce McRoberts's, Green World Coalition volunteer Laura Cromartie's, Mary the groupie's, radio interviewers', and those of sundry other minor walk-on characters). Perhaps just as significantly, these voices tend to be filtered to us, as Baker has already indicated, via a number of different media: letters, faxes, phone messages, graffiti, John's tour diary, and so on. Moreover, the exterior projection of these narrative voices is also contrasted, in the book, by Turner's use of interior monologues (signalled typographically in the text through italics[18]) for Billy, John, and Pipe, which often serve as ironic commentaries on what Joe is saying – or not saying, as the case may be.

It is significant that Joe, the front man, who is all bluster and bluff external representation, is denied these inner reflective moments. After the visit to Bucky Haight, for example, we never get Joe's own impressions of what happened; rather, we get commentary from John and Billy, as well as Joe's announcement to the audience in Saskatoon that Bucky has died (*HCL* 143) – a lie that nevertheless symbolically represents Joe's Oedipal slaying of his father-hero. Joe is always depicted as speaking directly to someone in the novel (whether it be us as readers [see *HCL* 14], his fellow bandmates, interviewers, or the audiences at Hard Core Logo's concerts through the songs he sings). Ironically, these so-called instances of direct speech are all about *indirection*, about Joe saying something other than what he really means. Indeed, the only time we get Joe apparently verbalizing an approximation of the truth about how he feels is near the very end of the novel, in a poetic fragment significantly titled 'Joe to Himself to Billy':

This is it, isn't it, Billy?
It's really over now, isn't it,
Billy? (*HCL* 193)

In its deliberately vague pronoun references, negative syntax, and apparent rhetoricism, this poem is of a piece with the lyrics to 'Something's Gonna Die Tonight,' which presumably stand in as the discursive fulfilment of the physical violence with which Joe threatens Billy in Edmonton when he learns of the latter's defection, but which at the same time are rigorously non-declarative in their phrasing (note especially the repetition of 'what,' 'whatever,' and of course 'some thing' in the final stanza; *HCL* 181). In other words, if Joe is unable to say exactly what or who has died, been lost, is over, this perhaps has as much to do with the unstated (but nevertheless implicitly understood) limits of masculine self-(dis)closure as it does with what remains unstated (but equally understood) about his relationship with Billy. This masculine 'conundrum' of not being able to articulate out loud one's affective desires, and therefore of not having those desires heard by others, is materialized on Joe's body in the book via his description of his 'old [musical] wounds' – namely, a 90 per cent hearing loss in his right ear and two inoperable vocal nodes on his throat:

People are always telling me
that I'm too loud, that I shout.
Half the time I can't even hear
what the hell I'm saying.

It's a conundrum, really.
The more your hearing goes,
the louder you become.
And the louder you become,
the more strain you put on the vocal.
If the strain goes untrained
you get nodes on your throat
Overgrown nodes cause complete
loss of voice. (*HCL* 19)

Ironically, while in Turner's book Joe subsequently presents this to Billy as the reason for the band 'going acoustic' on their initial reunion gig (*HCL* 19), and while John for one rejoices at finally being able to '*hear the words*' to their songs (*HCL* 36), as Billy notes to himself, with characteristic understatement, when it comes to Hard Core Logo – and even more pertinently its two front men – if '*You take away the volume, you have nothing*' (*HCL* 32).

The dilemma is no less vexing for the filmmakers: How, to paraphrase Beaty, does one render the unspoken (no matter how loudly unspoken) in visual terms?[19] For Baker, as screenwriter, this question led to a fundamental reconceptualization of the adaptation process, during which he found himself thanking Turner for 'writing so little but suggesting so much. Adapting novels to the screen is usually a process of subtraction. In this case it's not and I've had a great time filling in the blanks.'[20] Moreover, I contend that Baker and McDonald respond to the *unsaid* in Turner's book by *saying* and – even more so – by *showing* as much as they can. Here, the film's own hybrid generic status as a fictional narrative film masquerading as a documentary comes crucially into play, for McDonald's (that is, Bruce McDonald, the character) documentary camera captures things visually and acoustically that various band members would otherwise prefer remain unseen and un-overheard (most notably, in the case of Bucky still very much having the use of both legs; Joe and Billy conspiring to cut out on Pipe and John in forming a new band after the tour; and, finally, Billy cutting out on Joe when he learns of the *Jenifur* gig).

As well, there is the deliberate contrast between what the characters say (which is a lot) one on one to Bruce's camera (sequences which are mostly filmed in black and white) and what they don't say to one another, or what they say in very coded ways to one another. This finds its visual corollary in terms of the differences between the band members' performance of a hypermasculine erotics of display and exhibitionism on stage (note, for example, the kisses and expectorate exchanged between Joe, Billy, and John at the benefit gig that opens the film) and their studied 'non-performance' of masculinity – through the mostly successful withholding of theatrical effect and emotional affect – off stage (largely by hiding behind and under coats, hats, sunglasses, beer bottles, and other sundry props of masculine detachment).

Many of these issues come to the fore in a subtly self-reflexive sequence in the film, when, in a quiet moment on the road in the van, Joe and Billy play the 'Cool Film Game,' during the course of which *Hard Core Logo*'s most immediate filmic antecedent (at least in terms of the 'mockumentary' genre) – that is, Rob Reiner's *This Is Spinal Tap* – is directly referenced. I think a lot is going on in this three-minute clip, the various components of which can be parsed in any number of interesting ways. First, the tight *cinéma vérité*-style POV close-ups on Joe and Billy, intercut with shots of Pipe listening but not participating in the back of the van, serve to accentuate the exclusive and exclusionary intimacy between the band's two front men. Next, the structure of the game and the intertextual references to the films named – all of them, until Joe's stumble at coming up with one that begins with 'Y,' representing major works by auteurs like Welles, Fellini, Godard, Kubrick, Cronenberg, Antonioni, Polanski, and so on – serve to highlight interesting questions of male competition and authorship. The questions play out both intra-diegetically in terms of who is the band's animating force musically (Billy wins the game and, not so coincidentally, the lucrative contract with *Jenifur*), and extra-diegetically in terms of Bruce McDonald allowing his on-screen persona to take a self-parodying hit.

Bruce clearly understands the basic premise of the 'Cool Film Game' (that the last letter of one movie title becomes the first letter of the next), but he underestimates the seriousness with which Joe and Billy play it. Thus, when Billy mentions *Spinal Tap*, Bruce, from behind the camera, fills in the blank of Joe's initial non-response with the Ron Howard comedy *Parenthood*, a suggestion that both Billy and Joe greet with derision. This at once acknowledges – and therefore derails –

the obvious critical discourse that will accrue around *Hard Core Logo* being a pale imitation of its filmic forebear (a principle of genealogical influence/homage that is also foregrounded by the fact that films by both Rob Reiner [*Spinal Tap*] and his father, Carl Reiner [*Dead Men Don't Wear Plaid*] are referenced in this sequence, a link further compounded by the fact that Steve Martin played the lead in both Reiner *père*'s film and Howard's *Parenthood*). At the same time, it self-consciously deflates any pretensions McDonald might have, as a filmmaker, towards auteurship (in the same way that later scenes show Pipe and Bucky berating Bruce for his sophomoric *Highway 61* and *Roadkill* efforts).

Finally, Joe's losing film reference, following his stumbling effort over the letter 'Y,' to *Young at Heart* (Gordon Douglas, 1954), once again draws our attention as viewers to the issue of romance as it has been generically recoded along male–male lines in this film. Here I quote once again from Noel Baker's screenwriter's diary, because he lets us know that this last reference is a very deliberate one:

> Thought it a good idea to get the *Spinal Tap* issue right into the open here. Acknowledge the ancestor, as it were. The other issue is romantic: Joe's inability to think of a cool film that starts with a Y (as in 'Why') leads him to choose a 1950s Technicolor romance about a self-destructive musician who goes to the brink of death for love, but is delivered unto a happy ending with Doris Day (a weirdly idealized Billy Tallent). Billy's scorn for *Young at Heart* warns Joe not to expect any happy ending to his renewed 'courtship.'[21]

That Joe is indeed courting Billy, both artistically and interpersonally, is revealed even further if we examine the scene that immediately precedes this one. There, following the show in Calgary, Joe and Billy are being interviewed by a young local reporter named Tiffany (Nicole Parker), who quotes their former manager, Ed Festus, on how 'you two fought like some tanked-up, white trash married couple in a trailer park.' Joe, after leaning in flirtatiously to a suddenly girlish and giggling Billy (see Figure 7.1), responds by saying: 'Well, some of that might be true. But that's what makes our music and our art great.' To which Billy, doing his best Doris Day, interjects: 'I suffer for his art.' Warming to 'this romance theme,' Baker goes on to note in *Hardcore Roadshow* that later on in the script he is planning to '[drop] a bomb into one of John's fragile monologues, suggesting that the real source of the Joe-Billy tension lies in the fact that Joe once anally raped Billy, creating what the critics will doubtless call a tense homoerotic subtext.'[22]

Contributing to this subtext are two further sets of genre codes that get operationalized in this scene and, indeed, at multiple points throughout the movie. First, the scene's final superimposed and animated shots of the highway and its centre line foreground the film's equally hybrid generic status as a buddy/road movie. To be sure, Bruce McDonald's on- and off-screen presence as filmmaker serves to accentuate this reading, via his inextricable association – in both his documentary subjects' and his audience's minds – with his earlier classics *Roadkill* and *Highway 61*. But I want to throw the issue of the film's status as road movie into the mix here for the ways in which it comments on representations of masculine affect. That is, the road movie genre, while not necessarily gender-specific in

7.1   *Hard Core Logo*: Joe Dick (Hugh Dillon, l) and Billy Tallent (Callum Keith Rennie) kibbitz during a post-show interview in Calgary.

terms of subject matter, characters, or target audience (although maybe it does lean towards a more 'masculine' as opposed to 'feminine' constituency in all of these respects), does – very uniquely, it seems to me – tend to take as one of its structuring principles the documenting of the various permutations of non-sexual same-sex affective relationships: from *Easy Rider* to *Priscilla*; from *Thelma and Louise* to *Boys on the Side*.

Freed from the social conventions and gender policing of normative society, the men in particular in these films can more easily express both their self-alienation and their desire for the other, producing what Stuart Aitken and Christopher Lukinbeal have called a 'mobile' or 'hysterical' masculinity, one 'disassociated' but not completely emancipated from the domestic and capitalist constraints of hegemonic masculinity (to this end, the ubiquitous presence of McDonald's documentary camera means that the men in Hard Core Logo remain under surveillance).[23] This is also a characteristic feature – along with its episodic, retrospective, and pseudo-autobiographical narrative construction, its focus on the material level of daily existence, and its rogue's gallery of socially marginal and outsider character types – of the picaresque novel, from *Don Quixote* (both Cervantes's and Kathy Acker's) to Jack Kerouac's *On the Road*. Indeed, Joe and Billy's relationship is similar in many ways to that of Sal Paradise and Dean Moriarty, and Turner's novel in particular, in documenting the band's horizontal movement through space and Joe and Billy's opposing vertical trajectories through society, owes much to the circular narrative structure of Kerouac's novel.[24]

Moreover, two early and perceptive critics of the film especially attuned to its homoerotic subtext also separately point out that *Hard Core Logo* at times very much reads like a melodrama. In her review 'Hard Core Logo: A Love Story,' Noreen Golfman describes the film as 'a powerful melodrama of two men bound to each other with grudging inevitability.'[25] And in calling *Hard Core Logo* 'a buddy film not afraid to be a love story,' Ken Anderlini notes that it is also 'a melodrama full of cinematic poetry and humour … worthy of Douglas Sirk or Rainer Werner Fassbinder.'[26] Indeed, as Anderlini goes on to point out, a key feature of classic Hollywood melodramas – the threat to the sanctity of the family unit by some outside force – is represented in the film 'in the form of Jenifur, a band in Los Angeles which promises money and success to Billy,' but that in turn threatens the stability of Joe and Billy's personal and professional relationship.[27] To be sure, the visible absence of prominent women characters in both the film and Turner's novel complicates any reading of *Hard Core Logo* as a traditional melodrama, a form whose 'visible generic existence,' according to Linda Williams, has most often been tied to its status as a 'woman's film.'[28] Indeed, where women are present in the film, they are seen, in Golfman's words, to 'threaten the enclosed masculine economy of power and desire' rather than acting to stabilize the hetero-domestic norm.[29] One thinks, in this regard, of the hookers outside Calgary who roll Joe and Billy for all the band's money, or the scene backstage in Regina with Mary, the fan, whose temporary occupation of that space with her bourgeois family (she introduces the band members to her conservatively dressed husband and her daughter, also named Billie) is offset by John's aforementioned revelations about Joe's supposed rape of Billy, and by Joe and Billy's subsequent post-performance discussions about each having had sex with Mary during the band's heyday.

At the same time, it does seem appropriate here to mention women's participation in the libidinal economy of *Hard Core Logo*'s ongoing adaptation on the Internet via the production and dissemination of slash fan fiction that – as with Kirk and Spock, Starsky and Hutch, Mulder and Krycek, and any number of other male pop culture couples – makes sexually explicit the sublimated romantic relationship between Joe and Billy. A search of the Slash Page Database Project yields thirty-one hits for websites that feature *Hard Core Logo* slash fiction, often as part of complicated crossover narratives with other favourite Canadian televisual slash sources like *Due South* or *Da Vinci's Inquest*.[30] What my admittedly very cursory and wholly ad hoc survey of some of these narratives reveals is – as with Constance Penley's reading of *Star Trek* slash fiction – a complex suturing of female fantasy and phallic identification that completely renovates not only the genres of romance and pornography, but also the gender fixity of masculine and feminine viewing positions as they have been theorized, especially in relation to melodrama, by classic feminist film theory.[31]

Film scholar Peter Lehman has noted a similar crossbreeding of male fantasy and phallic disidentification, or alienation, in what he calls the 'male melodramatic rock tradition,' many of whose songs 'frequently have the word "crying" in their titles.'[32] While none of Hard Core Logo's lyrics contain overt allusions to crying, I want to adapt Lehman's insights elsewhere in the same article about the function of the 'melodramatic penis' in the representation of masculinity in films from the 1990s to comment on the suicide of the aptly named Joe Dick, which serves as the shocking conclusion to McDonald's film.

Following the on-screen McDonald's revelation to Joe of Billy's imminent departure from the band in order to begin his gig with *Jenifur*, we witness a montage of Hard Core Logo songs being performed on stage in Edmonton. We're back in the stylistic realm of the classic rock documentary here, and McDonald's frenetic hand-held camera intercuts reaction shots of a manically cavorting audience with shots of a lasciviously grinning Billy circling and butting against Joe, who stands rigidly erect in the middle of the stage in front of his microphone stand (see Figure 7.2). When Joe can stand this teasing foreplay no longer he explodes, punching Billy in the face, before jumping and fighting his long-time friend to John's spoken-word refrain of 'In the end, it's love.' The two men eventually separate, clothing ripped and askew, sweaty, bleeding, and breathing heavily; Joe goes back on stage, picks up the phallic extension of Billy's new Stratocaster guitar (only recently bestowed on him in a scene of patriarchal anointment by father-figure Bucky), and smashes it to pieces. He then grabs a whiskey bottle and two glasses and makes as if to gather Billy in a post-coital embrace. Billy, however, rejects the overture and leaves the club. We then cut to a long shot of Joe on the steps outside the club, whiskey bottle in hand, foot resting tellingly on what would have been Billy's glass. Acknowledging McDonald's hovering presence, Joe knowingly asks the director if he got all the footage he needs, before supplying one last Norma Desmondish close-up. Placing himself directly in front of the camera, Joe shares a final drink with McDonald, and then calmly pulls a gun from his coat pocket and blows his brains out, a Dick shot as melodramatic in its withheld masculine significations as are ridiculously comic the overdeveloped masculine significations on offer in the closing shot of Dirk Diggler's famous member in *Boogie Nights*.

In the brief and frenzied aftermath of Joe's suicide at the end of the film, one of the things we hear uttered – whether by a crew member or a passer-by remains unclear – is the phrase 'Was that for real?' I conclude my discussion of the operations of gender and genre in *Hard Core Logo* by returning to its formal construction as a quasi-documentary, especially as this necessarily intersects with and foregrounds issues of 'the real.' Following on my preceding discussion, we might well

7.2   *Hard Core Logo*: Billy and Joe on stage in Edmonton.

ask: How does a film that presents itself as a documentary reconcile itself as a melodrama? For, as Williams notes, melodrama has most often been read as 'antithetical to cinematic realism.'[33] However, Williams complicates this reading by arguing that melodrama employs various 'realist cinematic effects – whether of setting, action, acting or narrative motivation' – precisely in order to heighten emotional affect through 'a dialectic of pathos and action.'[34] Before I examine how McDonald employs this dialectic in his film to document the various lines of masculine affiliation and alienation among Hard Core Logo's band members, and particularly between the front men Billy and Joe, let me first address the documentary status of Turner's source text.

To be sure, the documentary genre has just as long a history in Canadian literature as it does in Canadian film, Dorothy Livesay having first drawn our attention
to its particular poetic manifestations in this country in her classic 1971 essay 'The
Documentary Poem: A Canadian Genre' (she traces the tradition as far back as the
nineteenth century and the poetry of Isabella Valancy Crawford).[35] It was Stephen
Scobie, however, who elaborated Livesay's rather amorphous dialectical theories
into the set of axioms by which critics (myself among them) continue to assess
examples of the form today.[36] According to Scobie, the Canadian documentary
poem is usually (a) of book length (that is, a long poem or series of linked poems)
and narrative in structure; (b) an amalgam of historical events and 'fictional inci-
dents'; (c) focalized through a single character who took part/is taking part in
these events/incidents, and around whose 'life story' the text is arranged; (d) supplemented with primary 'documents' such as journals, maps, photographic
images, and other artefacts and ephemera kept by this character, who is very
often some sort of 'artist'; and (e) noted for the dramatic irony and dialectical tension established in the relationship between and the representation of this character's objective 'persona' and the poet's own subjective 'voice.'[37] Included among
Scobie's examples of texts that conform to these criteria are, besides Margaret
Atwood's *The Journals of Susanna Moodie* (1970), three works that – interestingly
enough in the context of this chapter – centre on characters of what it only seems
appropriate to call questionable and/or troubled masculinity: Michael Ondaatje's
The Collected Works of Billy the Kid (1970), Scobie's own *McAlmon's Chinese Opera*
(1980), and Gwendolyn McEwen's *The T.E. Lawrence Poems* (1982).

We might well add *Hard Core Logo* to this list. While I don't propose to enumer-
ate the various ways in which Turner's text conforms to Scobie's documentary
model, I do wish to pause briefly over the relationship between the photographs
and other 'found' documents included in Turner's book and the text that sur-
rounds them. The collage-like effect this produces helps sustain, I would argue, a
peculiarly documentary representational aesthetic in the book between the objective record of events (the bills, the scrawled set lists, the invoices, the contracts,
the recorded phone messages, the photographs, found bits of graffiti, and so on)
and each of the band members' subjective interpretations of those events (which
are often included on facing pages). For example, a reproduction of the contract
signed between the band and the owner of the club where they're to perform in
Calgary, which clearly lists Joe as 'leader' of the band, is sandwiched between
Joe's division of the labour for the upcoming gig (noticeably he supplies himself
with no evident task to perform) and John's bathetic version of how things actually went at the club in his subsequent diary entry (*HCL* 97–9). And Pipe's interior
monologue about the 'easy' money he anticipates making on the tour is immediately followed by two receipts for Joe's initial – and very large – outlay of
expenses, which hints ominously at the band's final degradation in Edmonton,
when they are 'paid in quarters,' which makes Pipe in particular feel 'like a busk-
ing band' (*HCL* 78–80, 185).

In the film, McDonald self-reflexively foregrounds himself, as documentarian,
as the visible (and acoustic – for when he is not seen on screen he is nevertheless
heard) agent of mediation between the objective presentation of events ('Is the

camera still rolling?' we hear more than once during the course of this film) and our (as extra-diegetic spectators) and the band members' (as diegetic participants) subjective interpretation of those events. More specifically, there are numerous examples of McDonald's so-called invisible hand as documentary filmmaker making visible the various lines of male homosocial desire – and equally importantly, male homosexual cathexis – that anchor the relationship between Billy and Joe. As 'evidence' of this, one might point to the fact that Billy and Joe are most often filmed together in two-shots and tight close-ups, whereas Pipe and John are shot with their respective girlfriends at the beginning, mostly alone subsequently, or, when with the whole band, in long shots (and frequently in shadow). The scene in the Niagara Hotel bar following the benefit concert that opens the film, during which Billy and Joe play at stopping time by freezing in mid-movement, and during which Joe first pitches his idea of reuniting the band to Billy, is a good example of this. Certainly McDonald's splicing in of found Super 8 footage of Billy and Joe's first band, Peckerhead, during this sequence would seem to attest to his desire to construct, albeit retrospectively, a melodramatic narrative of adolescent male bonding and adult male estrangement.

More generally, it is also important to note the non-linear cutting of the film as a whole. Specifically, the splicing and intercutting of one-on-one band member interviews is used to comment (again retrospectively) on the increasing tensions among individuals. Moreover, following the time lapse sequence where Pipe and John await the arrival of Joe and their tour van in a Vancouver alley, there is a noticeable stylistic shift from a more quintessentially documentary style (replete with hand-held shots, quick cuts, lots of exterior and talking-head sequences, and so on) to what it only seems appropriate to call a more recognizably fictional narrative style.

That is, two noticeable changes seem to take place: first, the preponderance of intertitles and textual passages projected against a black screen (two recognizable documentary features) largely disappears (only to reappear at the end, in the case of the textual passages that flash up on screen during the closing credit sequence, when, perhaps, a now off-screen Bruce wants to reimpose an objective, documentary aesthetic, as if to eschew any responsibility he might have for Joe's death); and second, the quick cuts of the opening benefit concert sequence are replaced by much longer takes and by a tendency of Bruce's 'documentary' camera to cut away from the subjects and action it is purportedly enlisted to document to largely extraneous (that is to say, deliberately constructed) shots of the horizon, the road the boys are travelling down, and so on (often accompanied either by John's voice-over reading from his diary, or by appropriately suggestive extradiegetic music). All of this coalesces in the climactic acid sequence, where all pretense around documentary realism is thrown out the window, as – under the further mediating (or medicating) influence of a hallucinogen – Bruce responds to Bucky's implicit challenge about showing them what he can do cinematically by experimenting with all sorts of avant-garde visual techniques (both images and cuts) in the manner of Francis Ford Coppola's *Apocalypse Now* or Luis Buñuel's *Un chien andalou*. We can only read this sequence as encoding all sorts of visual and auditory cues/clues regarding the death of the band and of Joe.

Indeed, the film's coda arguably (and very melodramatically) shows death as the logical extension of our thoroughly mediatized culture's appetite for such ritualized performance, whether on stage or off, as well as Joe's inability to negotiate any longer the performative codes of his particular subcultural masculinity. To quote that old pop song from the early 1980s: 'Video killed the radio star.' Having visually exposed his hitherto unspoken feelings for Billy to Bruce's camera, it is wholly appropriate that Joe should choose the very medium that was supposed to remake him (in all gendered and generic senses of that word) to also be the end of him. Moreover, Joe's on-camera suicide, when compared to the final entry in Turner's book, where it is indicated that the singer trades in his stage pseudonym (Joe Dick) for a return to his 'real' name (Joe Mulgrew) as he sets about trying to put together yet another band, suggests that masculinity can never fully be achieved, only endlessly rehearsed. Or, to put this another way, where the book reveals Joe's final and perhaps most calculated performance to be the donning of the pretence of an authentic masculine identity (Joe Mulgrew), the film's closing frames, read in the context of Joe's diegetic and McDonald's extra-diegetic hoaxing of the viewer, reveal the impossibility of ever literally embodying such an identity: 'Was that for real?'

It's a question that needs to be extrapolated and asked not only of Bruce McDonald's generically hybrid film as a whole, but also of the various performances of gender recorded therein (which are the sum of its parts). Indeed, given that heteronormative white masculinity is all too often constructed as having an exclusive purchase on the real, and given (as I mentioned in the last chapter)[38] that Lacanian film theory has for the most part been inattentive to discussions of the real, posing such a question – and in such a melodramatic fashion – would seem to be essential if, to paraphrase Jane Gaines on the *vérité* claims of documentary and pornography,[39] either heteronormative masculinity *or* Lacanian film theory is to give up its affective secrets.

That masculinity is as much a masquerade as femininity, and that its *unmasking* as such might carry with it violent and even deadly repercussions, is something that Turner explores in all of his work, not least in *American Whiskey Bar*, another generically hybrid novel, which McDonald adapted for live television broadcast on Toronto's CityTV in the fall of 1998. Indeed, taking a page from McDonald (who, fittingly, appears briefly as a character in the book), Turner constructs his novel as a faux-memoir about the making and/or 'unmaking' of a film he was commissioned to write. To this end, the script proper, which comprises the bulk of the novel, and which draws liberally on the conventions of both porn and film noir – not least in the masculine aporia specific to each – is framed by a series of critically reflexive apparatuses that seek to disavow ownership of the finished product: a preface by screenwriter Turner that decries the film because it was shot *exactly* as he wrote it; an introduction by director Monika Herendy that details how her high ambitions for the film were thwarted by her eventual removal from the set; and an afterword by critic Milena Jagoda – one of the few people to have seen the film, and who, in reviewing it, is permitted only to say 'what this film is not' (*AWB* 180). This is an allegory of authorship that intersects with the broader

7.3   *American Whiskey Bar*: Moses Znaimer introduces Bruce McDonald's live television adaptation of Michael Turner's novel.

metanarrative of masculinity through the figure of Klaus 9, the shadowy producer who cleverly absents himself from the circuit of representation encapsulated by the film by seizing control (quite literally) of the mechanisms of its production, distribution, and reception.

All of this is something that McDonald's live television broadcast of *American Whiskey Bar* is only able to hint at. In his taped introduction, CityTV impresario Moses Znaimer offers a subtly ironic disclaimer about the events about to follow. He is filmed standing in the middle of the set on the main floor of the CHUM/CityTV building, ponytailed and sharply suited, speaking directly to the camera in his characteristically impassive monotone (see Figure 7.3). In pulling away from Znaimer, McDonald, as in *Hard Core Logo*, very deliberately foregrounds the presence of his camera. I argue that this sets up from the very beginning a dialectic in which the invisible operations of Znaimer's 'non-performance' of a normative masculinity paradoxically render all the more visible the performances of masculinity in the ensuing broadcast as hyperbolic and hyperstylized (dis)figurations of this norm. Hence the working-class garbage men (one or more of whom may be a serial cop killer) arguing about who to cast in their gay porn prison drama at table one; the undercover cops masquerading as famous American porn producers at table two; the gay black man and his Hispanic boxer boyfriend who are arrested on suspicion of murder while talking to the black man's lawyer sister and her white male colleague at table three; and the sexually potent Liberian who is recalled with fetishistic fondness by one of the white women at table four.

In this sense, the medium in which McDonald has chosen to adapt Turner's work is an important reminder that what is being 'remediated' is not only a prior technology of representation (Philip Auslander contends that television, and particularly live television, 'colonizes' and remakes both theatrical performance *and* film[40]) but also a prior technology of gender.[41] The blurring of boundaries between 'live' and 'mediatized' masculinities begs the question about the ontological differences between performative effect and embodied affect, between identity and image, between real men and fakes. This, then, is the paradoxical 'theorem' confronting all of Turner's and McDonald's male characters (including themselves): that, to quote the passage from Pasolini that serves as one of the epigraphs to Turner's *American Whiskey Bar*, 'the symbol of reality has something reality does not have: it does not represent any meaning yet it adds to it – by its very representative nature – a new meaning' (quoted in *AWB*, ix).

Arguably, this is something Turner himself trades on in his star turn as the caller in McDonald's *Elimination Dance*, an award-winning short film based on Michael Ondaatje's 1978 poetry chapbook of the same name, and co-directed by Ondaatje and Don McKellar.[42] As with Hugh Dillon's take on his own day job as Headstones' front man in playing Joe in *Hard Core Logo*, in *Elimination Dance* Turner's smoothly suave on-screen performance starts to merge with his off-screen personas: former indie rock star, bad boy author, and emerging Vancouver arts and culture czar. Having had a wordless cameo as the bartender in the live television broadcast of *American Whiskey Bar*, Turner here gets most of the dialogue – and the limelight – presiding over the desperate dancing couples (including our erstwhile hero and heroine, played by Don McKellar and Tracy Wright) with just the right combination of big band sophistication and cabaret-style sexual menace (see Figure 7.4). Equal parts Guy Lombardo and Joel Grey, Turner's caller supplies his (and, by extension, the film's) own autocritique of the gendered social symbolic to which these couples aspire via the flashcards from which he reads, which consistently expose – and eliminate – masculinity as the more fraudulent masquerade.

Similarly, the Joe Gillis-like narrator of Turner's most recent novel, *The Pornographer's Poem* (1999), finds himself trapped in a film loop of his own making, supplying an abject and (we later learn) from-the-grave voice-over narration to the story of his apprenticeship in blue-movie making.[43] Specifically, he recounts how he traded his and best friend Nettie Smart's youthful feminist ideals about the political and artistic merits of the social production of the pornographic image (both are devotees of Angela Carter's *The Sadeian Woman*) for Svengali-like producer Marty Flynn's more brutal and masculinist lessons about the economics of the repetition of that image. (Voice-over narration is also an integral element of the classic Mitchell Brothers porn film from 1972, *Behind the Green Door*, which, along with its AIDS-era sequel, serves as another important intertext for Turner's novel.) Thus, the narrator learns 'a lot about the male species' (not to mention makes 'most of [his] dough') in screening his first pornographic film, *The Family*

7.4   *Elimination Dance*: Don McKellar and Tracy Wright as the desperate dancing partners, with Michael Turner as the caller in the background.

Dog, at various 'stags and frats' around the city.[44] Furthermore, to paraphrase Linda Williams from *Hardcore*, the 'visual evidence of the mechanical "truth"' of his own bodily *male* pleasure – that is, the 'money shot' that we as readers/viewers have been waiting for – coincides with his literal disconnection from the narrative diegesis and from the *female* amanuensis that, for all intents and purposes, supplies the pleasure of the text[45]:

> ME
> (whispering)
>
> I love you, Nettie.
>
> Nettie's face collapses even more.
>
> I am about to come, so I pull out. I make a sound. A yell. Which is odd for me because I'm more a moaner than a shouter. But whatever. Something taps against the back of my head, something cold and metallic. I think it's the boom mike, but I guess I should've known better. I look down to see my cum dot Nettie's scar. The next spurt would be my third, and that one's always the best.

This time I went with it, my head propelling faster than any ride I'd ever been on. By the time the rest of me caught up to it, I was long gone. It was as if I passed right into the wall's flesh. That's when everything went white on white. In the distance, well behind me, the echo of something loud. A backfire.[46]

'White on white' and 'the echo of something loud': these are potentially very useful metaphors with which to talk about the functions of (hetero)normative masculinity. That is, like whiteness as a racial signifier, (white) masculinity remains largely invisible (or is made to seem invisible) as a socially constructed category of gender precisely because of its hypervisibility, in patriarchal culture, as the constitutive ground of *all* gender relations. At the same time, masculinity's endless repetition as ur-identity is also a diminution, ensuring that it becomes, in the words of Judith Butler, a copy without an original.[47] Or, to adapt the second of Turner's metaphors to a discursive formation invoked earlier in this chapter, unable to say with any declarative certainty what it is ('something loud,' perhaps?), it can only echo what it is not. The question remains, however: How does one render these echoes visible? I have already demonstrated, in my reading of the adaptation of *Hard Core Logo*, how Bruce McDonald cinematically exposes some of the loud silences around masculinity operating in Turner's text. I will now examine very briefly the asynchronous visual and aural representations of masculinity on offer in Turner's collaboration with internationally renowned Vancouver media artist Stan Douglas on Douglas's 2001 video installation *Journey into Fear*.

First shown at the Serpentine Gallery in London in the spring of 2002 before travelling on to Hanover's Kestner Gesellschaft Gallery and Vancouver's Contemporary Art Gallery later the same year, *Journey into Fear*, co-scripted by Douglas and Turner, is a complex adaptation, via Herman Melville's *The Confidence Man*, of the 1975 Daniel Mann film of the same name, itself a remake of Norman Foster's 1942 film, which is in turn based on the 1940 literary thriller by Eric Ambler. The plot of both Ambler's novel and Foster's original film adaptation (Orson Welles was replaced as director part way through filming) revolves around the internecine conspiratorial politics of Second World War arms trading. An independent dealer, Mr Graham (Joseph Cotten), is forced to hop a commercial cargo ship sailing from Turkey after becoming the target of an assassination plot as a result of a sale he has just made. Unbeknownst to Graham, however, his would-be assassins are also on board – something he only discovers definitively when the absent-minded archaeology professor, Herr Haller (Eustace Wyatt), sheds this disguise and reveals himself to Graham as Möller, a mercenary German counter-intelligence operative. The moral and narrative crux of the film revolves around the deal Möller offers Graham: death right then and there on the ship; or the opportunity to feign illness and be transported ashore in Italy, which would prevent Graham from ensuring the safe and timely arrival of his arms shipment to Turkey and thereby help give Germany the upper hand in the war.

Filmed on location in Vancouver, Mann's remake retains the basic plot structure of Foster's film and Ambler's novel; however, key changes have been made to the lead characters, no doubt reflecting – as Douglas himself points out in an essay included in the catalogue to the Serpentine exhibition – the 1973 oil crisis that served as a backdrop to the making of the film.[48] As such, in the 1975 *Journey into Fear*, Graham (Sam Waterston) has been turned into an engineer who is returning from scouting out possible oil deposits in Turkey, and his nemesis Möller (played here by Vincent Price at his leering best) is now an undercover operative for a nameless multinational that would score much-needed economic leverage if Graham's findings were to happen to arrive in the United States six weeks behind schedule.

Douglas and Turner's remake – or, to use Sven Lütticken's term, 'meta-remake'[49] – of *Journey into Fear* in turn adapts Mann's film for the new global economy. As Douglas summarizes the plot, Graham, a pilot on board the container ship *Fidèle* (also the name of the ship in Melville's novel), and Möller, a mysterious cargo handler, 'argue over the details of an arbitrage scheme Möller's associates have assigned him to engineer. Apparently, if a particular container were to arrive a day late, confidence in a certain Asian contractor would be shaken and either the services offered by his Export Production Zone, or shares in the contractor's company, would be up for grabs.'[50] Edited as a continuous fifteen-minute loop, the film's image track is comprised of four different montages: two exterior chase sequences, and two interior dialogue sequences. However, this dialogue is also looped, with the soundtrack comprised of five separately recorded dialogue variations that are randomly accessed at four different computer-generated juncture points in the film's time line, allowing for 625 different segmentations of dialogue in total, which unspool over a total elapsed time of 157 hours.

Much of the dialogue in Turner and Douglas's script is composed of lines mined from Melville's novel, in which the eponymous title character, an allegorical master of disguise, dupes unwitting passengers aboard a Mississippi steamboat. This is an important clue that the 'endless, circular con-game'[51] in which Möller and Graham are engaged is not just about the 'so-called New Economy' of global capital;[52] it is also, I would argue, about the new economy of gender. To this end, Möller's (Rob LaBelle) bluff posturing in speech is quite literally out of sync with his screen image; the discordant and constantly shifting sound and visual loops ensure that he can never effectively say what he purports to 'sincerely mean' – including the verbalized if not visualized threat of 'Man Overboard.'[53] And indeed, that masculinity might be the one confidence trick, the one masquerade, he can't quite pull off is nowhere more spectacularly visualized than in the casting of the pilot Graham as a woman (played here with steely-eyed determination by Jill Teed; see Figure 7.5).

On this point, in the introductory chapter to her important and ground-breaking 1998 book *Female Masculinity*, Judith Halberstam has written perceptively, stating categorically that 'masculinity must not and cannot and should not reduce down to the male body and its effects.'[54] Furthermore, she argues that 'if what we call "dominant masculinity" appears to be a naturalized relation between maleness and power, then it makes little sense to examine men for the contours of that masculinity's social construction'; indeed, according to Halberstam, dominant masculinity only becomes visible or 'legible' as such (that is, dominant and masculine) 'where and when it leaves the white male middle-class body.'[55]

7.5   *Journey into Fear*: Graham (Jill Teed, l) confronts Möller (Rob LaBelle).

In *Marked Men*, Sally Robinson has likewise theorized the visible/invisible dialectics of white heteronormative masculinity. She notes that the traditional privileges of what she calls white masculinity's 'unmarkedness' have since the 1960s
been accompanied by a concomitant mobilization of a contradictory 'identity politics of the dominant,' whereby white men 'mark' themselves as a persecuted and
oppressed class through visible signs of bodily trauma and psychic wounding.
However, as a visible marker of difference, even here the male body remains a
cipher. For according to Robinson, in the rhetoric of 'crisis' surrounding white
masculinity, the 'realness' of the crisis is superseded by the 'representation' of crisis.[56] Yet while theoretically we may find it easy to separate the 'political expression' of masculinity from the biological embodiment of maleness, as Halberstam
notes in her subsequent discussion of 'the bathroom problem,' the hermeneutics
of gender in our culture are still very much tied to how we read bodies. With masculinity, let me hazard to say, this is even more the case, as, coextensively with
biological maleness, masculinity is still largely judged in our culture by whether
or not one has a penis (and I do think, pace Freud and Lacan, I want to use that
word here rather than phallus).[57]

This paradox was very much at the centre of discussion in a recent graduate
seminar I taught called 'Adapting Masculinity: From Stage to Screen,' on film
treatments of stage plays ranging from *A Streetcar Named Desire* and *Look Back in
Anger* to *M. Butterfly* and *Hedwig and the Angry Inch*. Or perhaps I should say that
it was the absent centre of our discussion, in that over the course of the plays,
films, and critical articles we were analysing, we gradually developed a very curious discourse around dominant white middle-class masculinity. That is, following from the plays themselves, we often found ourselves talking about how
difficult it is to talk about what constitutes this masculinity as dominant; we

struggled with a general inarticulacy around its absent centre (words like 'nobody' and 'something' kept coming up in the texts and in our conversation), and we defined this particular masculinity, once again, in terms of what it *is not*: not female; not homosexual; not black; not working-class; and so on.

Why, I asked my students around week ten of the course, were we finding it so difficult – despite our general loquaciousness on other matters – to express what white middle-class masculinity *is*? Did it have anything to do with PC-induced fears about masculinity and maleness automatically being associated with patriarchal power? Couldn't we collectively come up with some positive signs of maleness? Or was it because this particular masculinity hadn't had to define itself in positive or even positivist terms because it has assumed in our culture the status of an a priori given? And did this explain the paradox – as Halberstam and Robinson and other theorists have suggested – that precisely when this 'dominant' masculinity finds itself under attack and asked to start defining itself, it chooses to do so in negative terms, marshalling a host of other marginal masculinities (female, queer, of colour) from which it needs to differentiate itself?

Coincidentally, around the same time as this was happening, my undergraduate class, which was also on the topic of gender and genre in literature-to-film adaptations, was in the midst of discussing *Hard Core Logo*. Reading through the essays that subsequently came in comparing Turner's text and McDonald's film, I was struck by how articulately my students talked about the various gender and genre codes circumscribing the band members' relations with one another, and about the broader applications of these codes to representations of masculinity in/as social discourse. Indeed, so taken was I with what my undergraduates had to say about *Hard Core Logo*, that I adapted many of their remarks into a set of axioms for my graduate students to mull over in connection with some of the texts we were studying. I reprint those axioms here, in somewhat modified form, in order to highlight some of the broader theoretical premises underscoring not just this chapter but the book as a whole:

(Dominant White Heteronormative) Masculinity is ...

1. ... a statement that doesn't say anything, what Robert Vorlicky, in connection with the work of David Mamet, calls 'cooperative communication *without* self-disclosure.'[58] (Compare, again, what the members of Hard Core Logo say, and don't say, to one another, and what they say, and say some more, to Bruce's camera.)
2. ... not effectively tied to the male body, but has bodily effects, one of which may be the expression – and reception – of a presumptive maleness. (Both the screen version of John Herbert's Queenie and the textual version of Susan Swan's Paulie discover this in their different ways.)
3. ... in this way, prosthetic, dependent on detachable props, accessories, and icons. (Think of the cassocks and bibles of Fathers Laforgue and Massicotte, or the lighters and cigarettes of Rocky, Billy, and Joe.)
4. Moreover, these prosthetic effects are often generated through the with-

holding of affect – that is, through a masquerade that refuses for the most part to call attention to itself, or through a non-performative performance. (Compare, in this regard, the generally affectless screen performances Lepage has variously solicited from Lothaire Bluteau, Patrick Goyette, Tom McCamus, and even himself.)

5. Indeed, the performance of masculinity only becomes visible as such through an 'aesthetic of masochism,'[59] through a representation of crisis as a self-wounding. (This can be witnessed at its most extreme in the respective suicides of Rocky in *Fortune and Men's Eyes* and Joe in *Hard Core Logo*.)

6. As an ideology/discourse/identity, masculinity constitutes itself through abjection, disavowal, and disidentification – that is, in relation to what it is not (not feminine, not homosexual, not child-like, not raced, and so on), to a loss, or to the potential/threat of a loss. (In this regard, note once again the curious phrasing of Joe's unspoken final query to Billy in Turner's *Hard Core Logo*: 'This is it, isn't it, Billy?' [*HCL* 193].)

7. Precisely because of masculinity's negative dialectics – what Robinson calls the 'privileges of its unmarkedness' – speaking about it tends to compel a discursive essentialism (that is, 'Unlike most women, all men are [fill in the blank],' or any number of the comments made by Kate, Elisabeth, Rose, Sarah, Gloria, or Florence in connection with the feckless males in the texts/films under discussion in chapter 2).

8. Like the cinema, masculinity's dominant narrative mode is realism ('Real men don't eat quiche …'); the conflation of social actor with his screen image (for example, Hugh Dillon is Joe Dick) serves in the end only to reify the status quo of patriarchal culture.

9. Masculinity is adaptive, responding synchronically in terms of space (*mise-en-scène*) and diachronically in terms of time (montage) (cf. the concert footage in Vancouver and Edmonton that brackets McDonald's *Hard Core Logo*, or the sauna scenes in Lepage's *Le confessionnal* and *La face cachée de la lune*).

10. Only by according masculinity's specific adaptations (in any of the titles listed above, for example) as much attention and careful scrutiny as those of femininity will there emerge a more nuanced and critically reflexive account of the patterns of genre recognition and gender identification that shore up the institutional apparatuses of literary and cinematic production.

In the end, then, what should be most apparent from this quasi-manifesto is that I am advocating an instrumentalist approach to adaptation studies generally, and to the study of adaptation in the Canadian context more specifically. Transforming the written word into the language of film (if indeed, pace Christian Metz and others, we can even say that film has a 'language'[60]) is a fraught and complicated process. However, as I have argued in this book, a careful examination of those complexities can prove especially useful for broader discussions of *gender* as they relate to the specific *generic* conventions of each medium, as well as to the different national contexts underscoring both the production and the reception of those conventions. (As a final example, in this regard, one might cite the aesthetic and ideological debates that necessarily arise around the classification of certain film adaptations like *Lost and Delirious* and *Hard Core Logo* as either 'chick flicks' or 'dick flicks.')

Much more basically, however, as a teacher of literature who came late to film studies,[61] and, moreover, who developed the initial idea for this project while teaching genre theory to a first-year undergraduate writing class via a discussion of the conventions of horror films being parodied in the *Scream* franchise, I have wanted to stress, in this book, how reading Canadian literature *through* film – and vice versa – can provide short cuts not only to narrative but also to pedagogical pleasure. Besides the course cited above, I have taught Turner's novel-in-verse and McDonald's film (as well as, tangentially, Craine's comic) in four different undergraduate courses: a Canadian literature survey course (with a featured component on Vancouver writing); an introduction-to-the-novel course and a 'critical approaches' course (both of which were loosely organized around the picaresque); and, finally, a gender studies course devoted to cultural 'remediations'[62] of masculinity (in which our discussions ranged from Ernest Hemingway's 'The Killers' and the film adaptations it has spawned[63] to *Fight Club, Austin Powers*, and reality television). While the discussions that ensued in each of these situations were, like the textual (re)productions of *Hard Core Logo* itself, very different, my students' reactions to the ending of McDonald's film remained remarkably consistent: shock and dismay greeted Joe Dick's suicide each time it was replayed on the screen.

This is, of course, to be expected. Having invested upwards of two or three weeks dissecting a favourite novel or play's narrative, analysing its characters, and examining its themes, students – if the instructor is doing his/her properly, and the class is suitably engaged – will have formed strong opinions, and are likely to be outraged if, in witnessing the story unfold before them on screen, a beloved character has been eliminated or made into a composite, important events are left out for the sake of narrative compression, or – and this is the real kicker – the ending has been changed. Students (and not just American ones) are – to bring us back to this book's opening epigraph from Turner – equally distressed if, having seen the film first, the written text doesn't correspond faithfully (and increasingly, this latter situation is the one I have found myself having to deal with in the classroom).

I do not wish to rehearse, at the end of this book, the specific points about textual mediation, translation, and (inter)semiosis that I made at the outset, in chapter 1. I merely wish to emphasize, as with my discussion there of Atwood's *The Handmaid's Tale* (and it's curious, isn't it, the extent to which the figure of Atwood haunts my reading of Turner here?), how one can likewise use a film like *Hard Core Logo* (or any of those discussed in previous chapters, for that matter) to exploit pedagogically the differences between literary text and film text. Indeed, the phenomenon of adaptation allows one to make expressly political points about the *gendered* experience of narrative, and about how narrative *and* gender operate differently in different representational media/contexts.

In this regard, as I hope I have demonstrated in this book, questions of *infidelity*, *incoherence*, and *non-equivalency* often provide more productive starting points for adaptation studies than the traditional measuring sticks of *fidelity*, *coherence*, and *equivalency*. For, just as there is often a disconnect between the physical and psychical experience of one's gender and the reception of that gender by others, or between a country's national self-representation and how it is collectively perceived on the international stage (all too apparent in the different aesthetic, political, and economic ideologies that govern the different 'national' film industries of English Canada and Quebec), so will a film adapted from a work of literature (or any other medium) necessarily call upon different institutional and cultural codes (including different codes of genre and gender) in hailing its ideal viewer, who, crucially, may not be the same as the source text's ideal reader. In this, I am reminded once again of the comment made by David Hare in the introduction to the published screenplay for *The Hours*, which I used as an epigraph in chapter 2: 'The great mystery of adaptation is that true fidelity can only be achieved through lavish promiscuity.'[64] Judging from my own indiscriminate and at times quite extravagant readings of Canadian literature and film in this book, one might say the same thing about criticism.

Filmography

8 Women, François Ozon, France, 2002.
The 400 Blows, François Truffaut, France, 1959.
Ada (TV), Claude Jutra, Canada, 1976.
The Adventures of Priscilla, Queen of the Desert, Stephen Elliott, Australia, 1994.
The Adventures of Sebastian Cole, Todd Williams, USA, 1998.
All About Eve, Joseph Mankiewicz, USA, 1950.
All About My Mother, Pedro Almodóvar, Spain, 1999.
All the Years of Her Life, Robert Fortier, Canada, 1974.
American Whiskey Bar (TV), Bruce McDonald, Canada, 1998.
Angel Square, Anne Wheeler, Canada, 1990.
Angel Walk, Mitch Gabourie, Canada, 1998.
Anne of a Thousand Days, Charles Jarrott, UK, 1969.
Anne of Green Gables, William Desmond Taylor, USA, 1919.
Anne of Green Gables, George Nichols, Jr, USA, 1934.
Anne of Green Gables (TV), Norman Campbell (producer), Canada, 1956.
Anne of Green Gables (TV), Kevin Sullivan, Canada, 1985.
Anne of Green Gables: The Sequel (TV), Kevin Sullivan, Canada, 1987.
Anne Trister, Léa Pool, Canada, 1986.
Apocalypse Now, Francis Ford Coppola, USA, 1979.
The Apprenticeship of Duddy Kravitz, Ted Kotcheff, Canada, 1974.
Atanarjuat: The Fast Runner, Zacharias Kunuk, Canada, 2002.
Autobiography of Red, Adrienne Campbell-Holt, USA, 2002.
Back to God's Country, David Hartford, Canada, 1919.
Bad Education, Pedro Almodóvar, Spain, 2004.
Bagdad Café, Percy Adlon, Germany, 1988.
Behind the Green Door, Mitchell Brothers, USA, 1972.
Behind the Green Door – The Sequel, Mitchell Brothers and Sharon McKnight, USA, 1986.
Being at Home with Claude, Jean Beaudin, Canada, 1991.
Bent, Sean Mathias, UK, 1997.
Better Than Chocolate, Anne Wheeler, Canada, 1998.
Betty (TV), Marni Banack, Canada, 2003.
Big Bear (TV), Gil Cardinal, Canada, 1998.

The Birdcage, Mike Nichols, USA, 1996.
Birth of a Nation, D.W. Griffith, USA, 1915.
Black Robe, Bruce Beresford, Canada/Australia, 1991.
Blue Water, David M. Hartford, Canada, 1924.
Bonheur d'occasion [aka *The Tin Flute*], Claude Fournier, Canada, 1983.
Boogie Nights, Paul Thomas Anderson, USA, 1997.
Les boys, Louis Saïa, Canada, 1997.
Les boys 2, Louis Saïa, Canada, 1998.
Les boys 3, Louis Saïa, Canada, 2001.
Boys and Girls, Don McBrearty, Canada, 1982.
Boys Don't Cry, Kimberley Pierce, USA, 1999.
The Boys in the Band, William Friedkin, USA, 1970.
Boys on the Side, Herbert Ross, USA, 1995.
Les brûlés, Bernard Devlin, Canada, 1959.
The Brandon Teena Story, Susan Muska and Gréta Ólafsdóttir, USA, 1998.
Caïn, Pierre Patry, Canada, 1967.
Cameron of the Royal Mounted, Henry MacRae, Canada, 1921.
La canne à pêche, Fernand Dansereau, Canada, 1959.
Carry on Crime and Punishment, Michael Ondaatje, Canada, 1970.
Catholics (TV), Jack Gold, UK, 1973.
Caught, Max Ophüls, USA, 1949.
Un chant d'amour, Jean Genet, France, 1947.
Cheyenne Autumn, John Ford, USA, 1964.
Un chien andalou, Luis Buñuel, France, 1929.
The Children's Hour, William Wyler, USA, 1961.
Clancy of the Mounted Police, Ray Taylor, USA, 1933.
Clearcut, Richard Bugajski, Canada, 1991.
Clinton Special: A Film About The Farm Show, Michael Ondaatje, Canada, 1974.
Cold Heaven, Nicholas Roeg, USA, 1991.
The Color Purple, Stephen Spielberg, USA, 1985.
Comment faire l'amour avec un nègre sans se fatiguer, Jacques Benoît, Canada, 1989.
Le confessionnal, Robert Lepage, Canada, 1995.
La corde au cou, Pierre Patry, Canada, 1965.
Cornet at Night, Stanley Jackson, Canada, 1963.
Cowboys Don't Cry, Anne Wheeler, Canada, 1987.
Crash, David Cronenberg, Canada, 1996.
The Cremation of Sam McGee, Bob Jacob, Canada, 1982.
The Cremation of Sam McGee, Eva Szasz, Canada, 1990.
Le crime d'Ovide Plouffe, Denys Arcand, Canada, 1984.
The Critical Age, Henry MacRae, Canada, 1922.
Cruising, William Friedkin, USA, 1980.
The Crying Game, Neil Jordan, UK, 1992.
Dance Me Outside, Bruce McDonald, Canada, 1995.
Dances with Wolves, Kevin Costner, USA, 1991.
Dangerous Dan McFoo, USA, 1939.
A Day in the Country, Jean Renoir, France, 1936.

Dead Ringers, David Cronenberg, Canada, 1988.

Dead Man, Jim Jarmusch, USA, 1996.

Dead Men Don't Wear Plaid, Carl Reiner, USA, 1982.

Death by Landscape (TV), Stacey Stewart Curtis, Canada, 2003.

Le déclin de l'empire américain, Denys Arcand, 1986.

Deliverance, John Boorman, USA, 1972.

Déliverez-nous du mal, Jean-Claude Lord, Canada, 1965.

La demoiselle sauvage, Léa Pool, Canada, 1991.

Dial M for Murder, Alfred Hitchcock, USA, 1954.

Different for Girls, Richard Spence, UK, 1997.

The Diviners (TV), Anne Wheeler, Canada, 1992.

Dragonwyck, Joseph L. Mankiewicz, 1946.

Dreamspeaker (TV), Claude Jutra, Canada, 1977.

Each Man's Son, Roger Blais, Canada, 1954.

Earth, Deepa Mehta, India, 1998.

Easy Rider, Dennis Hopper, USA, 1969.

Edge of Madness, Anne Wheeler, Canada, 2002.

Elimination Dance, Bruce McDonald, Don McKellar, and Michael Ondaatje, Canada, 1998.

Emporte-moi, Léa Pool, Canada, 1999.

The English Patient, Anthony Minghella, UK, 1996.

Evangeline, E.P. Sullivan and William Cavanaugh, Canada, 1913.

Even Cowgirls Get the Blues, Gus Van Sant, USA, 1993.

The Exorcist, William Friedkin, USA, 1973.

La face cachée de la lune, Robert Lepage, Canada, 2004.

Falling Angels, Scott Smith, Canada, 2003.

La famille Plouffe [aka *The Plouffe Family*] (TV), Canada, 1952-9.

The Favourite Game, Bernar Hébert, Canada, 2003.

Felicia's Journey, Atom Egoyan, Canada/UK, 1999.

La femme de l'hotel, Léa Pool, Canada, 1984.

Field of Dreams, Phil Alden Robinson, USA, 1989.

Fight Club, David Fincher, USA, 1999.

Les filles de Caleb (TV), Jean Beaudin, Canada, 1990.

Fire, Deepa Mehta, Canada/India, 1996.

Five Senses, Jeremy Podeswa, Canada, 1999.

Flawless, Joel Schumacher, USA, 1999.

Flow, Quentin Lee, USA, 1997.

Forrest Gump, Robert Zemeckis, USA, 1994.

Fort Apache, John Ford, USA, 1948.

Fortune and Men's Eyes, Harvey Hart, Canada, 1971.

Les fous de bassan, Yves Simoneau, Canada, 1988.

Fried Green Tomatoes, Jon Avnet, USA, 1991.

Full Blast, Rodrigue Jean, Canada, 1999.

Further Tales of the City (TV), Pierre Gang, Canada/USA, 2001.

Gaslight, George Cukor, USA, 1944.

The Gay Deceivers, Bruce Kessler, USA, 1969.

Il giorno prima, Giuliano Montaldo, Italy, 1987.
God's Crucible, Henry MacRae, Canada, 1920.
Goin' Down the Road, Don Shebib, Canada, 1972.
Gone With the Wind, Victor Fleming, USA, 1939.
Gypsy Boys, Brian Shepp, USA, 2000.
The Handmaid's Tale, Volker Schlöndorff, USA, 1990.
Hard Core Logo, Bruce McDonald, Canada, 1996.
The Harp (TV), Sarah Polley, Canada, 2004.
Hazel (TV), Norma Bailey, Canada, 2004.
Heaven, Scott Reynolds, UK, 1998.
Hedwig and the Angry Inch, John Cameron Mitchell, USA, 2001.
Heirs to a Felt Fortune, Michael Turner, Canada, 1998.
L'héritage, Bernard Devlin, Canada, 1960.
Hiawatha: The Messiah of the Ojibway, Joe Rosenthal (producer), Canada, 1903.
High Plains Drifter, Clint Eastwood, USA, 1973.
Highway 61, Bruce McDonald, Canada, 1991.
Hiroshima, mon amour, Alain Resnais, France, 1959.
The Hockey Sweater [aka *Le chandail*], Sheldon Cohen, Canada, 1980.
L'homme aux oiseaux, Bernard Devlin and Jean Palardy, Canada, 1955.
The Hours, Stephen Daldry, USA, 2002.
Hustler White, Bruce LaBruce and Rick Castro, Canada/Germany, 1996.
I Confess, Alfred Hitchcock, USA, 1953.
I Shot Andy Warhol, Mary Harron, USA, 1996.
Il était une fois dans l'est, André Brassard, Canada, 1974.
In Praise of Older Women, George Kaczender, 1978.
An Interview with Kevin and Dodie, Michael Turner, Canada, 1999.
Les invasions barbares, Denys Arcand, Canada, 2003.
Isis in Darkness (TV), Norma Bailey, Canada, 2003.
Jalna, John Cromwell, USA, 1935.
Jalna (TV), Philippe Marnier, Canada/France, 1994.
Jane Eyre, Robert Stevenson, USA, 1944.
Jaws, Stephen Spielberg, USA, 1975.
Jésus de Montréal, Denys Arcand, Canada, 1989.
Johnny Mnemonic, Robert Longo, USA, 1995.
Joshua Then and Now, Ted Kotcheff, Canada/USA, 1985.
The Journals of Susanna Moodie, Todd Southgate, Canada, 1997.
Journey into Fear, Norman Foster, USA, 1942.
Journey into Fear, Daniel Mann, Canada/USA, 1975.
Journey into Fear, Stan Douglas, Canada, 2001.
Kamouraska, Claude Jutra, Canada, 1973.
The Killers, Robert Siodmak, USA, 1946.
The Killers, Andrei Tarkovsky, USSR, 1956.
The Killers, Don Siegal, USA, 1964.
Kingsway, Clancy Dennehy, Canada, 1999.
Kissed, Lynne Stopkewich, Canada, 1996.
Knock! Knock!, Bruce McDonald, Canada, 1985.

Laura, Otto Preminger, USA, 1944.

The Last of the Mohicans, Theodore Marston, USA, 1911.

The Last of the Mohicans, Clarence Brown and Maurice Tourneur, USA, 1920.

The Last of the Mohicans, Ford Beebe and B. Reeves Eason, USA, 1932.

The Last of the Mohicans, George B. Steitz, USA, 1936.

The Last of the Mohicans, Michael Mann, USA, 1995.

The Law of the Yukon, Charles Miller, USA, 1920.

Leaving Metropolis, Brad Fraser, Canada, 2002.

Léolo, Jean-Claude Lauzon, Canada/France, 1992.

Lilies, John Greyson, Canada, 1996.

Little Big Man, Arthur Penn, 1970.

Look Back in Anger, Tony Richardson, UK, 1958.

The Lonely Passion of Judith Hearne, Jack Clayton, UK, 1987.

Lost and Delirious, Léa Pool, Canada, 2001.

Love and Human Remains, Denys Arcand, Canada, 1994.

The Luck of Ginger Coffey, Irvin Kershner, Canada, 1964.

The Lure of the Heart's Desire, Francis J. Gordon, USA, 1916.

M. Butterfly, David Cronenberg, USA, 1993.

Ma vie en rose, Alain Berliner, France, 1997.

Mädchen in Uniform, Leontine Sagan, Germany, 1931.

The Maltese Falcon, John Huston, USA, 1941.

The Man from Glengarry, Henry MacRae, Canada, 1924.

Man from Mars (TV), Lynne Stopkewich, Canada, 2003.

Margaret's Museum, Mort Ransen, Canada, 1995.

Maria Chapdelaine, Julien Duvivier, France, 1934.

Maria Chapdelaine [aka *The Naked Heart*], Marc Allégret, France/UK, 1950.

Maria Chapdelaine, Gilles Carle, Canada, 1983.

Marine Life, Anne Wheeler, Canada, 2000.

Mario, Jean Beaudin, Canada, 1994.

Marion Bridge, Wiebke von Carolsfeld, Canada, 2002.

Le matou, Jean Beaudin, Canada, 1985.

Meatballs, Ivan Reitman, Canada, 1979.

Midnight in the Garden of Good and Evil, Clint Eastwood, USA, 1997.

Midnight Sun, Larry McLaughlin, Canada, 2000.

Moby Dick, John Huston, UK, 1956.

Mon oncle Antoine, Claude Jutra, Canada, 1971.

Montréal vu par ..., Patricia Rozema, Jacques Leduc, Michel Brault, Atom Egoyan, Denys Arcand, and Léa Pool, Canada, 1991.

More Tales of the City (TV), Pierre Gang, Canada/UK/USA, 1998.

Morning on the Lièvre, David Bairstow, Canada, 1961.

Mouvements du désir, Léa Pool, Canada, 1994.

Mrs Dalloway, Marleen Gorris, UK, 1997.

Les muses orphelines, Robert Favreau, Canada, 2000.

My Madonna, Alice Blaché, USA, 1915.

Naked Lunch, David Cronenberg, Canada/UK/Japan, 1991.

Nanook of the North, Robert Flaherty, USA/France, 1922.

Nô, Robert Lepage, Canada, 1998.

Nobody Waved Goodbye, Don Owen, Canada, 1964.

Nunaqpa/Going Inland, Zacharias Kunuk, Canada, 1991.

Nunavut/Our Land (TV), Zacharias Kunuk, Canada, 1994–5.

Oliver Twist, J. Stuart Blackton, USA, 1909.

Oliver Twist, Thomas Bentley, UK, 1912.

Olivia, Jacqueline Audry, France, 1951.

On the Waterfront, Elia Kazan, USA, 1954.

One's a Heifer, Anne Wheeler, Canada, 1984.

One Flew Over the Cukoo's Nest, Milos Forman, USA, 1975.

The Outlaw Josey Wales, Clint Eastwood, USA, 1976.

Outrageous!, Richard Benner, Canada, 1977.

Orlando, Sally Potter, UK, 1992.

Oz (TV), Tom Fontana, USA, 1997–2003.

The Painted Door, Bruce Pittman, Canada, 1984.

Pale Rider, Clint Eastwood, USA, 1985.

Paperback Hero, Peter Pearson, Canada, 1975.

Parenthood, Ron Howard, USA, 1989.

Paris Is Burning, Jennie Livingston, USA, 1991.

The Piano Man's Daughter (TV), Kevin Sullivan, Canada, 2003.

Picnic at Hanging Rock, Peter Weir, Australia, 1976.

Picture Claire, Bruce McDonald, Canada, 2001.

Planet Claire: The Unmaking of a Movie [aka: *Claire's Hat*], Bruce McDonald, Canada, 2004.

Les Plouffe (TV), Gilles Carle, Canada, 1981.

Pocahontas, Eric Goldberg, USA, 1995.

Poisoned Paradise, Louis J. Gasnier, USA, 1924.

Polarities (TV), Lori Spring, Canada, 2003.

Le polygraphe, Robert Lepage, Canada, 1997.

Porky's, Bob Clark, Canada/USA, 1982.

Les portes tournantes, Francis Mankiewicz, Canada, 1988.

Possible Worlds, Robert Lepage, Canada, 2000.

Poussière sur la ville, Arthur Lamothe, Canada, 1967.

Pouvoir intime, Yves Simoneau, Canada, 1986.

The Prime of Miss Jean Brodie, Ronald Neame, UK, 1969.

Prom Night, Paul Lynch, Canada, 1980.

Pulp Fiction, Quentin Tarantino, USA, 1994.

The Pyx, Harvey Hart, Canada, 1973.

Qaggiq/The Gathering Place, Zacharias Kunuk, Canada, 1989.

Quest for Fire, Jean-Jacques Annaud, Canada/France/USA, 1981.

Quo Vadis?, Enrico Guazzoni, Italy, 1912.

Rachel, Rachel, Paul Newman, USA, 1968.

Rebecca, Alfred Hitchcock, UK, 1940.

The Republic of Love, Deepa Mehta, Canada, 2003.

The Rez (TV), T.W. Peacocke, Milan Cheylov, Gary Harvey, and John L'Ecuyer, Canada, 1996.

Rio Grande, John Ford, USA, 1950.

Rispondetemi, Léa Pool, Canada, 1992.

Road to Avonlea (TV), Kevin Sullivan (producer), Canada, 1989–96.

Roadkill, Bruce McDonald, Canada, 1989.

Rope, Alfred Hitchcock, USA, 1948.

The Roughneck, Jack Conway, USA, 1924.

Une saison dans la vie d'Emmanuel, Claude Weisz, Canada, 1973.

Salmonberries, Percy Adlon, Germany, 1991.

Sam and Me, Deepa Mehta, Canada, 1991.

Le sang des autres, Claude Chabrol, France, 1987.

Saputi/Fish Traps, Zacharias Kunuk, Canada, 1993.

The Searchers, John Ford, USA, 1956.

The Secret Agent, Alfred Hitchcock, UK, 1936.

Les sept branches de la rivière ota (TV), Francis Leclerc, Canada, 1997.

Séraphin, Paul Gury, Canada, 1950.

Séraphin, Charles Binamé, Canada, 2002.

Le sexe des étoiles, Paule Baillargeon, Canada, 1993.

Shadow of the Wolf [aka *Agaguk*], Jacques Dorfmann, Canada/France, 1993.

She Wore a Yellow Ribbon, John Ford, USA, 1949.

The Shooting of Dan McGoo, USA, 1945.

The Shooting of Dan McGrew, Herbert Blaché, USA, 1915.

The Shooting of Dan McGrew, Clarence G. Badger, USA, 1924.

Sling Blade, Billy Bob Thornton, USA, 1996.

Smoke Signals, Chris Eyre, USA, 1998.

Some Like It Hot, Billy Wilder, USA, 1959.

Sonatine, Micheline Lanctôt, Canada, 1984.

The Song of the Wage Slave, Herbert and Alice Blaché, USA, 1915.

The Sons of Captain Poetry, Michael Ondaatje, Canada, 1970.

Le sourd dans la ville, Mireille Dansereau, Canada, 1987.

Southern Comfort, Kate Davis, USA, 2001.

The Spell of the Yukon, Burton L. King, USA, 1916.

Spider, David Cronenberg, Canada/France/UK, 2002.

Stagecoach, John Ford, USA, 1939.

Stargaze, Jason McBride, Canada, 1998.

The Statement, Norman Jewison, USA, 2003.

Strange Brew [aka: *The Adventures of Bob and Doug McKenzie*], Rick Moranis and
   Dave Thomas, Canada/USA, 1983.

A Streetcar Named Desire, Elia Kazan, USA, 1951.

Such a Long Journey, Sturla Gunnarson, Canada, 1999.

The Sunrise (TV), Francine Zuckerman, Canada, 2003.

Sunshine Sketches of a Small Town (TV), Robert Allen (producer), Canada, 1952–3.

Surfacing, Claude Jutra, Canada, 1981.

Suspicion, Alfred Hitchcock, USA, 1941.

Swann, Anna Benson Gyles, Canada/UK, 1996.

The Sweet Hereafter, Atom Egoyan, Canada, 1997.

Tales of the City (TV), Alastair Reid, UK/USA, 1993.

Taxi Driver, Martin Scorsese, USA, 1976.
Tectonic Plates, Peter Mettler, Canada, 1992.
Thelma and Louise, Ridley Scott, USA, 1991.
These Three, William Wyler, USA, 1936.
This Is Spinal Tap, Rob Reiner, USA, 1984.
Tit-Coq, Gratien Gélinas and René Delacroix, Canada, 1954.
Titanic, James Cameron, USA, 1997.
To Kill a Mockingbird, Robert Milligan, USA, 1962.
To Set Our House in Order, Anne Wheeler, Canada, 1985.
To Wong Foo, Thanks for Everything, Julie Newmar, Beeban Kidron, USA, 1995.
Too Outrageous, Richard Benner, Canada, 1987.
Torn Curtain, Alfred Hitchcock, USA, 1966.
Touch, Jeremy Podeswa, Canada, 2001.
The Trail of 98, Clarence Brown, USA, 1928.
Transamerica, Duncan Tucker, USA, 2005.
Trick, Jim Fall, USA, 1999.
The Trojan Women, Michael Cacoyannis, UK/USA/Greece, 1971.
The Two Mrs Carrolls, Peter Godfrey, USA, 1947.
Two Rode Together, John Ford, USA, 1961.
Unforgiven, Clint Eastwood, USA, 1992.
Various Miracles (TV), Mina Shum, Canada, 2004.
Le viellard et l'enfant, Claude Grenier, Canada, 1985.
Victor/Victoria, Blake Edwards, UK/USA, 1982.
Vivre sa vie, Jean-Luc Godard, France, 1962.
Water, Deepa Mehta, Canada, 2005.
Whale Music, Richard J. Lewis, Canada, 1994.
Whale Rider, Niki Caro, New Zealand, 2002.
When Night Is Falling, Patricia Rozema, Canada, 1995.
The Whiteoaks of Jalna (TV), John Trent, Canada, 1972.
Who Has Seen the Wind, Allan King, Canada, 1977.
Wild Geese, Phil Goldstone, USA, 1927.
Wild Geese [aka: *After the Harvest*] (TV), Jeremy Podeswa, Canada, 2000.
Windows (TV), Lynne Stopkewich, 2004.
Winter Kept Us Warm, David Secter, Canada, 1965.
A Word (TV), Lori Spring, Canada, 2004.
The World According to Garp, George Roy Hill, USA, 1982.
Young at Heart, Gordon Douglas, USA, 1954.
Un zoo la nuit, Jean-Claude Lauzon, Canada, 1987.

Notes

Introduction

1 M. Turner, *American Whiskey Bar*, 7.
2 See Parpart, 'Adapting Emotions'; Plantinga, 'Notes on Spectator Emotion.'
3 Ondaatje, *The English Patient*, 282. Further references to the novel will be cited paren-thetically in the text as *EP*.
4 As representative of this scholarship, see Lowry, 'Between *The English Patients*'; Pesch, 'Dropping the Bomb?'; Roberts, '"Sins of Omission"'; and Younis, 'Nationhood and Decolonization in *The English Patient*.'
5 Williams, 'Film Bodies,' 143.
6 As several critics have noted, Minghella's visual poetics on screen are for the most part very successful in conveying Ondaatje's highly elliptical and intensely lyrical narrative style on the page; see Thomas, '"Piecing Together a Mirage."' Indeed, Minghella has repeatedly been applauded – and not just by the Academy of Motion Picture Arts and Sciences – for the success with which he adapted such a 'difficult' and 'literary' novel to the screen. Minghella deserves much of this credit, but at the same time we should not ignore the cinematic elements in Ondaatje's writing that lend themselves to visual adaptation – for example, his tendency to write juxtapositional, non-linear, and frag-mentary scenes is akin to montage, and his polyphonic narration and overlapping of voices is the literary equivalent of a camera's capacity to show multiple points of view, often simultaneously.
7 In this regard, note also the temporally anterior scene in both the novel and the film that spatially reconstructs the moment Almásy fell in love with Katharine. In the desert with her husband, Almásy, and the rest of the all-male members of the Gilf Kebir mapmaking expedition, Katharine celebrates their most recent findings by read-ing aloud from Herodotus's version of 'the story of Candaules and his queen,' about a besotted husband who, in seeking to convince his friend, Gyges, of his wife's inesti-mable charms, succeeds in having Gyges fall in love with her. As the English patient is the first to note, the parallels with his own story are all too obvious: 'This is a story of how I fell in love with a woman, who read me a specific story from Herodotus' (*EP* 232, 233).
8 Mulvey, 'Visual Pleasure and Narrative Cinema.'
9 Younis, 'Nationhood,' 6.

10 See in particular Simpson, 'Minefield Readings.'

11 Mulvey, 'Visual Pleasure,' 808–9.

12 See in this regard two recent books that respectively read English-Canadian and Québécois cinema within the framework of nationalism and national identity formation: Gittings, *Canadian National Cinema*; and Marshall, *Quebec National Cinema*. Jim Leach complicates the model of dual national cinemas in this country as follows: 'The old questions of national duality and the influence of US popular culture continue to preoccupy English Canadian and Québécois filmmakers in their different cultural contexts. However, these themes now often become entangled with the new interest in cultural diversity, and Canada has recently produced a number of films that engage with this experience on several levels and in terms that link their national contexts to the broader experience of globalization and postmodernity.' See Leach, 'The Reel Nation,' 8.

13 Neale, *Genre and Hollywood*, 2, 39 and ff. In adopting the word 'inter-textual relay' to refer to the institutionalized advertising, publicity, and marketing practices central to Hollywood's construction of a generic 'narrative image' for individual films (39), Neale is drawing on the work of Gregory Lukow and Steven Ricci; see their 'The "Audience" Goes "Public."' See also Derrida, 'The Law of Genre'; and Gerhart, *Genre Choices*.

14 Stam, *Literature through Film*, 6.

15 See Mulvey, 'Afterthoughts.'

16 Neale, *Genre*, 56.

17 Butler, *Gender Trouble*, 35–78. I will be returning to Butler's work, as it specifically applies to Canadian adaptation studies, in chapters 4, 5, and 6.

18 Ibid., 140–1.

19 Neale, *Genre*, 56.

20 Perez, *The Material Ghost*, 225.

21 See Loiselle, *Stage-Bound*.

22 Dyer, *Stars*, 162.

1 Sex Maidens and Yankee Skunks

1 In Rubio and Waterston, eds., *The Selected Journals of L.M. Montgomery*, vol. 2, 373.

2 In Malcolm, 'Margaret Atwood Reflects on a Hit.'

3 Murch, perhaps not so coincidentally, also cut – and later recut – another classic film adaptation of an equally classic work of literature, Francis Ford Coppola's *Apocalypse Now*, based on Joseph Conrad's *Heart of Darkness*. Ondaatje has said more than once that as a writer, he feels the greatest affinity with editing in the filmmaking process. His ongoing, five-year conversations with Murch resulted in an award-winning book, *The Conversations: The Art of Editing Film*. Ondaatje, it should be noted, has long had an interest in the cinema, producing three short films in the 1970s: *The Sons of Captain Poetry* (1970), *Carry on Crime and Punishment* (1970), and *Clinton Special: A Film about The Farm Show* (1974). And, as I note at greater length in chapter 7, after *The English Patient* was released he collaborated with Canadian filmmakers Bruce McDonald and Don McKellar in adapting his 1976 book of poetry, *Elimination Dance*, as a short film.

4 At a 4 April 1998 lecture at the Vancouver Institute.

5 A co-production of Toronto's Shaftesbury Films and Winnipeg's Original Pictures, each anthology series comprised six short films based on well-known stories by the respective authors, and directed by noted Canadian women filmmakers. The Atwood Stories, broadcast in 2003, included *Polarities* (dir. Lori Spring), *Betty* (dir. Marni Banack), *Man from Mars* (dir. Lynne Stopkewich), *Death by Landscape* (dir. Stacey Stewart Curtis), *Isis in Darkness* (dir. Norma Bailey), and *The Sunrise* (dir. Francine Zuckerman). Airing the following spring, The Shields Stories included *Various Miracles* (dir. Mina Shum), *Hazel* (dir. Norma Bailey), *A Word* (dir. Lori Spring), *The Harp* (dir. Sarah Polley), and *Windows* (dir. Lynne Stopkewich). Plans were underway to screen The Munro Stories in 2005.

6 See Naremore, 'Introduction,' 4.

7 Peter Morris notes that the first dramatic short filmed in Canada, *Hiawatha: The Messiah of the Ojibway* (1903; prod. Joe Rosenthal), was also based on a Longfellow poem, *The Song of Hiawatha*. See Morris, *Embattled Shadows*, 36.

8 Several filmographies and reference guides have been published on the subject of Canadian film. See, for example, Easterbrook et al., *Canada and Canadians in Feature Films*; Lerner, ed., *Canadian Film and Video*; Lever, *Histoire générale du cinéma au Québec*; J.D. Turner, ed., *Canadian Feature Film Index*; and Wise, ed., *Take One's Essential Guide to Canadian Film*. However, so far as I can tell, there are only two guides specifically devoted to the subject of adaptations: Godard, *Filmography of Canadian and Quebec Literatures*; and Hu Xiangwen and Gagnon, *Adaptations filmiques au Québec*.

9 See Morris, *Embattled Shadows*, 95–126. For a thorough assessment of Nell Shipman's important contributions to the history of Canadian and American cinema, see Armatage, *The Girl from God's Country*.

10 A Canadian film mogul equivalent to Shipman's stature in the contemporary era would no doubt be Robert Lantos, whose production credits include several adaptations: *In Praise of Older Women* (1978), *Joshua Then and Now* (1985), *Black Robe* (1991), *Whale Music* (1994), *Johnny Mnemonic* (1995), *Crash* (1996), and *The Sweet Hereafter* (1997). Lantos has recently purchased the rights to Ondaatje's *In the Skin of the Lion* and Mordecai Richler's *Barney's Version*. The company he once headed, Alliance Atlantis, is competing by securing options on works by David Gilmour (*Lost Between Houses*) and Michael Turner (*The Pornographer's Poem*).

11 'The Shooting of Dan McGrew' would spawn two further film adaptations, both directed by Tex Avery, and mostly distinguishable only by the rather uninspired changes made to their titles: *Dangerous Dan McFoo* (1939, USA) and *The Shooting of Dan McGoo* (1945, USA). Interestingly, Service's more famous narrative poem, 'The Cremation of Sam McGee,' was brought to the screen for the first time only in 1982, with Bob Jacob's short film *The Cremation of Sam McGee: A Poem by Robert W. Service*. As with 'The Shooting of Dan McGrew,' however, further adaptations followed: an NFB short directed by Eva Szasz in 1990 and, most recently, *Midnight Sun* (2000), directed by Larry McLaughlin.

12 This kind of hybrid feature film/TV miniseries adaptation became something of a hallmark in Canada during the 1980s. Other examples include Claude Fournier's bilingually shot *Bonheur d'occasion/The Tin Flute* (1983; based on the novel by Gabrielle Roy), Denys Arcand and Gilles Carle's *Le crime d'Ovide Plouffe* (1984; based on the novel by

Roger Lemelin), and Ted Kotcheff's *Joshua Then and Now* (1985; based on the novel by Mordecai Richler).

13 Sheckels, 'Anne in Hollywood,' 185. See also Benjamin Lefebvre's discussion of the Anne films in 'Stand by Your Man'; and Patsy Kotsopoulos's theorization of 'borderless romance' as it relates to Sullivan Entertainment's popular television series *Road to Avonlea* in 'Avonlea as Main Street USA.'

14 Lefebvre, 'Stand by Your Man,' 150. For the most extended compilation of adaptations based on Montgomery's texts, see also Lefebvre, 'L.M. Montgomery: An Annotated Filmography.'

15 Sheckles, 'Anne in Hollywood,' 188.

16 See Givner, *Mazo de la Roche*.

17 For relevant histories of John Grierson and the NFB, see Evans, *John Grierson and the NFB*; Evans, *In the National Interest*; and Nelson, *The Colonized Eye*. For a discussion of how the ONF provided an entrée into filmmaking for a generation of Quebec directors, and for a history of Quebec cinema more generally, see Lever, *Histoire générale du cinéma au Québec*.

18 The film, like the play, was produced in both French and English, and became the most successful feature shot in Quebec during this period. It also won Film of the Year at the 1953 Canadian Film Awards. See Wise, 84.

19 See, for example, Luc Perreault's review of the film in *La Presse*, 11 mai 1968; and Patry, 'Arthur Lamothe.'

20 Waugh, 'Cinemas, Nations, Masculinities,' 39.

21 This is not to say that Canada's rural regions were not also captured on film during the same period. Indeed, the legendary director Claude Jutra gave us two of the most spectacular and enduring representations of the Quebec landscape when he produced, within the space of two years, *Mon oncle Antoine* (1971) and *Kamouraska* (1973), the latter based on Anne Hébert's celebrated novel. In the specific context of film adaptations from this period, we should also not forget the rural Quebec on view in Claude Weisz's 1973 adaptation of Marie-Claire Blais's *Une saison dans la vie d'Emmanuel*, or the dust bowl prairies recreated by Allan King in his 1977 adaptation of W.O. Mitchell's *Who Has Seen the Wind*.

22 Waugh, 'Fairy Tales of Two Cities,' 289. Waugh discusses the material consequences of one such intersection when he notes the debates that arose in this country when Brassard's *Il était une fois* was chosen over Kotcheff's *Duddy Kravitz* to represent Canada at the 1973 Cannes Film Festival; see 'Fairy Tales,' 295.

23 Carrière, 'Les images de femmes dans le cinéma masculin,' 58.

24 See Waugh, 'Nègres blancs, tapettes, et "butch."'

25 Yves Lever, 'Contenu sur *Déliverez-nous du mal*.'

26 Pevere and Dymond, *Mondo Canuck*, 216.

27 Ibid.

28 See, for example, Slott, 'From Agent of Destruction to Object of Desire'; and Tulloch, '"Yves Simoneau's Rewriting ....' For representative comments by Hébert on the film, see Hébert, 'Anne Hébert et *Les fous de bassan*.'

29 Tulloch, 84–5.

30 Ibid., 109.

31 Ibid., 111.

32 Quoted in Pallister, *The Cinema of Québec*, 210.

33 Atwood, *The Handmaid's Tail*, 252. Subsequent references will be cited in-text as *HT*.

34 Kirtz, 'Teaching Literature Through Film,' 144.

35 Atwood does something similarly McLuhanesque with space and time in *Cat's Eye*; on how McLuhan's theories can provide insight into both the novel and film of *The Handmaid's Tale*, see Willmott, 'O Say, Can You See,' 167–90.

36 Willmott, 171.

37 See Cooper, 'Sexual Surveillance and Medical Authority,' 57–8; see also Willmott, 181, who in this regard notes the prevalence of video and television newscasts within the film – an effect that creates a kind of *mise-en-abîme*, or 'a screen within a screen.'

38 Cf., in this regard, Cooper, who notes that 'the immediacy of the visual medium traps the viewer of *The Handmaid's Tale* in an especially piquant double bind, by its radical alteration of the terms of readerly engagement with the written text. Transforming the indirect, more abstract and generalized voyeurism of reading into the physically prompt voyeurism of watching, the movie invites the viewer to the very pleasures of looking reproved in the novel' (58).

39 Recent critical interventions include Pendakur, *Canadian Dreams and American Control*; Magder, *Canada's Hollywood*; and Dorland, *So Close to the State/s*.

40 As outlined in Canadian Heritage's recent report *From Script to Screen*.

41 In this regard, Vancouver film reviewer Katherine Monk hasn't helped matters much with the publication of her critically jejune and woefully under-researched *Weird Sex and Snowshoes and Other Canadian Film Phenomena*.

42 *From Script to Screen*, 7.

43 Ibid., 8.

44 Adams, 'Have You Seen These Movies?'

45 Petras, letter to *The Globe and Mail*, A14. To be sure, the ongoing issue of fostering a 'national cinema' for a 'national audience' in this country needs to be contextualized intranationally by noting that this is largely an English-Canadian problem. Not only do Quebec films make up most of the feature productions each year, but they also regularly account for the lion's share of the domestic box office gross – a fact that the *Les boys* phenomenon has consistently demonstrated.

46 See in this regard 'Moment of Truth for CBA,' Jennifer Pike's recent prescription for independent booksellers in the wake of the Indigo-Chapters merger.

47 Examples of films that have been produced so far through the fund include Bruce McDonald, Don McKellar, and Michael Ondaatje's *Elimination Dance* (based on Ondaatje's book of poems), Mitch Gabourie's *Angel Walk* (based on the novel by Katherine Govier), and Todd Southgate's *The Journals of Susanna Moodie* (based on the book of poems by Margaret Atwood).

48 Several critics have used the term 'intersemiotic translation' to describe the process of exchange that occurs between overlapping, extra-linguistic sign systems. For one of many applications of this term to the literature-into-film process, see Helman and Osadnik, 'Film and Literature.' On 'intermediality' as it applies to film adaptation, see Kirtz, 'Teaching Literature through Film,' 140, and Gaudreault and Groensteen, *La transécriture*.

49 Naremore, 'Introduction,' 6. See also Bluestone, *Novels into Film*.

50 Orr, 'The Discourse on Adaptation,' 72.

51 Chatman, *Coming to Terms*, 4–5, 203.
52 McFarlane, *Novel to Film*, 21-2.
53 Ibid., 20.
54 See Gay, 'Bonheur d'occasion.'
55 See Groen, 'TV version of Tin Flute,' M7. Among English-speaking critics, only Jay Scott was willing to critique the film along political lines, arguing that the bicultural production elided important material issues relevant both to the source text and to its setting: 'The division between French and English, which has more than a tiny bit to do with the social and political reality of Montreal, simply does not exist in this movie ... Did the producers think Canadians, English or French, wouldn't notice? Or was the film made for an "international" audience?' See Scott, '"The Tin Flute" in English ...,' 3. For a summary of the specific 'four-movies-in-one' logistics of the production, see Bailey, 'Making of "The Tin Flute."'
56 For a summary of some of the controversy surrounding *Black Robe*, see, for example, Dumont, 'Black Robe: A Jesuit World'; Harris, 'Black Robe Faces Attack on Two Fronts'; and Rubinoff, 'Why Were Critics So Kind to "Black Robe"?'
57 See Waugh, 'Fairy Tales' and 'Nègres blancs.'
58 Andrew, *Concepts in Film Theory*, 104, 106.
59 Baker, *Hard Core Roadshow*, 23.
60 See Kotsopoulos, 'Avonlea as Main Street USA.'
61 Swan, *The Wives of Bath*, v–vi.
62 Loiselle, *Stage-Bound*, 160–87.
63 See Shaviro, *The Cinematic Body*, esp. ch. 1, 'Film Theory and Visual Fascination,' 1–65; Metz, *The Imaginary Signifier*, esp. 61–8; Bazin, *What Is Cinema?*, vol. 1, esp. 76–124; and Benjamin, 'The Work of Art in the Age of Mechanical Reproduction.'
64 Benjamin, 228.
65 Bazin, *What Is Cinema?*, 101–2.
66 Ibid., 104–5.
67 See Loiselle, 11–12 and ff.
68 Metz, 66-7.
69 Ibid., 66.
70 Ibid., 62, 65.
71 Ibid., 65.
72 Parpart, 'Adapting Emotions,' 57.
73 Ibid.
74 See Lowry, 'Between *The English Patients*'; and Roberts, '"Sins of Omission."' Other critics have made similar points about adaptations ranging from *Gone With the Wind* and *To Kill a Mockingbird* to *Fried Green Tomatoes* and *Forrest Gump*. See Maria St John, '"It Ain't Fittin'"'; Nicholson, 'Hollywood and Race,' 151–9; Lu, 'Excuse Me, Did We See the Same Movie?'; and Wang, '"A Struggle of Contending Stories."'
75 See Kotsopoulos, 'Avonlea as Main Street USA.'
76 Corrigan, *Film and Literature*, 48.
77 Mayne, *Private Novels, Public Films*, 102, 103. Three contemporary producers in Canada to rival Selznick in commercial acumen, especially where the market value of literature-to-film adaptations is concerned, are Kevin Sullivan, Robert Lantos, and – though he has recently fallen from grace – Garth Drabinsky.

78 Barthes, *Image–Music–Text.*
79 Teresa de Lauretis, *Alice Doesn't*, 103–57.
80 Roberts, 'Sins of Omission.'
81 Eberle-Sinatra, 'Quelques réflexions sur l'adaptation cinématographique.'
82 Parpart, 'Adapting Emotions,' 59.
83 More critics of English-Canadian literature and film would do well to pay closer atten-
    tion to what their Quebec counterparts have to say about theories of adaptation, espe-
    cially as they both overlap with and depart from theories of translation. See, again,
    Gaudreault and Groensteen, *La transécriture.*
84 Rifkin, *Semiotics of Narration*, 10.
85 Stam, 'Beyond Fidelity,' 64. Stam adapts and incorporates portions of this article in the
    introduction to his recent book-length study, *Literature through Film*, in which he notes:
    'Adaptation theory has available a rich constellation of terms and tropes – translation,
    actualization, reading critique, dialogization, cannibalization, transmutation, transfigu-
    ration, incarnation, transmogrification, transcoding, performance, signifying, rewriting,
    detournement – all of which shed light on a different dimension of adaptation. The
    trope of adaptation as a "reading" of the source novel, one which is inevitably partial,
    personal, conjunctural, for example, suggests that just as any literary text can generate
    an infinity of readings, so any novel can generate any number of adaptations. An adap-
    tation is thus less a resuscitation of an originary word than a turn in an ongoing dialog-
    ical process. Intertextual dialogism, then, helps us transcend the aporias of "fidelity"'
    (4). Drawing, in particular, on the integration of theories of Bakhtinian dialogism and
    Kristevan intertextuality within Genette's theory of 'transtextuality,' which he defines
    in *Palimpsests* as 'the textual transcendence of the text,' or '"all that sets the text in a rela-
    tionship, whether obvious or concealed, with other texts,"' Stam notes that Genette's
    fourth 'type' of transtextuality, what he calls 'hypertextuality' – which 'refers to the
    relation between one text [the 'hypertext'] to an anterior text or "hypotext," which the
    former transforms, modifies, elaborates, or extends' – is 'especially productive in terms
    of adaptation.' See Genette, *Palimpsests*, 1, 5; and Stam, *Literature through Film*, 5.
86 Naremore, 'Introduction,' 9.
87 Telmissany, 'La citation filmique comme anachronisme.'
88 Metz, *Film Language*, 44.

2 Feminism, Fidelity, and the Female Gothic

1 Gilbert and Gubar, *The Madwoman in the Attic*, 356.
2 David Hare, *The Hours: A Screenplay*, ix.
3 Freud, 'The "Uncanny,"' 220.
4 Sedgwick, *The Coherence of Gothic Conventions.*
5 Moers, *Literary Women.*
6 Gilbert and Gubar, 361, 362.
7 See Freud, 'Fragment of an Analysis,' 7–122; and 'Hysterical Phantasies,' 155–66;
   and Freud and Breuer, *Studies on Hysteria.* At Thornfield, as her anxieties about her
   impending marriage to Rochester mount, Jane starts 'to reexperience the dangerous
   sense of doubleness that had begun in the red-room' – the room at Gateshead where her
   surrogate-father, Mr Reed, had died, and into which his 'tyrannical son,' John, locks her

at the outset of the novel. Gilbert and Gubar's excellent reading of how this occurs confirms how hysteria overlaps with uncanniness in the female gothic; see *The Madwoman in the Attic*, 357, 340.

8 Freud, 'The "Uncanny,"' 245.

9 See Hume, 'Gothic versus Romantic,' 287; and Massé, 'Gothic Repetition,' 679. Fiedler, in *Love and Death in the American Novel*, has, like Hume, prioritized the gothic as a male genre, one that reflects the son's Oedipal conflicts with patriarchal authority. Bruhm is representative of a generation of postmodern gothic critics who have applied Kristeva's insights to the abject male at the heart of the genre's late twentieth-century incarnations – in Bruhm's case the queerly gothic oeuvre of Stephen King; see his 'Picture This: Stephen King's Queer Gothic,' 269–80. See also Kristeva, *Powers of Horror*.

10 Massé, 680.

11 Ibid., 681.

12 Lupack, 'Vision/Re-Vision,' 12.

13 Ellis and Kaplan, 'Feminism in Brontë's *Jane Eyre*,' 196.

14 Doane, *The Desire to Desire*, 125.

15 Ibid., 141–2.

16 Ibid., 147.

17 Massé, 682.

18 See, for example, Margot Northey, *The Haunted Wilderness*, 53–61, 62–9; Davidson, 'Canadian Gothic and Anne Hébert's *Kamouraska*'; and Godard, 'My (m)Other, My Self.'

19 Hébert, *Kamouraska*, 10. The quotation in French is from the 1970 Paris edition. All subsequent references to this text will be cited parenthetically, along with their English translations, which are reproduced from the Shapiro translation published in 1982; this quotation is from page 4.

20 Margaret Atwood, *Surfacing*, 108. All subsequent references to this text will be cited parenthetically.

21 In this regard, see also *Ada* (1976), adapted by Jutra from a short story by Margaret Gibson; and *Dreamspeaker* (1976), based on the book by Anne Cameron.

22 Doane, 147.

23 Blais, *Le sourd dans la ville*, 37. All subsequent references to this text will be cited parenthetically, along with their English translations, which are reproduced from the translation by Carol Dunlop: *Deaf to the City*; this quotation is from page 35.

24 See Leach, *Claude Jutra*, 150 and ff. Leach notes that the references to the Selznick epic rankled Jutra, and that its $750,000 budget meant that '*Kamouraska* was hardly a large-budget film by Hollywood standards' (151).

25 Ibid., 155.

26 In his chapter on *Kamouraska*, Leach does an excellent job summarizing the critical response to the film. For a representative sampling of this criticism, see in particular Perreault, 'À la recherche de l'enfance' and 'Copie trop conforme'; Scully, 'L'oeuvre de notre grande bourgeoisie'; and J. Lefebvre, 'La Cohérence dans le cinéma québécois.'

27 Leach, *Claude Jutra*, paraphrasing Perreault ('Copie trop conforme'), 155.

28 Freud, 'The "Uncanny,"' 233–4.

29 Ibid., 235.

30 'To go on dreaming at the risk of life and limb, as if you were acting out your own death. Just to see if you can. Well, don't delude yourself. Someday reality and its imag-

ined double are going to be one and the same. No difference at all between them. Every premonition, true. Every alibi, flat. Every escape, blocked off. Doom will lie clinging to my bones. They'll find me guilty, guilty before the world. It's time to break free, break out of this stagnation, now. To stifle the dream before it's too late. Quick, into the sunshine. Shake it off. Throw off the specters' (17).

31 Davidson, 253.

32 Doane, 142, 143.

33 Freud, 'The "Uncanny,"' 235-6.

34 'Then all at once the nightmare breaks again. Dashes its winds against Elisabeth d'Aulinières. While on the surface everything seems so calm. The model wife, clasping her husband's hands in hers, poised on the sheet. And yet ... Off in a parched field, under the rocks, they've dug up a woman, all black but still alive, buried there long ago, some far-off, savage time. Strangely preserved. Then they've gone and let her loose on the town. And all the people have locked themselves in. So deathly afraid of this woman. And everyone thinks that she must have an utterly awesome lust for life, buried alive so long. A hunger growing and growing inside the earth for centuries on end! Unlike any other that's ever been known. And whenever she runs through the town, begging and weeping, they sound the alarm. Nothing before her but doors shut tight, and the empty, unpaved streets. Nothing to do now but let herself die. Alone and hungry' (249–50).

35 Doane, 141.

36 This was a strategy consciously employed by Jutra at other points in the diegesis in order to work against a teleological reading of the film as 'mere' melodrama; see Leach, *Claude Jutra,* 156.

37 See Doane, 138; and Leach, *Claude Jutra,* 158–61.

38 Leach, *Claude Jutra,* 158. For his part, Guy Lavorel argues that the 'distanciated' aspect the film adopts towards the 'moi multiple et impossible' ('the multiple and impossible self') of the novel is necessarily compromised, noting that the film, 'plus psychologique que métaphysique, n'a pu traduire que d'une façon artificielle et plaquée le modernisme propre à l'écriture hébertienne' ('more psychological than metaphysical, can only translate in an artificial and somewhat cheapened way the high modernism of Hébert's writing'; my translation). See Lavorel, 'Kamouraska,' 56, 54.

39 Freud, 'The "Uncanny,"' 232–3.

40 See Mandel, 'Atwood Gothic.'

41 Mycak, *In Search of the Split Subject,* 48.

42 The term 'sociological gothic' is Northey's. See her reading of Atwood's novel in *The Haunted Wilderness,* 62–9.

43 See her interview with Graeme Gibson in Gibson, *Eleven Canadian Novelists,* 20.

44 Kirtz, 'Teaching Literature through Film,' 142.

45 See Leach, *Claude Jutra,* 214–16.

46 Knelman, 'Mum's the Word,' 22.

47 See Kirtz, 142–3; and Monk, *Weird Sex and Snowshoes,* 27–31.

48 Jacobwitz, 'Surfacing,' 35.

49 Ibid.; and Leach, *Claude Jutra,* 220.

50 Leach, *Claude Jutra,* 221.

51 Davidson, 'Canadian Gothic,' 247.

52 Besides Davidson, see Northey, *The Haunted Wilderness*, 70–8; Coldwell, 'Mad Shadows as Psychological Fiction'; Godard, '"Blais,"' 159–75; Slama, '*La belle bête*, ou la double scène'; and Green, *Marie-Claire Blais*, 8–14.

53 Green, 109.

54 'Now the only humiliation that tormented her was the thoughtlessness of the two lovers who had given themselves over to the joys of life while a silent death had lain in wait for them, death had been present, she thought, in each of their abandonments, they had never been aware of its breath passing over their cheeks, they hadn't moved, hadn't spoken, hadn't run away, it had shut itself up in their house with them, it had slipped between the sheets with them and had drunk up all the warmth and fragrance of the fine summer in bloom at the window' (211–12).

55 Green, 109.

56 See Viswanathan, "Échanger sa vie pour une autre.'

57 See Gravili, 'Entre le livre et l'écran,' 76.

58 Dansereau, 'Entretien avec Mireille Dansereau,' 31. 'I couldn't do justice to the brilliant form of the mosaic-like *Sourd dans la ville*, even though I love its collages, its fragments of conversation, its movement. I had to simplify it, if only to obtain the approval of investors' (my translation).

59 Doane, 136; emphasis in original. I will return to the importance of staircases – specifically as they figure in the adaptive genre of lesbian boarding school films – in chapter 6.

60 Marshall, *Quebec National Cinema*, 224–6.

61 Ibid., 226. See also Deleuze, *Cinema 1: The Movement-Image*, 87 and ff.

62 Gravili, 76. In addition to director and co-screenwriter Dansereau, those involved included producers Louise Carré, Suzanne Laverdière, and Claire Stevens, editor Louise Coté, co-screenwriter Michèle Mailhot, art director Gaudeline Sauriol, and composer and sound designer Ginette Bellavance.

63 Stam, 'Beyond Fidelity,' 73.

64 Tulloch, 'Yves Simoneau's Rewriting,' 111. For my own brief reading of Simoneau's film, see chapter 1.

65 Shields, *Swann*, 13, 14, 15.

3 Images of the Indigene

1 Prats, *Invisible Natives*, 24.

2 Rony, *The Third Eye*, 5–6.

3 Goldie, *Fear and Temptation*, 4, 6.

4 The adaptations include two silent versions, one directed by Theodore Marston in 1911 and one co-directed by Clarence Brown and Maurice Tourneur in 1920, and three talkies: a 1932 twelve-part serial directed by Ford Beebe and B. Reeves Eason; a 1936 version directed by George B. Seitz and starring Cary Grant's lover Randolph Scott as Hawkeye; and Michael Mann's 1995 big-budget epic, with Daniel Day Lewis in the lead role.

5 Rony, 5.

6 James Fenimore Cooper provided the source text for the various versions of *The Last of the Mohicans*. *Little Big Man* was based on the novel by Thomas Berger; *Dances with*

Wolves on a novel by Michael Blake; *Stagecoach* on a story by Ernest Haycox; *Fort Apache*, *She Wore a Yellow Ribbon*, and *Rio Grande* on stories by James Warner Bellah; *The Searchers* on the novel by Alan LeMay; *Two Rode Together* on the novel by Will Cook; and *Cheyenne Autumn* on the novel by Mari Sandoz. *The Outlaw Josey Wales* was based on the novel *Gone to Texas* by Forrest Carter, and *One Flew Over the Cuckoo's Nest* on the novel by Ken Kesey. Even Jarmusch's *Dead Man* can be seen as a quasi-adaptation of the poetry of William Blake, which Nobody quotes to the onscreen Blake (Johnny Depp) at great length.

7 Gittings, *Canadian National Cinema*, 200.
8 Kilpatrick, *Celluloid Indians*, 98.
9 Kesey, *One Flew Over the Cuckoo's Nest*, 13.
10 Kilpatrick, 100.
11 Rony, 7.
12 Ibid., 101–2.
13 Prats, 27.
14 Ibid., 36.
15 Li, *The Neo-Primitivist Turn*, ix. Li borrows the term 'chronopolitics' from Johannes Fabian's *Time and the Other*, a work to which Rony is likewise indebted.
16 See Leahy, 'History: Its Contradictions and Absence,' 312, 313; and Ben-Z. Shek, 'Yves Thériault,' 120.
17 Made for $14 million Canadian, *Black Robe* took in just over US$8 million at the box office, earning it the Golden Reel Award for top-grossing feature at the 1992 Genie Awards, where it also won awards for Best Picture, Director, Adapted Screenplay, Supporting Actor (August Schellenberg), Cinematography (Peter James), and Art Direction. Jay Scott's breathless, four-star review of the film in the *Globe in Mail* is typical of the sort of press it received across the country: '*Black Robe*, the visually extravagant Canada/Australia co-production … is exhilaratingly shocking, an intelligent priests-and-Indians costume dra-ma that frequently provokes uncomfortable thoughts and intermittently incites unpleasant emotions.' See Scott, 'A Hideous Period of History,' C1. By contrast, *Shadow of the Wolf*, at the time the most expensive film ever made in Canada, earned only US$1.4 million and sank almost immediately, due in part to what Patricia Hluchy, reviewing the film in *Maclean's*, identified as its 'cartoonish characters,' 'heavy allegorical overlay,' and 'bizarre to laughable' acting; see Hluchy, 'Lost in the Barrens,' 50.
18 Pevere, 'Hostiles,' 36.
19 Coincidentally, Greene has publicly expressed a desire to play Lasagna, one of the more prominent Mohawk militants involved in the Oka standoff, should a feature film ever be made of the crisis. See Johnson, 'Dances with Oscars,' 60.
20 A sixth novel by Moore, *Catholics*, was adapted for American television in 1973, and Moore wrote or co-wrote the screenplays for Alfred Hitchcock's *Torn Curtain*, Claude Chabrol's *Le sang des autres* (1987), and Giuliano Montaldo's *Il giorno prima* (1987).
21 Moore, *Black Robe*, 41.
22 Freud, in 'A Child Is Being Beaten,' distinguishes masochism in women from 'feminine masochism,' which he defines as an exclusively male pathology, in terms of the following comparative framework:

masochism in women	masochism in men
Phase 1 (oedipal/genital)	
'My father is beating the child [whom I hate].'	'I am being loved by my father.'
– Sadistic/positive	– Passive (masochistic)/negative
– Feminine attitude: jealousy	– Feminine attitude: love
Phase 2 (unconscious)	
'I am being beaten by my father.'	'I am being beaten by my father.'
– Masochistic	– Masochistic
– Feminine attitude: submission	– Feminine attitude: submission
Phase 3 (conscious)	
'Some boys are being beaten. [I am probably looking on.]'	'I am being beaten by my mother.'
– Sadistic/positive	– Masochistic/negative
– Masculine attitude: success of masculine protest	– Feminine attitude: failure of masculine protest
– Repression	– Regression

In other words, sexual fantasies involving corporal punishment produce 'unmanly boys' (cowering from their phallic mothers) and 'unwomanly girls' (who identify with schoolyard boys being beaten). Or, as Freud puts it, 'a trait of femininity in the boy and of masculinity in the girl … must be made responsible' for the fantasy (202). All of this Freud further links up to the theory of 'masculine protest' as it relates to beating fantasies involving children and their fathers, and in particular the motive force of repression (the agent of which is always a 'masculine instinctual response,' while that which is being 'repressed would be a feminine one' [201]). Based on his comparison of the cases of four female analysands and two male analysands, Freud posits that girls seem to be more successful than boys in repressing their masochistic fantasies, suggesting that masculine protest is successful in Phase 3 (conscious) of the female masochistic fantasy, but not always so in the male Phase 3, with the attendant consequence that, if acted upon, the fantasy will result in regressive behaviour in men: 'In the case of both boys and girls the beating-phantasy corresponds with a feminine attitude – one, that is, in which the individual is lingering on the "feminine line" – and both sexes hasten to get free from this attitude by repressing the phantasy. Nevertheless, it seems to be only with the girl that the masculine protest is attended with complete success, and in that instance, indeed, an ideal example is to be found of the operation of the masculine protest. With the boy the result is not entirely satisfactory; the feminine line is not given up, and the boy is certainly not "on top" in his conscious masochistic phantasy' (202–3).

23 Moore, *Black Robe,* 171.
24 Scott, 'A Hideous Period of History,' C1.
25 Moore, *Black Robe,* 41.
26 Churchill, 'And They Did It Like Dogs in the Dirt,' 23.
27 Dumont, 'Black Robe,' 13.
28 Pevere, 'Hostiles,' 36.

29 Perron, *Semiotics and the Modern Quebec Novel*, 17.

30 See Smart, *Writing in the Father's House*.

31 Thériault, *Agaguk*, n.p. All subsequent references to this text will be cited parenthetically, along with their English translations, which are reproduced from the Chapin translation; this quotation, n.p.

32 'Then slowly, from the depths of his subconscious, Agaguk felt his rage rising, not in a sharp rush of blood to the head, but in a slow implacable anger, which mounted from his entrails to take over his whole being. A new force existed in him, an extraordinary power which would decide the event. His hands braced against the ice wall, the muscles of his legs taut, his knees bent, he panted, his rage in rhythm with the moans of Iriook, with the fury of her cries … At that instant the vagina opened like a mouth, a sort of dark orifice, a monstrosity carved in the lower belly. The woman's cries filled the hut and reverberated in terrifying echoes along the walls and up to the ice dome. Still against the wall, Agaguk had become more beast than man' (58–9).

33 'Since Iriook had first become pregnant, he had never possessed her without at the same time thinking of the child. First of the unknown, mysterious, anonymous being lying within his wife's body, then of Tayaout, this Tayaout in whom he placed all his hopes and joys. By instinct he linked these two things, refusing to shut off the pleasure of sex and the pleasure he drew from this being he had procreated and who had now come to live so close to him. Without knowing it, Agaguk reached back to man's original philosophy, his first thought' (84–5).

34 Pevere, 'Harpooned,' 23.

35 Pevere, 'Hostiles,' 37.

36 Ibid.

37 Kelly, *A Dream Like Mine*, 20, 42–3, 150.

38 Ibid., 44.

39 Ibid., 9–10, 152.

40 See note 21.

41 Pevere, 'Dances with Natives,' C2.

42 As with McDonald's next film, *Hard Core Logo* (see chapter 7), the film adaptation of *Dance Me Outside*, combined with its source text by Kinsella, was further adapted by artist Nick Craine as a graphic novel. See his *Dance Me Outside: The Illustrated Screenplay*.

43 Lusty, '*Dance Me Outside* Maintains Stereotypes,' 15.

44 Gittings, 213.

45 Ibid.

46 Pevere, 'Dances with Natives,' C2.

47 Kinsella, *Dance Me Outside*, 49.

48 Ibid., 5.

49 Prats, 149.

50 Kilpatrick, 231.

51 Quoted in Kilpatrick, 231.

52 Gittings, citing Paul Chaat Smith, has identified Mohawk filmmaker Shelley Niro's 1998 *Honey Moccasin* 'as the first independent Canadian feature film written by, directed by and starring Natives'; see Gittings, 226–7. However, the film was produced as part of an exhibit of contemporary Aboriginal art at the Canadian Museum of Civilization and

never released theatrically. Thus, in terms of representing a real commercial break-
through for Aboriginal filmmaking in this country, *Atanarjuat* has the greater claim.
53 Rony, 213.
54 Kunuk, quoted in Hendrick and Fleming, 'Zacharias Kunuk,' 26.
55 Rony, 125.
56 See McCall, '"A Life Has Only One Author."'
57 Norman Cohn, 'The Art of Community-Based Filmmaking,' 25.
58 See Rony, 124.
59 Sophie McCall, '"I Can Only Sing This Song,"' 26.
60 Here I am deliberately counterposing Kunuk's technique to what Rony, drawing on the
work of Johannes Fabian, has discussed in terms of the '"naturalized-spatialized Time"'
of ethnographic exposition, where, for example, 'artefacts extracted from a distant place
and past, placed within the context of the museum, embodied an evolutionary "real."'
See Rony, 130.
61 Apak Angilirq and Cohn, *Atanarjuat: The Fast Runner*, 193; ellipses in original.
62 For Kunuk's discussion of the benefits of digital video technology for his kind of cinematic storytelling, including the facilitation of tight close-ups and the ability 'to correct
your mistakes right on the set,' see Chun, 'Storytelling in the Arctic Circle,' 23. Moreover, in terms of the role this technology plays in inverting the traditional ethnographic
gaze, consider the following excerpt from the 'Production Diary' posted to the film's
official website (www.atanarjuat.com/production_diary/index.html): 'The film's
visual strategy was designed to heighten the audience's sense of being there, despite
the exotic locale. Even state-of-the-art digital cameras can take you places a film camera
could never go. The goal of Atanarjuat is to make the viewer feel *inside* the action, looking out, rather than outside looking in. This lets people forget how far away they really
are, and to identify with the story and characters as if they were just like us.'
63 Hall, 'Cultural Identity and Cinematic Representation,' 708.
64 Ibid., 704.

4 Critically Queenie

1 Herbert, *Fortune and Men's Eyes*, 70. Subsequent references will be cited parenthetically
in the text as *F*.
2 Grossman, 'Transvestism in Film.'
3 The series ran from 1998 to 2003 on the HBO network in the United States and on Showcase in Canada.
4 Loiselle, *Stage-Bound*, 6, 12, 4.
5 Ibid., 11.
6 Originally published in 1981, *The Celluloid Closet* was republished in a revised edition in
1987.
7 He was later incarcerated in another Toronto-area reformatory after he was arrested for
appearing in public in drag. See the obituary by Kate Taylor, 'John Herbert.'
8 See, for example, Jerry Wasserman, who in his introduction to the canonical anthology
Modern Canadian Drama lists 1967 as the 'key date' for the beginning of modern drama
in English Canada, citing such defining moments as the Centennial, Expo 67, and the
Dominion Drama Festival, alongside contemporaneous productions of James Coulter's
Louis Riel, George Ryga's *The Ecstasy of Rita Joe*, and Herbert's *Fortune and Men's Eyes*.

9 The 1975 production of the play was staged at the Phoenix Theatre in Toronto, directed by Graham Harley. It promptly won the Chalmers Award for Best Play. Herbert accepted this 'belated Canadian acknowledgement' with 'a mixture of humour and irony'; see Anthony, ed., *Stage Voices*, 166. Lest the national slight against Herbert be overemphasized (not that the author himself didn't interpret it this way), it should also be pointed out that a touring production of the off-Broadway show (with the original cast) did visit Toronto in October 1967 for a brief run, and that it was enthusiastically reviewed by Nathan Cohen ('Fortune and Men's Eyes Rich in Reality').

10 See Sullivan, 'Theater: A Distressing "Fortune and Men's Eyes,"' 29; and Oliver, Review of *Fortune and Men's Eyes*, 134.

11 Whittaker, 'Toronto's Jack Brundage Has a Winner,' 18.

12 Cohen, 'Prison Drama Softened,' 22.

13 Barnes, 'Theater: "Boys in the Band" Opens Off Broadway,' 48. Of the comparisons with Albee, Barnes made sure he was first off the mark: 'As the conventional thing to say about Mart Crowley's "The Boys in the Band" will be something to the effect that it makes Edward Albee's "Who's Afraid of Virginia Woolf?" seem like a vicarage tea party, let me at least take the opportunity of saying it first' (48).

14 Oliver, Review, 134.

15 Barnes, 'Theater: Question Marks at Stage 73,' 55.

16 So intensely did Mineo's production chafe against the sensibilities of bourgeois theatre-goers that Barnes's negative response to the show continued to be echoed by other critics several years after its closing; see Hofsess, 'Fortune and Men's Eyes – a Report'; Carson, 'Sexuality and Identity in *Fortune and Men's Eyes*,' 208; and Russo, *The Celluloid Closet*, 198.

17 Russo, 198. Schwerin, a left-leaning documentarian and educational filmmaker from New York, saw *Fortune* 'in the greatest tradition of cinema and social drama' (see Lanken, 'Director Has Credentials,' 37). By contrast, Hart was a journeyman director who had worked mostly in television, and whose job it was to wrap up an overbudget production as quickly as possible. Thus, if the film's narrative seems at times to unspool at generic cross-purposes, this has as much to do with each director's different film training as it does with any additional exigencies experienced on the set. Hart, incidentally, would follow up his work on *Fortune* with another adaptation of a work of Canadian literature. *The Pyx* (1973), based on John Buell's 1959 novel, features Christopher Plummer as a detective who, in the course of investigating the death of a heroin-addicted prostitute played by Karen Black, stumbles onto a Satanic cult. A not unstylish paranoid/possession thriller that makes innovative use of flashbacks, Hart's second feature had the misfortune of being released the same year as yet another William Friedkin film in the same vein, *The Exorcist*.

18 Russo, 98, 199.

19 See, for example, the capsule reviews in *Newsweek* (5 July 1971, 72) and the *New York Times* (2 September 1971, 125).

20 Byron, 'Finally – Two Films Dealing With the Issues of Gay Lib,' 12. Byron and Russo both decried the tag line that accompanied MGM's advertising and promotion of the film – 'What goes on in prison is a crime' – rightly suggesting that the 'crime' being alluded to was homosexuality.

21 Quoted in Russo, 199.

22 Quoted in Russo, 200. Interestingly, fellow British gay film critic Richard Dyer explicitly

places *Fortune* in a tradition of films 'that have the Genet flavour'; see his *Now You See It*, 101.

23 Russo, 198.

24 See the final chapter of Butler's *Bodies That Matter*, 223–42.

25 Ibid., 235.

26 Wallace, 'Defying Category,' 304, 305. Reid Gilbert has likewise argued that 'it is around the character of Mona that gender debate [in *Fortune*] centres.' However, Gilbert conflates key differences in the play and the film in his description of Queenie's and Mona's drag performances. See Gilbert, '"My Mother Wants Me to Play Romeo Before It's Too Late,"' 127. For other interesting readings of Mona's cross-gender performance within the play, specifically as it contrasts with Queenie's, see Messenger, 'Damnation at Christmas,' 174–5; and Carson, 'Sexuality and Identity in *Fortune and Men's Eyes*,' 214.

27 Butler, *Bodies That Matter*, 236, 235.

28 For a reading of how different productions of *Hosanna*, the play, have accomplished similar allegorical shifts, see Schwartzwald, 'From Authenticity to Ambivalence'; see as well my own *Here is Queer*, 108–15. Loiselle has demonstrated, in this regard, how the film, coming as it does in the middle of Tremblay's Belles Soeurs cycle, in many ways 'frees' Tremblay's later plays from the burden of nationalist allegorization and overdetermination, although Waugh has also shown that the film was itself subject to just this kind of nationalist overdetermination from several reviewers in Quebec. See Loiselle, 'The Function of André Brassard's *Il était une fois dans l'est*'; and Waugh, 'Fairy Tales of Two Cities,' 285–305.

29 Tremblay, quoted in Anthony, ed., *Stage Voices*, 284.

30 Butler, *Gender Trouble*, 137, 138.

31 The story is based on Gibson's real-life struggle with mental illness and her friendship with Craig Russell.

32 Gibson, 'Making It,' 118.

33 Newton, *Mother Camp*, 103–4.

34 See Trow, 'Once Upon a Time in the East,' 21; and Riordon, '*Outrageous!*' 15.

35 See, for example, *Flow* (1997), *Trick* (1999), and *Gypsy Boys* (2000).

36 See Butler, *Gender Trouble*. See also Garber, *Vested Interests*; Tyler, 'Boys Will be Girls'; and Champagne, *The Ethics of Marginality*.

37 Straayer, 'Redressing the "Natural,"' 429.

38 Butler, *Gender Trouble*, 137.

39 Butler, *Bodies That Matter*, 230.

40 Champagne, 105.

41 I direct readers instead to Prosser's critique of Butler's reading of the film, and of Venus Xtravaganza's body in particular; see Prosser, *Second Skins*.

42 Halberstam, 'The Transgender Gaze in *Boys Don't Cry*,' 296.

43 Ibid., 297.

44 Ibid.

45 Mitchell and Trask, *Hedwig and the Angry Inch*, 83–4.

46 Anna Madrigal (Olympia Dukakis) is the wise and motherly transgendered landlady in Armistead Maupin's fictional *Tales of the City* miniseries: *Tales of the City* (1993); *More Tales of the City* (1998); and *Further Tales of the City* (2001). Roberta Muldoon (John Lith-

gow) is the former pro football player who becomes Jenny Fields's (Glenn Close) body-guard in *The World According to Garp* (1982). Dil (Jaye Davidson) and Heaven (Danny Edwards) are the soulful trans entertainers of colour in Neil Jordan's *The Crying Game* (1992) and Scott Reynolds's *Heaven* (1998), respectively. Kim/Karl Foyle (Steven Mack-intosh) is a career girl pursued by a former school chum in *Different for Girls* (1997). Rob-ert Eads, an FTM diagnosed with ovarian cancer, and Lola Cola, his demure MTF partner, are members of a southern American transsexual community featured in Kate Davis's *Southern Comfort* (2001). Finally, for a much more brutal look at the fate of Bran-don Teena/Teena Brandon, see Susan Muska and Gréta Ólafsdóttir's *The Brandon Teena Story* (1998).

47 Fraser, *Poor Super Man*, 79.
48 Ibid., 12, 13.
49 Proulx, *Le sexe des étoiles*, 229; ellipsis in original. Matt Cohen's English translation (173) reads as follows: 'you love the idea I represent, you love in me the woman with a capital W, that's what it is ... My dear, you are tremendously excited by my capital W. Don't count on me to solve your problems.'
50 See Eberle-Sinatra, 'Quelques réflexions sur l'adaptation cinématographique.'
51 Namaste, *Invisible Lives*, 107, 108. Namaste, it should be noted, in condemning the way that *Le sexe des étoiles* represents transsexuals as 'alien' and outside the normative (sub-urban) system of reproductive heterosexuality, extends her critique to Proulx's novel.
52 Proulx, *Le sexe des étoiles*, 159; 'the most fantastic paradox: black holes and quasars' (*Sex of the Stars*, 117).
53 Butler, *Bodies That Matter*, 239.

5 Space, Time, Auteurity, and the Queer Male Body

1 Deleuze, *Cinema 2*, 81.
2 For Pavis's theorization of intercultural theatre, see his *Theatre at the Crossroads of Cul-ture*. Hodgdon has applied Pavis's theories to an analysis of Lepage's updating of Shakespeare in 'Robert Lepage's Intercultural Dream Machine.'
3 Simon, 'Robert Lepage and the Languages of Spectacle,' 227. See also Simon, 'Robert Lepage and Intercultural Theatre'; Godard, 'Between Performative and Performance'; and Carson, 'From *Dragons' Trilogy* to *The Seven Streams of the River Ota*.'
4 Harvie, 'Transnationalism, Orientalism, and Cultural Tourism,' 123.
5 See Marshall, *Quebec National Cinema*; Garrity, 'Robert Lepage's Cinema of Time and Space'; Lefebvre, 'A Sense of Time and Place'; Telmissany, 'La citation filmique comme anachronisme'; and Dundjerovic, *The Cinema of Robert Lepage*.
6 See Garrity, 102, 105–6; on Deleuze's definition of the 'recollection-image,' see *Cinema 2*, 54.
7 On how the presence of a narrator need not be a precondition of narration in film, and on how film narration 'presupposes a perceiver, but not any sender, of a message,' see Bordwell, *Narration in the Fiction Film*, 62.
8 In an earlier version of this chapter, I had used the word 'gay' instead of 'queer' in for-mulating the argument that follows. However, as one of that version's anonymous reviewers pointed out, this presupposes a somewhat essentialist conception of male homosexual identity formation (and deformation) – one that is belied both by the theo-

retical framework of the chapter itself and by the imaging of several of the sexually polymorphous characters in Lepage's films. At the same time, it might be argued that 'gay' is one of the signifiers lost in translation in Lepage's reauthorizing of his 'queer' male bodies from stage to screen.

9 Corber, *Homosexuality in Cold War America*, 10. See also Dyer, 'Homosexuality and Film Noir,' 52–73.
10 Corber, 11, 53–4.
11 Dundjerovic, 63.
12 See Thérien, 'Cinéma québécois.'
13 See Schwartzwald, '"Symbolic" Homosexuality'; and Marshall, 129 ff.
14 Lefebvre, 'A Sense of Time and Place,' 96.
15 Ibid.
16 Alenka Zupančič, 'A Perfect Place to Die,' 80 (italics in original).
17 See Loiselle, 'Cinema, Theatre and Red Gushing Blood'; and 'The Corpse Lies in *Lilies*.'
18 Dominique Lafon, 'Pour servir à la petite histoire,' 49; 'presents singular similarities with the text of Daoust, independent of their common source, the play by Anthelme' (my translation). See as well Vaïs, 'Robert Lepage,' 125.
19 Lepage (with Rémy Charest), *Connecting Flights*, 33, 34.
20 Ibid., 35.
21 Ibid., 42.
22 To be sure, Pierre is just as nervous and uncomfortable in the strip club in Charny where Manon performs. Moreover, it is important to note that any reading of Pierre's screen sexuality necessarily overlaps with such extra-diegetic considerations as Bluteau's own sexuality and his previous acting roles. Again as one of the reviewers of an earlier version of this chapter put it, 'Bluteau, although fiercely private, may well have a personal identity that matches his onscreen queer personae in such New Queer films as *Bent*, *Orlando*, and *I Shot Andy Warhol*, but his public persona as well as his onscreen sensibility in such films as *Black Robe* and *Jésus de Montréal* are basically asexual, and the character of Pierre surely appropriates that asexual aura.'
23 'In the city where I was born, the past carries the present like a child on its shoulders' (translation courtesy English subtitles to film).
24 Obviously, my reading of Lepage's panoptical camera and the disciplined gay male body in *Le confessionnal* owes much to Foucault's analysis of the Ben-thamite panopticon in *Discipline and Punish*. In the first volume of *The History of Sexuality*, Foucault famously reads the seventeenth-century confession as one of the sites of the production of a discourse of sexuality, arguing that this 'unrelenting system of confession' puts 'sex into discourse' by '[compelling] individuals to articulate their sexual peculiarity – no matter how extreme': 'For us, it is in the confession that truth and sex are joined, through the obligatory and exhaustive expression of an individual secret. But this time it is truth that serves as a medium for sex and its manifestations' (61). Along these lines, Gittings reminds us that in Lepage's film 'the booths in which … Manon table-dances are referred to as confessionals. Formerly a ritualized space of containment in which Rachel confesses her sin of adultery before a male priest, the confessional becomes a ritualized space for the performance of female sexuality for the male gaze'; Gittings, *Canadian National Cinema*, 134.

25 Garrity, 103. See, also Durgnat, *The Strange Case of Alfred Hitchcock*; and Bazin, 'Hitchcock versus Hitchcock.'

26 Deleuze, *Cinema 2*, 77.

27 See Brassard and Lepage, *Polygraph*, 647–83. Further references to this play will be cited in-text as *P*.

28 See Sidnell, 'Polygraph.'

29 Deleuze, *Cinema 2*, 77.

30 'When I masturbate, I strangle myself with this. I pull then let go, pull then let go. Then, just before coming, I pull harder and harder … But once over, you have to let go – if you don't want to come for the last time' (my translation).

31 Shaviro, *The Cinematic Body*, 44, 46.

32 Ibid., 62. See also Bersani, *The Freudian Body*; Silverman, *Male Subjectivity at the Margins*; and Deleuze, *Masochism*. In this regard, consider as well Loiselle's comments on *Le polygraphe*'s adaptation: 'What most critics failed to perceive is that *Le polygraphe* does not (merely) seek to tell the complicated story of people involved in a crime and the film version of the crime. Rather, the film itself is the crime, as it proceeds very purposefully to kill the original play'; Loiselle, *Stage-Bound*, 197.

33 Schwartzwald, 'Fear of Federasty,' 176, 178, 183.

34 Ibid., 184–5. Interestingly, in Arcand's latest film, *Les invasions barbares*, a sequel to *Le déclin*, the director seems to reverse the equation between homosexuality and family/community dissolution, showing a still very much alive Claude to be the only one of the original movie's characters still in a stable relationship.

35 See Vaïs, 123–4. For a review of Leclerc's television adaptation of *Seven Streams*, see Lévesque, 'L'autonomie d'un oeuvre.'

36 Lepage and Morency, *Nô*, 57; 'Pushing against her interlocutor, the landlady enters energetically and stops just as quickly when she sees the other police officer stretched out nonchalantly on the hide-a-bed. Outraged, believing she's dealing with a homosexual couple, she gives them a dirty look. Under the same impression about the sexual identity of the cops, the visitors, themselves homosexuals, exchange knowing looks, attempting to establish a complicity that singularly embarrasses the representatives of the forces of order' (my translation).

37 Gittings reads Lepage's cut 'from a low-angled close-up shot of blood running down the inside of Sophie's legs to Sophie and Michel watching television coverage of the results of the May 1980 Referendum' somewhat differently, arguing that it constitutes Lepage's 'rather heavy-handed point about the failure of Québécois separatists to carry the embryonic Québec nation to full term'; see *Canadian National Cinema*, 191.

38 Lepage and Morency, 87; 'People with a collective project are always a little disadvantaged next to people who don't have a project. In the sense that those without a project always have the force of inertia with them. The idea is that it always takes more energy to change political institutions, social institutions than … to do nothing' (my translation).

39 Ibid.; 'It's a bit static as a project, isn't it?' (my translation).

40 Ibid., 89; 'Ten years ago, we were occupied with changing the world … Times have changed' (my translation).

41 Lepage and Ex Machina, *The Seven Streams of the River Ota*, 147.

42 See, in this regard, the scene in *Nô* in which Sophie encounters twin Québécoise airline

hostesses smoking up in the bathroom of a bar at the Quebec pavilion in Osaka. Putting a small piece of plastic over her little finger and waving it in the direction of her sister, one of the hostesses says 'Un condom japonais.' To which the other, laughing hysterically, replies: 'Ah mon dieu! Je comprends pourquoi c'est eux autres qui ont inventé le transistor'; see Lepage and Morency, 77.

43 Mighton, *Possible Worlds*, 23; further references to this play will be cited in-text as *PW*.

44 Wittig, *The Straight Mind and Other Essays*, 28; see also Rubin, 'The Traffic in Women,' 180: 'The incest taboo presupposes a prior, less articulate taboo on homosexuality. A prohibition against *some* heterosexual unions assumes a taboo against *non*heterosexual unions. Gender is not only an identification with one sex; it also entails that sexual desire be directed toward the other sex. The sexual division of labour is implicated in both aspects of gender – male and female it creates them, and it creates them heterosexual.'

45 See Butler, *Gender Trouble*, 63ff; see also Butler, *Bodies That Matter*, 235–6 and ff; and Butler, *Antigone's Claim*.

46 See 'The Mark of Gender' and 'On the Social Contract,' both in *The Straight Mind*.

47 Loiselle, *Stage-Bound*, 191.

48 On the 'heterosexual matrix,' see Butler, *Gender Trouble*, 35–78.

49 Lepage, *Connecting Flights*, 90–1.

50 Loiselle, 'The Corpse,' 124, 133.

51 Ibid., 131; see also Bouchard, 'Contraintes et libertés de la scénarisation,' 50–1.

52 Dubois, *Being at home with Claude*, 403. In the French version of the play it is specified that Claude is a member of the RIN, a radical separatist group active in the 1960s; but in the film we are offered only a vague reference to Claude working for the Parti Québécois.

53 See my own *Here Is Queer*, 121.

54 Marshall, 127; Marshall does go on to note, however, that the casting of Quebec superstar Roy Dupuis in the central role of Yves is 'replete with connotations of national masculinity,' especially when one considers his star-making performance in Beaudin's television adaptation of Arlette Couture's *Les filles de Caleb* the previous year, in which he played no less of a Quebec national icon than a *coureur de bois*. See Marshall, 128.

55 Loiselle, 'Cinema,' 31.

56 In *Le confessionnal*, it should be noted, blood is also used as a visual signifier of loss when Françoise miscarries in the bathtub with Paul-Émile.

57 Lepage, *Connecting Flights*, 32.

58 Zupančič, 80.

59 Deleuze, *Cinema 2*, 77–8; second ellipsis in original.

6 Ghosts In and Out of the Machine

1 Castle, *The Apparitional Lesbian*, 4.

2 White, *Uninvited*, 61.

3 Mulvey, 'Visual Pleasure and Narrative Cinema,' 808–9.

4 Mulvey, 'Afterthoughts,' 15.

5 Doane, *The Desire to Desire*, 7, 12.

6 Ibid., 13.

7 See Kaplan, *Women and Film*; Kuhn, *Women's Pictures*; Silverman, *The Subject of Semiotics* and *The Acoustic Mirror*; and Stacey, *Star Gazing*.

8 De Lauretis, *Alice Doesn't*, 144.

9 See, in particular, Stacey's important article 'Desperately Seeking Difference.'

10 White, 72.

11 Mulvey, 'Afterthoughts,' 12.

12 Doane, 8, 157.

13 White, 75.

14 Perez, *The Material Ghost*, 25.

15 Metz, *The Imaginary Signifier*, 48–9.

16 Perez, 25, 26.

17 Mulvey, 'Visual Pleasure,' 810.

18 Ibid.

19 My use of the term 'real' here should remind us that if, in a Lacanian reading of cine-matic identification, the male gaze represents a flight (under threat of castration) from the symbolic order of language and the law of the father to that of the imaginary order of visual fantasy and fetishistic scopophilia, then the female spectator can perhaps resist both symbolization and fetishization by staying within the realm of the real. As Perez notes, mainstream Lacanian film theory has tended to concern 'itself exclusively with the imaginary and the symbolic,' and to de-emphasize the importance of the real; see Perez, 420n34. A notable exception in this regard is Slavoj Žižek; see his *Enjoy Your Symp-tom!* For a critique of Žižek's reading of the real, see Butler, *Bodies That Matter*, 187–222. I will briefly return to questions of the 'real' in the next chapter.

20 Mayne, *Cinema and Spectatorship*, 64–5.

21 Ibid., 162.

22 On the importance of the 'star image' for gay male audiences, see Dyer, *Stars*; and also his *Heavenly Bodies*.

23 Metz, *The Imaginary Signifier*, 47.

24 Kabir, *Daughters of Desire*, 186.

25 Ibid., 185.

26 On how doubleness relates to both the woman spectator generally, and the lesbian spec-tator particularly, see de Lauretis, *Alice Doesn't*, as well as her essay 'Film and the Visi-ble,' 223–76.

27 Butler, *Bodies That Matter*, 13, 15.

28 Kabir, 196.

29 Allen, '*Salmonberries*,' 74.

30 Kabir, 195.

31 Ibid.

32 Ibid., 192.

33 See Korinek, *Roughing It in the Suburbs*.

34 The soundtrack of *Lost and Delirious* also works to extend the chain of lesbian spectato-rial identifications set in motion by the film, containing as it does contributions from queer singing icons Me'Shell Ndegéecello ('Beautiful') and Ani Di Franco ('You Had Time').

35 Kabir, 204.

36 See, for example, Patel, 'On Fire,' and Bachmann, 'After the Fire.'

37 Gopinath, 'On Fire,' 295, 297. See as well her 'Local Sites/Global Contexts,' 149–61.
38 Butler, *Bodies That Matter*, 242.
39 Swan, *The Wives of Bath*, ix. Subsequent references will be cited parenthetically in the text as *WB*.
40 Fuss, *Identification Papers*, 110.
41 Spark, *The Prime of Miss Jean Brodie*, 120.
42 Bussy, *Olivia*, 10, 9, 11. The novel, based on Bussy's own time at Marie Souvestre's famous finishing school outside Paris in the 1880s, was first published under an eponymous pseudonym in 1949 by Leonard Woolf's Hogarth Press, publishers, beginning four years later, of brother James's twenty-four-volume *Standard Edition of the Complete Psychological Works of Sigmund Freud*. In a further bit of Bloomsburian incestuousness, Bussy dedicated her Sapphic autobiographical musings to the memory of Virginia Woolf. For a fascinating reading of the pedagogically and sexually 'contagious' operations of lesbian identification in Bussy's novel, see Fuss, 107–40. For more on the historical context behind boarding school friendships between girls and their teachers during the late nineteenth and early twentieth centuries – not to mention an account of the real-life models for some of Bussy's characters (including Eleanor Roosevelt) – see Vicinus, 'Distance and Desire,' 600–22.
43 Hall, *The Well of Loneliness*, 207. Subsequent references will be cited parenthetically in the text as *WL*.
44 Ellis, 'Sexual Inversion in Women,' 222. For a critique of the inherent misogyny of Ellis's 'ascending scale of inversion,' especially as it applies to readings of Hall's novel, see Newton, 'The Mythic Mannish Lesbian,' 567 ff.
45 Ellis, 'Sexual Inversion,' 218.
46 Halberstam, *Female Masculinity*, 99.
47 See Lacan, 'The Mirror Stage,' 1–7.
48 For two opposing readings of this scene, one negative and one positive, see, for example, de Lauretis, *The Practice of Love*, 203–53; and Halberstam, *Female Masculinity*, 75–110.
49 Martin, 'From Book to Screen.'
50 Thomas Waugh, in a discussion of *Lost and Delirious* in the context of what he identifies as the 'lesbian coming-of-age-in-the-country film,' regrets that Thompson's 'ill-advised decision to update' Swan's source text to the twenty-first century resulted in the film adaptation becoming 'not Canada's *Boys Don't Cry* (USA, 1999), but our belated entry into the hoary seventy-year lesbian girls' school film genre, in which all have had somber if not tragic endings.' See his *The Romance of Transgression in Canada*, 131–2.
51 Martin, 'From Book to Screen.'
52 See, in this regard, Wilton's reading of Mulvey: 'If Laura Mulvey is to be believed, it is impossible for any woman to get pleasure from a mainstream narrative film without temporarily unsexing herself in order to carry out what is understood to be an intrinsically male set of behaviours, *à la* Lady Macbeth'; Wilton, 'On Not Being Lady Macbeth,' 144.
53 As Fuss likewise notes in connection with the title of Bussy's novel, the author was not only paying homage to 'a younger sister named Olivia who died in infancy,' but 'also surely had another Olivia in mind when she named her fictional alter ego: the heroine of the Shakespearean comedy *Twelfth Night* … A tangled romance of sartorial masquerade and comic impersonation, of sexual confusion and gender ambiguity, *Twelfth Night*

serves as the perfect analogue for Strachey's literary exploration of the improbability of her own "unheard of" passions'; see Fuss, *Identification Papers*, 132.

54 Shakespeare, *Antony and Cleopatra*, in *The Complete Works of William Shakespeare*, ll. 60-62.

55 See Russo, *The Celluloid Closet*, 63.

56 A curious side note to this case is that Roughead makes much of the fact that the teachers' accuser, Miss Jane Cumming, was 'patently what is termed a person of colour,' and thus overplayed the link between her mixed-raced identity and the 'divers physical and moral drawbacks later manifested' in her; see Roughead, *Bad Companions*, 116. The (post)colonial element to the story is something that both Hellman and Wyler have chosen to delete from their fictionalized versions, and that few critics have paid much attention to. Notable exceptions in this regard include Faderman, *Scotch Verdict*; Moore, '"Something More Tender Still than Friendship,"'; Martin, 'The Children's Hour'; and Halberstam, *Female Masculinity*, 62–5. Halberstam, in particular, is highly critical of both the original court transcripts and Faderman's 'use of Orientalist rhetoric to downplay the seriousness of Cumming's charges,' noting that 'the imbrication of racial difference and sexual perversity in the various representations of this trial become sensational precisely where and when competing definitions of lesbianism are at stake' (64, 63).

57 An earlier published version of the play uses as its opening Shakespearean intertext Portia's 'quality of mercy' speech from *The Merchant of Venice.*

58 My thanks to Patsy Aspasia Kotsopoulos for bringing this to my attention.

59 See the publisher's note to the original English translation of Winsloe's novel, *The Child Manuela*, n.p.

60 Rich, 'From Repressive Tolerance to Erotic Liberation,' 102.

61 Weiss, *Vampires and Violets*, 8–9.

62 Ibid., 10.

63 Ibid.

64 Rich, 106.

65 White, 197.

66 Ibid.

7 Adapting Masculinity

1 Cohan and Hark, *Screening the Male*, 3.

2 Turner, *American Whiskey Bar*, 71. Subsequent references will be cited parenthetically in the text as *AWB*.

3 Neale, 'Masculinity as Spectacle,' 4. Dyer provided another early intervention into the theorization of masculinity as spectacle in 'Don't Look Now.'

4 See Lehman, ed., *Masculinity*; Cohan and Hark, eds., *Screening the Male*; and Stukator, ed., *Cinemas, Nations, Masculinities*.

5 Neale, 'Masculinity,' 16.

6 See Waugh, 'Cinemas, Nations, Masculinities,' 21–2. In particular, Waugh singles out an article by Robert Fothergill, originally published in *Take One* in 1973, as having singularly 'bedevilled' subsequent scholarship on English-Canadian cinematic masculinities. Fothergill's thesis, which remains remarkably resilient in much film studies discourse in this country, is that repeated representations of what he identifies as male 'victims' and 'losers' in films from the 1970s such as Don Shebib's *Goin' Down the Road* (1970) and

Peter Pearson's *Paperback Hero* (1972) are symptomatic of our collectively colonized national identity, with Canada forced to play emasculated younger brother to bully America; see Fothergill, 'Coward, Bully, or Clown.' For an important critique of Fothergill, see also Ramsay, 'Canadian Narrative Cinema from the Margins.'

7 Waugh, 'Cinemas, Nations, Masculinities,' 22.

8 See Mellen, *Big Bad Wolves*.

9 As with his graphic novelization of an earlier McDonald adaptation, *Dance Me Outside* (see chapter 3), Craine's comic book occupies a middle ground between McDonald's film and Turner's source text, incorporating aspects of each. See Craine, *Hard Core Logo*. For an astute analysis of Craine's works as doubly mediated adaptations (that is, aesthetically and culturally), see Beaty, 'Imagining the Written Word.'

10 Turner, *Hard Core Logo*, 173. Subsequent references will be cited parenthetically in the text as *HCL*.

11 Beaty, 35.

12 Turner, 'An Interview with the Author,' 419.

13 McDonald has lately returned to the genre with *Planet Claire* [aka: *Claire's Hat*]: *The Unmaking of a Movie* (2004), another highly self-referential commentary – this one on the filmmaking disaster that was *Picture Claire* (2001), McDonald's first high-budget picture with Hollywood stars (Juliette Lewis, Gina Gershon), which remains unreleased.

14 Baker, *Hard Core Roadshow*, 242–3.

15 On the four 'basic victim positions' in Canadian literature identified by Atwood, and on the 'basic game' rules that attend each, see her *Survival*, 36–9. Turner's *Survivial* was published as a limited-edition chapbook by Vancouver's Canlit Classics in Transition in 1997.

16 Baker, 10.

17 Beaty, 35.

18 See, for example, *HCL* 18, 22, 25, 32, 36, 40, 60, 73, 76, 78, 116, 147, 148, 156, 170, and 173.

19 Beaty, 35.

20 Baker, 14.

21 Ibid., 105.

22 Ibid.

23 Aitken and Lukinbeal, 'Disassociated Masculinities,' 353–4. On male hysteria in the road movie genre, see also Corrigan, *A Cinema Without Walls*. Finally, for an insightful critique of 'just how radically opposed to patriarchal capitalism even the most self-congratulatory examples of the "wild" and "alienated" American road mythos actually are,' particularly as that mythos attempted to reinvent itself in the 're-emergent buddy-road movie of the late 1980s,' see Hark, 'Fear of Flying,' 206.

24 For a fuller list of the characteristic features of the picaresque novel, see Guillén, 'Toward a Definition of the Picaresque'; Wicks, 'The Nature of the Picaresque Narrative'; and Sherrill, *Road-Book America*.

25 Golfman, 'Hard Core Logo: A Love Story,' 30.

26 Anderlini, 'Hard Core Logo,' 43.

27 Ibid., 44.

28 Williams, 'Melodrama Revised,' 43.

29 Golfman, 31.

30 The Slash Page Database Project, a searchable website that lists thousands of slash fic-

tion Internet sites by genre, theme, and character pairings can be accessed at www.squidge.org/~minotaur/5data.html.

31 See Penley, 'Feminism, Psychoanalysis,' 488–9 and ff.
32 Lehman, 'Crying Over the Melodramatic Penis,' 26, 25.
33 Williams, 'Melodrama,' 42.
34 Ibid., 42.
35 See Livesay, 'The Documentary Poem.'
36 See Scobie, 'Amelia'; and Dickinson, '"Documenting "North."'
37 Scobie, 269 and ff.
38 See chapter 6, note 18, above.
39 See Gaines, 'Lonely Boy and the Vérité of Sexuality.'
40 See Auslander, Liveness, 12–13 and passim. In using the word 'remediation' (7 and passim), Auslander is drawing on the work of Jay Bolter and Richard Grusin. In Remediation, Bolter and Grusin argue that new visual media achieve their cultural significance precisely by reinventing and recycling earlier media, with photography, for example, remediating perspectival painting, film remediating photography (and, according to Auslander, theatre), television remediating film, and the Internet and new digital technologies remediating all of the above. They further argue that the resulting media adopt one of two principal styles or strategies: 'transparent immediacy,' which seeks to deny the presence of both prior and anterior media; or 'hypermediacy,' which seeks to foreground the presence of both media. Of course, it needs to be pointed out that Bolter and Grusin owe much of the substance of their notion of remediation to McLuhan's concept of 'retrieval,' one of his laws of media; see his Understanding Media.
41 On gender as a technology, and how this intersects with film, see de Lauretis, Technologies of Gender.
42 Turner also had a cameo in McDonald's adaptation of American Whiskey Bar, playing the role of the bartender. It should also be pointed out that Turner, a prolific poet, fiction writer, screenwriter, and visual arts critic, has made two short films of his own: Heirs to a Felt Fortune (1998), a piece Turner describes as an example of 'found pornography'; and An Interview with Kevin and Dodie, a Warholesque silent black-and-white, ten-minute, single-take close-up of San Francisco authors Kevin Killian and Dodie Bellamy. Finally, as noted above, one other text by Turner has been adapted for the screen, Clancy Dennehy having turned the 1997 poetry collection Kingsway into a film-poem reminiscent of the silent 'city symphonies' of the 1920s with the aid of funds from Bravo!FACT.
43 The Sunset Boulevard intertext is worth pursuing further (the film is alluded to directly on page 250 of Turner's novel via porn ingenue Tanya's parroting of Norma Desmond's final line), if only for how the famously 'illogical' narrative construction of Billy Wilder's film is echoed in other recent literary and filmic representations of illogical masculinity. One thinks, in this regard, of Chuck Palahniuk's novel Fight Club (but not necessarily David Fincher's more famous film adaptation), or Canadian filmmaker Bruce LaBruce's Hustler White. LaBruce and Turner are currently collaborating on a film based on the life of photographer Willem Von Gloeden. Meanwhile, the proposed film adaptation of Turner's Pornographer's Poem languishes in development limbo.
44 Turner, The Pornographer's Poem, 215.
45 Williams, Hardcore, 101.
46 Turner, The Pornographer's Poem, 317–18.

47 See, for example, Butler, 'Imitation and Gender Insubordination,' 25 and passim.
48 Douglas, *Journey into Fear*, 135.
49 Lütticken, 'Planet of the Remakes,' 118.
50 Douglas, 136.
51 Lütticken, 118.
52 Douglas, 137.
53 Ibid., 129.
54 Halberstam, *Female Masculinity*, 1.
55 Ibid., 2.
56 Robinson, *Marked Men*, 3, 10-11.
57 On the potential overdeterminations of the male penis as visual signifier on screen, especially as a symbol of phallic power and/or abjection, see Lehman, 'Crying Over the Melodramatic Penis'; and, in the Canadian context, Parpart, 'The Nation and the Nude.'
58 Vorlicky, *Act Like a Man*, 27.
59 The phrase is Robinson's; see her *Marked Men*, 13. For further useful analyses of the operations of male masochism, see Silverman, *Male Subjectivity at the Margins*; Savran, *Taking It Like a Man*; and, of course, Freud, 'A Child is Being Beaten.' See also note 32 in chapter 5.
60 See Metz, *Film Language*.
61 On how lateness has more or less defined my scholarly career, see the introduction to my *Here Is Queer*.
62 See note 37.
63 The various adaptations of Hemingway's story include Robert Siodmak's 1946 version; Andrei Tarkovsky's 1956 student short; Don Siegal's 1964 version, originally meant to be broadcast as the first made-for-television movie in the United States, but released theatrically instead in the wake of John F. Kennedy's assassination; and, arguably, Quentin Tarantino's 1994 *Pulp Fiction*, with the hit men played by John Travolta and Samuel L. Jackson bearing more than a passing resemblance to Hemingway's Al and Max.
64 David Hare, *The Hours: A Screenplay*, ix.

Bibliography

Adams, James. 'Have You Seen These Movies?' *Globe and Mail*, 2 February 2002, R1, R4.

Aitken, Stuart C., and Christopher Lee Lukinbeal. 'Disassociated Masculinities and Geographies of the Road.' In Cohan and Hark, *The Road Movie Book*. 349–70.

Allen, Louise. '*Salmonberries*: Consuming kd lang.' In Wilton, *Immortal, Invisible*. 70–84.

Anderlini, Ken. 'Hard Core Logo.' *Take One* 5.13 (1996): 43–4.

Andrew, J. Dudley. *Concepts in Film Theory*. New York: Oxford University Press, 1984.

Anthony, Geraldine, ed. *Stage Voices: Twelve Canadian Playwrights Talk About Their Lives and Work*. Toronto: Doubleday, 1978.

Apak Angilirq, Paul, et al. *Atanarjuat: The Fast Runner: The Original Story and Screenplay*. Toronto: Coach House Books and Isuma Publishing, 2002.

Armatage, Kay. *The Girl from God's Country: Nell Shipman and the Silent Cinema*. Toronto: University of Toronto Press, 2003.

Atwood, Margaret. *Cat's Eye*. Toronto: McClelland & Stewart, 1988.

– *The Handmaid's Tale*. 1985. Toronto: Seal, 1986.

– *Surfacing*. Toronto: McClelland & Stewart, 1972.

– *Survival: A Thematic Guide to Canadian Literature*. Toronto: Anansi, 1972.

Auslander, Philip. *Liveness: Performance in a Mediatized Culture*. New York: Routledge, 1999.

Bachman, Monica. 'After the Fire.' In Vanita, *Queering India*. 234–43.

Bailey, Bruce. 'Making of "The Tin Flute": How to Shoot Four Movies at Once in Two Languages.' *Montreal Gazette*, 9 July 1982, D1.

Baker, Noel S. *Hard Core Roadshow: A Screenwriter's Diary*. Toronto: Anansi, 1997.

Barnes, Clive. 'Theater: "Boys in the Band" Opens Off Broadway.' *New York Times*, 15 April 1968, 48.

– 'Theater: Question Marks at Stage 73.' *New York Times*, 23 October 1969, 55.

Barthes, Roland. *Image–Music–Text*. Trans. Stephen Heath. New York: Fontana, 1977.

Bazin, André. 'Hitchcock versus Hitchcock.' In Albert J. Lavelly, ed., *Focus on Hitchcock*. Englewood Cliffs, NJ: Prentice Hall, 1972. 60–9.

– *What Is Cinema?* Vol. I. Trans. Hugh Gray. Berkeley: University of California Press, 1967.

Beaty, Bart. 'Imagining the Written Word: Adaptation in the Work of Bruce McDonald and Nick Craine.' *Canadian Journal of Film Studies* 13.2 (2004): 22–44.

Benjamin, Walter. 'The Work of Art in the Age of Mechanical Reproduction.' *Illuminations*. Ed. Hannah Arendt. New York: Schocken, 1968. 217–51.

Bersani, Leo. *The Freudian Body: Psychoanalysis and Art*. New York: Columbia University Press, 1986.

Blais, Marie-Claire. *La belle bête*. 1959. Montreal: Pierre Tisseyre, 1977.

− *Deaf to the City*. Trans. Carol Dunlop. Toronto: Lester and Orpen Dennys, 1981.

− *Le sourd dans la ville*. Paris: Gallimard, 1980.

Bluestone, George. *Novels into Film*. Berkeley: University of California Press, 1957.

Bolter, Jay, and Richard Grusin. *Remediation: Understanding New Media*. Cambridge, MA: MIT Press, 1999.

Bordwell, David. *Narration in the Fiction Film*. Madison: University of Wisconsin Press, 1985.

Bouchard, Michel Marc. 'Contraintes et libertés de la scénarisation: Entrentien avec Michel Marc Bouchard.' With Patricia Belzil. *Jeu* 88.3 (1998): 46–67.

Brassard, Marie, and Robert Lepage, *Polygraph*. Trans. Gyllian Raby. In Filewod, *The* CTR *Anthology*. 647–83.

Bruhm, Steven. 'Picture This: Stephen King's Queer Gothic.' In David Punter, ed., *A Companion to the Gothic*. Oxford: Blackwell, 2000. 269–80.

Bussy, Dorothy Strachey. *Olivia*. 1949. London: Virago, 1987.

Butler, Judith. *Antigone's Claim: Kinship between Life and Death*. New York: Columbia University Press, 2001.

− *Bodies That Matter: On the Discursive Limits of 'Sex.'* New York: Routledge, 1993.

− *Gender Trouble: Feminism and the Subversion of Identity*. New York: Routledge, 1990.

− 'Imitation and Gender Insubordination.' In Fuss, *Inside/Out*. 13-31.

Byron, Stuart. 'Finally – Two Films Dealing With the Issues of Gay Lib.' *New York Times*, 18 July 1971, 12.

Carrière, Louise. 'Les images de femmes dans le cinéma masculin.' In Carrière et al., eds., *Femmes et cinéma québécois*. Montreal: Boréal Express, 1983. 53–112.

Carson, Christie. 'From *Dragons' Trilogy* to *The Seven Streams of the River Ota*: The Intercultural Experiments of Robert Lepage.' In Donohoe and Koustas, *Theater sans frontières*. 43–78.

Carson, Neil. 'Sexuality and Identity in *Fortune and Men's Eyes*.' *Twentieth Century Literature* 18.3 (1972): 207–18.

Castle, Terry. *The Apparitional Lesbian: Female Homosexuality and Modern Culture*. New York: Columbia University Press, 1993.

Champagne, John. *The Ethics of Marginality: A New Approach to Gay Studies*. Minneapolis: University of Minnesota Press, 1995.

Chatman, Seymour. *Coming to Terms: The Rhetoric of Narrative in Fiction and Film*. Ithaca, NY: Cornell University Press, 1990.

Chun, Kimberly. 'Storytelling in the Arctic Circle: An Interview with Zacharias Kunuk.' *Cineaste* 28.1 (2002): 21–3.

Churchill, Ward. 'And They Did It Like Dogs in the Dirt …' *Z Magazine* 12 (December 1992): 20–4.

Cohan, Steven, and Ina Rae Hark, eds. *The Road Movie Book*. New York: Routledge, 1997.

− *Screening the Male: Exploring Masculinities in Hollywood Cinema*. New York: Routledge, 1993.

Cohen, Nathan. '"Fortune and Men's Eyes" Rich in Reality.' *Toronto Daily Star*, 20 October 1967, 23.

– 'Prison Drama Softened.' *Toronto Daily Star*, 17 April 1967, 22.

Cohn, Norman. 'The Art of Community-Based Filmmaking.' In Apak Angilirq et al., *Atanarjuat*. 25–7.

Coldwell, Joan. '*Mad Shadows* as Psychological Fiction.' *Journal of Canadian Fiction* 2.4 (1973): 65–7.

Cooper, Pamela. 'Sexual Surveillance and Medical Authority in Two Versions of *The Handmaid's Tale*.' *Journal of Popular Culture* 28.4 (1995): 49–66.

Corber, Richard J. *Homosexuality in Cold War America: Resistance and the Crisis of Masculinity*. Durham, NC: Duke University Press, 1997.

Corrigan, Tim. *A Cinema without Walls: Movies and Culture after Vietnam*. New Brunswick, NJ: Rutgers University Press, 1991.

– *Film and Literature: An Introduction and Reader*. Upper Saddle River, NJ: Prentice Hall, 1999.

Craine, Nick. *Dance Me Outside: The Illustrated Screenplay*. Cambridge, ON: Black Eye Books, 1994.

– *Hard Core Logo: Portrait of A Thousand Punks*. Concord, ON: Anansi, 1997.

Dansereau, Mireille. 'Entretien avec Mireille Dansereau.' With Denis Bélanger and Michel Coulombe. *Cinébulles* 7.1 (1987): 30–4.

Davidson, Arnold E. 'Canadian Gothic and Anne Hébert's *Kamouraska*.' *Modern Fiction Studies* 27.2 (1981): 243–54.

de Lauretis, Teresa. *Alice Doesn't: Feminism, Semiotics, Cinema*. Bloomington: Indiana University Press, 1984.

– 'Film and the Visible.' In Bad Object-Choices, eds., *How Do I Look? Queer Film and Video*. Seattle: Bay Press, 1991. 223–76.

– *The Practice of Love: Lesbian Sexuality and Perverse Desire*. Bloomington: Indiana University Press, 1994.

– *Technologies of Gender: Essays on Theory, Film, and Fiction*. Bloomington: Indiana University Press, 1987.

Deleuze, Gilles. *Cinema 1: The Movement-Image*. Trans. Hugh Tomlinson and Robert Galeta. Minneapolis: University of Minnesota Press, 1986.

– *Cinema 2: The Time-Image*. Trans. Hugh Tomlinson and Robert Galeta. Minneapolis: University of Minnesota Press, 1989.

– *Masochism: An Interpretation of Coldness and Cruelty*. Trans. Jean McNeil. New York: George Braziller, 1971.

Derrida, Jacques. 'The Law of Genre.' In Derrick Attridge, ed., *Acts of Literature*. New York: Routledge, 1992. 221–52.

Dickinson, Peter. 'Documenting "North" in Canadian Poetry and Music.' *Essays on Canadian Writing* 59 (1996): 105-22.

– *Here Is Queer: Nationalisms, Sexualities, and the Literatures of Canada*. Toronto: University of Toronto Press, 1999.

Doane, Mary Ann. *The Desire to Desire: The Woman's Film of the 1940s*. Bloomington: Indiana University Press, 1987.

Donohoe, Joseph I., and Jane M. Koustas, eds. *Theater sans frontières: Essays on the Dramatic Universe of Robert Lepage*. East Lansing: Michigan State University Press, 2000.

Dorland, Michael. *So Close to the State/s: The Emergence of Canadian Feature Film Policy.* Toronto: University of Toronto Press, 1998.

Douglas, Stan. *Journey into Fear.* Köln: Walther König/Serpentine Gallery, 2002.

Dubois, René-Daniel. *Being at home with Claude.* Trans. Linda Gaboriau. In Filewod, *The CTR Anthology.* 389–433.

Dumont, Marilyn. 'Black Robe: A Jesuit World Review.' *Windspeaker,* 25 October 1991, 13.

Dundjerovic, Aleksandar. *The Cinema of Robert Lepage: The Poetics of Memory.* London: Wallflower Press, 2003.

Dupuis, G., C. Fratta, and M. Riopel, eds. *Littérature et cinéma du québec.* Rome: Bulzoni Editore, 1997.

Durgnat, Raymond. *The Strange Case of Alfred Hitchcock.* Cambridge, MA: MIT Press, 1974.

Dyer, Richard. 'Don't Look Now: The Male Pin-Up.' *Screen* 23.3–4 (1982): 61–73.

– *Heavenly Bodies: Film Stars and Society.* New York: St Martin's Press, 1986.

– 'Homosexuality and Film Noir.' In *The Matter of Images: Essays on Representations.* London: Routledge, 1993. 52–73.

– *Now You See It: Studies on Lesbian and Gay Film.* London: Routledge, 1990.

– *Stars.* 1979. New edition, with a supplementary chapter and bibliography by Paul McDonald. London: BFI Publishing, 1998.

Easterbrook, Ian K., et al. *Canada and Canadians in Feature Films: A Filmography, 1928–1990.* Guelph, ON: University of Guelph, 1996.

Eberle-Sinatra, Michael. 'Quelques réflexions sur l'adaptation cinématographique du roman de Monique Proulx, *Le sexe des étoiles.' Essays on Canadian Writing* 76 (2002): 139–48.

Ellis, Havelock. 'Sexual Inversion in Women.' 1895. In *Studies on the Psychology of Sex.* Vol. I. Part IV. New York: Random House, 1942. 195–263.

Ellis, Kate, and E. Ann Kaplan. 'Feminism in Brontë's *Jane Eyre* and Its Film Versions.' In Barbara Tepa Lupack, ed., *Nineteenth-Century Women at the Movies: Adapting Classic Women's Fiction to Film.* Bowling Green, OH: Bowling Green State University Press, 1999. 192–206.

Evans, Gary. *In the National Interest: A Chronicle of the National Film Board of Canada from 1949 to 1989.* Toronto: University of Toronto Press, 1991.

– *John Grierson and the NFB: The Politics of Wartime Propaganda.* Toronto: University of Toronto Press, 1984.

Fabian, Johannes. *Time and the Other: How Anthropology Makes Its Others.* New York: Columbia University Press, 1983.

Faderman, Lillian. *Scotch Verdict.* New York: Quill, 1983.

Fiedler, Leslie. *Love and Death in the American Novel.* New York: Dell, 1966.

Filewod, Alan, ed. *The CTR Anthology: Fifteen Plays from Canadian Theatre Review.* Toronto: University of Toronto Press, 1993.

Fothergill, Robert. 'Coward, Bully, or Clown: The Dream-Life of a Younger Brother.' In Seth Feldman and Joyce Nelson, eds., *Canadian Film Reader.* Toronto: Peter Martin, 1977. 234–51.

Foucault, Michel. *Discipline and Punish: The Birth of the Prison.* Trans. Alan Sheridan. New York: Pantheon, 1977.

– *The History of Sexuality, Vol. 1: An Introduction.* Trans. Robert Hurley. New York: Vintage, 1990.

Fraser, Brad. *Poor Super Man*. Edmonton: NeWest, 1995.

Freud, Sigmund. 'A Child Is Being Beaten.' In *The Standard Edition of the Complete Psychological Works of Sigmund Freud*. Vol. 17. Trans. and ed. James Strachey. London: Hogarth, 1955. 179–204.

– 'Fragment of an Analysis of a Case of Hysteria.' In *The Standard Edition of the Complete Psychological Works of Sigmund Freud*. Vol. 7. Trans. and ed. James Strachey. London: Hogarth, 1953. 7–122.

– 'Hysterical Phantasies and their Relation to Bisexuality.' In *The Standard Edition of the Complete Psychological Works of Sigmund Freud*. Vol. 9. Trans. and ed. James Strachey. London: Hogarth, 1959. 155–66.

– 'The "Uncanny."' In *The Standard Edition of the Complete Psychological Works of Sigmund Freud*. Vol. 17. Trans. and ed. James Strachey. London: Hogarth, 1955. 219–56.

Freud, Sigmund, and Josef Breuer. *Studies on Hysteria*. Vol. 2 of *The Standard Edition of the Complete Psychological Works of Sigmund Freud*. Trans and ed. James Strachey. London: Hogarth, 1955.

From Script to Screen: New Policy Directions. Ottawa: Canadian Heritage, 2000.

Fuss, Diana. *Identification Papers*. New York: Routledge, 1995.

– ed. *Inside/Out: Lesbian Studies, Gay Studies*. New York: Routledge, 1991.

Gaines, Jane. '*Lonely Boy* and the *Vérité* of Sexuality.' *Canadian Journal of Film Studies* 8.1 (1998): 108.

Garber, Marjorie. *Vested Interests: Cross-Dressing and Cultural Anxiety*. New York: Routledge, 1992.

Garrity, Henry A. 'Robert Lepage's Cinema of Time and Space.' In Donohoe and Koustas, *Theater sans frontières*. 95–107.

Gaudreault, André, and Thierry Groensteen. *La transécriture: pour une théorie de l'adaptation, littérature, cinéma, bande dessinée, théâtre, clip*. Quebec: Éditions Note Bene, 1998.

Gay, Richard. 'Bonheur d'occasion: la vertu d'émouvoir.' *Le Devoir*, 3 septembre 1983, 15.

Genette, Gérard. *Palimpsests: Literature in the Second Degree*. Trans. Channa Newman and Claude Doubinsky. Lincoln: University of Nebraska Press, 1997.

Gerhart, Mary. *Genre Choices, Gender Questions*. Norman: University of Oklahoma Press, 1992.

Gibson, Graeme. *Eleven Canadian Novelists*. Toronto: Anansi, 1973.

Gibson, Margaret. 'Making It.' In *The Butterfly Ward*. Toronto: Oberon, 1976. 96–118.

Gilbert, Reid. '"My Mother Wants Me to Play Romeo before It's Too Late": Framing Gender on Stage.' *Theatre Research in Canada* 14.2 (1993): 123–43.

Gilbert, Sandra M., and Susan Gubar. *The Madwoman in the Attic: The Woman Writer and the Nineteenth-Century Literary Imagination*. 2nd edition. New Haven, CT: Yale University Press, 2000.

Gittings, Christopher. *Canadian National Cinema: Ideology, Difference and Representation*. London: Routledge, 2002.

Givner, Joan. *Mazo de la Roche: The Hidden Life*. Toronto: Oxford University Press, 1989.

Godard, Barbara. 'Between Performative and Performance: Translation and Theatre in the Canadian/Quebec Context.' *Modern Drama* 43.3 (2000): 327–58.

– 'Blais' *La belle bête*: Infernal Fairy Tale.' In Virginia Harper Grinling and Terry Goldie, eds., *Violence in the Canadian Novel*. St John's: Memorial University Press, 1981. 159–75.

- *Filmography of Canadian and Quebec Literatures.* Association of Canadian and Quebec Literatures. No date.
- 'My (m)Other, My Self: Strategies for Subversion in Atwood and Hébert.' *Essays on Canadian Writing* 26 (1983): 13–44.
Goldie, Terry. *Fear and Temptation: The Image of the Indigene in Canadian, Australian, and New Zealand Literatures.* Montreal: McGill–Queen's University Press, 1993.
Golfman, Noreen. 'Hard Core Logo: A Love Story.' *Canadian Forum* 75.857 (1997): 30–1.
Gopinath, Gayatri. 'Local Sites/Global Contexts: The Transnational Trajectories of Deepa Mehta's *Fire.*' In Arnaldo Cruz-Malavé and Martin F. Manalansan, eds., *Queer Globalizations: Citizenship and the Afterlife of Colonialism.* New York: New York University Press, 2002. 149–61.
- 'On Fire.' In Peter X. Feng, ed., *Screening Asian Americans.* New Brunswick, NJ: Rutgers University Press, 2002. 293–8.
Grant, Barry Keith, ed. *Film Genre Reader III.* Austin: University of Texas Press, 2003.
Gravili, Anne de Vaucher. 'Entre le livre et l'écran: *Le sourd dans la ville* de Marie-Claire Blais et de Mireille Dansereau.' In Dupuis et al., *Littérature et cinéma du Québec.* 75-83.
Green, Mary Jean. *Marie-Claire Blais.* New York: Twayne, 1995.
Greyson, John. 'The Coconut Strategy.' *Essays on Canadian Writing* 76 (2002): 263–6.
Groen, Rick. 'TV version of Tin Flute Hits a Few Sour Notes.' *Globe and Mail,* 2 January 1985, M7.
Grossman, Andrew. 'Transvestism in Film.' *glbtq: an encyclopedia of gay, lesbian, bisexual, transgender, and queer culture.* <www.glbtq.com/arts/transvestism_film.html>
Guillén, Claudio. 'Toward a Definition of the Picaresque.' In Gustavo Pellon and Julio Rodriguez-Luis, eds., *Upstarts, Wanderers or Swindlers: Anatomy of the Picaro.* Amsterdam: Rodopi, 1986. 81–102.
Halberstam, Judith. *Female Masculinity.* Durham, NC: Duke University Press, 1998.
- 'The Transgender Gaze in *Boys Don't Cry.*' *Screen* 42.3 (2001): 294–8.
Hall, Radclyffe. *The Well of Loneliness.* 1928. London: Virago, 1982.
Hall, Stuart. 'Cultural Identity and Cinematic Representation.' In Robert Stam and Toby Miller, eds., *Film and Theory: An Anthology.* Oxford: Blackwell, 2000. 704–14.
Hare, David. *The Hours: A Screenplay.* New York: Miramax Books, 2002.
Hark, Ina Rae. 'Fear of Flying: Yuppie Critique and the Buddy-Road Movie in the 1980s.' In Cohan and Hark, *The Road Movie Book.* 204–29.
Harris, Christopher. 'Black Robe Faces Attack on Two Fronts.' *Globe and Mail,* 7 September 1991, C4.
Harvie, Jennifer. 'Transnationalism, Orientalism, and Cultural Tourism: *La Trilogie des dragons* and *The Seven Streams of the River Ota.*' In Donohoe and Koustas, *Theater sans frontières.* 109–25.
Hébert, Anne. 'Anne Hébert et *Les fous de bassan.*' Entrevue avec Simone Suchet. *Séquences* 124 (1987): 54.
- *Les fous de bassan.* Paris: Éditions de Seuil, 1982.
- *Kamouraska.* Paris: Éditions du Seuil, 1970.
- *Kamouraska.* Trans. Norman Shapiro. Toronto: General Publishing, 1982.
Hellman, Lillian. *The Children's Hour.* New York: Dramatists Play Service, 1953.
Helman, Alicja, and Waclaw M. Osadnik. 'Film and Literature: Historical Models of Film

Adaptation and a Proposal for a (Poly)System Approach.' *Canadian Review of Comparative Literature* 23.3 (1996): 645–57.

Hendrick, Stephen, and Kathleen Fleming. 'Zacharias Kunuk: Video Maker and Inuit Historian.' *Inuit Art Quarterly* 6.2 (1991): 25–8.

Herbert, John. *Fortune and Men's Eyes*. New York: Grove, 1967.

– *Some Angry Summer Songs*. Vancouver: Talonbooks, 1976.

Hluchy, Patricia. 'Lost in the Barrens.' *Maclean's*, 15 March 1993, 50.

Hofsess, John. 'Fortune and Men's Eyes – a Report from the Set in a Quebec City Prison.' *Maclean's*, December 1970, 81.

Hodgdon, Barbara. 'Robert Lepage's Intercultural Dream Machine.' In Robert Shaughnessy, ed., *New Casebooks: Shakespeare in Performance*. London: Macmillan, 2000. 194–217.

Hu, Xiangwen, and François Gagnon. *Adaptations filmiques au Québec. Répertoire: 1922–1996*. Montreal: Université de Montréal et La cinémathèque québécoise, 1997.

Hume, Robert. 'Gothic versus Romantic: A Revaluation of the Gothic Novel.' *PMLA* 84 (1969): 282–90.

Jacobwitz, Florence. '*Surfacing*.' *Cinema Canada* 80 (December/January 1981–2): 35.

Jasmin, Claude. *Déliverez-nous du mal*. 1961. Montreal: Éditions internationales A. Stanké, 1980.

Johnson, Brian D. 'Dances with Oscars.' *Maclean's*, 25 March 1991, 60–1.

Kabir, Shameem. *Daughters of Desire: Lesbian Representations in Film*. London: Cassell, 1998.

Kaplan, E. Ann. *Women and Film: Both Sides of the Camera*. New York: Methuen, 1983.

Kelly, M.T. *A Dream Like Mine*. Toronto: General Publishing, 1987.

Kesey, Ken. *One Flew Over the Cuckoo's Nest*. New York: Signet, 1962.

Kilpatrick, Jacquelyn. *Celluloid Indians: Native Americans and Film*. Lincoln: University of Nebraska Press, 1999.

Kinsella, W.P. *Dance Me Outside*. Ottawa: Oberon, 1977.

Kirtz, Mary K. 'Teaching Literature through Film: An Interdisciplinary Approach to *Surfacing* and *The Handmaid's Tale*.' In Shannon Hengen, ed., *Approaches to Teaching Margaret Atwood's* The Handmaid's Tale *and Other Works*. New York: MLA, 1996. 140–5.

Knelman, Martin. 'Mum's the Word.' In Seth Feldman, ed., *Take Two*. Toronto: Irwin, 1984. 21–3.

Korinek, Valerie. *Roughing It in the Suburbs: Reading* Chatelaine *in the Fifties and Sixties*. Toronto: University of Toronto Press, 2000.

Kotsopoulos, Patsy Aspasia. 'Avonlea as Main Street USA: Genre, Adaptation, and the Making of a Borderless Romance.' *Essays on Canadian Writing* 76 (2002): 170–94.

Kristeva, Julia. *Powers of Horror: An Essay in Abjection*. Trans. Leon S. Roudiez. New York: Columbia University Press, 1982.

Kuhn, Annette. *Women's Pictures: Feminism and Cinema*. London: Routledge, 1982.

Lacan, Jacques. 'The Mirror Stage as Formative of the Function of the I.' In *Écrits*. Trans. Alan Sheridan. New York: Norton, 1977. 1–7.

Laferrière, Dany. *Comment faire l'amour avec un nègre sans se fatiguer*. Montreal: Vlb éditeur, 1985.

Lafon, Dominique. 'Pour servir à la petite histoire d'un mélodrame québécois: la leçon d'un tapuscrit.' *L'Annuaire théâtral* 17 (1995): 37–51.

Lanken, Dane. 'Director has credentials.' *Montreal Gazette*, 7 November 1970, 37.

Laurence, Margaret. *A Jest of God*. 1966. Toronto: McClelland & Stewart, 1988.

Lavorel, Guy. '*Kamouraska*: Du roman au film: la modification.' In Dupuis et al., *Littérature et cinéma du Québec*. 49–56.

Leach, Jim. *Claude Jutra: Filmmaker*. Montreal: McGill–Queen's University Press, 1999.

– 'The Reel Nation: Image and Reality in Contemporary Canadian Cinema.' *Canadian Journal of Film Studies* 11.2 (2002): 2–18.

Leahy, David. 'History: Its Contradictions and Absence in Brian Moore's *The Revolution Script* and *Black Robe*.' *World Literature Written in English* 28.2 (1988): 308–17.

Lefebvre, Benjamin. 'L.M. Montgomery: An Annotated Filmography.' *Canadian Children's Literature* 99: 26.3 (2000): 43–73.

– 'Stand by Your Man: Adapting L.M. Montgomery's *Anne of Green Gables*.' *Essays on Canadian Writing* 76 (2002): 149–69.

Lefebvre, Jean Pierre. 'La cohérence dans le cinéma québécois.' *Cinéma Québec* 4.9–10 (1976): 42–5.

Lefebvre, Martin. 'A Sense of Time and Place: The Chronotope in *I Confess* and *Le Confessionnal*.' *Quebec Studies* 26 (Fall 1998/Winter 1999): 88–98.

Lehman, Peter. 'Crying Over the Melodramatic Penis: Melodrama and Male Nudity in Films of the 90s.' In Lehman, *Masculinity*. 25–41.

– ed. *Masculinity: Bodies, Movies, Culture*. New York: Routledge, 2001.

Lepage, Robert. *Connecting Flights*. With Rémy Charest. Trans. Wanda Romer Taylor. London: Methuen, 1997.

Lepage, Robert, and Ex Machina. *The Seven Streams of the River Ota*. London: Methuen, 1996.

Lepage, Robert, and André Morency. *Nô*. Laval and Montreal: Les 400 Coups/Alliance Vivafilm, 1998.

Lerner, Loren R., ed. *Canadian Film and Video: A Bibliography and Guide to the Literature*. 2 vols. Toronto: University of Toronto Press, 1997.

Lever, Yves. 'Contenu sur *Déliverez-nous du mal*.' <www.cam.org/~lever/Films/Deliverez.html>

– *Histoire générale du cinéma au Québec*. 2ième édition. Montreal: Éditions du Boréal, 1995.

Lévesque, Solange. 'L'autonomie d'un oeuvre.' *Jeu* 88.3 (1998): 144–5.

Li, Victor: *The Neo-Primitivist Turn: Critical Reflections on Alterity, Culture, and Modernity*. Toronto: University of Toronto Press, 2006.

Livesay, Dorothy. 'The Documentary Poem: A Canadian Genre.' In Eli Mandel, ed., *Contexts of Canadian Criticism*. Toronto: University of Toronto Press, 1971. 267–81.

Loiselle, André. 'Cinema, Theater and Red Gushing Blood in Jean Beaudin's *Being at home with Claude*.' *Canadian Journal of Film Studies* 5.2 (1996): 17–33

– 'The Corpse Lies in *Lilies*: The Stage, the Screen, and the Dead Body.' *Essays on Canadian Writing* 76 (2002): 117–38.

– 'The Function of André Brassard's Film *Il était une fois dans l'est* in the Context of Michel Tremblay's "Cycle des Belles-Sœurs."' MA thesis, University of British Columbia, 1989.

– 'Scenes from a Failed Marriage: A Brief Analytical History of Canadian and Québécois Feature Film Adaptations of Drama from 1942 to 1992.' *Theatre Research in Canada* 17.1 (1996): 46–66.

– *Stage-Bound: Feature Film Adaptations of Canadian and Québécois Drama.* Montreal: McGill–Queen's University Press, 2003.

Lowry, Glen. 'Between *The English Patients*: "Race" and the Cultural Politics of Adapting CanLit.' *Essays on Canadian Writing* 76 (2002): 216–46.

Lu, Vickers. 'Excuse Me, Did We See the Same Movie? *Fried Green Tomoatoes.' Jump-Cut: A Review of Contemporary Media* 39 (1994): 25–30.

Lukow Gregory, and Steven Ricci. 'The "Audience" Goes "Public": Inter-Textuality, Genre and the Responsibilities of Film Literacy.' *On Film* 12.3 (1984): 28–36.

Lupack, Barbara Tepa. 'Vision/Re-Vision: Adapting Contemporary American Fiction by Women to Film.' In Lupack, ed., *Vision/Re-Vision: Adapting Contemporary American Fiction by Women to Film.* Bowling Green, OH: Bowling Green University Press, 1996. 1–44.

Lusty, Terry. '*Dance Me Outside* Maintains Stereotypes.' *Windspeaker,* April 1995, 18.

Lütticken, Sven. 'Planet of the Remakes.' *New Left Review* 25 (January/February 2004): 103–19.

Magder, Ted. *Canada's Hollywood: The Canadian State and Feature Films.* Toronto: University of Toronto Press, 1993.

Malcolm, Andrew H. 'Margaret Atwood Reflects on a Hit,' *New York Times,* 14 April 1990.

Mandel, Eli. 'Atwood Gothic.' *Malahat Review* 41 (1977): 165–74.

Marshall, Bill. *Quebec National Cinema.* Montreal: McGill–Queen's University Press, 2001.

Martin, Robert K. '*The Children's Hour*: A Postcolonial *Turn of the Screw.' Canadian Review of American Studies* 31.1 (2001): 401–7.

Martin, Sandra. 'From Book to Screen: A Story in Three Acts.' *Globe and Mail,* 7 July 2001.

Massé, Michelle A. 'Gothic Repetition: Husbands, Horrors, and Things that Go Bump in the Night.' *Signs* 15.4 (1990): 679–709.

Mayne, Judith. *Cinema and Spectatorship.* New York: Routledge, 1993.

– *Private Novels, Public Films.* Athens: University of Georgia Press, 1988.

McCall, Sophie. '"A Life Has Only One Author": Twice-Told Aboriginal Life Narratives.' *Canadian Literature* 172 (2002): 70–90.

– '"I Can Only Sing This Song to Someone Who Understands It": Community Filmmaking and the Politics of Partial Translation in *Atanarjuat, the Fast Runner.' Essays on Canadian Writing* 83 (2004): 18–46.

McFarlane, Brian. *Novel to Film: An Introduction to the Theory of Adaptation.* Oxford, UK: Clarendon, 1996.

McLuhan, Marshall. *Understanding Media: The Extensions of Man.* Toronto: McGraw-Hill, 1964.

Mellen, Joan. *Big Bad Wolves: Masculinity in American Film.* New York: Pantheon, 1977.

Messenger, Ann P. 'Damnation at Christmas: John Herbert's "Fortune and Men's Eyes."' In William New, ed., *Dramatists in Canada: Selected Essays.* Vancouver: UBC Press, 1972. 173–8.

Metz, Christian. *Film Language: A Semiotics of the Cinema.* Trans. Michael Taylor. New York: Oxford University Press, 1974.

– *The Imaginary Signifier: Psychoanalysis and the Cinema.* Trans. Celia Britton, Annwyl Williams, Ben Brewster, and Alfred Guzzetti. Bloomington: Indiana University Press, 1982.

Mighton, John. *Possible Worlds.* Toronto: Playwrights Canada Press, 1988.

Mitchell, John Cameron, and Steven Trask. *Hedwig and the Angry Inch*. Woodstock, NY: Overlook Press, 2000.

Moers, Ellen. *Literary Women*. Garden City, NY: Doubleday, 1977.

Monk, Katherine. *Weird Sex and Snowshoes: and Other Canadian Film Phenomena*. Vancouver: Raincoast, 2001.

Montgomery, L.M. *Anne of Green Gables*. 1908. Toronto: Ryerson, 1942.

– *The Selected Journals of L.M. Montgomery*. Vol. 2. Eds. Mary Rubio and Elizabeth Waterston. Toronto: Oxford University Press, 1987.

Moore, Brian. *Black Robe*. 1985. Toronto: Penguin Canada, 1996.

Moore, Lisa. '"Something More Tender Still than Friendship": Romantic Friendship in Early Nineteenth-Century England.' *Feminist Studies* 18.3 (1992): 499–521.

Morris, Peter. *Embattled Shadows: A History of Canadian Cinema, 1895–1939*. Montreal: McGill–Queen's University Press, 1978.

Mulvey, Laura. 'Afterthoughts on "Visual Pleasure and Narrative Cinema" Inspired by *Duel in the Sun*.' *Framework* 15/16/17 (1981): 12–25.

– 'Visual Pleasure and Narrative Cinema.' 1975. In Gerald Mast and Marshall Cohen, eds., *Film Theory and Criticism: Introductory Readings*, 3rd ed. New York: Oxford University Press, 1985. 803–16.

Mycak, Sonia. *In Search of the Split Subject: Psychoanalysis, Phenomenology, and the Novels of Margaret Atwood*. Toronto: ECW Press, 1996.

Namaste, Viviane K. *Invisible Lives: The Erasure of Transsexual and Transgendered People*. Chicago: University of Chicago Press, 2000.

Naremore, James, ed. *Film Adaptation*. New Brunswick, NJ: Rutgers University Press, 2000.

– 'Introduction: Film and the Reign of Adaptation.' In Naremore, *Film Adaptation*. 1–16.

Neale, Steve. *Genre*. London: BFI Publishing, 1980.

– *Genre and Hollywood*. New York: Routledge, 2000.

– 'Masculinity as Spectacle.' *Screen* 24.6 (1983): 2–16.

Nelson, Joyce. *The Colonized Eye: Rethinking the Grierson Legend*. Toronto: Between the Lines, 1988.

Newton, Esther. *Mother Camp: Female Impersonators in America*. Englewood Cliffs, NJ: Prentice Hall, 1972.

– 'The Mythic Mannish Lesbian: Radclyffe Hall and the New Woman.' *Signs* 9.4 (1984): 557–75.

Nicholson, Colin. 'Hollywood and Race: *To Kill a Mockingbird*.' In John Orr and Colin Nicholson, eds., *Cinema and Fiction: New Modes of Adapting, 1950–90*. Edinburgh: Edinburgh University Press, 1992. 151–9.

Northey, Margot. *The Haunted Wilderness: The Gothic and Grotesque in Canadian Fiction*. Toronto: University of Toronto Press, 1976.

Oliver, Edith. Review of *Fortune and Men's Eyes*. *The New Yorker*, 4 March 1967, 134.

Ondaatje, Michael. *The Conversations: The Art of Editing Film*. Toronto: Vintage, 2002.

– *Elimination Dance*. Ilderton, ON: Nairn Coldstream, 1978.

– *The English Patient*. Toronto: McClelland & Stewart, 1991.

Orr, Christopher. 'The Discourse on Adaptation.' *Wide Angle* 6.2 (1984): 72–6.

Pallister, Janis L. *The Cinema of Québec: Masters in their Own House*. London: Associated University Presses, 1995.

Parpart, Lee. 'Adapting Emotions: Notes on the Transformation of Affect and Ideology from "We So Seldom Look on Love" to *Kissed.' Essays on Canadian Writing* 76 (2002): 51–82.

– 'The Nation and the Nude: Colonial Masculinity and the Spectacle of the Male Body in Recent Canadian Cinema(s).' In Lehman, *Masculinity.* 167–92.

Patel, Geeta. 'On Fire: Sexuality and Its Incitements.' In Vanita, *Queering India.* 222–33.

Patry, Yvan. 'Arthur Lamothe.' In Yvan Patry et al., eds., *Le cinéma québécois: tendances et prolongements.* Montreal: Éditions Sainte-Marie, 1968. 116–20.

Pavis, Patrice. *Theatre at the Crossroads of Culture.* Trans. Loren Kruger. London: Routledge, 1992.

Pendakur, Manjunath. *Canadian Dreams and American Control: The Political Economy of the Canadian Film Industry.* Toronto: Garamond, 1990.

Penley, Constance. 'Feminism, Psychoanalysis, and the Study of Popular Culture.' In Lawrence Grossberg et al., eds., *Cultural Studies.* New York: Routledge, 1992. 479–500.

Perez, Gilberto. *The Material Ghost: Films and Their Medium.* Baltimore, MD: Johns Hopkins University Press, 1998.

Perreault, Luc. 'À la recherche de l'enfance.' *La Presse,* 31 mars 1973.

– 'Copie trop conforme.' *La Presse,* 31 mars 1973.

– Review of *Poussière sur la ville. La Presse,* 11 mai 1968.

Perron, Paul. *Semiotics and the Modern Quebec Novel: A Greimassian Analysis of Thériault's Agaguk.* Toronto: University of Toronto Press, 1996.

Pesch, Josef. 'Dropping the Bomb? On Critical and Cinematic Responses to Michael Ondaatje's *The English Patient.'* In J.H. Lacroix and Michael Ondaatje, eds., *Re-Constructing the Fragments of Michael Ondaatje's Work: La diversité déconstruite et réconstruite de l'oeuvre de Michael Ondaatje.* Paris: Presses de la Sorbonne, 1999. 229–46.

Petras, Elias. Letter to editor. *Globe and Mail,* 6 February 2002, A14.

Pevere, Geoff. 'Dances with Natives.' *Globe and Mail,* 10 March 1995, C2.

– 'Harpooned.' *Canadian Forum* 76 (April 1993): 22–3.

– 'Hostiles.' *Canadian Forum* 71 (November 1992): 35–7.

Pevere, Geoff, and Greig Dymond. *Mondo Canuck: A Canadian Pop Culture Odyssey.* Scarborough: Prentice Hall Canada, 1996.

Pike, Jennifer. 'Moment of Truth for CBA.' *Quill & Quire* 68.2 (February 2002): 17.

Plantinga, Carl. 'Notes on Spectator Emotion and Ideological Film Criticism.' In Richard Allen and Murray Smith, eds., *Film Theory and Philosophy.* Oxford: Clarendon, 1997. 372–93.

Prats, Armando José. *Invisible Natives: Myth and Identity in the American Western.* Ithaca, NY: Cornell University Press, 2002.

'Production Diary: Filmmaking Inuit-Style.' *Atanarjuat: The Official Website* www.atanarjuat.com/production_diary/index.html.

Prosser, Jay. *Second Skins: The Body Narratives of Transsexuality.* New York: Columbia University Press, 1998.

Proulx, Monique. *Le sexe des étoiles.* Montreal: Québec/Amérique, 1987.

– *Sex of the Stars.* Trans. Matt Cohen. Vancouver: Douglas and McIntyre, 1996.

Ramsay, Christine. 'Canadian Narrative Cinema from the Margins: "The Nation" and Masculinity in *Goin' Down the Road.' Canadian Journal of Film Studies* 2.2–3 (1993): 27–50.

Review of *Fortune and Men's Eyes*. *Newsweek*, 5 July 1971, 72.

Review of *Fortune and Men's Eyes*. *The New York Times*, 2 September 1971, 125.

Rich, B. Ruby. 'From Repressive Tolerance to Erotic Liberation: *Maedchen in Uniform*.' In Mary Anne Doane, Patricia Mellencamp, and Linda Williams, eds., *Re-Vision: Essays in Feminist Film Criticism*. Frederick, MD: University Publications of America/ AFI, 1984. 100–30.

Rifkin, Benjamin. *Semiotics of Narration in Film and Prose Fiction*. New York: Peter Lang, 1994.

Riordan, Michael. '*Outrageous!* How Can You Argue with Success?' *The Body Politic* 37 (October 1977): 15.

Roberts, Gillian. '"Sins of Omission": *The English Patient*, THE ENGLISH PATIENT, and the Critics.' *Essays on Canadian Writing* 76 (2002): 195–215.

Robinson, Sally. *Marked Men: White Masculinity in Crisis*. New York: Columbia University Press, 2000.

Rony, Fatimah Tobing. *The Third Eye: Race, Cinema, and Ethnographic Spectacle*. Durham, NC: Duke University Press, 1996.

Roughead, William. *Bad Companions*. Edinburgh: W. Green and Son, 1930.

Rubin, Gayle. 'The Traffic in Women: "The Political Economy" of Sex.' In Rayna R. Reiter, ed., *Toward an Anthropology of Women*. New York: Monthly Review Press, 1975. 157–210.

Rubinoff, Joel. 'Why Were Critics So Kind to "Black Robe"?' *Montreal Gazette*, 2 November 1991, E9.

Russo, Vito. *The Celluloid Closet: Homosexuality in the Movies*. Rev. ed. New York: Harper and Row, 1987.

St John, Maria. '"It Ain't Fittin": Cinematic Contours of Mammy in *Gone with the Wind* and Beyond.' *Qui Parle* 11.2 (1999): 127–36.

Savoie, Jacques. *Les portes tournantes*. 1984. Montreal: Boréal, 1990.

Savran, David. *Taking It Like a Man: White Masculinity, Masochism, and Contemporary American Culture*. Princeton, NJ: Princeton University Press, 1998.

Schwartzwald, Robert. 'Fear of Federasty: Québec's Inverted Fictions.' In Hortense Spillers, ed., *Comparative American Identities: Race, Sex, and Natonality in the Modern Text*. New York: Routledge, 1991. 175–95.

– 'From Authenticity to Ambivalence: Michel Tremblay's *Hosanna*.' *American Review of Canadian Studies* 22.4 (1992): 499–510.

– '"Symbolic" Homosexuality, "False Feminine," and the Problematics of Identity in Québec.' In Michael Warner, ed., *Fear of a Queer Planet: Queer Politics and Social Theory*. Minneapolis: University of Minnesota Press, 1993. 264–99.

Scobie, Stephen. 'Amelia, Or: Who Do You Think You Are? Documentary and Identity in Canadian Literature.' *Canadian Literature* 100 (1984): 264–85.

Scott, Jay. 'A Hideous Period of History Wrapped in a Frosty, Ebony Shroud.' *Globe and Mail*, 5 September 1991, C1.

– '"The Tin Flute" in English Betrays Its Subject Matter.' *Globe and Mail*, 17 September 1983, 3.

Scully, Robert Guy. 'L'oeuvre de notre grande bourgeoisie.' *Le Devoir*, 31 mars 1973.

Sedgwick, Eve Kosofsky. *The Coherence of Gothic Conventions*. New York: Arno, 1980.

Shakespeare, William. *The Complete Works of William Shakespeare*. Ed. W.J. Craig. London: Oxford University Press, 1945.

Shaviro, Steven. *The Cinematic Body.* Minneapolis: University of Minnesota Press, 1993.

Sheckels, Theodore F. 'Anne in Hollywood: The Americanization of a Canadian Icon.' In Irene Gammel and Elizabeth Epperley, eds., *L.M. Montgomery and Canadian Culture.* Toronto: University of Toronto Press, 1999. 183–91.

Shek, Ben-Z. 'Yves Thériault: The Would-Be Amerindian and His Imaginary Inuit.' In Jorn Carlsen and Bengt Steijffert, eds., *The Canadian North: Essays in Culture and Literature.* Lund, Sweden: Nordic Association for Canadian Studies Text Series, 1989. 119–28.

Sherrill, Rowland A. *Road-Book America: Contemporary Culture and the New Picaresque.* Urbana: University of Illinois Press, 2000.

Shields, Carol. Lecture. Vancouver Institute, University of British Columbia. Vancouver, 4 April 1998.

– *Swann: A Literary Mystery.* 1987. Toronto: General Publishing, 1989.

Sidnell, Michael. 'Polygraph: Somatic Truth and the Art of Presence.' *Canadian Theatre Review* 64 (Fall 1990): 45–8.

Silverman, Kaja. *The Acoustic Mirror: The Female Voice in Psychoanalysis and Cinema.* Bloomington: Indiana University Press, 1988.

– *Male Subjectivity at the Margins.* New York: Routledge, 1993.

– *The Subject of Semiotics.* New York: Oxford University Press, 1983.

Simon, Sherry. 'Robert Lepage and Intercultural Theatre.' In Stephen Totosy-de-Zepetnek and Yiu-nam Leung, eds., *Canadian Culture and Literature and a Taiwan Perspective.* Edmonton: University of Alberta Press, 1998. 125–43.

– 'Robert Lepage and the Languages of Spectacle.' In Donohoe and Koustas, *Theater sans frontières.* 215–30.

Simpson, D. Mark. 'Minefield Readings: The Postcolonial *English Patient.*' *Essays on Canadian Writing* 53 (1994): 216–37.

Slama, Beatrice. '*La belle bête,* ou la double scène.' *Voix et Images* 8 (1983): 213–28.

The Slash Page Database Project. <www.sqidge.org/~minotaur/5data.html>

Slott, Kathryn. 'From Agent of Destruction to Object of Desire: The Cinematic Transformation of Stevens Brown in *Les fous de bassan.*' *Quebec Studies* 9 (1989-90): 17–28.

Smart, Patricia. *Writing in the Father's House: The Emergence of the Feminine in the Quebec Literary Tradition.* Toronto: University of Toronto Press, 1991.

Spark, Muriel. *The Prime of Miss Jean Brodie.* 1961. London: Penguin, 1965.

Stacey, Jackie. 'Desperately Seeking Difference.' *Screen* 28.1 (1987): 48–61.

– *Star Gazing: Hollywood Cinema and Female Spectatorship.* London: Routledge, 1994.

Stam, Robert. 'Beyond Fidelity: The Dialogics of Adaptation.' In Naremore, *Film Adaptation.* 54–76.

– *Literature through Film: Realism, Magic, and the Art of Adaptation.* Oxford: Blackwell, 2005.

Straayer, Chris. 'Redressing the "Natural": The Temporary Transvestite Film.' In Grant, *Film Genre Reader III.* 417–42.

Stukator, Angela, ed. *Cinemas, Nations, Masculinities.* Special issue of the *Canadian Journal of Film Studies* 8.1 (1999).

Sullivan, Dan. 'Theater: A Distressing "Fortune and Men's Eyes."' *New York Times,* 24 February 1967, 29.

Swan, Susan. *The Wives of Bath.* 1993. Toronto: Vintage Canada, 2001.

Taylor, Kate. 'John Herbert: Playwright Wrote Landmark Drama.' *Globe and Mail,* 26 June 2001, R7.

Telmissany, May. 'La citation filmique comme anachronisme.' *Essays on Canadian Writing* 76 (2002): 247–62.

Thériault, Yves. *Agaguk*. 1958. Montreal: Le Dernier havre, 2003.

– *Agaguk*. Trans. Miriam Chapin. Toronto: Ryerson Press, 1963.

Thérien, Gilles. 'Cinéma québécois: La difficile conquête de l'altérité.' *Littérature* 66 (1987): 101–14.

Thomas, Bronwen. '"Piecing together a mirage": Adapting *The English Patient* for the Screen.' In Robert Giddings and Eric Sheen, eds., *The Classic Novel: From Page to Screen*. New York: St Martin's Press, 2000. 197–232.

Trow, Robert. 'Once Upon a Time in the East.' *The Body Politic* 9 (July/August 1975): 21.

Tulloch, Elspeth. 'Yves Simoneau's Rewriting of the Troubled Manhood Script in Anne Hébert's *Les fous de Bassan*.' *Essays on Canadian Writing* 76 (2002): 83–116.

Turner, John D., ed. *Canadian Feature Film Index, 1913–1985*. Ottawa: Public Archives of Canada, 1987.

Turner, Michael. *American Whiskey Bar*. Vancouver: Arsenal Pulp, 1997.

– *Hard Core Logo*. 1993. Vancouver: Arsenal Pulp, 1998.

– 'An Interview with the Author.' With Michelle Berry. In Michelle Berry and Natalee Caplee, eds., *The Notebooks: Interviews and New Fiction from Contemporary Writers*. Toronto: Anchor Canada, 2002.

– *The Pornographer's Poem*. Toronto: Doubleday Canada, 1999.

– *Survival: A Strobic Guide*. Vancouver: Canlit Classics in Transition, 1997.

Tyler, Carole-Anne. 'Boys Will be Girls: The Politics of Gay Drag.' In Fuss, *Inside/Out*. 32–70.

Vaïs, Michael. 'Robert Lepage: un homme de théâtre au cinéma.' *Jeu* 88.3 (1998): 123–30.

Vanita, Ruth, ed. *Queering India: Same-Sex Love and Eroticism in Indian Culture and Society*. New York: Routledge, 2002.

Vicinus, Martha. 'Distance and Desire: English Boarding-School Friendships.' *Signs* 9.4 (1984): 600–22.

Viswanathan, Jacqueline. 'Échanger sa vie pour une autre: Focalisation multiple dans *Mrs Dalloway* et *Le sourd dans la ville*.' *Arcadia* 20.2 (1985): 179–84.

Vorlicky, Robert. *Act Like a Man: Challenging Masculinities in American Drama*. Ann Arbor: University of Michigan Press, 1995.

Wallace, Robert. 'Defying Category: Re/viewing John Herbert's *Fortune and Men's Eyes*.' In Marc Maufort and Franca Bellarsi, eds., *Siting the Other: Re-visions of Marginality in Australian and English Canadian Drama*. Brussels: Peter Lang, 2001. 291–310.

Wang, Jennifer Hyland. '"A Struggle of Contending Stories": Race, Gender, and Political Memory in *Forrest Gump*.' *Cinema Journal* 39.3 (2000): 92–115.

Wasserman, Jerry, ed. *Modern Canadian Drama*. Vancouver: Talonbooks, 1986.

Waugh, Thomas. 'Cinemas, Nations, Masculinities.' In Stukator, *Cinemas, Nations, Masculinities*. 8–44.

– 'Fairy Tales of Two Cities: Queer Nation(s)–National Cinema(s).' In Terry Goldie, ed., *In a Queer Country: Gay and Lesbian Studies in the Canadian Context*. Vancouver: Arsenal Pulp, 2001. 285–305.

– 'Nègres blancs, tapettes et "butch": images des lesbiennes et des gais dans le cinéma québécois.' *Copie zéro* 11 (1981): 12–29.

– *The Romance of Transgression in Canada: Queering Sexualities, Nations, Cinemas*. Montreal: McGill-Queen's University Press, 2006.

Weiss, Andrea. *Vampires and Violets: Lesbians in the Cinema*. London: Jonathan Cape, 1992.

White, Patricia. *UnInvited: Classical Hollywood Cinema and Lesbian Representability*. Bloomington: Indiana University Press, 1999.

Whittaker, Herbert. 'Toronto's Jack Brundage Has a Winner.' *Globe and Mail*, 4 March 1967, 18.

Wicks, Ulrich. 'The Nature of the Picaresque Narrative: A Modal Approach.' *PMLA* 89 (1974): 240–9.

Williams, Linda. 'Film Bodies: Gender, Genre, and Excess.' In Grant, *Film Genre Reader III*. 141–59.

– *Hardcore: Power, Pleasure, and the 'Frenzy of the Visible.'* Berkeley: University of California Press, 1989.

– 'Melodrama Revised.' In Nick Browne, ed., *Refiguring American Film Genres*. Berkeley: University of California Press, 1998. 42–88.

Willmott, Glenn. 'O Say, Can You See: *The Handmaid's Tale* in Novel and Film.' In Lorraine York, ed., *Various Atwoods*. Toronto: Anansi, 1995. 167–90.

Wilton, Tamsin, ed. *Immortal, Invisible: Lesbians and the Moving Image*. London: Routledge, 1995.

– 'On Not Being Lady Macbeth: Some (Troubled) Thoughts on Lesbian Spectatorship.' In Wilton, *Immortal Invisible*. 143–62.

Winsloe, Christa. *The Child Manuela*. Trans. Agnes Neil Scott. New York: Farrar & Rinehart, 1933.

Wise, Wyndham, ed. *Take One's Essential Guide to Canadian Film*. Toronto: University of Toronto Press, 2001.

Wittig, Monique. *The Straight Mind and Other Essays*. Boston: Beacon Press, 1992.

Younis, Raymond Aaron. 'Nationhood and Decolonization in *The English Patient*.' *Literature/Film Quarterly* 26.1 (1998): 2–9.

Žižek, Slavoj. *Enjoy Your Symptom! Jacques Lacan in Hollywood and Out*. New York: Routledge, 1992.

Zupančič, Alenka. 'A Perfect Place to Die: Theatre in Hitchcock's Films.' In Slavoj Žižek ed., *Everything You Always Wanted to Know about Lacan (but Were Afraid to Ask Hitchcock)*. London: Verso, 1992. 73–105.

Illustration Credits

Alliance Atlantis Communications Inc.: *Black Robe* (3.1)

British Film Institute: *Mädchen in Uniform* (6.5)

British Film Institute and Metro-Goldwyn-Mayer Inc.: *The Handmaid's Tale* (1.4).

British Film Institute and David Hamilton Productions: *Fire* (6.2), photograph by Dilip Mehta.

Cinémaginaire: *Le confessionnal* (5.1–5.4)

La cinémathèque québécoise: *Les fous de bassan* (1.3), *Surfacing* (2.2, 2.3)

La cinémathèque québécoise (copyright Les productions Pierre Lamy): *Kamouraska* (2.1), photograph by Bruno Massenet; *Il était une fois dans l'est* (4.2), photograph by Attila Dory.

La cinémathèque québécoise and Metro-Goldwyn-Mayer Inc. *Fortune and Men's Eyes* (4.1).

La cinémathèque québécoise and Les productions Thalie Inc.: *Le sexe des étoiles* (4.6), photograph by Roger Dufresne.

La cinémathèque québécoise and Transfilm Inc.: *Shadow of the Wolf* (3.2)

La cinémathèque québécoise and Warner Brothers Entertainment Inc.: *Rachel, Rachel* (1.1).

La cinémathèque québécoise and Pierre Patry: *Déliverez-nous du mal* (1.2)

La cinémathèque québécoise and Louise Carré: *Le sourd dans la ville* (2.4), photograph by Attila Dory.

Cinexus Distribution Corp.: *Clearcut* (3.2)

Cité Amérique Inc.: *Lost and Delirious* (6.3), photograph by Michel Gravel; (6.4), photograph by Christine Powell

Ex Aequo Films: *Le polygraphe* (5.5–5.7); *Nô* (5.8, 5.9); *Possible Worlds* (5.10); *La face cachée de la lune* (5.11)

Igloolik Isuma Productions: *Atanarjuat* (3.5)

Mark Peacock: The B-Girlz (4.4)

Miramax Film Corp.: *The English Patient* (I.1).

Percy Adlon and Leora Films: *Salmonberries* (6.1)

Rave Film: *Better Than Chocolate* (4.5), photograph by Rosamond Norbury

Shadow Shows Inc.: *Dance Me Outside* (3.4); *Hard Core Logo* (7.1, 7.2); *American Whiskey Bar* (7.3); *Elimination Dance* (7.4)

Shaftesbury Films: *Swann* (2.5)

Stan Douglas Studio Inc.: *Journey into Fear* (7.5)

Xybermedia Inc.: *Outrageous!* (4.3)

Index

Page numbers in italics refer to illustrations.

abjection: and homosexuality, in work of Robert Lepage, 156; Julia Kristeva on, 50; and masculinity, 89, 209

Adams, Evan, 97, 98

Adams, James, 38

adaptation: and audience response/identification, 3–4, 7–8; and auteurism, 10, 13–14, 45–6; and auteurism, in work of Robert Lepage, 129–61; critical frameworks used to evaluate, 3; and (de)construction of gender as mode of address, 4, 5, 7–8; and fidelity, 3–4, 5, 8, 39–41, 45, 49–76; and genre classification/recognition, 3–4, 7–8; history of, in film, 21; ideology of, 3–4, 7–8; and (in)visibility of the Indigene, in *Black Robe, Shadow of the Wolf, Clearcut,* and *Dance Me Outside,* 77–103; and lesbian citationality, in *The Wives of Bath* and *Lost and Delirious,* 162–85; of masculinity, in work of Michael Turner and Bruce McDonald, 14–15, 185–211; and 'queering' of narrative and sexual epistemologies, in *Fortune and Men's Eyes, Il était une fois dans l'est, Outrageous!* and *Le sexe des étoiles,* 104–28; theories of, 10, 12, 38–48; uncanny art of, in *Kamouraska, Surfacing,* and *Le sourd dans la ville,* 49–76

Adlon, Percy, 15; *Bagdad Café,* 167–8; *Salmonberries,* 14, 165, 166–9

Adventures of Priscilla, Queen of the Desert, The (Elliott), 122, 195

affect: embodiment of, vs performative effect, 203; and female friendship, in lesbian boarding school films, 165, 172–84; and female friendship, in *Rachel, Rachel* and *Anne of Green Gables,* 18, 23; lack of, in performance by Will Sampson in *One Flew Over the Cuckoo's Nest,* 79; and production of meaning in literature vs film, 46; solicitation of, in *Lost and Delirious,* 181; and spectatorship, 44; withholding of, in performance of masculinity, 189, 193, 201, 209. *See also* emotion

Agaguk (Thériault/Dorfmann), 11, 13, 80–1, 86–91. *See also Shadow of the Wolf*

Aitken, Stuart, and Christopher Lukinbeal, on road movies and 'hysterical' masculinity, 195–6

Albee, Edward, 108, 235n13

Alexie, Sherman, 15, 96–7

All About Eve (Orr/Mankiewicz), 185

Allégret, Marc, 22

Allen, Louise, 166, 167

Allende, Isabelle, 49

Alliance Atlantis, 10, 37, 223n10

Almodóvar, Pedro, 122

Ambler, Eric, 15, 205

American Whiskey Bar (Turner/McDonald), 3, 15, 38, 186, 187, 188, 189, 201–3

Anderlini, Ken, 196

Anderson, Judith, 57

Andrew, Dudley, 41

Andrews, Naveen, 3

Anne of Green Gables (Montgomery/Various): 1919 film adaptation of, by William Desmond Taylor, 17, 21; 1934 film adaptation of, by George Nichols, Jr, 12, 22–3, 46; 1956 TV musical adaptation of, by Don Harron and Norman Campbell, 24, 46; 1985 TV adaptation of, by Kevin Sullivan, 20

Apak, Paul, 100–1, 102

Apocalypse Now (Coppola), 200, 222n3

Apprenticeship of Duddy Kravitz, The (Richler/Kotcheff), 12, 18, 25, 224n22

Aquin, Hubert, 24, 25

Arcand, Denys, 47; *Le crime d'Ovide Plouffe*, 24, 223n12; *Le déclin de l'empire américain*, 28, 147, 239n34; *Love and Human Remains*, 37

Armatage, Kay, 223n9

Atanarjuat: The Fast Runner (Kunuk), 13, 82, 98–103, 233n52

Atwood, Margaret, 10, 20; *The Blind Assassin*, 20, 62; *The Edible Woman*, 62; gothic elements in writing of, 61–2; *The Handmaid's Tale* 11, 12, 17, 29, 32, 32–7, 210; *The Journals of Susanna Moodie*, 61, 199, 225n47; *Lady Oracle*, 62; *Surfacing*, 11, 12, 29, 52–4, 62–9; *Survival*, 62, 190, 244n15

audience(s): and Canadian film distribution policy, 37–8; Canadian vs American, and reception of *Fortune and Men's Eyes*, 105–6, 107–8; differences in English-Canadian and Québécois, 40; gay and lesbian, identificatory strategies of, 164; gendered and generic construction of, 7–8; Native vs non-Native, and reception of images of indigeneity, 40, 78, 81, 86, 95; responses of, to film adaptations, 3–4, 10, 210; in theatre vs film, 43–4; Western vs non–Western, and reception of *Fire*, 170–1

Audry, Jacquline: *Olivia*, 15, 180, 182

Auslander, Philip, 203, 245n40

authorship/auteurship: allegorizing of, and masculinity in *Hard Core Logo* and

American Whiskey Bar, 193–4, 201–2; relationship between, in literature and film, 10, 45–6; in work of Robert Lepage, 14, 129–61

Azmi, Shabana, in *Fire*, 169, *170*

B Girlz, The, 120, *121*

Babuscio, Jack, on *Fortune and Men's Eyes*, 110

Bagdad Café (Adlon), 167–8, 172

Baillargeon, Paule, 28; *Le sexe des étoiles*, 46, 106, 126–8

Baker, Josephine, 98

Baker, Noel S., *Hard Core Roadshow*, 41, 188, 189–91, 192–3, 194

Bakhtin, Mikhail, 47, 227n85

Ballard, J.G., 37

Banks, Russell, 37

Banner, Steve: in *Les fous de bassan*, 29, *30*

Barnes, Clive: on *The Boys in the Band*, 108, 235n13; on *Fortune and Men's Eyes*, 109, 235n16

Barthes, Roland, 15, 39, 45, 130

Barton, Mischa: in *Lost and Delirious*, 173, *178*

Baxter, Anne, 139

Bazin, André, 12; on Alfred Hitchcock, 138; on theatre vs film, 42–3

Beach, Adam, 95, 97, 98

Beaty, Bart, 189, 191, 192, 244n9

Beauchemin, Yves, 28

Beaudin, Jean, 12, 28, 132, 133, 156–8

Being at home with Claude (Dubois/Beaudin), 12, 28, 133, 156–8, 240n52

Beller, Kathleen, in *Surfacing*, 64, *66*, 68

Benjamin, Walter, on theatre vs film, 42–3

Benner, Richard: *Outrageous!* 13, 25, 41, 106, 119

Benoît, Jacques, 28, 31

Benson Gyles, Anna: *Swann*, 20, 73–6

Berenger, Tom, 12, 27

Beresford, Bruce: *Black Robe*, 13, 40, 81, 83–6, 91

Bernhard, Sandra, 164

Bersani, Leo, 146

Better Than Chocolate (Wheeler), 124

Binamé, Charles, 37

Binoche, Juliette, in *The English Patient*, 3, 5, 6, 19

Birth of a Nation/The Clansman (Griffith/ Dixon Jr), 21, 77

Black, Ryan: in *Dance Me Outside*, 95, 97

Black Robe (Moore/Beresford), 11, 13, 40, 80–1, 82–6, 91, 92, 94, 223n10, 232n17

Blais, Marie-Claire: *La belle bête*, 69; *Une saison dans la vie d'Emmanuel*, 224n21; *Le sourd dans la ville*, 12, 28, 29, 31, 54–5, 69–73

Blais, Roger, 24

Blanchett, Cate, 20

Bluestone, George, 12, 39

Bluteau, Lothaire: in *Black Robe*, 13, 83, *84*; in *Le confessionnal*, 132; in *Les fous de bassan* 29, *30*; generally affectless and desexualized performances of, 209, 238n22

body: inscription of, in film adaptation, 9–10; legibility of transvestite and transsexual, 113–28; male horror of female, as represented in *Shadow of the Wolf*, 89; male horror of female, as theorized by Freud in 'The "Uncanny,"' 50; reframing of queer male, in films of Robert Lepage, 14, 129–61; representation of, in melodrama, 5; secret terrors of, in female gothic, 50–1; uncovering of female, in *Surfacing*, 65–9; uncovering of indigenous, in *Black Robe*, 83; wounding of, as symptom of male crisis, 207, 209

Bolter, Jay, and Richard Grusin: *Remediation*, 245n40

Bonheur d'occasion/The Tin Flute (Roy/ Fournier), 24, 40, 223n12

Boorman, John, 65

Bottoms, Joseph: in *Surfacing*, 64, *66*

Bouchard, Lucien, 151

Bouchard, Michel Marc: 130; *Lilies*, 12, 37, 42, 43, 114, 156–7; *Les muses orphelines*, 37, 114

Boys Don't Cry (Pierce), 122–3, 124, 179

Boys in the Band, The (Crowley/Friedkin), 108–9, 235n13

Brassard, André: *Il était une fois dans l'est*, 11, 13, 25, 41, 106, 116–17, 119

Brassard, Marie, 131; in *Nô*, 148; and *Le polygraphe*, 140, 143, *144*

Brault, Michel, 28, 65

Bravo!FACT, 10, 11, 38, 245n42

Brecht, Bertolt, 44

Brontë, Charlotte, 15, 59, 174

Bugajski, Richard: *Clearcut*, 13, 40, 81, 91–4

Bujold, Genviève, in *Kamouraska*, 55, *56*

Burroughs, Jackie, 173, 180

Burroughs, William, 37

Burton, Richard, 55

Bussy, Dorothy Strachey: *Olivia*, 14, 15, 166, 174, 175, 180, 242n42

Butler, Judith, 14, 15, 111, 205; and 'gender melancholia,' as applied to *Fortune and Men's Eyes*, 113; and 'gender melancholia,' as applied to *Possible Worlds*, 153–4; on 'gender performativity' and drag, 120, 128; on 'heterosexual matrix,' 9, 155; and theory of 'citationality,' 165, 172; on Žižek's theorization of 'the real,' 241n19

Byatt, A.S., 73

Byron, Stuart, on *Fortune and Men's Eyes*, 110

Cadieux, Anne–Marie: in *Le confessionnal*, 132; in *La face cachée de la lune*, 159; in *Nô*, 148, *149*

Callaghan, Morley, 24

Campbell-Holt, Adrienne, 11

Canadian Broadcasting Corporation/ Société Radio-Canada, 10, 12, 23, 24, 41, 94, 190

Canadian Film Development Corporation, 11, 25, 41, 53, 108

Canadian Heritage, 10, 225n40

Cardinal, Gil, 40

Cardinal, Tantoo, 78, 85, 97

Carle, Gilles, 22, 24, 28, 223n12

Carpenter, Edward: *The Intermediate Sex*, 175

Carrier, Roch, 24

Carson, Anne, 11

Carter, Angela: *The Sadeian Woman*, 203

Carver, Brent, 157
Castle, Terry, 162
Cavanaugh, William, 21
Champagne, John, 120
Channing, Stockard, 20
Chant d'amour, Un (Genet), 110
Charest, Rémy, 133
Chatman, Seymour, 39, 41, 44
Chetwynd, Lionel, 18, 25
Chien andalou, Un (Buñuel), 200
Children's Hour, The (Hellman/Wyler), 14, 165, 179–80
Chowdhry, Ranjit, 169, 172
Chrétien, Jean, 151
Churchill, Ward: on *Black Robe*, 86
citationality: in film, as theorized by May Telmassiny, 47–8; as mode of lesbian cinematic address, 14, 162–85
Clearcut/A Dream Like Mine (Bugjaski/Kelly), 13, 40, 81, 91–4
Clift, Montgomery, 135, 137, 139
Cohan, Steven, and Ina Rae Hark: *Screening the Male*, 186
Cohen, Leonard, 37
Cohen, Nathan, on *Fortune and Men's Eyes*, 107, 108
Cohen, Sheldon, 24
Cohn, Norman, 100–1, 102
Color Purple, The (Walker/Spielberg), 44, 185
Comment faire l'amour avec un nègre sans se fatiguer (Laferrière/Benoît), 28, 31–2
Confessionnal, Le (Lepage), 130, 132, 133–40, 158, 209, 240n56
Connor, Ralph, 21
Cooper, James Fenimore, 77, 230n6
Cooper, Pamela, on *The Handmaid's Tale*, 36, 225n38
Coquelicot Mercier, Marianne: in *Le sexe des étoiles*, 127
Corber, Robert, 131
Corrigan, Timothy, 45, 244n23
Coupland, Douglas, 20
Craine, Nick, 188, 189, 210, 233n42, 244n9
Crime d'Ovide Plouffe (Lemelin/Arcand and Carle), 24, 223n12

Cromwell, John, 23
Cronenberg, David, 28, 37, 74, 193
Crowley, Mart, 15, 108, 235n13
Cunningham, Michael, 15, 71
Currie, Sheldon, 37
Curwood, James Oliver, 21

Dafoe, Willem, 3
Daldry, Stephen, 15, 71
Damnée Manon, sacré Sandra (Tremblay), 116–17
Dance Me Outside (Kinsella/McDonald), 13, 40, 81–2, 94–7
Dances with Wolves (Costner/Blake), 77, 78, 86, 96, 231n6
Dansereau, Mireille: *Le sourd dans la ville*, 12, 28, 31, 54–5, 70–3, 74
Das, Nandita in *Fire*, 169, *170*
Davidson, Arnold, 57
Davis, Bette, 119, 164
De La Roche, Mazo, 23
De Lauretis, Teresa, 14, 45–6; and female spectatorship, 163, 241n16; on gender as a technology, 245n41; on *The Well of Loneliness*, 242n48
De Maupassant, Guy, 11
Dead Man (Jarmusch), 77–8, 230n6
Déclin de l'empire américain, Le (Arcand), 28, 147, 239n34
Deleuze, Gilles, 14, 15, 73; and crystalline images of time, in films of Robert Lepage, 129–31, 139, 150, 158–9, 161; on masochism, 146
Déliverez–nous du mal (Jasmin/Lord), 25–7
desire: heteronormative representation of, in *Surfacing*, 68; lesbian, representation of, in film and feminist film theory, 162–85; and looking, in *Kamouraska*, 59–60; male homosocial, in *Hard Core Logo*, 200; and narcissism, in gothic woman's film of 1940s, 52; and/in narrative, 10, 16, 45–6; regulation of, in *Fortune and Men's Eyes*, 113; sexual, and gender identification, 9, 128
Derrida, Jacques, 8
Devlin, Bernard, 24, 25

Dillon, Hugh: in *Dance Me Outside*, 95; in *Hard Core Logo*, 187, *195*, *198*, 203, 209

Doane, Mary Ann, 14; on gothic woman's film of 1940s, 52, 54, 59, 60, 72; on *Rebecca*, 57–8; on woman as spectator, 162–3

documentary: and Canadian poetry, 199; and ethnography, in *Clearcut*, 91; and ethnography, in *Nanook of the North*, 78; and NFB under John Grierson, 24; operations of, in *Hard Core Logo*, 14, 187, 189–90, 193, 197–201; relationship to melodrama, 198; relationship to pornography, 201

Dorfmann, Jacques: *Shadow of the Wolf*, 13, 81, 87–91

Douglas, Stan: *Journey into Fear*, 15, 187, 205–6

Doyle, Brian, 20

drag: Judith Butler on, 120; rehabilitation of, in popular culture and queer theory, 119–22; as sign of gender and narrative ambivalence in film, 13, 104–28; and transgenderism, 120–8

Dragons' Trilogy, The (Lepage and Théâtre Repère), 129, 133, 147

Dragu, Margaret: in *Surfacing*, 64, *67*

Dreyfuss, Richard, 12, 27

Du Maurier, Daphne, 15, 52, 57

Dubois, René-Daniel: *Being at home with Claude*, 12, 28, 130, 133, 156–8

Ducharme, Réjean, 28

Dumont, Marilyn, on *Black Robe*, 86, 226n56

Dundjerovic, Aleksandar, 130, 132

Dupuis, Roy, 31, 156, 240n54

Durgnat, Raymond, 138

Duvivier, Julien, 22

Dyer, Richard, 15, 131, 235n22, 241n22, 243n3

Dymond, Greig, 27–8

Eastwood, Clint, 77, 122

Easy Rider (Hopper), 195

Eberle-Sinatra, Michael, 46, 126

Egoyan, Atom, 37

Elimination Dance (Ondaatje/McDonald/ McKellar), 15, 187, 203, 222n3, 225n47

Elliott, Stephen, 15

Ellis, Havelock: 'Sexual Inversion in Women,' 175, 242n44

emotion: investments of, in literature vs film, 46; and spectatorial response to *The English Patient*, 4–6; stylistics of, in *Lost and Delirious*, 181; and textual fidelity, 44. *See also* affect

English Patient, The (Ondaatje/Minghella), 3–7, 12, 15, 18–19, 44–5, 46, 221n7

ethnography, and representation of indigenous peoples on film, 13, 77–103

Even Cowgirls Get the Blues (Robbins/Van Sant), 169

Ex Machina, 129, 131, 147–8. *See also* Lepage, Robert

Eyre, Chris, 15, 97

Fabian, Johannes, 231n15, 234n60

Face cachée de la lune, La (Lepage), 155–61, 209

Falling Angels (Gowdy/Smith), 37, 74

Farmer, Gary, 77, 97, 157

Favreau, Robert, 37, 114

female/feminine: interiority, as represented in *Kamouraska*, *Surfacing*, and *Le sourd dans la ville*, 49–76; masquerade of, in *Hedwig and the Angry Inch*, 123–4; masquerade of, in *Lost and Delirious*, 177; monstrous representation of, in *Black Robe* and *Shadow of the Wolf*, 81–90; silencing of, in *Les fous de bassan*, 28–8; spectatorship, theories of, 162–5

fidelity: criticism, as applied to film adaptation, 3–4, 5, 8, 39, 45, 49–76, 211; critiques of, 39–41; feminist caveats to critiques of, 12, 15, 29, 36–7, 44, 51–2, 73, 185; and gothic marriage plot, 12, 49–76; Susan Swan on, 174

Fiedler, Leslie, 228n9

Field of Dreams/Shoeless Joe (Robinson/ Kinsella), 17

Fiennes, Ralph, in *The English Patient*, 3, *6*

Fight Club (Palahniuk/Fincher), 210, 245n43

film language, 3, 209; of Percy Adlon, 168
film noir, conventions of, 131–2, 136
Findley, Timothy, 20, 23
Fire (Mehta), 14, 165, 169–72
Flaherty, Robert, 78, 102
Flawless (Schumacher), 120, 122
FLQ, 149
Follows, Megan, 18
Fontaine, Joan, 51, 57
Fontana, Tom: creator of *Oz*, 104
Ford, John, 77, 96
Forman, Milos, 15; *One Flew Over the Cuckoo's Nest*, 77, 79–80
Fortune and Men's Eyes (Herbert/Hart), 12, 13, 25, 103, 104–15, 119, 125, 128, 153, 209
Fothergill, Robert, 243n6
Foucault, Michel, 137, 239–40n24
Fournier, Claude, 24, 28, 40, 223n12
Fous de bassan, Les (Hébert/Simoneau), 11, 28–30, 73
Fox, Beryl, 65
Fraser, Brad, 37, 119; *Leaving Metropolis*, 106, 124–6
Fréchette, Richard, 134, 148
Freud, Sigmund: on female hysteria, 49, 227n7; on homosexual cathexis and Oedipus complex, 155; on masochism, in 'A Child Is Being Beaten,' 85, 94, 231n22, 246n59; and Strachey family, 175; on 'The "Uncanny,"' 49, 50, 52, 55–6, 57, 61
Fricker, Brenda: in *Swann*, 20, 74, 75
Fried Green Tomatoes (Flagg/Avnet), 185, 226n74
Friedkin, William, 15, 108–9, 235n17
Fuss, Diana, 174, 242n42, 53

Gable, Clark, 55
Gaines, Jane, 201
Garber, Marjorie, 120–1
Garbo, Greta, 164
Garrity, Henry A., 130, 138–9
Gay Deceivers, The (Kessler), 110–11
gaze: and ethnographic representations of indigenous people on film, 13, 79, 83, 85, 94; Laura Mulvey on masculine dimensions of, in film, 6, 8–9, 162–3; male, vs

female image, 162–3; Mary Ann Doane on woman's relation to, 52, 72, 162–3; operations of, in 1944 film version of *Jane Eyre*, 50; operations of, in *Le sourd dans la ville*, 72–3; operations of, in theatre vs film, 44; and relation to point-of-view shots, in *Kamouraska*, 60–1; returning of, in *Atanarjuat*, 82, 98–103; tourist, in work of Robert Lepage, 129; transgender, as theorized by Judith Halberstam, 122–3; and voyeurism, in *Surfacing*, 66–7
Gélinas, Gratien, 25
gender: and genre recognition, 7–9; and ghosting of lesbianism, in *The Wives of Bath* and *Lost and Delirious*, 162–85; ideological representation of, in film and literature, 7–8; as lens through which to examine film adaptation, 4, 8; as mode of address, in *The English Patient*, 5–7; and narrative ambivalence, in *Fortune and Men's Eyes*, *Il était une fois dans l'est*, *Outrageous!* and *Le sexe des étoiles*, 13, 104–28; performativity, as theorized by Judith Butler, 15, 165; policing of, in film adaptations of Robert Lepage, 129–61; and psychoanalytical approaches to gothic literature, as applied to *Kamouraska*, *Surfacing*, and *Le sourd dans la ville*, 49–76; 'repatriarchalization' of, in *The Handmaid's Tale*, 32–7; and representations of masculinity, in the work of Michael Turner and Bruce McDonald, 186–211; and the screen Indigene, in *Black Robe*, *Shadow of the Wolf*, *Clearcut*, and *Dance Me Outside*, 77–103; and sexual desire, 9; and social space, 18, 23
Genet, Jean, 110, 235n22
Genette, Gérard, 39, 47, 227n85
genre: and conventions of, in female gothic, 49–76; economic dimensions of, 45; and gender identification, 7–8; hybrid nature of, in work of Michael Turner and Bruce McDonald, 186–211; and institutionalized codes of sex and power, in prison drama, 104–15; and lesbian boarding school films, 162–85; and

narrative coherence, in literature, 4; and policed images of the queer male, 129–61; Steve Neale on gendered conventions of, 8–10; synecdochic and 'taxidermic' conventions of, in romantic ethnography and classic westerns, 77–103

George, Chief Dan, 77

Gibson, Margaret: 'Making It' as source for *Outrageous!*, 13, 25, 106, 117–8, 236n31

Gignac, Marie, 134, 148

Gilbert, Reid, on *Fortune and Men's Eyes*, 236n26

Gilbert, Sandra, and Susan Gubar: *The Madwoman in the Attic*, 49, 50, 227n7

Gittings, Christopher, 78, 222n12, 233n52; on *Le confessionnal*, 238n24; on *Nô*, 239n37

Godard, Jean-Luc, 181, 193

Godbout, Jacques, 24

Goin' Down the Road (Shebib), 25, 243n6

Goldberg, Whoopi, 20

Golfman, Noreen, 196

Goldie, Terry, 77

Goldstone, Phil, 21

Gone With the Wind (Mitchell/Fleming), 23, 55, 226n74

Gopinath, Gayatri: on *Fire*, 171

Gorris, Marleen, 71

gothic: as female form, 49–52; Mary Ann Doane on conventions of, in woman's film of 1940s, 52; and representation of fragmented feminine consciousness, in *Kamouraska*, *Surfacing*, and *Le sourd dans la ville*, 12, 49–76

Gowdy, Barbara, 4, 37, 74

Goyette, Patrick: in *Le confessionnal*, 132, *138*, *139*, *140*; in *Le polygraphe*, *142*, *144*, *145*, 209

Green, Jean, 69

Greene, Graham: in *Clearcut*, 91, *92*; in *Dances with Wolves*, 77, 78; 231n19

Greer, Michael: in *Fortune and Men's Eyes*, 109, 114, 115, *116*; in *The Gay Deceivers*, 110–11, 115

Greyson, John: *Lilies*, 12, 37, 42, 43, 114, 133, 156–7

Grierson, John, 24, 224n17

Griffith, D.W., 21, 77

Grignon, Claude-Henri, 25

Grossman, Andrew, 104

Gunnarsson, Sturla, 37, 40

Gury, Paul, 25

Halberstam, Judith: on *Boys Don't Cry*, 122–3; on 'female masculinity,' in *The Well of Loneliness*, 176, 242n48; on legibility of dominant masculinity, 206–7; on William Roughead's *Bad Companions*, 243n56

Hall, Radclyffe: *The Well of Loneliness*, 14, 15, 174–8

Hall, Stuart: and 'Third Cinema,' 102–3

Halvorson, Marilyn, 20

Handmaid's Tale, The (Atwood/Schlöndorff), 11, 12, 17, 20, 29, 32–7, 210

Hard Core Logo (Turner/McDonald), 14–15, 41, 96, 185, 187–201, 202–3, 205, 208–10

Hare, David, and screenplay for *The Hours*, 49, 54, 71, 211

Hart, Harvey: *Fortune and Men's Eyes*, 12, 13, 25, 41, 104–15, 235n17

Hartford, David, 21

Harvie, Jennifer, 129

Hébert, Anne: *La canne à pêche*, 24; *Les fous de bassan*, 11, 28–9, 31, 73; *Kamouraska*, 11, 12, 29, 52–4, 55–61, 63, 224n21

Hébert, Bernar, 37

Hedwig and the Angry Inch (Mitchell and Trask/Mitchell), 106, 122–4, 207

Hellman, Lillian: *The Children's Hour*, 14, 15, 166, 179–80, 185

Hemingway, Ernest, 210, 246n63

Hémon, Louis, 22

Hepburn, Katherine, 55

Herbert, John: *Fortune and Men's Eyes*, 12, 13, 25, 104–15, 208; imprisonment of, 106, 234n7; *Some Angry Summer Songs*, 115

Hiroshima, mon amour (Duras/Resnais), 45

history: epic representation of, in *The English Patient*, 5–6; erasure of Indigene from, in cinema, 13, 77–103; fictionalization of, in *Black Robe* and *Shadow of the*

Wolf, 81, 82, 87; of film adaptation, in Canada, 21–38; reclaiming of, by Zacharias Kunuk, 98–9

Hitchcock, Alfred, 15, 48, 57, 231n20; and connection to Robert Lepage, 130–5, 138–9, 158

Hoffman, Philip Seymour, 120, 122

Holt, Sandrine: in *Black Robe*, 85; in *Dance Me Outside*, 96

homosexuality: 'death' of images of, in films of Robert Lepage, 129–61; debates around positive images of, in film adaptation, 41, 157, 178; and dynamics of sex and power, in *Fortune and Men's Eyes*, 13, 104–15; and film noir, 131–2; as metaphor for unrealized national identity, in Quebec cinema, 132, 147, 151–2, 157; representation of, in *Déliverez–nous du mal*, 25–7. *See also* lesbian; queer

Hopkins, Miriam, 179–80

Hosanna (Tremblay), 115–17, 236n28

The Hours (Cunningham/Daldry), 49, 71, 211

Hume, Robert, 50, 228n9

Hurston, Zora Neale, 98

I Confess (Hitchcock), 132, 133–5, 137–9

identification: and/with female image, in feminist theories of spectatorship, 162–3; gendered and generic rules of, 9; heterosexual, as form of melancholia, 113, 153–4; in literature vs film, 10; and sex/gender system, 107, 109, 128; and spectatorship, 9, 162–5; and transgender representation, in *Hedwig and the Angry Inch*, 123–4

Igloolik Isuma Productions, 98, 100

Il était une fois dans l'est (Brassard/Tremblay), 11, 13, 25, 106, 116–17, 119, 128, 224n22

In Praise of Older Women (Vizinczey/Kaczender), 12, 25, 223n10

Indigene: detemporalized images of, in Canadian film adaptations, 11, 12–13, 40, 77–103

Innuksuk, Pakkak: in *Atanarjuat*, 99, *100*

intertextuality: adaptation as mode of, 12, 47; in *Hard Core Logo*, 193–4; and lesbian citationality in film, 14, 162–85

Ivalu, Madeline, 99, 102

Ivalu, Sylvia, 99, 102

Jaaferi, Jaaved, 169, 171–2

Jacobwitz, Florence, 65, 68

Jalna (De La Roche/Cromwell), 23

Jane Eyre (Brontë/Stevenson), 49, 50–2, 76, 174

Jasmin, Claude, 25, *26*, 27

Jean, Rodrigue, 37

Jésus de Montréal (Arcand), 28

Jordan, Richard: in *Kamouraska*, 55, *56*, 60

Joshua Then and Now (Kotcheff/Richler), 12, 223nn10, 12

Journey into Fear (Ambler/Foster/Mann), 205–6

Journey into Fear (Douglas/Turner), 15, 187, 205–6

Jutra, Claude, 24, 25, 28, 74, 224n21; *Kamouraska*, 12, 29, 54, 55–61, 62–3, 66; *Mon oncle Antoine*, 55, 224n21; *Surfacing*, 12, 20, 29, 54, 62–9

Kabir, Shameem: on 'extratextual' cinematic identifications for lesbian spectator, 164, 165; on *Fire*, 170; on *Salmonberries*, 166, 168

Kaczender, George, 25, 27

Kafka, Franz, 69

Kamouraska (Hébert/Juta), 11, 12, 24, 29; as female gothic, 52–4, 55–61, 62–3, 66

Kaplan, E. Ann: and Kate Ellis on Stevenson's *Jane Eyre*, 51; on woman as spectator, 162

Kelly, M.T.: *A Dream Like Mine*, 13, 40, 81, 92–4

Kershner, Irvin, 25

Kesey, Ken, 15, 79–80, 230n6

Kharbanda, Kulbushan, 169, 172

Killers, The (Hemingway/Siodmak/Tarkovsky/Siegel), 210, 246n63

Kilpatrick, Jacquelyn: *Celluloid Indians*, 79

King, Thomas, 20

Kingsway (Turner/Dennehy), 189, 245n42
Kinsella, W.P.: *Dance Me Outside*, 13, 40, 81–2, 95–7; *Shoeless Joe*, 17, 40
Kirtz, Mary, 34, 65
Kissed/'We So Seldom Look on Love' (Stopkewich/Gowdy), 4, 37
Knelman, Martin, 65
Kotcheff, Ted, 25, 27, 223n12
Kotsopoulos, Patsy, 41, 224n13, 243n58
Kristeva, Julia, 47, 50, 52, 227n85, 228n9
Kuhn, Annette, 162
Kunuk, Zacharias: *Atanarjuat*, 13, 82, 98–103, 234n62

LaBelle, Rob: in *Journey into Fear*, 206, *207*
Lacan, Jacques, 15, 155, 201; on 'mirror stage,' 163, 176–7; on 'the real,' 241n19
Laferrière, Dany, 28, 31
Lamothe, Arthur, 25
Lampman, Archibald, 24
Lancaster, Burt, 91
Lanctôt, Micheline, 132
lang, k.d.: in *Salmonberries*, 165, 166, *167*, 168–9; and soundtrack for *Even Cowgirls Get the Blues*, 169
Langevin, André, 25
Lantos, Robert, 223n10, 226n77
Last of the Mohicans, The (Cooper/Various), 77, 230n4
Laurence, Margaret, 12, 17–18, 20
Lauzon, Jean-Claude, 28, 47
Lavorel, Guy, on *Kamouraska*, 229n38
Lea, Ron, in *Clearcut*, 91, *92*
Leach, Jim: on *Kamouraska*, 55, 59–60, 228nn24, 26; on 'national duality' of Canadian cinema, 222n12; on *Surfacing*, 68–9
Leacock, Stephen, 24
Leahy, David, 81
Lean, David, 6
Leaving Metropolis/Poor Super Man (Fraser), 106, 124–6
Leclerc, Francis, 147
Lefebvre, Benjamin, 23, 224n13
Lefebvre, Martin, 130, 132, 135
Léger, Claude, 90

Lehman, Peter, 186, 197, 246n57
Leigh, Vivien, 55
Lemay-Thivièrge, Guillaume, in *Le sourd dans la ville*, 31, 71, *72*
Lemelin, Roger, 24, 223n12
Lepage, Robert, 10, 40, 47, 101, 187, 209; as actor, in *La face cachée de la lune*, 159, *160*, 209; and Alfred Hitchcock, 48, 130–5, 137–9, 158; *Le confessionnal*, 130, 132, 133–40, 158, 209; *The Dragons' Trilogy*, 129, 133, 147; and Ex Machina, 129, 131, 147–8; *La face cachée de la lune*, 131, 155–61, 209; intersection of auteurism and adaptation in films of, 13–14, 42, 46, 129–61; and Marie Brassard, 131, 140; *Nô*, 45–6, 133, 147–52, 154, 158; operations of space and time in films of, 129–61; *Le polygraphe*, 140–6, 155; *Possible Worlds*, 146, 152–5, 158; queer imagery in films of, 13–14, 15, 129–61, 237n8; *The Seven Streams of the River Ota*, 129, 133, 134, 147–8, 151–2, 155; *Tectonic Plates*, 124, 148; and Théâtre Repère, 124, 129, 131, 140; and theories of Gilles Deleuze, 15, 129–31, 139, 150, 158–9, 161
lesbian: citationality, in *Lost and Delirious/The Wives of Bath*, 14, 162–85; desire; and female spectatorship, 163–5; ghosting of, in Hollywood film and feminist film theory, 14, 162–4, 184–5. *See also* homosexuality
Lever, Yves, 25
Lewis, Richard, 37
Li, Victor: and 'neo-primitivism,' 80, 231n15
Lilies (Bouchard/Greyson), 12, 37, 42–3, 114, 133, 156–7
Lindsay, Joan, 166
Little Big Man (Berger/Penn), 77, 230n6
Livesay, Dorothy, 199
Livingston, Jennie, 15; *Paris Is Burning*, 120
Loiselle, André, 12; on *Being at home with Claude* and *Lilies*, 133, 156–8; on *Il était une fois dans l'est*, 236n28; on *Le polygraphe*, 154–5, 239n32; on spatial dynamics

of film adaptations of Canadian plays, 42–3, 105

Longfellow, Henry Wadsworth, 21, 223n7

Lord, Jean-Claude, 25, *26*, 27

Lost and Delirious/The Wives of Bath (Pool/ Swan), 14, 28, 42, 161, 165–6, 172–85, 210, 241n34

Lowry, Glen, 44

Lusty, Terry: on *Dance Me Outside*, 94–5

Lütticken, Sven, 206

MacDonald, Ann-Marie, 20, 49, 124

MacIvor, Daniel, 37

MacLennan, Hugh, 24

MacRae, Henry, 21

Mamet, David, 208

Mandel, Eli, 61

Mankiewicz, Francis, 28, 31

Mann, Daniel, 15, 205–6

Maria Chapdelaine (Hémon/Duvivier/Allégret/Carle), 22, 23, 24

Marshall, Bill: on *Being at home with Claude*, 157, 240n54; and response to Gilles Thérien, 132; on national context of Quebec cinema, 222n12; on Robert Lepage, 130; on *Le sourd dans la ville*, 73

masculinity: abject representation of, in *Black Robe, Shadow of the Wolf, Clearcut*, and *Dance Me Outside*, 81–97; and crises of, in Canadian film, 25, 187; dominant, axioms relating to, 208–9; dominant, Judith Halberstam and Sally Robinson on 'legibility' and 'marking' of, 206–7; female, in *The Wives of Bath, The Well of Loneliness*, and *Lost and Delirious*, 173–84; and identity formation, in *Fortune and Men's Eyes*, 13, 104–15; as masquerade, 201, 203, 209; and narcissism, in *Hedwig and the Angry Inch*, 123; representation of, in work of Michael Turner and Bruce McDonald, 14–15; 185–211; studies relating to, in film theory, 186–7; white, (in)visibility of, 205

masochism: feminine, as theorized by Freud, 85, 95, 231n22; and masculine self-representation, 209; Steven Shaviro

on film and, 146

Massé, Michelle A.: on 'marital Gothic,' 50–1, 52

Mayer, Louis B., 19

Mayne, Judith, 14, 45, 164

McBride, Jason, 11

McCall, Sophie, 100–1

McCamus, Tom, in *Possible Worlds*, 152, *154*, 209

McCann, Sean, in *Possible Worlds*, 152, *154*

McCormack, Derek, 11

McDonald, Bruce: *American Whiskey Bar*, 3, 38, 187, 201–3; *Dance Me Outside*, 13, 40, 81–2, 94–7; *Elimination Dance*, 15, 187, 203, 222n3; *Hard Core Logo*, 14–15, 41, 96, 187–201, 202–3, 205, 208–10; *Highway 61*, 190, 194; *Knock! Knock!* 190; *Roadkill*, 190, 194

McFarlane, Brian, 12, 41, 44–5; on filmic 'enunciation,' 39–40

McGrath, Patrick, 74

McGuiness, Richard: on *Fortune and Men's Eyes*, 110

McKellar, Don, 96; and *Elimination Dance*, 203, *204*, 222n3

McLaren, Norman, 24

McLuhan, Marshall: *Understanding Media*, 245n40

Mehta, Deepa: *Bollywood/Hollywood*, 172; *Earth*, 170; *Fire*, 14, 165, 169–72; *The Republic of Love*, 20, 172; *Sam and Me*, 172; *Water*, 170

Mellen, Joan, 187

melodrama: and *Bonheur d'occasion/The Tin Flute*, 40; and *The English Patient*, 5–6; and *Hard Core Logo*, 14, 187, 196, 198, 200, 201; and *Kamouraska*, 229n38; and lesbian boarding school films, 181; Linda Williams on, 5, 196, 198; and *Rachel, Rachel*, 18

Melville, Herman: *The Confidence Man*, 15, 205–6

Mercier, Denis: in *Le sexe des étoiles*, *127*

Mettler, Peter, 124, 148

Metz, Christian, 39, 42; on adaptation, 48; on 'film language,' 209; on identification and the gaze, in theatre vs film, 43–4; and the 'imaginary signifier' of cinema, 163

Michaels, Anne, 20

Mighton, John: *Possible Worlds*, 152–5

Millette, Jean-Louis: in *Le confessionnal*, 132, 139; in *Les fous de bassan*, 29

Mineo, Sal: directs New York remount of *Fortune and Men's Eyes*, 107, 109, 235n16

Minghella, Anthony: *The English Patient*, 3–7, 18–19, 32, 44–5, 221n6; relationship with Michael Ondaatje, 18, 46

Mistry, Rohinton, 37, 40

Mitchell, John Cameron, 15; *Hedwig and the Angry Inch*, 106, 122–4

Mitchell, Margaret, 23

Moers, Ellen: on female gothic, 50

Mon oncle Antoine (Jutra), 55, 224n21

Montgomery, L.M.: and various film adaptations of *Anne of Green Gables*, 12, 17, 21–3; and Sullivan Entertainment's *Road to Avonlea*, 41, 180

Montmorency, André, in *Il était une fois dans l'est*, 117

Moore, Brian: *Black Robe*, 11, 13, 40, 80–1, 82–6; *The Luck of Ginger Coffey*, 25, 82

Morency, André, 150

Morris, Peter, 21, 223n7

Mrs Dalloway (Woolf/Gorris), 54, 70–1

Mulvey, Laura: on identification and the gaze, as theorized in 'Visual Pleasure and Narrative Cinema,' 7–9, 14, 36, 51, 102, 162, 164, 186; on 'masculinization' of female spectator, 162–3, 242n52

Munro, Alice, 11, 18, 20

Murch, Walter, relationship with Michael Ondaatje, 18, 222n3

music: in *Dance Me Outside*, 94; in *Fire*, 171; and k.d. lang, 168, 169; in *Kamouraska*, 54, 59, 60; and piano score of *The Hours*, 71; and soundtrack of *Lost and Delirious*, 241n34; and soundtracks of *Salmonberries* and *Bagdad Café*, 168; and theme song of *Surfacing*, 65, 66. *See also* sound

Muses orphelines, Les (Bouchard/Favreau), 37, 114

Namaste, Viviane: on *Le sexe des étoiles*, 237n51

Nanook of the North (Flaherty), 78, 80, 102

narcissism: Freud on, in 'The "Uncanny,"' 58; patterns of, in gothic woman's film, 52, 57; representation of, in *Hedwig and the Angry Inch*, 123; theme of, in *La face cachée de la lune*, 159–60; and woman spectator, 162

Naremore, James, 21

narration: and 'enunciation,' as theorized by Brian McFarlane, 39–40; in film, as theorized by David Bordwell, 237n7; first-person, in *Dance Me Outside* and *The Lone Ranger and Tonto Fistfight in Heaven*, 97; first-person, in *One Flew Over the Cuckoo's Nest*, 79; first-person, and representation of female selfhood in *Kamouraska* and *Surfacing*, 53–4; polyphonic and intersubjective construction of, in *Le sourd dans la ville*, 70–1; through voice-over, 18, 54, 71

narrative: desire, 10, 16, 45–6; framing, in *Le confessionnal*, 134–9; gendered experience of, 210; infidelity, in *Swann*, 74; syntax, in fiction and film, 4; voice, in *Hard Core Logo*, 191–2

National Film Board of Canada/Office National du film de Canada, 10–12, 23–4, 41, 98, 190, 224n17

nationality/national identity: allegorized in *Hosanna*, 116; and Canadian film and literature, 8, 10; vs gender identity, in *Surfacing*, 62; and heterosexual masculinity, in Canadian film, 186–7; and reception of *Fortune and Men's Eyes*, 107–8; selling of, during tax shelter era of Canadian filmmaking, 27–8; and symbolic representation of homosexuality, in Quebec cinema, 132, 147, 151–2, 157

Neale, Steve, 8–10, 186–7, 222n13

Neame, Ronald, 15, 180

Newman, Paul: *Rachel, Rachel*, 12, 17–18

Newton, Esther: *Mother Camp*, 119; 'The Mythic Mannish Lesbian,' 242n44

Nichols Jr, George: *Anne of Green Gables* (1934), 22–3
Nicholson, Jack, 79
Nô (Lepage), 45, 133, 147–52, 154, 158

O'Connor, Flannery, 69
Oka standoff (1990), 80, 81, 231n19
Oliver, Edith, and *New Yorker* review of *Fortune and Men's Eyes*, 107–8, 109
Olivia (Bussy/Audry), 14, 165, 174, 175, 180, 242n42
Ondaatje, Michael: *The Collected Works of Billy the Kid*, 199; *Elimination Dance*, 15, 187, 203, 222n3; *The English Patient*, 3–7, 12, 32–3, 45, 221n6; relationship with Anthony Minghella, 18, 46; relationship with Walter Murch, 18, 222n3; short films of, 222n3
One Flew Over the Cuckoo's Nest (Kesey/Forman), 77, 79–80, 230n6
Orality, adaptation of, in *Atanarjuat*, 99–101
Orr, Christopher, 39, 41, 44
Ostenso, Martha, 21
Outerbridge, Peter: in *Better Than Chocolate*, 124, *125*
Outrageous!/'Making It' (Benner/Gibson), 13, 25, 106, 117–19, 128
Owen, Don, 25

Paré, Jessica: in *Lost and Delirious*, *173*
Paris Is Burning (Livingston), 120–1
Parizeau, Jacques, 80, 151
Parker, Molly, 37
Parpart, Lee, 4, 44, 246n57
Parsons, Estelle: in *Rachel, Rachel*, 18, *19*
Patry, Pierre, 25, 27
Pavis, Patrice, 129, 237n2
Penley, Constance, 197
Perabo, Piper: in *Lost and Delirious*, *173*, *178*
Perez, Gilberto, 11, 163–4, 241n19
performativity: and drag, in film, 104–28; of gender, as theorized by Judith Butler, 15, 120, 165; and masculinity, 193; in theatre vs film, 41–4, 105
Persky, Lester, 109
Pevere, Geoff, 27–8; on *Black Robe* and *Shadow of the Wolf*, 81–2, 86, 90–1; on *Clearcut*, 91; on *Dance Me Outside*, 94, 95
Philip, Jules, 149, *150*
Phillips, Lou Diamond, in *Shadow of the Wolf*, 13, 81, *88*, 91
Picard, Béatrice: in *Le sourd dans la ville*, 31, 54, 71, *72*
picaresque: and Michael Turner's *Hard Core Logo*, 187, 196; narrative features of, 244n24
Picnic at Hanging Rock (Weir/Lindsay), 165
Pickford, Mary, 19
Pierce, Kimberley, 15; *Boys Don't Cry*, 122–3, 178–9
Pinter, Harold, 32, 35
Plantinga, Carl, 4
Podemski, Jennifer: in *Dance Me Outside*, 96, *97*
Podeswa, Jeremy, 11, 21
Polygraphe, Le (Lepage and Brassard/Lepage), 140–6, 155
Pool, Léa: *Anne Trister*, 14, 132, 165, 181; *Emporte-moi*, 14, 165, 181; *Lost and Delirious*, 14, 28, 42, 161, 165–6, 172–85
pornography: Linda Williams on, 204; in work of Michael Turner, 201, 203–5; relationship to documentary, 201; redeployed conventions of, in slash fan fiction, 197; remount of *Fortune and Men's Eyes* accused of being, 109
Portes tournantes, Les (Savoie/Mankiewicz), 28, 31
Possible Worlds (Mighton/Lepage), 146, 152–5, 158
Poulin, Marco: in *La face cachée de la lune*, *160*
Prats, Armando José: on synecdochic representations of the Native on screen, 77, 80, 96, 102
Prime of Miss Jean Brodie, The (Spark/Neame), 14, 165, 174, 180
Prosser, Jay: *Second Skins*, 236n41
Proulx, Monique: *Le sexe des étoiles*, 28, 46, 106, 126–8

Quarrington, Paul, 37

Quebec referenda (1980, 1995), as represented in *Nô*, 149, 151
queer: critical representation of, in *Fortune and Men's Eyes*, 104–15; and representations of the male body, in films of Robert Lepage, 13–14, 129–61. *See also* homosexuality

race: dehistoricization of, in *The English Patient*, 44–5; and gender hierarchies, in *Salmonberries*, 166–7; and masculinity, in work of Michael Turner, 202–3, 205; and sexuality, in *Comment faire l'amour avec un nègre sans se fatiguer*, 32; screening of, in films focusing on Native peoples, 77–103
Rachel, Rachel / A Jest of God (Newman / Laurence), 12, 17–18
Radcliffe, Ann, 49
Ransen, Mort, 37
'real,' the / realness: in films focusing on Native peoples, 78; in *Hard Core Logo*, 197–8, 201; in Lacanian film theory, 241n19; and masculinity, 207, 209; in *Paris Is Burning*, 120; in theatre vs film, 44
Rebecca (Du Maurier / Hitchcock), 52, 57–8, 185
Redgrave, Vanessa, 55, 71
Reiner, Rob, 15; *This Is Spinal Tap*, 189, 193–4
'remediation': and / as adaptation 203, 210; as defined by Bolter and Grusin, 245n40; and primitivism, in recycled images of the Indigene on film, 77–8
Rennie, Callum Keith: in *Hard Core Logo*, 187, *195, 198*
Renoir, Jean, 11
Republic of Love, The (Shields / Mehta), 20, 172
Resnais, Alain, 45, 130
Rich, B. Ruby, 181
Richardson, Miranda, 20, 74
Richardson, Natasha, in *The Handmaid's Tale*, 32
Richler, Mordecai, 12, 18, 25, 223n12
Rifkin, Benjamin, 47

Ringuet (Philippe Panneton), 25
Road to Avonlea, 41, 180, 224n13
road movie: genre and gender codes in, 194–6; *Hard Core Logo* as example of, 14, 187, 194; relationship to picaresque, 196; *Smoke Signals* as example of, 97
Roberts, Gillian, 44–5, 46
Robinson, Phil, 17
Robinson, Sally, 207, 209, 246n59
romance: and ethnography, in representation of indigenous peoples on film, 13, 77–103; and relationship to melodrama, in *The English Patient*, 6–7; and slash fan fiction, 197; and sublimated homoerotic theme, in *Hard Core Logo*, 14, 188, 194; and *Surfacing*, 62, 64
Rony, Fatimah: on romantic ethnography and the screen Indigene, 77, 78, 80, 98, 99; and theories of Johannes Fabian, 231n15, 234n60
Roscoe, Patrick, 11
Ross, Sinclair, 18, 20, 24
Roughead, William: *Bad Companions*, 179, 243n56
Roy, Gabrielle, 11, 24, 40, 223n12
Rubin, Gayle: 'The Traffic in Women,' 240n44
Russell, Craig: in *Outrageous!* 106, 117, *118*, 236n31
Russo, Vito, 104; assails *Fortune and Men's Eyes* in *The Celluloid Closet*, 106, 109–11

Sagan, Leontine, 15
Salmonberries (Adlon), 14, 165, 166–9
Sampson, Will, 77, 79
Savoie, Jacques, 28
Savran, David, 246n59
Schellenberg, August, in *Black Robe*, 83, *84*
Schlöndorff, Volker: *The Handmaid's Tale*, 20, 29, 32–7
Schwartzwald, Robert: on *Le déclin de l'empire américain*, 147; response to Gilles Thérien, 132; on Michel Tremblay's *Hosanna*, 236n28
Schwerin, Jules, 109, 235n17
Scobie, Stephen, 199

scopophilia: in *The English Patient*, 7; Mary Ann Doane on female vs male, in gothic woman's film of 1940s, 52; representation of, in *Kamouraska*, 59; and romantic ethnography, 80; in theatre vs film, as theorized by Christian Metz, 43–4

Scott, Cynthia, 20

Scott, Jay, 86, 226n55, 231n17

Scott Thomas, Kristin: in *Le confessionnal*, 135; in *The English Patient*, 3, 5

Secter, David, 25

Sedgwick, Eve Kosofsky, 49

Selznick, David O., 45, 226n77, 228n24

serialization, and relationship to history of film adaptation, in Canada, 11, 21–4

Service, Robert, 21–2, 223n11

Seven Streams of the River Ota, The (Lepage and Ex Machina/Leclerc), 129, 133, 134, 147–8, 151–2, 155

Sexe des étoiles, Le (Proulx/Baillargeon), 28, 46, 106, 126–8

sexuality: and gender, 9; heteronormative representation of, in *Surfacing*, 68; ideological representation of, in film and literature, 7; and national identity, in Quebec cinema, 132, 147, 151–2, 157; and race, in *Comment faire l'amour avec un nègre sans se fatiguer*, 32; regulation of, in *Fortune and Men's Eyes*, 104–15; reproductive, as normatively reinscribed in film adaptation of *The Handmaid's Tale*, 32–7; reproductive, and 'Making It,' 117

Shadow of the Wolf (Dorfmann/Thériault), 11, 13, 40, 80–1, 86–91, 231n17. *See also* Agaguk

Shakespeare, William: and *The Children's Hour*, 179–80, 243n57; and *Fortune and Men's Eyes*, 112–14; and *Lost and Delirious*, 179; and *Olivia*, 242n53

Shaviro, Steven, 42, 146

Shearer, Norma, 21

Shebib, Don, 25

Sheckels, Theodore F., 22–3

Shepard, Sam, 21

Shepherd, Cybill, 20

Shields, Carol: *The Republic of Love*, 20, 172; *Swann*, 73–6

Shipman, Ernest, 21

Shipman, Nell, 21, 223n9

Sidnell, Michael, 141

Silverman, Kaja, 146, 162, 246n59

Simon, Sherry, 129

Simoneau, Yves: *Les fous de bassan*, 28–9, 31; *Pouvoir intime*, 132

slash fan fiction: *Hard Core Logo* a target of, 188, 196–7

Smart, Patricia, 87

Smith, Maggie, 180

Smith, Scott, 37, 74

Smoke Signals/The Lone Ranger and Tonto Fistfight in Heaven, (Eyre/Alexie), 97–8

sound: bridging of and absence of, in *Le sourd dans la ville*, 54, 71; use of, in *Lost and Delirious* and *Mädchen in Uniform*. *See also* music

Sourd dans la ville, Le (Blais/Dansereau), 12, 28, 31; as female gothic, 54–5, 61, 69–73

space: architectural framing of, in *Lost and Delirious* and *Mädchen in Uniform*, 182–4; function of, in theatre vs film, 43–4, 105; and time, in films of Robert Lepage, 129–61

Spark, Muriel, 14, 15, 166, 174, 180

spectatorship: and desire, 13, 162–5; and emotion, 4–5, 44; female, feminist theories of, 162–5; and gothic woman's film of 1940s, 52; and lesbian citationality, 162–85; in theatre vs film, 43–4, 146

Spider (McGrath/Cronenberg), 74

Stacey, Jackie, 162–3

Stagecoach/'Stage to Lordsburg' (Ford/Haycox), 77, 96, 230n6

staircases: importance of, in gothic woman's films and lesbian boarding school films, 72, 230n59; in *Kamouraska*, 61; in *Le sourd dans la ville*, 72–3; visual representation of, in *Lost and Delirious* and *Mädchen in Uniform*, 182–4

Stam, Robert, 8, 12, 47, 73, 227n85

Stevenson, Robert, 15, 51

Stopkewich, Lynne, 4, 37, 223n5

Straayer, Chris, 120

Streetcar Named Desire, A (Williams/Kazan), 207

Such a Long Journey (Mistry/Gunnarsson), 37, 40

Sullivan, E.P., 21

Sullivan, Kevin, 20, 226n77

Sunset Boulevard (Wilder), 245n43

Surfacing (Atwood/Jutra), 11, 12, 20, 24, 29; as female gothic, 52–4, 62–9

surveillance: in *The English Patient*, 7; in the films of Robert Lepage, 129–61; Gilles Deleuze on, 139

Sutherland, Donald, 89

Swan, Susan: *The Wives of Bath*, 14, 28, 42, 161, 165, 172–85, 208

Swann (Shields/Benson Gyles), 20, 73–6

Swinton, Tilda, 152, 164

Tarantino, Quentin, 246n63

Taylor, Ray, 22

Taylor, William Desmond, 21

Tectonic Places (Lepage and Théâtre Repère/Mettler), 124, 148

Teed, Jill: in *Journey into Fear*, 206, *207*

Teena, Brandon, 122–3, 124, 179, 236–7n46

Telefilm Canada, 10, 11, 25, 37, 41, 190

television: *American Whiskey Bar* and live broadcast on, 15, 38, 202–3; broadcast of re-edited version of *Kamouraska* on, 55; *Dance Me Outside* developed into spin-off series, 94; place of, in history of Canadian literary adaptation, 11, 12, 21–38; and remediation of film and theatre, 203; and work of Robert Lepage, 147

Telmissany, May, 47–8, 130

Thalberg, Irving, 21

theatre: and film, differences in performative frameworks of, 41–4, 105, 129–61; Leontine Sagan's training in, 182; Susan Swan's background in, 42

Théâtre Repère, 124, 129, 131, 140. *See also* Lepage, Robert

Thériault, Yves: *Agaguk*, 11, 13, 80–1, 86–91

Thérien, Gilles, 132, 135

Thiele, Hertha: in *Mädchen in Uniform*, 180, *183*

Third Cinema, 13; Stuart Hall on, 102–3

This Is Spinal Tap (Reiner), 189, 193–4

Thompson, Judith, 42, 172, 178

Thomson, R.H.: in *Surfacing*, 64, *67*

Till, Eric, 65

Tilly, Jennifer: in *Shadow of the Wolf*, 13, 81, 86, 89

time: Indigene placed outside of, in filmic representations, 80; re-emplotting of Indigene within, in *Atanarjuat*, 101–2; rupturing of, through shot sequencing in *Kamouraska*, 58–61; and space, in films of Robert Lepage, 129–61; and visual memory, 48

transgenderism: representation of, in film, 106, 120–8

translation: adaptation as form of, 12, 46–7; in work of Robert Lepage, 129, 131, 144, 148

Tremblay, Michel, 11, 13, 25, 106, 115–17, 119

Trevor, William, 37

Trudeau, Pierre, 149

Tulloch, Elspeth, 29, 73

Tulugarjuk, Lucy, 99, 102

Turner, Michael, 10, 185; *American Whiskey Bar*, 3, 15, 38, 186–9, 201–3, 245n42; and collaboration with Stan Douglas on *Journey into Fear*, 15, 187, 205–6; *Company Town*, 189; *Hard Core Logo*, 14–15, 41, 187–201, 202–3, 205, 208–10; hybrid writing style of, 189; *Kingsway*, 189, 245n42; and participation in *Elimination Dance*, 15, 187, 203, *204*; *The Pornographer's Poem*, 187, 189, 203–5, 223n10, 245n43; representations of masculinity in work of, 14–15, 186–211; *Survivial*, 190, 244n15

Tyler, Carole–Anne, 120

uncanny: as metaphor for adaptation, 12, 49–76. *See also* Freud, Sigmund

Ungalaak, Natar, in *Atanarjuat*, 99, *100*

Unidentified Human Remains and the True

Nature of Love/Love and Human Remains (Fraser/Arcand), 24, 37

Vanderhaege, Guy, 20
Vizinczey, Stephen, 12, 25
Vivre sa vie, 181
Voice-over: in *Dance Me Outside*, 96–7; in *The Handmaid's Tale*, 32; and film noir, 131; in *Kamouraska*, 54, 59; lack of, in *Black Robe*, 85; lack of, in films by Zacharias Kunuk, 99; lack of, in *Le sourd dans la ville*, 54; in *Mrs Dalloway*, 71; in *The Pornographer's Poem*, 203; in *Rachel, Rachel*, 18; single instance of, in *Surfacing*, 65; in *Smoke Signals*, 97
Von Carolsfeld, Wiebke, 37
Vorlicky, Robert, 208
voyeurism: in *Black Robe* and *Shadow of the Wolf*, 81; in *Kamouraska*, 60; in *Surfacing*, 66–8; vs fetishism, in theories of cinematic spectatorship, 162

W Network, 11
Wallace, Frederick William, 21
Wallace, Robert, on *Fortune and Men's Eyes*, 113–14
Warner, Jack, 19
Waugh, Thomas, 25, 41; critiques Robert Fothergill, 243n6; on *Il était une fois dans l'est*, 224n22, 236n28; on *Lost and Delirious*, 242n50; on masculinity in Canadian film, 186–7
Well of Loneliness, The (Hall): and *The Wives of Bath*, 14, 165, 174–8, 184
Welles, Orson, 51, 193, 205
Whale Rider (Caro/Ihimaera), 98
Wheeler, Anne, 20, 124
When Night Is Falling (Rozema), 181
White, Patricia, 14; on 'ghosting' of lesbian representability in Hollywood film and feminist film theory, 162, 163, 169; and theory of 'retrospectatorship,' 165, 184–5
Whiteoaks of Jalna, The (De La Roche/Trent), 23
Whittaker, Herbert, on *Fortune and Men's Eyes*, 107–8
Who Has Seen the Wind (Mitchell/King), 224n21
Who's Afraid of Virginia Woolf (Albee/Nichols), 109
Wiebe, Rudy, 40
Wild Geese, The (Ostenso/Goldstone), 21
Williams, Linda: on melodrama, 5, 196, 198; on pornography, 204
Willmott, Glenn, 35, 36, 225n37
Winsloe, Christa: *The Child Manuela*, 14, 15, 166, 180
Wittig, Monique, 153–4, 155
Wives of Bath, The (Swan): 14, 28, 42, 161, 165–6, 172–85. See also *Lost and Delirious*; Swan, Susan
Woods, James, 12
Woodward, Joanne, in *Rachel, Rachel*, 17, *19*
Woolf, Virginia, 54, 70–1, 175, 242n42
Wright, Tracy, in *Elimination Dance*, 203, *204*
Wyler, William, 15, 179–80

Yared, Gabriel, 6
Young at Heart (Douglas), 194

Zech, Rosel: in *Salmonberries*, 166, *167*
Žižek, Slavoj, 241n19
Znaimer, Moses, and *American Whiskey Bar*, 38, *202*
Zoo la nuit, Un (Lauzon), 28
Zupančič, Alenka, on theatre-to-film adaptations, 132–3, 158